Scilly At War

The Constant Warwick *was one of Robert Blake's principal warships helping in the Reduction of Scilly in 1651. The vessel was part-owned by Batten and had the reputation at the time of being the fastest frigate in the navy. She was one of the ships which, under Blake's personal direction, helped to bombard Tresco Castle (later called King Charles's Castle) and to capture two rebel Royalist frigates in Scilly. This contemporary drawing of the* Constant Warwick *is by Van de Velde the Elder and is reproduced by permission of the British National Maritime Museum.*

Scilly At War

by
R.L. Bowley
author of
The Fortunate Islands: The Story of the Isles of Scilly
and of *The Isles of Scilly Standard Guidebook*

Part I
Robert Blake and the Reduction of Scilly, 1651

Part II
The First World War, 1914-18
and Developments in the Air
between the Wars. 1918-39

Part III
The Second World War, 1939-45
and postwar Air Communications with Scilly

Bowley Publications Ltd
P.O. Box 1, St Mary's, Isles of Scilly TR21 0PR
Isbn 0 900184 34 5

1st Edition 2001

ACKNOWLEDGEMENTS

Thanks are due in compiling this book to the late John Pickwell for his help and enthusiasm, and to Frank Gibson for allowing me to use some of his wonderful collection of photographs, and to Glenda Pattenden for valuable help in improving the manuscript. Thanks are due to Belinda Rowe for her expert typing, and also especially due to the following for information and/or photographs: Lieutenant Commander C.R. Perrin, former commander of RML542; David Rogers of Scilly, former Hurricane pilot based on St. Mary's during the Second World War; Wing Commander G.R. Leatherbarrow of Scilly, former Sunderland pilot; and to, Matt Lethbridge, former coxswain of the St. Mary's lifeboat – as his father and grandfather had been.

Among books (and their authors) which have been especially helpful in the completion of this work are Captain A.B. Sainsbury's splendid *The Royal Navy Day By Day*, M.J. Ingham's informative *To The Sunset Bound* and *Atlantic Helicopter* – and eagerly awaited is his book on the Tresco air station in the 1st World War – Paul Kemp's *U-Boats Destroyed*, Robert M. Grant's book of the same name and his *U-Boat Intelligence*, Peter London's *Aviation in Cornwall* and his *U-Boat Hunters*, *Osborne's War Diaries*, the magazine *The Scillonian*, *U-Boat Hunters: Cornwall's Air War, 1916-19* by Peter Hunter and *U-Boat Fact File* by Peter Sharpe.

Inspiration for Part One of this book was largely owing to the encouragement of the late John Hamilton who, before moving to Hugh Town, lived for many years in the house nearest to the quay at Old Grimsby overlooking the beaches where fighting took place in the 17th century. Thanks are due also to Robert Dorrien Smith for permitting the reproduction of Jos. Lereck's fine contemporary account of the events.

Readers who have interesting reminiscences of Scilly in the 2nd World War, which they would be willing to permit being included in a second edition of this book – before time washes away memory – are asked to write to the author at P.O. Box 1, St Mary's, Isles of Scilly TR21 0PR. Also, anyone who finds and points out any errors in the text will be most gratefully appreciated.

PREFACE

It seems almost a contradiction in terms to be writing about Scilly in the context of war, when the Islands today seem the very embodiment of peace. But the present prosperous and tranquil state has not always prevailed; the isolation of the Islands in the Middle Ages meant periods of privation and the ravages of pirates – and starvation faced the islanders even in the decades after the ending of the Napoleonic War in 1815. This book is concerned with a 17th century episode which occurred in Scilly when Royalists and Roundheads fought one of their last actions in England; and with two world wars in the 20th century, when the Islands played a role of some importance mainly because of their position in the Western Approaches and the need to combat the menace of the U-boats.

Considering a wordy book such as this, sensible folk may legitimately question whether it was worthwhile sacrificing all those fine trees to print it – quite apart from the time and attention required trying to read it. After all, it is only about happenings from long ago – deeds done that cannot be undone, or, as Wordsworth put it, of 'Old unhappy far-off things and battles long ago.' Would we not be better to live in the present, plan for the future and recognise that what is written about the past may contain as much to mislead as to inform?

We cannot be sure that what we read presents an accurate picture of what really happened, even though we might not go as far as Napoleon Bonaparte who declared that 'History is a set of lies agreed upon'. Even when the facts written about the past can be shown to be accurate, they are unlikely always to be complete, and may not be fairly representative, not necessarily because of any deliberate attempt to falsify, but because those given happen to be the only ones available. Some facts may be given greater weight than others because of the individual historian's attitude and interests, for, as Samuel Butler wrote, 'God cannot alter the past, but historians can'. Even where an historical writer avoids the excesses of such matters as political correctness, his interpretation of events will inevitably be hard to divorce from current concerns and preoccupations; and can he afford, in practice, entirely to offend or to discount the known prejudices and preferences of his readership? The historian, E.H. Carr, in his book of lectures on *What is History?*, may not be far off the mark when he suggests (p. 23) that received history could be described as 'a hard core of interpretation surrounded by a pulp of disputable facts'.

H.L. Mencken, 1880-1956, the American philologist, satirist and influential editor of the *American Mercury*, overstated the case forcefully when he wrote: 'No normal human being wants to hear the truth. It is the passion of a small and abherrant minority of men, most of them pathological. They are hated for telling it while they live, and when they die are swiftly forgotten. What remains ... is a series of long tested and solidly agreeable lies.'

'Progress' is a difficult word to use of matters historical, somehow suggestive of straight lines onwards and upwards to the glorious present. Herbert Butterfield's well-known book of 1931, *The Whig Interpretation of History,* rejected such an interpretation, and claimed that 'the study of the past with one eye, so to speak, upon the present ... is unhistorical'. However, in his wartime book *The Englishman and His History*, 1944, Butterfield appeared to reflect something of the approach which twelve years before he had denounced. This is corroboration that historians move with their times, and are unable entirely to be free of contemporary influences.

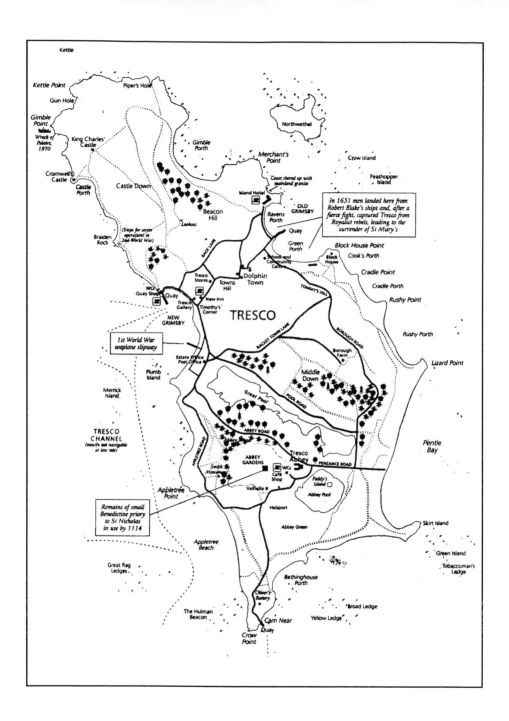

Tresco in 2001

I

PART I

ROBERT BLAKE AND THE REDUCTION OF SCILLY IN 1651

'War makes rattling good history;
but Peace is poor reading' – Thomas Hardy

The most important single military event in Scilly's recorded history is the part played by the Islands in the Civil War period, culminating in the drama of the assault upon and defeat of the Royalist rebels in 1651 by government forces led by one of England's greatest commanders, Robert Blake.

The Civil War in England from 1642 to 1646 that preceded this event had been a struggle of conflicting ideas and competing loyalties, often dividing families and alienating friends. Of West Cornwall families, the Boscawens, Trefusises and Eriseys declared for Parliament, the Arundells, Bassets and Vyvyans for the King, and the Godolphin and Courtenay families were both divided. As the Roundhead commander, Sir William Waller, wrote to his friend and former colleague in arms, Sir Ralph Hopton, the Cavalier commander, on the eve of the Battle of Lansdown in 1643 against each other: 'The great God … knows with what a sad sense I go upon this service, and with what a perfect hatred I detest this war without an enemy'.

In Scilly, as in Cornwall generally, the King's cause was supported by the more conservative elements among its landowners; only in the towns and ports, such as Penryn and St Ives, where trade or fishing were important, was the parliamentary cause predominant. Thus, the inhabitants of Scilly generally – whatever their individual private views, if any – in their practice had little choice but to support the cause of the King. By 1646, this proved to be the losing side and, with Royalist resistance crumbling in the West Country, Charles, the Prince of Wales, accompanied by Sir Edward Hyde, Lord Culpepper and a large retinue, fled westwards from Pendennis Castle to Marazion, where the Prince is claimed to have rested on March 2nd, 1646, at the house immediately opposite what is now the Godolphin Hotel, his room on the first floor overlooking the causeway. Here, the retinue awaited the lowering of the tide before crossing to the Mount, and Charles is believed to have given orders that the chapel on Chapel Rock should be dismantled. The next day the party boarded a frigate called *The Phoenix*, which would carry them over to the Scillies; unfortunately for the Royal Party, this ship was not an English vessel but a foreign privateer that happened to be available, as the following may explain.

3

In April, 1645, the Self-Denying Ordinance (removing MPs from military command and intended really to get rid of lethargic and lukewarm commanders such as the Earl of Manchester), had obliged Warwick to resign as Lord Admiral, and his deputy, William Batten, took his place. At that time there were about 50 Parliamentary vessels in the West Country based mainly at Milford Haven and Plymouth; but Charles I, although his Royalist vessels were much in the minority, still employed them during the war, mostly as privateers. He had issued letters of marque allowing his Royalist ships to prey upon Parliamentary vessels entering the Western Approaches, which was, in effect, tantamount to legalising piracy. At one period there were scores of these ships, and they were joined by a number of ships of owners and masters from cross-channel ports in Brittany and at Dunkirk, who jumped at the opportunity to plunder English shipping under guise of helping the English King. *The Phoenix* was one such vessel from Dunkirk, belonging to Jan van Haesdonck, who owned several ships. For this voyage she was captained by Baldwin Walke, one of a small number of English ex-navy captains who supported the King rather than Parliament. However, the crew of *The Phoenix* were ruffians of Haesdonck's and quite undisciplined, so that when the ship arrived in Scilly on March 4, the Prince's retinue found that many of their valuable possessions had been stolen, and there was nothing they could do about it.

In February, 1646, Charles I appointed Lord Hopton to command all Royalist armies in Cornwall and, after many of his soldiers had deserted, he sent a trumpeter to Sir Thomas Fairfax seeking peace and made the final surrender of these forces to the Parliamentary army at Tresillian Bridge, Truro, on March 14, fleeing afterwards with Lord Capel to join Prince Charles at Star Castle in Scilly.

Prince Charles chose to flee to Scilly rather than to the Channel Islands because, in Clarendon's words, 'Jersey was so near to France and so might give the greater umbrage'. Charles was informed by his ministers of the indisposition that they perceived in his loyal subjects towards His Highness leaving the Kingdom and must 'prefer the continuing of him still within His Majesty's own dominions'. Scilly was within this, and so it could not be said that he had fled abroad. Lord Culpepper was sent to France to notify the Queen, Henrietta Maria, and ask her for supplies, as there was in Scilly 'a scarcity of provision'. But the Queen apparently was not very impressed with her son going to Scilly, and wrote that it was 'not sufficiently fortified and is accessible in divers places'. Charles stayed in Scilly, together with Sir Edward Hyde (later made Earl of Clarendon and, after 1660, the King's chief minister), from Wednesday, March 4, 1646, to Thursday, April 16, and was joined by Lord Capel and Lord Hopton on Saturday, April 11. Sir Richard Fanshawe, secretary to the Prince's Council, and his wife, Lady Ann Fanshawe, arrived in Scilly in an accompanying craft, but they found the

Scillonians reluctant to share with such incoming 'persons of quality' their shelter, food and drink, when they had so little for themselves. Much has been written of the hardships suffered by the entourage of Prince Charles, but little of the poverty which was part of the everyday life of the ordinary islander, a disparity which was, of course, a reflection of divisions in society found in the rest of England in the 17th century.

In her memoirs, Lady Fanshawe describes some of the discomforts she suffered both on the voyage to Scilly and in the subsequent accommodation arrangements upon her arrival, made worse for her by her pregnancy at the time:

> We having put all our present estate into two trunks, and carried them aboard with us in a ship commanded by Sir Nicholas Crispe, whose skill and honesty the master and seamen had no opinion of, my husband was forced to appease their mutiny which his miscarriage caused, and he taking out money to pay the seamen, that night following they broke open one of our trunks and took out a bag of sixty pounds and a quantity of gold lace, with our best clothes and linen, and all my combs, gloves and ribbons, which amounted to near three hundred pounds more.
>
> The next day after, having been pillaged, and extremely sick, and big with child, I was set ashore almost dead in the Island of Scilly. When we had got to our quarters near the Castle, where the Prince lay, I went immediately to bed, which was so vile, that my footman ever lay in a better; and we had but three in the whole house, which consisted of four rooms, or rather partitions, two low rooms and two little lofts, with a ladder to go up. In one of these they kept dry fish (which was their trade), and in this my husband's two clerks lay; one there was for my sister, and one for myself, and one amongst the rest of our servants. But when I awaked in the morning, I was so cold I knew not what to do; but the daylight discovered that our bed was near swimming with the sea, which, the owner told us afterwards, it never did so but at spring tides.
>
> With this we were destitute of clothes; and meat or fuel for half the Court, to serve them a month, was not to be had in the whole island. And truly we begged our daily bread of God, for we thought every meal our last.

Accommodation in Scilly proved primitive and uncomfortable for everyone in the Royal Party and, after a frustrating six weeks at Star Castle, Charles was persuaded by Hyde to leave for Jersey. Hyde was particularly conscious of the danger to Prince Charles as, on April 12, a squadron of nine Parliamentary ships commanded by Batten was sighted near Scilly by observers on St Mary's, but was keeping its distance from the islands because of a gale blowing. Hyde persuaded Charles that, to avoid capture, he must leave the Scillies the moment the wind abated; and so, on April 16, Charles and his retinue – said to have numbered nearly 300 – embarked on Baldwin Walke's own frigate, *The Proud Black Eagle*, which had a well-disciplined crew. They evaded Batten's squadron and also – more by luck than judgement – a fleet of 20 sail out of Plymouth, and arrived in Jersey the next day; then, on being told of the approach of Parliamentary warships, Charles sailed to France on June 25th. Here he joined his mother at the French Court – a step which, as Sir Charles Petrie has written, 'his father had said should only be taken in the last resort'. Hyde also thoroughly disapproved of Prince Charles going to Paris, for he disliked Henrietta Maria as much because she was French, Roman Catholic and indiscreet as for her poor judgement of people. His perceptive comment was that she was inclined to remember those who could be of service to her rather than those who had been.

Thereafter, except for a brief return to England leading to the Battle of Worcester, Charles 'travelled' (his word) more or less as a wandering exile for most of the intervening years, until unexpectedly recalled to England by his countrymen in 1660. Leaving Scilly on April 16, 1646, the Prince just missed the arrival of Lord Digby and two frigates sent by the Marquis of Ormonde in Ireland to persuade the Prince to come to Dublin. Whether Charles would have been so persuaded is unclear; in any event, Hyde's advice to Prince Charles to leave Scilly on April 16, 1646, proved timely because, on the day they sailed away from the islands, they learnt that the Royalist stronghold at St Michael's Mount, held by Sir Arthur Bassett, and formerly regarded as impregnable, had been surrendered after a short siege but without much of a fight to Parliamentary forces under Colonel Hammond and Colonel John St Aubyn – this latter the Roundhead who was later to command and to purchase the Mount in 1659, and whose descendants, in the person of Lord St Levan, still live there today. It was Sir Francis Bassett who had owned and held the Mount during the Civil War, using his tin sales to buy munitions, improve the Mount's defences and pay the garrison. Writers have tended to overlook the fact that, before the Civil War began, St Michael's Mount was owned by William Cecil, Earl of Salisbury, who declared for Parliament. However, Sir Francis Bassett had been negotiating his purchase of the Mount since 1640, and the King welcomed Bassett's fortification of it on behalf of the Royalists. Prince Maurice, Rupert's brother, visited it in February, 1643, and must have been satisfied as to the Mount's defensive capability, its steep sides and the fact that it was 'both land and water twice a day', which had for long led to the presumption that it was impregnable. However, such natural defences, even with adequate armaments, cannot prevail for ever once supplies are denied, and its surrender was in a sense a return into Parliament's hands. It came about because Sir Francis died in 1645 leaving the Mount to his brother, Sir Arthur Bassett, who found the burden of all this just too much, even though he had ample means of resistance on the Mount, including 30 guns and 100 barrels of gunpowder; but he had lost some men, who had deserted his garrison, and another dozen or so were said to have been rounded-up in Market Jew Street, Penzance, and the local population had practically ceased to provide the Royalists with food supplies; moreover, Colonel St Aubyn offered to allow Bassett free passage to the Scillies, and Bassett's officers free passage to their homes. Thus Bassett's plea for surrender terms was a rational and sensible decision because, with the King a virtual prisoner, Prince Charles embarking upon exile, and the war really over, there was no possible advantage to be gained from continued resistance. This sensible logic contrasts with what happened at Pendennis Castle, where the obstinate, elderly commander and Governor since 1646, Colonel John Arundell (nicknamed 'Old Tilbury' because he claimed he had been at Tilbury and heard Queen Elizabeth's famous speech defying the Armada in 1588), put his garrison through unnecessary and excruciating hardships because he feared damage to his reputation if he should be thought to have surrendered too early, despite the fact that the St Mawes Castle across the bay had surrendered on March 12 without opprobrium.

In 1644, Arundell had helped the Queen, Henrietta Maria, escape via Pendennis Castle to Brest in her native France, but when, on March 17, 1646, Fairfax had taken over beautiful Arwenack House, fortunately before the retreating Royalists entirely destroyed it (but they did set fire to it), further resistance at the castle was little short of suffering for its own sake. Arundell maintained that to surrender would be 'a blemish on his honour' and claimed 'I will here bury myself before I deliver this castle', and so, for nearly six months, the 1,000 or so castle defenders held out, though blockaded by William Batten from the sea and besieged by Colonels Hammond and Fortescue from the land, in the end reduced to killing and eating their horses before their commander would face reality and give in, which eventually he did on August 17, 1646. By then he was ruined in health and wealth and his garrison were ill and facing complete starvation. His boast had proved an empty one. He was later reduced to beseeching Cromwell for help and, rather abjectly, tried to maintain that the earlier Arundells and the Cromwells had once been kindred and friends. At the surrender, his men – 924 of them – were allowed by Fairfax to march out with full military honours, 'colours flying, trumpets sounding, bullets in their mouths and each man with twelve charges of gunpowder', and this was deserved, for they had fought well.

By the time of Arundell's surrender at Pendennis Castle, except for Raglan and Harlech on the mainland, plus Scilly, Jersey, the Isle of Man, the Castle of Cornet on Guernsey and the West Indies, all other major Royalist strongholds had surrendered. Exeter surrendered on April 16 and Oxford on June 24. Moreover, further resistance could not be justified on the grounds that the consequences of surrender were feared, because Fairfax, the Parliamentary commander, had a reputation as a fair and decent man whose troops were well under control; and from those defeated Royalists who had already surrendered, there were few complaints of cruelties or destruction or even of much looting. This situation may be compared with some of the dreadful happenings which had taken place on the Continent between 1618 and 1648 during the Thirty Years War – the sack of Magdeburg in 1629 being one awful example. In relative terms, the Civil War in England, though hard fought, was not a catalogue of similar excesses; rather was it – in Waller's words – 'a war without an enemy'.

On June 17, 1646, Colonel John St Aubyn was nominated by Parliament to be Captain of the Mount. With firmness he quelled the local Royalist rising in 1648, and in 1659 purchased the Mount from Sir Arthur Bassett. Scilly surrendered on August 25, 1646, like St Michael's Mount without bloodshed; below is a contemporary letter concerning this surrender of the Royalist forces in Scilly to Admiral Batten:

A true and perfect relation of the surrender of the strong and impregnable Garrison on the Island of Scillie to Captain Batten, Vice-Admiral of the Parliaments Navie at Sea, Aug. 15. 1646, by Mr John Hoselock, chyrurgion to the Vice-Admiral Captain Batten in the St Andrew.
(London, Printed by B.I., 1646, and published from the original copies by order of Parliament)

Loving friend,
In my last I writ to you at large of all our proceedings at Pendennis; but since I have been in the castle, I can give you more true and just account: of which more in the ensuing Letter, because I thought it meet to insert in this place, the gallant proceedings of our Vice-Admirall in the reducing of the Island of Silly, viz. Upon the 24 of August, 1646. Some of the chiefe Commanders of the Garrison of the Island of Silly, (having before sent a Trumpeteer to the Vice-Admirall for a Treaty), came aboard the Andrew, where they laid open and presented their propositions for the surrendering of that Island. Where, after some consultation between the Vice-Admirall and the rest of his Officers, their earnest requests were admitted and immediately began to debate upon the Articles, and at last concluded that the Garrison and Island of Silly, with all the Ordnance, Armes, and Ammunition, should be surrendered to Captain Batten, Vice-Admirall of the Parliament's Navie, upon the 25. of August, 1646.
Your loving friend
John Haslock

From this surrender in 1646, the Scillies were peaceful and settled for 2 years; but, in September, 1648, a rising took place in the Islands at about the same time as other Royalist risings on the mainland. These synchronised with a Scottish invasion of England which was defeated by Parliamentary forces at the Battle of Preston, and the Royalist risings on the mainland of England were everywhere suppressed in what has since been called the 2nd Civil War. However, in islands outside the mainland, such as Man, Jersey and the Scillies, Royalist resistance continued. In Scilly, young Sir John Grenville, son of Sir Bevil Grenville of Stowe was appointed governor by the King in November, 1648; and his brother, Bernard Grenville, brought reinforcements to his support after staying for a while in hiding at Menabilly, then a manor house owned by Mr Rashleigh, and in the 20th century made famous as the home of Daphne du Maurier. In addition, Prince Rupert brought Irish catholic soldiers to the Scillies from Kinsale. Sir John Grenville's uncle also brought aid; he was Sir Richard Grenville, the King's General in the West, but a man who, as Hyde wrote, 'made himself so many enemies and so few friends'. Sir

Richard had taken over command of the Cornish Royalists after Sir Bevil's death but his overbearing manner and quarrelsome nature tended to give offence to everyone he met. In September, 1644, the King gave command of all Royalist forces in Devon and Cornwall to Sir Richard Grenville, but others – particularly Sir John Berkeley – were jealous of this appointment, and Berkeley stepped with alacrity into Sir Richard's post when Sir Richard was wounded. On Sir Richard's recovery in June, 1645, he was restored by the King to his command; but, when he tried to assemble scattered Royalist forces, his rival commanders, out of pique, sabotaged his efforts. It was estimated that about 3,000 former Royalist soldiers were deterred from answering his summons. Sir Richard did succeed in raising 500 cavalry and, on January 17, was ordered by the King to act as Lieutenant General under Lord Hopton. Now it was Sir Richard's turn to show pique and he refused the subordinate role. He was cashiered, imprisoned and eventually sent to reside in St Michael's Mount, where his popularity with troops was demonstrated by a monster petition to the King asking for his restoration to command. The King refused and Sir Richard eventually went abroad. In a letter to Edward Hyde of May 4, 1650, Sir Edward Nicholas doubts Sir Richard's suitability to command. He wrote: 'I now perceive Sir Richard Grenville to be, as you say, of a very odd humour, and I doubt a person not fit to be trusted with so great employment and charges'. But, notwithstanding these adverse opinions, Sir Richard was loyal and competent enough to send help to his nephew. From St Malo in 1651 he wrote: 'There I employed my own monies and great labours to advantage in the King's service, as in supplying Sorlinges [Scilly] with what was in my power'. Thus, Sir Richard's nephew, Sir John Grenville, was not without assistance at first in holding the Scillies as a Royalist stronghold. He also enjoyed the support of Prince Charles. News of Charles I's execution on a scaffold in Whitehall on January 30, 1649, reached Scilly only slowly – actually only a few days after the ship carrying some of the Royal Family's possessions and, in particular, their wardrobes, was wrecked on Godrevy Island, where the lighthouse now stands. Of the 60 crew, 58 were drowned, and, for days, sodden garments of great value came ashore, strewn along the North Cornwall beaches – a bizarre event interpreted in Cornwall as an evil omen for the Royalist cause. Such a view was not shared by the faithful Grenville, who, as his letter to Nicholas of February 23 shows, was mainly concerned that he had been correct in the formalities he used when proclaiming in Scilly Prince Charles as King on February 22, 1649.

Sir John also had the advantage of possessing a great name in the West Country and of having a famous great-grandfather from whom he seems to have inherited some of his best and worst characteristics. His great-grandfather was the former and more famous Sir Richard Grenville, a cousin of Sir Walter Raleigh and Sheriff of Cornwall in 1577. He commanded one of the fleets sent out to colonise Virginia, but his greatest fame rests on his action in 1591, when his one ship engaged units of a Spanish fleet in a long but hopeless battle. Contrary to popular understanding, precise details of the action are unknown – there is no firsthand account – but the background and circumstances can be described.

The cost of the fleet action against the Spanish Armada in 1588 had been high, and Sir John Hawkins favoured less expensive warfare against Spain for the rest of the war, 1588-1604, especially after Drake's failure in 1589 when the Spanish treasure fleet got through and he lost many soldiers. In 1590, Hawkins's fleet was in home waters, and Frobisher's reached the Azores only in June, after that year's treasure shipment had already reached Spain. In the following year, a particularly large treasure fleet was anticipated; so, in the hope of intercepting it and capturing its cargo, Lord Thomas Howard, with a dozen or so ships, sailed for the Azores, anchored there and lay in wait for over 4 months. Then, in August, a fast pinnace arrived with the unwelcome news of the approach from Spain of an overwhelming fleet of 53 sail commanded by Don Alonzo de Bazan, brother of the late great admiral, the Marquis of Santa Cruz, and sent by Philip II with the object of escorting the American treasure fleet safely to Spain.

Howard weighed anchor and headed northwards to avoid the approaching Spaniards, but Sir Richard Grenville, his vice-admiral, sailing in the 43-gun, 500 ton *Revenge* – Drake's ship in the fight against the Spanish Armada 3 years before – was the last to leave, possibly because she was the fastest of Howard's ships and may have been embarking 90 sick crew who had gone ashore, although it is suggested that her sailing qualities may also have been reduced by her ballast being incompletely replaced. Whatever the reason for her delay, by the time the *Revenge* had put to sea, some of the Spanish ships had already positioned themselves between her and Howard's squadron; escape was, however, still possible by heading south, but instead – whether through obstinate bravado or misplaced pride – Grenville insisted on trying to pass to windward, so provoking the battle which, at 15 hours duration, was then believed to have been the longest night engagement ever fought at sea. Grenville hated his Catholic opponents, and had a history of hotheaded actions and brutality as someone who could never suffer fools or opponents gladly. In his student days in London, he had even stabbed a man to death in a street fight. Such behaviour seems something of an inherited characteristic – at least many Grenvilles met violent deaths. His father was Roger Grenville of Stowe, Captain of the *Mary Rose* and one of the 415 who drowned as, somewhat overloaded or badly loaded, that vessel listed to starboard and then overturned, watched from the shore on July 19, 1545, by a horrified Henry VIII and Lady Carew. Admiral Sir George Carew and Captain Roger Grenville had given orders which were not obeyed owing, it is alleged, to some poor discipline on board exacerbated by having heavy equipment and too many 'gentlemen' and too few hands. The gun ports had been left open

10

and took in water as the vessel reeled while turning. Only about 30 were saved from the stricken ship, which was raised from the seabed in 1970 and is now on show in Portsmouth.

Grenville's grandparents died taking part in the rebellion of 1549, when conservative Cornishmen objected to having to use Edward VI's new prayer book in English, not because they understood the old service in Latin, but because it was familiar and revered. Rendered in English, it sounded, as one critic put it, 'like a Christmas game'. But to Richard Grenville, the new protestantism was patriotism and, like many others, he increasingly associated Catholicism with the cause of Spain, especially after the Pope excommunicated Elizabeth I in 1567. Grenville also had a personal dislike of the Tregians of Tregony in Cornwall, a Catholic family originally from St Ives, who had prospered through trade. When Grenville was appointed Sheriff of Cornwall in 1576, he took the opportunity to root out Catholicism from the County – and at the same time to serve his personal interest – by arresting Francis Tregian, and ensuring that he was jailed for 26 years and all his property confiscated, such firm action – along with others – earning him a knighthood from Queen Elizabeth.

Even more severe was Grenville's treatment of the mild-mannered Cuthbert Mayne, Tregian's priest, who also served as his estate steward. Mayne had once been Chaplain of St John's College, Oxford, but had later been ordained at Douai. His sentence was to be hanged, drawn and quartered in the Market Place of Launceston on November 30, 1577, with his body parts hung up for all to see – the punishment then accorded to the worst of men. But Mayne was one of the best of men – at least as judged by 21st century standards – and, indeed, not unlike the saintly Campion who had influenced him, and who was later to suffer a similar fate in this time of intolerance and national danger. In 1970 Mayne was declared a saint by the Pope, and his figurehead, carved by the late Scillonian boatbuilder and craftsman Tom Chudleigh, now graces the garden of the Roman Catholic Chapel in the Strand of Hugh Town in Scilly. No other 17th century figure is so remembered in the Islands, although the statue is tucked away in a corner, unmarked and unremarked. The gardener, when asked about the statue in August, 2000, speculated only that the head might represent 'some Roman god or other'.

Nobody can deny Grenville his bravery, even though it may be fair to add a pejorative qualifying adjective such as 'foolhardy' or 'reckless'. Barring the way of the *Revenge* on August 31, 1591, was the great 3-decker, Spanish galleon *San Philip* of 1,500 tons, which took the wind out of *Revenge*'s sails, enabling other Spanish ships to come alongside the *Revenge* and attempt to board her. This they tried to do an alleged 15 times, yet the Spanish soldiers were repulsed on each occasion by the hundred or so still-active sailors on the *Revenge*, despite the 90 or so sick men below on lower decks. Such desperate

11

Cuthbert Mayne, mild and sincere, but catholic. Of his body, only the top of his skull remains, carried in procession each year.

heroism has been much applauded, especially as it was successful for so long in repelling the attempted incursions; but it leaves the question of just how laudable such a pointless fight was when viewed in retrospect.

In the evening Grenville was mortally wounded by musket shot, nearly all powder in his ship had been spent, 40 of his crew were dead, and by dawn the remainder had had enough and surrendered. What was remarkable was the large number of Spanish casualties, the sinking of two of their ships, and the length of time Grenville's men fought on for him – a heroic if wasteful action recorded in poems by Raleigh and Tennyson. Raleigh's poem was merely patriotic propaganda, but Tennyson's has served to keep the memory of the event alive.

Yet the main disaster occurred over the next two days, after the valuable treasure fleet had joined Don Alonzo's escorts; a great gale sprang up, sinking 108 ships in the two Spanish fleets, including the *Revenge* and its Spanish prize crew, with only 32 ships out of about 140 eventually reaching Spain. Tactically, the fight of the *Revenge* was a surprising achievement because of the odds; strategically, the operation was a failure because Howard signally failed once again to intercept the Spanish plate fleet; and it was the wind that had the last word on both protagonists, sending the majority of the precious cargoes to the seabed.

Sir Richard Grenville had two sons; John, who died at sea, and Bernard who died in 1605; but Bernard's son, Bevil, inherited all the family gifts of leadership, reckless bravado, and ability to inspire the men he led to great things, even to their deaths. Sir Bevil died in the Civil War from wounds incurred at the Battle of Lansdown, where his inspiring leadership of Cornishmen in Hopton's Royalist army successfully dislodged the Parliamentarians under Waller from the disputed ridge and forced them to withdraw. It was a barren victory and Grenville in the thick of the action, fell at the moment of his success, but there is no historical evidence for the pleasant story circulated later that Sir Bevil's 7-foot 4-inches high squire, retainer and minder, Anthony Payne, on seeing his master fall, lifted Bevil's son, John, onto his father's horse and shouted to the dispirited Cornishmen that they had another Grenville to lead them.

The story may have arisen because, when Sir Bevil passed away at the nearby manor house at Langbridge later that night of July 5, 1643, it fell to Payne to write to Lady Grace Grenville at Stowe, informing her of the sad event. This letter could be construed as suggesting the gratuitous embellishment, even though Bevil's son, John, was at the time a little older than the young boy which some have pictured. In his letter Payne wrote:

> Ill news flieth apace: the heavy tidings no doubt have already travelled to Stowe that we have lost our blessed master by the enemy's advantage. You must not, dear lady, grieve too much for your noble spouse. You know, as we all believe, that his soul was in heaven before his bones were cold. He delivered to me his last commands and with such tender words for you and for his children as are not to be set down with my poor pen, but must come to your ears upon my heart's breath. Master John, when I mounted him on his father's horse, rode him into war like a young prince, as he is, and our men followed him with their swords drawn and with tears in their eyes. They did say they would slay a rebel for every hair of Sir Bevil's beard, but I bade them remember their good master's word when he wiped his sword after Stamford fight; how he said (when their cry was 'stab and slay'): 'Halt men; God will avenge'.

John went on the fight at Worcester and, with such antecedents and from such a background, it is not altogether surprising that he inspired similar devotion and, despite his youth, was the natural as well as the appointed Royalist leader in Scilly, 1648-51. But it was not problems of leadership or lack of devotion in his followers that bothered him in those years; increasingly it was difficulties of supply and attendant privations that beset him during all the time he held the Scillies. Prince Rupert brought him men and supplies from Ireland in the early years, and his forces survived until 1651, but in the later years mainly by plundering passing ships, actions which led his fellow countrymen to refer to Scilly under Grenville's regime as 'a second Algiers'. In the Nicholas Papers (the correspondence of Sir Edward Nicholas, Secretary of State) there is the following letter from Grenville 'humbly beseeching' Nicholas to intercede with Charles to allocate more frigates to assist in the Royalist defence of Scilly, and asking to be pardoned if he was incorrect in the formalities of his proclamation of Charles II as King in the islands after he had learnt of the execution of Charles I on January 30, 1649. For all his faults, Charles I had died with bravery and dignity for a cause now discredited – dictatorship. He was a good husband, father, and a lover of art, who believed himself to be a good Christian; but he was politically untrustworthy, betrayed people and broke promises, all permissible, he thought, to save his arbitrary powers, because, as he put it, 'a subject and a sovereign are clean different things'. He was not someone 'to do business with' and, in Cromwell's words, his execution became 'a cruel necessity', otherwise none of the gains for which the Civil War had been fought would have lasted. But it is debatable how far one should blame Charles I for looking only to the past, wanting to preserve the present and fearing or failing to anticipate or contemplate adjustment to the future – such is the weakness of many conservatives, past and present. Certainly he could not have foreseen the consequences of marrying his daughter Mary at the age of 10 in 1642 to the 15-year-old William, Prince of Orange; they both died from smallpox in their 20s, but in 1689 their son – also William – became King of England and of Scotland, an accession which was to confirm and much extend the success of Parliament over the King in the Civil Wars and in the Restoration Settlement of 1660, and to see the end of Charles I's belief that he ruled by 'divine right'. But, in the curious way in which longstanding customs and beliefs tend to persist long after any justification for them has disappeared, the idea that touching the King's person was a cure for scrofula – a kind of tuberculosis – was prevalent in some places even after 1689. Some coins were given round holes called touch-pieces, and contact with these was thought by the more incorrigible of believers or desperate of sufferers to be a substitute for the King's physical presence, and to hold prospect of curing them. One of the beneficial effects in the 20th century of the Second World War was the enormous strides made in medical knowledge and treatment; in the 17th century, when so little was understood, a sufferer may be excused for clutching at almost anything that seemed to offer hope. It was not just in England that belief in the Royal Touch endured; Louis XIV (1660-1714), 'the Sun King', was believed by nearly everybody to be able to cure scrofula.

* * * * *

The Royalist risings in mainland Cornwall in 1648 were led mostly by inferior officers such as Major Gosse, but with the secret hopes, if not the connivance, of former more senior Royalist supporters. The ranks of the rebels were inflated by many who were incensed by bureaucratic delays that had meant that, of 274 Cornish estates sequestered during the Civil War, by 1648 only 30 had been redeemed. Many others felt oppressed by high taxation, the burdens of billeting and their hard lives, with general discontent fuelling their rebelliousness, and Royalism providing the focus of discontent rather than their having any passion for constitutional niceties.

Parliament appointed Sir Hardess Waller to keep the peace in the West Country but, even in 'puritan' Exeter, the people refused to give his troops billets. This helps to explain why troops often had to be quartered in churches, together with their horses, which – perhaps inevitably – led to accusations of vandalism. In Penzance, Royalist rebels plundered houses and shops demanding money with menaces, and looting from Gubbs's shop when he refused to pay them £300. Waller sent Colonel Robert Bennett, who restored law and order in the town, losing 2 of his men killed and 5 wounded, but leaving 60 of the rebels dead, and wounding as many more. At the same time 120 other Royalist rebels were menacing Helston, joined by over 300 from the Lizard area; the Mayor of Helston, with loyal forces in the town, sought help from troops in Penzance and from those of John St Aubyn on the Mount. These met the rebels in a hard fought engagement alongside the church at St Mawgan, during which the poorer discipline of the rebels led them to flee in panic from the old earthwork called 'The Gear', and to hide in caves and mineshafts, some even to jump headlong into the sea.

Thus were the Cornish mainland Royalist revolts of 1648 ended, with Waller, St Aubyn and other Cornish gentlemen who had played a part in putting them down, sent a letter of thanks by the House of Commons; only in the Scillies was a Royalist rising successful and lasting, when, on Sunday, September 30, the Islanders, resentful particularly of the unremunerated burden of providing lodgings for the garrison soldiers, seized Colonel Buller and his officers when they were at church. Unlike on the mainland, no immediate effort was made to suppress this Scilly rising because of the difficulty of doing so, and so Sir John Grenville was sent by Charles to exploit the situation in the Royalist interest, by making the islands a Royalist stronghold.

It is sometimes difficult in times of civil war to decide without bias whom to describe as rebels and whom to regard as the followers of the legitimate government. One unprejudiced solution is to see whichever side wins as the legitimate authority and those who oppose it as rebels – until, of course, the position changes. As Sir John Harrington wrote:

Treason doth never prosper; what's the reason?
For if it prosper, none dare call it treason.

Thus, although the Royalist cause was restored in 1648 in Scilly, it could be considered partisan to describe it as the legitimate authority when the rest of the country had by then rejected it. But for those who insist on coming down on one side or the other and are not comfortable sitting on fences, there are J.E. Logan's cautionary words:

Thar's good and bad in Injun,
And thar's good and bad in White;
But somehow, they is allus wrong,
And we is allus right.

Sir John Grenville commanded in Scilly for the Royalist cause for 3 years from 1648 and displayed qualities which included a steadfast loyalty to the

Stuarts. He was not popular with everyone for in April, 1650, there was a plot by disaffected Scillonians and some troops to murder him and seize control of Scilly. It was nipped in the bud on the day it was due to take place. In his letter below Grenville confesses that he had some difficulty in persuading the Scillonian inhabitants to be 'conformable to the advancement of His Majesty's service', but he soon came to realise that his most pressing problem was want of supplies.

In the Nicholas Papers there is the following letter from Grenville in Scilly, dated February 23, 1649, asking Nicholas if he would intercede with the King to allocate Grenville more frigates to assist the Royalist cause in Scilly.

Note. *Some of the spelling and punctuation in the following two letters have been modernised for clarity of meaning and ease of reading. There are some who hold the view that the wording of old documents, when quoted, should not be tampered with; but this is to overlook the fact that old wording can often be more misleading than an honest attempt to update it. One example is the Duke of Wellington's alleged remark that the Battle of Waterloo 'was won on the playing fields of Eton' which has been used to seek to justify organised games in the school curriculum. The Daily Telegraph on November 22, 1999, mentioned Wellington's remark in connection with the Wall Game between Collegers and Oppidans as 'a shoving match with arcane rules, the last goal in a St Andrew's Day contest was scored in 1909'. But organised games did not exist in schools in 1815; what Wellington was referring to were the disorganised fights frequently taking place between Eton boys and the town boys of Windsor on waste ground (where they 'played') and which toughened the Eton youngsters for war combat – a quite different matter. Also, the year in the documents appears originally as 1648; but it is a convenient and widespread convention – in order to reduce confusion – to render the dates in accordance with the Gregorian calendar adopted in the 18th century rather than in the older Julian calendar still in use in England in the 17th century.*

To Sir Edward Nicholas. Scilly. 23rd February, 1649.

Sir,

Hearing the necessity and ill-condition this place was in by reason of disorder, mutinies and wants, and His Majesty's service so much concerned therein, I thought it my duty, without consideration of myself, to hasten from Jersey with all the speed I could and, by Sir George Canteret's favourable means, I had Capt. Amye's little frigate to transport me thence and, having been five days at sea in a continual storm, very likely to be cast away, I arrived safely at last in these Islands, where I find the same disorder that I feared and heard at Jersey. I have with great industry endeavoured to regulate these people into some better condition and order, and have already brought them a little more conformable to the advancement of His Majesty's service; and I hope every day they will know more duty and obedience and they are at present seeming to be well satisfied. It hath been a great misfortune to the King's service that no frigate hath been appointed for the service of this place, its advantage and subsistence wholly depending upon the benefit it should receive by sea. I have acquainted His Majesty therewith, as likewise the condition I find this Island in, our wants growing very great. And, as concerning the ship and commodities seized on here, they were embezzled, lost and disposed of before my coming. Also the distraction of the Islanders could scarce be composed, so that our condition will be very bad without relief. Therefore, I have most humbly desired of His Majesty to supply us with such provision as we want, having sent a gentleman on purpose to His Majesty about that business. I have likewise dispatched another messenger to my Lord Lieutenant of Ireland to give his Lordship likewise account of my condition, and I hope I shall receive speedily a supply of soldiers from thence and some provision from His Majesty for our present maintenance, and then I doubt not by God's blessing to give His Majesty a good account of this place. And if His Majesty think fit to assign me some frigates, I am confident I shall not for the future put His Majesty to any further trouble of this kind, but on the contrary I hope to be in a condition to send His Majesty supply from hence. Therefore I shall humbly beseech you to be a mediation for me in your letters to the Court, the preservation of this place being of so great concernment to His Majesty's service.

The fleet called here as they passed by into Ireland, but we have heard no news of them since. Sir, the extraordinary news I have heard since my being here concerning the most horrid murder and treason committed on the person of his most sacred Majesty, has so transported me with grief as that I am not able to express it to you, this barbarous and most inhuman action being without precedent the greatest that ever has been committed, and I hope God will revenge it on the heads of the damned authors and contrivers of it. But since this greatest misfortune that ever befell us cannot be recalled, and seeing we cannot better show our deep sense hereof to his Majesty's memory than by performing our duty to his royal son in sacrificing our lives and fortunes to his service, and as soon as I was assured of this sad truth, and had solemnly paid here our abundant griefs in infinite tears having commanded throughout all these Islands a day of mourning and humiliation for our most fatal and incomparable loss, I thought it my particular duty to proclaim His Majesty that now is King, which was accordingly done on the 22nd of February with as much joy and cheerfulness as possibly could be expected after so sad news. I have been troubled very much; no person here had formerly seen a precedent of the like that I might have been able to have put the proclamation in a better form. But I hope yourself, and every worthy person besides, will pardon my errors, it being, I humbly conceive, a great fault to neglect the performance of such a duty of so high importance to the King's service and, for want of a form, to occasion by a delay a prejudice upon His Majesty's service here, which I hope during my life never to be guilty of in the least measure. This is all that I have to trouble you with at present

Your most faithful and obedient servant

John Grenville

In 1650 Charles wrote the following letter to Sir John which was obviously looking towards the future Royalist risings and invasion from Scotland, which took place the following year:

St Johnston's   2 of Sber, 1650

Sir John Grenville,

'Considering how important it would be for the good of my affairs to have a body of men in readiness – to countenance any attempt that shalbe made by my good subjects in the West for the recovering my just Rights, their owne Libertys, and suppressing the present barbarous and bloody usurpers, especially in a place soe neere and opportune for the seconding any such enterprize, as that under your charge; I have thought good to desire and require you to gather and entertaine as many soldiers and to provide what store of Armes and Munition you can possibly and as may consist with the necessary subsistence of ye Garrison under your command, to be ready to be seasonably transported on any good occasion. In we busines soe highly conducting to the good of my service, as I am very confident, your particular relation and affection to my Person and interests will prompt you to imploy your utmost industry and assistance; soe you may rest assured that what you shall therein performe shalbe acknowledged on any seasonable occasion that may manifest

your deserts and ye esteeme and kindness I have for you; who am'
Your very loving Friend
Charles R.

In the event, the Royalist risings in 1651 (the so-called 3rd Civil War) were all suppressed.

Charles sent Montrose to Scotland in 1650 to make Charles's nominal rule there a real one; but Montrose was soon captured, and then hanged and quartered in Edinburgh as a felon, whereupon Charles repudiated him and protested to the Scottish Parliament that he had never authorised Montrose to use violence – a deliberate lie, showing that, despite his surface geniality, he could be as mean and disloyal as the other Stuart Kings. However, Charles II's great political gift, which served him well in the long run, was his willingness to compromise on principles when reality required it, which neither his father nor his brother could do and other lesser men found hard to contemplate. With Cromwell's great victory at Dunbar, all Royalist hopes of re-establishing themselves had for the time being to be abandoned. Dunbar occurred on September 3rd, so afterwards this date was called by Cromwell 'my lucky day'; by a strange irony it was also on this day that he died in 1658. It is sometimes suggested that he need not have died then, if he had been willing to take quinine which had been available since the 1630s. It is thought that Cromwell was suffering from malaria, then known as marsh fever; quinine, made from the bark of the Cinchona tree, could have helped him, but he rejected it, as it was reported to be a catholic remedy – thus showing him to have been a man sadly prepared to face pain and death rather than compromise principle. As Milton wrote 'Cromwell ... was guided always by faith and matchless fortitude' and for all his rows and disappointments with different parliaments during his time, the debt parliamentary democracy owes to him is tacitly acknowledged today by the statue of him outside the House of Commons.

As for Charles II, he resigned himself to exile. One epitaph for him was composed by John Wilmot, Earl of Rochester:

> We have a pritty witty king
> Whose word no man relies on.
> He never said a foolish thing,
> Nor ever did a wise one.

But Charles II, one of whose redeeming graces was a ready wit, replied to it: 'That is very true: for my words are my own, and my actions are my ministers'. It was indeed by fair, if false, promises and other such means, including his undertaking to set up Presbyterianism in place of Anglicanism in Scotland, that the Scots were persuaded to back him and crown him 'King of the Scots' at Scone in January, 1651. But the Scottish army, on which his hopes rested, after advancing boldly into England, was convincingly defeated by Cromwell and a New Model Army half its size at Worcester; the result was that once more Charles had to flee, this time in disguise – and famously resorting to hiding in a tree on one occasion – transported by a favourable wind to France not to return for another nine years.

Charles made his escape from England from between Shoreham and Hove, with the help of Colonel Gounter and a boatman called Tettersfield – but who for some reason is referred to as Tattersall – and who was waiting upon the tide before he could float his ship, the coal-brig *Surprise*. That night the King slept in his daytime clothes in the company of Lord Wilmot; but, at two in the morning, the Colonel decided to summon the company awake, as horses had been heard being led by the back way to the building where the King was lodged, and it was presumed they were to help drag the *Surprise* to the water. However, it was not until 8 o'clock in the morning before all had gone aboard and the Colonel was able to watch the King and his companions set sail. With the wind holding good, they reached near Le Havre at about 10 o'clock that evening, it being Wednesday, October 15, 1651. They were fortunate to have voyaged without incident, for, after they had settled themselves ashore, a storm blew up and the boatman had to cut his cable and so lost his anchor, but later made a safe return to Chichester. At a subsequent date, they heard that, just two hours after their sailing from near Shoreham, soldiers entered the town seeking 'a tall, black [meaning 'dark'] man, 6 feet and nearly 4 inches tall'. It seems that Charles had made a timely escape once again.

That the King after the Restoration in 1660 failed to remember some who had been of service to him during his period of adversity, is well attested. But that old seaman, Tattersall, had an unusual way of reminding his King; he sailed the *Surprise* up the River Thames and moored it off Whitehall, where the King could not fail to observe it. To his credit, Charles responded and made ample amends by taking the brig into his navy as a 5th rate ship-of-war, and renaming her *Royal Escape*, with Tattersall appointed her salaried captain. In addition, Tattersall was awarded a pension of £100 per annum – a handsome amount which continued to be paid to Tattersall's descendants for several generations. Forgetfulness – if that is what Charles's omission had been – is forgivable when the atonement is sufficient. Charles had experienced somewhat uncomfortable years in exile; it is not altogether surprising that after 1660 he resolved 'never to go on his travels again'; but he developed a remarkable capacity for self-indulgence in compensation, well meriting the title of 'Merry Monarch'.

* * * * *

In Scilly, while Grenville was engaged from 1648 in holding the Islands for the Royalist cause, in the next year one of Parliament's commanders from the

Civil War of 1642 to 1646, Colonel Robert Blake (1599-1657), was appointed to be one of Parliament's three Generals-at-Sea – along with Colonels Popham and Deane – and in his subsequent career was to become one of this country's greatest maritime commanders. Yet he does not feature in school history syllabuses with anything like the prominence that has been given, for instance, to Francis Drake and Horatio Nelson. There are understandable reasons for this: Drake is regarded today (in England, if not in Spain) as a hero, whose plundering exploits on the Spanish Main 'every schoolboy knows'.

Less well known is Drake's pursuit of personal gain when pursuing the Armada. Actually, although Martin Frobisher was most critical and condemnatory, Drake's fleet abandonment at the engagement sounds worse in the 21st century than it was judged in the 16th century, when others were likely to have done the same, given the chance. On the night of July 1, 1588, Drake was leading the English fleet up the English Channel following the Spanish Armada in its strong crescent formation, when the flagship of one of the Spanish Squadrons, *Nuestra Senora del Rosario* commanded by Don Pedro de Valdes, broke its mainmast and bowsprit in an accidental collision. Drake, without consultation, doused the poop lamp – which his ship, the *Revenge*, had been carrying to show the English fleet the way – and sped off to capture the *Rosario*. This desertion caused confusion in the English fleet and nearly led to disaster when English ships began to follow the Spanish ships too closely; but the *Rosario* surrendered on July 21 to Drake off Start Point without a fight, and he (and his crew) found themselves with 50,000 ducats and other valuables. To the 21st century mind, Drake's conduct seems like serious dereliction of duty, but there is a defence of it. The action helped promote Drake's discipline over his crew in the *Revenge* and was a morale booster. Captains of men-of-war, just like commanders of units on land, were expected to reward their men for any success by allowing looting of the defeated enemy. This is, after all, what usually made them fight more keenly. Men may claim to fight for abstractions such as 'freedom', but usually this covers a multitude of motivations concerned with personal advantage, 'King and Country' being a favourite 20th century rallying cry, while religion and identification with one's local leader or land owner were 17th century ones. Valdes later became the honoured prisoner of Drake in London until a ransom was paid for his release, while the crew of *Rosario* became virtual slaves of gentry in the West Country. Another galleon, *San Salvador*, surrendered off Weymouth on the following day and her crew were likewise taken prisoner, after her gunpowder store accidentally exploded and blew off much of her stern.

Drake is often thought of as a rough-mannered West Country sailor rather than a polished courtier such as Sir Walter Raleigh, and this is in accord with Drake's piratical attacks on Spanish colonists on the Spanish Main. He was thought of by the Spanish as El Draque, the Devil's messenger, and episodes such as his sack of Valparaiso, made him much feared. But his career as a slave trader in his younger days need not be held against him as it was an activity widely accepted at the time. More surprisingly perhaps, Drake was also a member of the Middle Temple, although he never actually practised as a lawyer; but there is today a table in the Inn, made from a hatch-cover of the *Golden Hind*, the ship Drake took around the world in 1577, returning in 1580 with a fortune in Spanish silver and gold for his Queen, and £47 for every £1 investors had put into the voyage. Drake presented the table to the Inn after his circumnavigation, and it is used today by every aspiring barrister who is called to the bar of the Middle Temple, as he has to sign his / her name on the roll on this table. On a landing nearby is a framed copy of the welcome accorded to Drake after his epic voyage, but the *Golden Hind*'s poop deck lantern, which used to hang in the entrance hall, was destroyed by a bomb in the 2nd World War, being replaced now by a replica. It is sometimes overlooked that Drake was also a politician, a member of parliament, a mayor of Plymouth, and the man who organised the superb water supply to Plymouth from Dartmoor. Drake's water supply was used at least until 1880, after which 140 feet high dams were built between 1893 and 1898 at Burrator stemming the River Meavy and holding back over 1,000 million gallons of water at a depth of 87 feet. From a hard water area such as London one of the pleasures of visiting a soft water area such as Plymouth is the comparatively delicious taste of the water, but few would now think to raise their glass to Drake before sipping it.

* * * * *

The Spanish Armada of 1588 – otherwise known as the Enterprise of England – was an attempt by Spain to conquer an annoying rival power; but it was also a seaborne religious crusade to return Protestant England to Catholicism, and it was therefore blessed by the Pope and supported by the major powers of Western Europe. It consisted of about 130 ships, whose sails carried Christian crosses, and many of whose decks were packed with the 9,000 soldiers it was transporting. Its defeat was probably inevitable, given that the Duke of Parma's 30,000 army in the Netherlands was not ready to be transported across the English Channel to invade England as Philip II had planned; but certainly, after his *Rosario* diversion (or desertion), Drake played a major role in the Armada's discomfort after the fireships had panicked most of them out of their Calais anchorage. However, the wind, by changing direction, saved many Spanish vessels from grounding on the sandbanks and enabled them to run before it to the north, but then blew so hard that only half the ships returned to Spain, many being wrecked on the coasts of England, Scotland and Ireland along the way. Both fleets ran out of

There are a number of alleged portraits of Blake, some of them of dubious authenticity. Of the two which are considered the most reliable, the Pelly Portrait – of which this is a passable rendering – has, as part of its inscription:

O ever faithful, vigilant and brave,
Thou bold asserter of Britannia's
Fame,
Unconquerable Blake!

The other portrait hangs in Wadham College, Oxford, where Blake obtained his degree in 1618, and is of a young man, but with what some have averred are enough facial similarities with the Pelly Portrait to carry conviction that it genuinely represents Blake.

ammunition – the Spanish first, whereupon some soldiers on the crowded decks could only reply to English cannon with musket fire.

There was enormous relief in England at the Armada's defeat, but in fact Philip II planned three subsequent armadas which, although they did not reach England's shores, indicate that the victory was not seen, at any rate by him, as decisive at the time. But in the light of history – which means with the benefit of hindsight – the Spanish defeat marked not only the rise of England as a seapower but the beginning of the decline of Spain from its position of dominance in the sixteenth century, eventually by 1743 to be overtaken by France as Europe's superpower. While the sixteenth century in Europe may be said largely to have belonged to Spain, much of the seventeenth and eighteenth centuries are those of French ascendancy, politically and culturally as well as militarily. But, by the nineteenth century, it was Britain which had become the predominant power, based largely on her industrial revolution, but also on victories in arms. Thus, when Nelson won the Battle of Trafalgar in 1805, not only was Britain saved from threats of French invasions – and the fleets of France and Spain virtually destroyed – but the victory marked the establishment of Britain as the world's greatest naval power, measured by the fact that for most of the nineteenth century Britain's navy was at least twice as large as the next largest navy in the world; moreover, for most of the 19th century, Britain's merchant fleet carried almost half the world's total commerce. It is for these reasons that Nelson earned his post atop the 145 feet column in Trafalgar Square put up in 1843, the sculptor being E.H. Bailey, the builder of the column being W. Railton, and the bas-reliefs being made from captured enemy cannon – although Landseer's lions were not added until 1867. Nelson lost an eye at Corsica, an arm at Tenerife, and his life at Trafalgar in 1805 at the moment of his greatest victory; but an even taller column, erected for him at what later became the former tram-terminus in the centre of O'Connell Street, Dublin, and called Nelson's Pillar, was totally dismantled after the 1950s for political reasons – another instance of how history and historical reputations can change as time goes on and circumstances and allegiances alter.

The victories of Robert Blake are, by comparison with those of Drake and Nelson, today not viewed as so important nor as so lasting in their consequences, even though in 1657 at Santa Cruz, the Battle of Teneriffe was perhaps the single most complete victory ever won by any English fleet, and may have served to hasten the decline of Spain.

Yet, Blake was faced by opponents, some of whom – such as the Dutch Admirals Tromp and de Ruyter – equalled him in skill and excelled him in fame; by contrast, Drake, who in 1588 was vice-admiral to Lord Howard of Effingham, but with more influence than his superior on the conduct of the fight against the Spanish Armada, had the lofty but inexperienced Duke of Medina Sidonia as his opponent, while Nelson in 1805 had merely Admiral Villeneuve, honourable opponents but neither of them of conspicuous calibre – rather were they the obedient servants suffering the errors of judgement of their respective political masters, Philip II and Napoleon Bonaparte.

Even more important in explaining why Blake has remained relatively unregarded today is that he was one of Oliver Cromwell's commanders, supporting the cause of Parliament rather than that of the King, a choice which, in much popular understanding of the English Civil Wars – even with improved school history syllabuses – places him on the 'wrong' side in the 17th century conflict. Moreover, he joined the Parliamentary Army against the King in 1642, not as a professional soldier just doing his duty, but as a civilian who sincerely believed in the righteousness of the cause. The shadows of present-day politics, with the division in this country between Left and Right, cast a prejudice over seventeenth-century happenings, since many of present-day political divisions in Britain can be traced back to seventeenth-century struggles, as is revealed, for instance, in the debates of the New Model Army at Putney in 1648-9; and Blake, before he took to the sea, was a commander in this godly New Model Army. Not only books, but plays on radio and films on television and in the cinema, have tended to confirm the perception that the 'baddies' in the Civil War were the Roundheads, while the 'goodies' were the Royalists. For instance, the dashing Prince Rupert of the Rhine, Royalist fleet commander 1649-53, is portrayed as the hero and is the romantic figure in Margaret Irwin's historical novel, and he was certainly one of the best Royalist commanders and a man of wide interests; but Blake, who would be hard ever to classify as 'romantic', is mentioned merely as one of his opponents.

The political prejudice persists and confounds insidiously, as in a BBC television broadcast of 1996 about a Civil War engagement in the West Country, in which the supposedly impartial voice-over, with almost unconscious partisanship, spoke of the 'brave Royalists fighting their Parliamentary opponents'. Another common cause of historical distortion is judging the past only from the standpoint of current attitudes and concerns, for it is often hard to appreciate that what is politically correct at the moment may not be so either in the past or in the future.

But perhaps the tide of prejudice is beginning to turn, at least in Blake's delightful native town of Bridgwater where he was born in 1599, and where St Mary's church, which was old when Blake was young – indeed, he was baptised in it on September 27 – still sports a gilded cockerel atop one of England's tallest spires. After 300 years the town's most prominent former citizen – a man who shunned publicity – is becoming increasingly recognised, with his former home converted into a museum to his memory and his statue relocated to the town centre. Unlike Drake and Nelson – but like Monk – Blake was not a seaman, nor even a soldier, before war broke out in 1642; instead, he was a scholar, a merchant, and briefly an M.P. in the Short Parliament of 1640. Indeed, it is unlikely that he had ever been to sea other than occasionally as a trader in a merchant ship, and certainly he never captained a ship before, at the age of 50, being called upon to command a fleet. This may seem rather late in life until it is compared with some other notable commanders such as Oliver Cromwell and Julius Caesar, neither of whom took up militarism until they were in their 40s. But, like Cromwell and Caesar, Blake possessed the same special qualities of a great commander, the most outstanding of which were a firm discipline over and respect of his men, and a calm tenacity of purpose.

In appearance Blake was short, thick-set, a little ungainly, and even a little sullen in expression; but, except in films, depictions of great commanders have not been renowned for good looks. In the 20th century, the commander who won the Battle of Britain, Air Marshal Dowding of RAF Fighter Command, was said always to be gloomy in manner and appearance, and his nickname was 'stuffy'; while it is said of Admiral Earl Howe, 1725-99, that he never ever smiled, except when going into a battle, such as on *The Glorious 1st of June*, 1794. Blake was a bachelor, in a lifestyle noted for simplicity, dedication and freedom from personal ambition, with a deep religious conviction and a genuine contempt for personal gain. Clarendon (Sir Edward Hyde) in his *History of the Great Rebellion* was fulsome in his praise of Blake, even though they had served on opposite sides in the Civil War. He wrote: 'He was the first that infused that proportion of courage into seamen by making them see by experience what mighty things they could do if they were resolved.' In a letter to the Earl of St Vincent, Horatio Nelson was quite clear in his assessment; he wrote: 'I do not reckon myself equal to Blake ...'

* * * * *

Blake sailed from Plymouth on April 12th, 'with nine companies of infantry,' and arrived in Scilly on April 13th, some of his ships entering St Helen's Pool, which was regarded as the best anchorage in Scilly at that time. Blake's flagship was the *Phoenix*, a 4th rate ship-of-the-line commanded by John Taylor, his other principal ships being the *Constant Warwick* and the *Providence*, this latter ship having been built in 1637 – she ended her days wrecked in 1668. Both vessels were a little smaller than the *Phoenix* (sunk in 1664), but also ranked as 4th-raters; there was also the *Crowned Lion*, a prize captured earlier from the Royalists off Lisbon, and the *Swiftsure*. Also in Blake's squadron were two armed merchant-ships and a number of small vessels suitable for scouting or carrying orders which included the *Tenth Whelp*, the *Fox*, the *Truelove*, the *Convert*, the *Hoy*, the *Fellowship*, the *Concord* and the *Hector*. In addition, the fleet included the six ships of Sir George Ayscue's squadron, with Ayscue flying his flag in the 2nd rate ship-of-the-line *Rainbow*, which was accompanied by the *Amity*; the others in Ayscue's squadron were four armed-merchantmen, *Brazil*, *Success*, *Increase* and *Malaga Incident* which transported the nine companies of soldiers (up to about 1,000 men altogether) under Lieut-Colonels Clarke and Bawden. Blake's fleet was more powerful than Grenville's frigates, a number of whom were thought to be away from the Islands at the time, seeking and hoping to capture some passing merchant vessel, but whom Tromp had been hoping to intercept on their return to Scilly so as to enforce some restitution for Grenville's piracies. From the above, it would appear that Blake's fleet consisted of about 11 ships, plus up to a dozen smaller vessels, which would, if included, roughly confirm Bishop Leslie's estimate of 23 vessels altogether – not very different in terms of naval strength from Tromp's squadron, which Bishop Leslie estimates as 13 fighting ships. In terms of soldiers, Lereck estimates the Royalist forces in Scilly as 'about 1,200 or 1,300 men, a greater number by far than we were', Bishop Leslie, in his letter of May 13, 1651, mentions 400 Royalists defending Tresco – 120 of whom fled to St Mary's, 'the rest being killed and taken prisoners'. That would leave up to 900 defending St Mary's, of whom he says 'not 500 able to do duty'. This was possibly because of weakness or illness owing to shortage of food, and their ranks were probably encumbered by excessive numbers of senior personnel – too many 'chiefs', not enough 'injuns'. In terms of soldiers, Grenville was not 'considerably outnumbered', as is sometimes advanced as an excuse for his surrender, but his men were likely to have been less fit than Blake's. Figures suggesting an excess of 2,000 men in the Parliamentary forces may have included the sailors, as many of these played a part in the Tresco landings as Lereck's account shows, and this would leave about 1,000 or so soldiers as originally calculated.

None of the ships in Blake's fleet were damaged by enemy action during his reduction of Scilly in 1651. Peter Pett, nephew of the great designer

This photograph of Pomeroy's statue of Robert Blake shows him 'pointing the way that God ordains', and in the dress of an officer of the New Model Army. The statue was sited on the Cornhill in Blake's native town of Bridgwater in Somerset, and it was not until the 1990s that it was moved to a more suitable and prominent position in the town; at the same time, Blake's family home, where he was born and brought up, was converted into a museum to his memory. Blake's early ambition had been to become a don but, instead, he went to work hard but uneventfully for his father in Bridgwater, for a time becoming an M.P. for the town.

Phineas Pett, built the famous *Constant Warwick* in 1645 as a two-decker privateer for a syndicate of Batten, Swanley and Moulton, and headed by the Earl of Warwick – hence her name. She was purchased by the navy in 1649 because she was of a new design – the first English frigate of the new type which copied the successful Dunkirkers, slim and trim vessels without great castles, but fast enough to catch their prey – which had developed on the Continent. She had between 26 and 42 guns and a crew of about 150, and later gave good service after a rebuild in 1666. She was eventually captured by the French in 1691. According to John Evelyn in his diary, he, with Samuel Pepys and Anthony Deane, the naval architect who wrote the classic *The Doctrine of Naval Architecture*, dined together on March 7, 1690, and paid tribute during their conversation to the *Constant Warwick* as the first of England's light and swift frigates which did much to help her supremacy at sea. She was not called 'H.M...' because warships at that time did not have this title, but the definite article was often included before the name. In Ayscue's squadron was the *Amity* which was similar in size and armament to the *Constant Warwick*, but Blake chose as his flagship the *Phoenix*, then of 32 guns, built in 1647, which impressed the navy because she was very fast. To save weight the *Phoenix* had been designed with no proper forecastle – until given one in 1653 – so that she was said to 'cut through the water so that the waves went over her head in such a manner as that her commander ... has sometimes been afraid that she would never have appeared above water again.' Later, she had 40 guns and was classed as a 4th-rater, but in 1660 was given such heavy replacement guns that she became terribly slow and was known as a 'slug', ending her days when she was wrecked in 1664. Most of the ships of the mid-seventeenth century navy were built of English oak, with timbers often fastened by wooden treenails. Masts and spars were of fir, pine or spruce, much of this wood coming from the colony in New England.

One of the first ships constructed with her sides pierced with gun points was the 600 ton carrack *Mary Rose* of 1513, but at that date she still carried a couple of thousand bows and arrows in her armoury; it was not until after 1568 that guns were thought of as weapons to destroy ships as much as to kill men. Even by the time of the Spanish Armada in 1588, the Spanish still conceived a battle at sea as a land battle on water, ramming perhaps but to be followed by boarding; while the English ships – although not all that smaller than the Spanish ships except in looks – carried many more guns. It was not David against Goliath, more a fleet using newer tactics against a fleet relying on older ones. On paper the English even had more ships, mustering about 140 vessels, although some were small, against between 124 and 130 Spanish ships, although many of these were primarily for soldiers being transported to take part in the planned invasion of England. The English fleet was led by its overall commander, Lord Howard in the *Ark Royal*, Drake in the *Revenge*, Hawkins in the *Victory*, and Frobisher in the largest English ship, the *Triumph* – all men who were helping carve out an English maritime tradition, which was the foundation of future greatness. After the discovery of the mainland continent of America in 1497 by Cabot and in 1498 by Columbus, this New World disappointed, for it was found to be lacking in spices and the other luxuries of the East, and regarded rather as an obstacle to be negotiated by finding the Northwest Passage linking the Atlantic with the Pacific. From the reign of Elizabeth I, English explorers participated in the search for the route, an example being Franklin with two ships, *Terror* and *Erebus*, which were trapped in the ice for two winters in 1846 and 1847, Franklin dying, together with all the 135 men who made up their crews. The Norwegian explorer Roald Amundsen, the first man to show that the North Magnetic Pole moves, and that no magnetic compass points the same way two years running – and who was also in 1912 to be the first to reach the South Pole by just pipping Captain Scott to the post – was, in 1906, the first to make the voyage through, but it took him three years, two of them stuck fast in the ice as Franklin had been. Later, the submarine *Nautilus* voyaged through, and, in 1940, the patrol ship *Roch* also succeeded in order to substantiate Canadian sovereignty over the region, but the *Roch* was icebound for almost a year. The feat of a surface ship sailing through without being halted by ice was eventually achieved by the police patrol vessel *Nadon* in the summer of 2000, but the success scarcely occasioned much widespread celebration as it was seen as just another facet of supposed global warming. By 2001, there were plans to build reinforced merchant ships to sail through regularly, hoping to cut 5,000 miles off normal trips between London and Tokyo. Thus, what for hundreds of years had seemed an almost impossible accomplishment, and which had absorbed the energies and often lives of many brave men, is suddenly, possibly owing to climate change, a feat which could in the 21st century become almost routine, at least in the summer months.

* * * * *

In the English fleet the average size of ship taking part against the Armada was about 360 tons, which was about the size of the largest merchant ships sent by the leading south coast ports to aid Howard; but about a quarter of the 130 or so vessels in the fleet were warships of over 600 tons, while the flagship *Ark Royal* was said to be about 800 tons and 150 feet long. The word 'ton' stems from 'tun' meaning a wine barrel, and the measurement therefore represented the number of wine barrels (each holding 252 gallons), or its equivalent in merchandise, which the ship could carry – in other words it described the amount of cargo space rather than weight or water displacement. It was also inaccurate, made smaller by merchants seeking to reduce custom or port fees, and made larger by the navy wishing to impress. It was not until after the Restoration that a start was made to regulate this measurement, with tonnage acts of 1720 and 1835 laying down more reliable criteria. A gross ton – equivalent to 100 cubic feet – was a measurement of all the hull and upper deck housing, while a net ton was goods-carrying capacity or tons burden.

It was under the Tudors that shipbuilding began to spread and, in 1495, Henry VII ordered the first dry-dock to be built at Portsmouth, where there was deeper water than at the main dockyards of the 16th and 17th centuries at Woolwich, Deptford, Chatham and Plymouth, which had, in turn, largely replaced the medieval shipbuilding centre on the banks of the Hamble River.

The ships were constructed using little machinery, although saws operated by manpower cut the planks over saw-pits, the sawyers being or becoming men of incredible strength. Treenails held the planking in place and were not replaced by iron spikes and bolts until after 1810 – but these latter tended to corrode more rapidly in the more acidic English oaks than they did in the hardwoods of which Indian and other Eastern ships were made. One huge warship, the 102 gun *Sovereign of the Seas*, described by Trinity House as 'beyond the art or wit of man' was 170 feet long and of 1,637 tons: she was laid down in 1634 by Phineas Pitt, Commissioner at Chatham Dockyard, on Charles I's orders after he had visited Woolwich dockyard. She was a one-off prestige vessel, built in response to French naval building, and the only ship with over 100 guns in the English navy, massively decorated especially on

Continental
transom or square
stern of the
17th century ships.

English round-tuck
stern, common in
English ships by
1651.

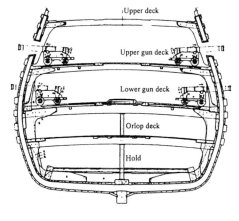

17th century Man-of-War:
cross section showing decks.

Upper deck

Upper gun deck

Lower gun deck

Orlop deck

Hold

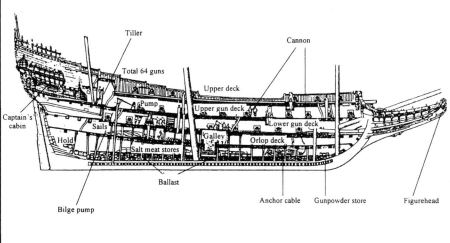

Tiller

Cannon

Total 64 guns

Upper deck

Pump

Upper gun deck

Lower gun deck

Captain's
cabin

Sails

Galley

Orlop deck

Hold

Salt meat stores

Ballast

Bilge pump

Anchor cable   Gunpowder store   Figurehead

17TH CENTURY MAN-OF-WAR

her stern, and costing nearly £66,000 at a time when an average 40-gun warship cost about £6,000. She was a 3-decker, one of the first in England's navy, and the epitome of Stuart magnificence and power, with Royal sails on her foremast and mainmast, and a topgallant sail on her mizzen, unique in English ships of the time, easily distinguished in battle with the Dutch and called by them 'The Golden Devil'. She was viewed by people in the 17th century in a fashion not dissimilar to the way the battlecruiser *Hood* was regarded in the 20th century between the two World Wars, when *Hood* was the largest capital ship in the Royal Navy, with even the postwar *Vanguard* – the very last and biggest Royal Navy battleship – barely exceeding her in tonnage.

The *Sovereign of the Seas* was finally destroyed accidentally by fire at Chatham in 1696, but it was its building that aroused so much comment; it seemed at the time to consume a remarkable number of trees. An even more extreme example is the 100-gun, 1st rater, the *Victory*, Nelson's flagship at the Battle of Trafalgar in 1805 and now on view to the public in Portsmouth dockyard. Launched in 1769, *Victory* required nearly 3,000 trees to be felled, of which about 700 were mature oaks. Although the trees came from a variety of woods, they represented in total about 200 acres of woodland. English elm was usually used for the keel because it held fastenings better, and shifted very little when in the water; but a big ship would require perhaps 7 elm trunks cut to a square shape, and much spar timber with nearly 13 miles of caulking to ensure watertight seams. Copper sheathing (some 17 tons of it) was later employed to help prevent worms boring through the wood, together with 30 hundredweight of copper nails; but iron was not common until the nineteenth century – even though Brunel's *Great Britain*, launched in 1843 and the first ocean-going, iron-screw ship in the world, had clearly shown the superiority of metal hulls. An abandoned hulk in the Falkland Islands in 1886, she is now restored and the pride of Bristol. The weakness of wooden ships to deal with shell fire was demonstrated in the Crimean War, 1854-56, and resulted in the French constructing the ironclad warship *La Gloire*. *Warrior* was Britain's answer in 1860, 380 feet long, 56 feet beam, 9,210 tons, and capable of making 14 knots under sail and engine. She has a most graceful clipper bow which conceals a ram, and it was said that, in her day, and armed with large 110 pounder guns, she could single-handed have sunk a whole hostile navy of wooden ships. After her service days were over, she became a floating oiling-jetty at Milford Haven, but is now saved and restored near the *Victory* at Portsmouth.

One painstaking task in the early days in constructing a wooden ship was to produce an accurate curvature on the timber beams, which involved suspending them over a fire and pouring water over them – a problem no more when building ironclads.

Among other old historic ships preserved and open to visitors in Britain, is the famous *Cutty Sark*, the 963 ton tea-clipper built in 1869, which had an iron frame and wooden planking and, with 32,000 square feet of canvas, was capable of a speed of 17 knots. She was designed to be one of the first to reach Britain with the early tea crops from China – a journey of a hundred days sail or more. *Cutty Sark* never was actually the fastest tea-clipper, and the opening of the Suez Canal in 1869 drove her from the tea trade to bringing wool from Australia instead; but she is also preserved in dry dock, but at Greenwich, after many years between the wars anchored and seemingly abandoned in Falmouth Harbour. One regret is that neither of Brunel's other great ships of the 19th century, *Great Western* (1836) and *Great Eastern* (1858) have survived, and none of the ships from the Civil War, such as the *Constant Warwick*, or, indeed from the 16th or 17th century – other than *Mary Rose*.

* * * * *

By 1642, at the start of the Civil War, the navy had only 34 larger ships between 300 and 850 tons, to which in the years between 1642 and 1660 were added another 207, with 154 still in service in 1660. In 1651, the entire English fleet totalled only about 85 ships as compared, for instance, with 115 in the Dutch fleet; but the English vessels tended to be superior in fire power, with 18 of them having 40 guns, compared with an average 20 or 30 guns in each of the Dutch ships, although Tromp's 59-gun flagship, the *Brederode*, was an exception. She was named after Count Brederode, the Netherlands rebel leader, whose followers were called 'beggars' disparagingly by their Spanish enemies, and who then proudly adopted the label, and when they operated against Spanish ships were known as 'Sea Beggars'. The reason for the smaller number of guns in Dutch ships was because they were designed to be capable of navigating and defending the shallow coastal waters and estuaries around the Dutch coast, and were therefore built with comparatively shallow draughts and limited to two short gun-decks.

One of the best known Dutch warships was the *Amelia*, Tromp's flagship at the *Battle of the Downs* against the Spanish in 1639. She had been launched at Rotterdam in 1637 and carried 56 guns. She was elaborately decorated with a towering stern rising 16 metres above the waterline, with square ports similar to most other Dutch vessels in the 17th century, and had two gun-decks; but the orlop deck was without ports as it was too near the waterline. The ship's complement was over 400, 300 of whom were soldiers. In time, as gunnery developed and improved, particularly during the period of the three Dutch wars with England (1652-54, 1664-67 and 1672), the numbers of soldiers carried declined and those of sailors increased. Most of the crew slept in hammocks on the orlop deck or on the lower gun-deck, but without concessions to comfort, and only the upper deck had gratings in its roof to let in light and air. The ship's hold had a meat store (the meat was well-salted to preserve it), a gunpowder magazine, an anchor and cable hold, and a ballast area usually used for ship's stores.

A report published in 1815, but relevant also to the centuries previous to that, showed that while the rate of lunacy in the population of the UK was about 1 in 7,000, in the Royal Navy it was about 1 in 1,000. This can in small measure be attributed to the seaman's increased consumption of alcohol (on top of rum issues) and to venereal disease (a girl in every port), but mainly it was reported to be due to men banging their heads on low beams 'tween decks. Average heights of men were inches shorter than today, but the difference was apparently insufficient to avoid accidental collisions.

In the reorganisation of the navy during the Commonwealth period between 1649 and 1660, such wasteful decorative extravagances as on the *Sovereign of the Seas* were ended, for they offended the puritan spirit and had served to glorify the monarchy rather than to fortify the state. A national tax was instituted to provide a permanent navy and became generally accepted, unlike Charles I's ship-money tax which had been so resented that it had figured as one of the causes of the Civil War. New ships in the Commonwealth period were of sturdier build, although sail area was still relatively small in relation to size. By the mid-17th century the complexity of the rigging in warships was greater than ever before, and three-deckers were becoming quite common, the first English one being the 1200 ton *Prince Royal* of 1610, which was also the first English warship known to have had an entrance hatch on her side, previous vessels having relied on ladders for entry. At the beginning of the century, armed merchant-ships were still fighting alongside warships, but the Dutch wars from 1652 showed the former to be at a disadvantage in battle and so the two types of ships increasingly diverged.

English warships tended to be more solidly-built than the lighter, slightly smaller Dutch vessels of the same period. The English ships could readily be distinguished from the Dutch by their round tuck sterns in contrast to the flat sterns of most continental ships; but, because the English ships often carried more and larger guns than the Dutch, this tended to make them slower sailers, outgunning their opponents but unable to outpace them.

Elaborate, baroque-style ornamentation and decoration, particularly on the stern, was a feature of many of the larger seventeenth-century warships generally, because the status and dignity of rulers tended to be reflected in their warships as much as in their palaces, although sometimes only achieved at a cost of a vessel's stability and seaworthiness. Figureheads were also impressive, the *Naseby* had one showing Oliver Cromwell trampling six nations underfoot, a reference to his rule as Lord Protector from 1653 to 1658 when England was militarily at its most successful in that century with defeats of Scots, Irish, French, Spanish, Dutch and the English Royalists. In

1660 Charles II sailed in the *Naseby* back to England from the Continent at the restoration of the monarchy, but tactfully the ship's figurehead, was changed – to one of Father Neptune. The first ironclad, the *Warrior*, lost her original figurehead in a collision with *Royal Oak*, after which Admiralty rules abolishing figureheads, and dating back to 1796, were tightened. But smaller figureheads continued to be produced, although few survive.

Early in the 17th century it became the practice for ships to be placed in categories, at first depending on crew numbers but, by Blake's time, on the number of guns carried. By the Battle of Trafalgar in 1805, the categories were as follows, rating requirements having increased a little during the Dutch wars because ships were larger by then and carried more armament:

100 guns - 1st rater
90 guns - 2nd rater
74 guns - 3rd rater
50 guns - 4th rater
44 guns - 5th rater
28 guns - 6th rater

The *Prince Royal*, of 88 guns, launched in 1610, was about four times as long as she was broad, the first English 3-decker man-of-war and one of the two 1st-raters inherited by Charles II in 1660 from the Commonwealth navy, in which she had been known as the *Resolution*. In the Four Days Battle of 1666, one of the greatest naval engagements with the Dutch of the century, Tromp's able successor, de Ruyter, captured her, and she was surrendered to him by Sir George Ayscue who had played major roles both in bringing about the surrender of Scilly in 1646 and in Blake's reduction of Scilly in 1651.

* * * * *

Such were the type of ships which Blake had with him when he arrived in Scilly on April 13, 1651, although none of them were 3-deckers. He was informed that Tromp's ships had been in the region since April 9th and were still lying nearby. Blake immediately instigated talks with Tromp but, despite the latter's protestations of peaceful purposes, Blake does not seem to have been entirely convinced. On April 20, a letter from the English Envoys, expressing fears of the Dutch intentions, was delivered to the Dutch States-General. It said: 'The Scillies have always belonged to England and were always in the possession of the Parliament which had a garrison there. At present they are in the possession of the enemies of Parliament, but the latter is employing every means that it considers necessary to win them back. But now Admiral Tromp has betaken himself to these Islands with a considerable fleet, with a considerable number of soldiers on board, and has taken up his station off the Islands, without clearly giving information of his intentions. He asserts it is only to force the Islands to give satisfaction for the damage caused to the Dutch by the ships of the Islands. He has not said a word as to whether he is, for this purpose, to make himself master of these Islands.'

The Dutch reaction to this letter was to instruct the Secretary of the States-General to confer with the English Envoys and allay their fears regarding Tromp's expedition. They issued the statement: 'We have no other intention but to cultivate and maintain honourable and sincere friendship with the English Republic. In order to remove all suspicion and mistrust from the Parliament respecting Tromp's expedition, we declare that we have given Tromp no instructions and no orders to seize the Islands; he is to do nothing to the detriment of the English Republic but is only to compel the Governor of the Islands to give back the confiscated ships and goods and, in case of refusal or delay, is to seize the ships of the Scillies and carry them off to sea or wherever else he is able to catch them'.

When Blake's fleet appeared, Tromp broke off his fruitless negotiations with Grenville and spent some time cruising off the Islands, with his fleet divided into two squadrons, hoping thereby to intercept some of Grenville's privateering ships returning with their spoils.

* * * * *

Robert Blake was born in 1599 and studied at Wadham College, Oxford, where he is reported to have enjoyed the classics. He hoped to become an Oxford don but, instead, joined his father in business in his native town of Bridgwater. When he was 25, his father died, leaving Blake to spend the next 15 years running the merchant business and helping to support and educate his 14 brothers and sisters.

When war came in 1642, he joined the Parliamentary army and rose to be a Lieutenant-Colonel, distinguishing himself first by organising the successful defence of Lyme Regis, when it was besieged by Charles I's nephew, Prince Maurice, and then of Taunton in 1644-45, when it was besieged by Maurice's brother, the impetuous but able Prince Rupert, born 1619, the brothers being the sons of Charles I's sister Elizabeth, wife of Frederick, Elector Palatine. Both towns were unwalled and so Blake had to arrange extempore defences, yet from Taunton the garrison on two occasions made sorties out to surprise and damage Rupert's besieging forces. Blake's success here established his military reputation, and he was especially successful against Rupert's subordinate, Goring, who was a good general, but only when sober. Goring was not a drunkard but a hard-drinking individualist, who exhibited characteristics all too common in the Royalist commanders – selfishness, irresponsibility, unreliability and quarrelsomeness – although such criticism does not apply to the admirable Prince Rupert or to Lord Hopton or to the youthful Sir John Grenville. Blake's resistance to the Royalists at Taunton was significant for it crucially tied down the King's forces which were badly needed in the Midlands, but the Taunton defenders had to endure great hardship; food became so short in the ruined town that it is said the defenders were reduced to the deception of whipping one of their last pigs around the town in the desperate hope that the besiegers would conclude that the starving defenders were actually well supplied. Another pleasant story from this siege, concerns an envoy that the Royalists sent into the town to demand their surrender; he happened to be dressed in rather less than neat clothing, and Blake sent him back with his refusal to surrender, but had him dressed in spotless new clothing.

In the following year, Taunton was at last relieved and the Royalist besiegers dispersed, the final military engagement of the 1st Civil War in England coming with the Royalist defeat at Stow-on-the-Wold in 1646.

* * * * *

In 1649, Blake, now 50 years old, was promoted. He may have been chosen by the Parliamentary Commission of 1649 as one of their three Generals-at-Sea because he had already commanded successfully against Prince Rupert at Taunton. Rupert was by this time in charge of the Royalist fleet-in-exile, and was harassing English shipping from bases across the English Channel, but was as equally inexperienced as Blake in seafaring matters. Blake showed his quality by keeping Rupert's fleet blockaded in Portugal's River Tagus for eight months in 1650 – including the winter months – something never achieved before. Rupert also showed enterprise by helping in the invention of a new weapon – what might be called today a sort of cross between a mine and a torpedo – but which was much before its time and proved ineffectual. Blake countered in a more practical way by seizing a number of Portuguese merchant ships and their cargoes, which had sailed from Brazil, in order to bring pressure on the King of Portugal to expel Rupert and his ships. In this Blake was successful, and he even facilitated Rupert by withdrawing his blockading ships temporarily from the Tagus, ostensibly to scrape their hulls but really to provide an opportunity for the Royalist fleet to make its escape. Obligingly, Rupert's six ships sailed out and into the Mediterranean, closely followed by Blake's seven vessels. In Cartagena Bay, Blake caught up with them and captured or forced ashore all six Royalist ships, the Prince making his escape over land. This virtually brought to a close Royalist fleet activity, except for isolated smaller squadrons such as those in Scilly, Man and the Channel Islands. Rupert then spent much of the Interregnum at his brother's court at Heidelberg, finally settling in Mainz where he turned his energies to experiments in chemistry and to developing the art of mezzotint. He came back to England at the Restoration in 1660, and Charles II granted him a handsome annual pension of £6,000. It was then that Rupert showed that he was not just a great cavalry leader but a man of parts: he fought at sea with Monk in the 2nd Dutch War, 1664-7, was one of the founders of the Royal Society and, from 1668, Governor of Windsor, where he experimented with firearms in his laboratory; he was also a leading light in the activities of the Hudson Bay Company of Canada. Although a bachelor, he had a mistress, an actress called Peg Hughes, and was a most talented tennis player; and when he died in 1682, he left to posterity some superb mezzotints. However, Pepys, found him rather bad-tempered.

* * * * *

In 1648, with the outbreak of the 2nd Civil War, Sir John Grenville was sent to Scilly to organise a strong Royalist base in the Islands. But, before the year was out, the Royalist cause had everywhere been defeated on the mainland, leaving Sir John with the task of making the best use he could of the base in Scilly. This consisted increasingly of using his fleet of frigates as privateers to attack passing shipping regardless of the states to which they belonged, so desperate did he become to replenish his stores, and it is arguable that, by so doing, he turned Scilly into a Royalist liability rather than an asset. He even tried to raid Welsh ports – for one of his frigates was captured by the Governor of Cardiff in June, 1649. The Dutch especially were annoyed by his piratical attacks on their vessels, and the States General tried hard to gain recompense for the 28 ships they alleged Grenville's privateers had captured and plundered, but they did not succeed mainly because Grenville had nothing tangible to offer. In fact, a profitable business was run by Grenville with some of the captured vessels; not only were their cargoes taken, but, in the case of one captured ship they even had the impertinence to sell it back to its previous Dutch owner from Rotterdam, together with a cargo of herrings as an additional item for him to purchase. This brazen and outrageous policy continued and, a while later when the ship was again under the Dutch flag at sea, one of Grenville's frigates intercepted her for the second time, and then calmly sold her to other Dutch merchants. Grenville's behaviour in this may have been inevitable, given the desperate isolation of his position, but it was no less appalling when one reflects that the Dutch had generously provided facilities for the King's ships during the Civil War and given them supplies, and had allowed Prince Charles, and his brother James, Duke of York, refuge in their country. The States General in the United Provinces took the action of summoning Charles's ambassador and demanding the return of their plundered ships and cargoes, which led merely to a modest attempt to placate matters by the Duke of York who wrote to Grenville in protest. Grenville maintained that the Dutch ships had been taken by Royalist privateers legitimately, as his ships carried letters of marque which had been issued earlier by the Royalists to merchants who had themselves lost ships and goods to Dutch privateers.

These letters of marque had at one time given a quasi-legitimate status to privateering. They began in Elizabeth's reign when the Crowns of both England and Spain issued letters of marque, allowing private ships to act on behalf of their respective sovereigns and attack the ships of the other. This enabled the two states to conduct a limited war without officially being at war and at no cost to the two governments. It had the added advantage that the sovereigns could disown their privateers if violence was excessive and it became politically advantageous so to do. When captured, the crew of a hostile privateer were invariably treated as proper prisoners of war, whereas if a privateer's captain did not carry a letter of marque, he was classified as a pirate and could be hanged as an outlaw.

However, to use such letters of marque as justification for attacking ships of any nation, could be seen as stretching their purpose. As Michael Baumber in his book *Blake: General-At-Sea* writes: 'For sheer effrontery, impertinence and stupidity, Grenville's attitude is hard to rival. The Dutch had given the Royalists supplies during the First Civil War; had sheltered their fleet during the Second Civil War; and now were giving asylum to the Prince of Wales and the Duke of York.' It is little wonder that the Dutch became increasingly irritated, and, when diplomatic channels achieved nothing, they sent Admiral Maarten Harpertzoon Tromp with three ships to remonstrate with Grenville in person. He arrived in Scilly on 30th March, 1651, only to discover that most of the captured Dutch vessels had been sold and their cargoes along with them, so that there was no chance of getting them back or of being recompensed. Frustrated in his purpose, Tromp was obliged to sail away empty-handed, his three ships and their crews being an insufficient force to persuade Grenville to a different course. All Tromp got from Grenville was a letter containing flowery compliments and the release of a few Dutch prisoners from the captured ships. The Dutch did not declare war on the Scillies, as is sometimes erroneously alleged; Tromp's concern was to seek restitution for losses the Dutch had suffered from the piratical attacks of Grenville's privateers, and a show of force could be a way of achieving this without recourse to violence. Remembered history can often be somewhat removed from what actually happened. Just as Nero never fiddled while Rome burned – nor even plucked a lyre – but actually took some part in leading the firefighters, so the Dutch did not make war on Scilly and never even fired a shot. However, when Tromp visited Pendennis Castle and laid his complaints there, he did seem to push his case by the threat of violence, and this possibility seems to have begun to be taken seriously by the English Government. The Council of State was so alarmed by the number of merchants captured by Grenville's frigates, that they issued an order to Major General Desborough to seize any relations of Grenville living in the West Country and hold them in confinement until Grenville released his civilian prisoners. The order was not put into effect as it was overtaken by events.

On April 17, 1986, an unnecessary but pleasant occasion was held on St Mary's, at which the Dutch ambassador presented a scroll 'officially' ending the 'war' between Scilly and the Netherlands; in fact, of course, there had been no war and, even if one had occurred in 1651, all matters pertaining would have been resolved in 1654 as part of the subsequent treaty between England and the United Provinces at the end of the 1st Dutch War.

When Tromp with about twelve ships (Leslie counted 13) came a second time to Scilly in 1651, he offered to assist Blake to suppress the rebels, but there was no question of conflict with Blake at that time. Curiously, at the 1986 ceremony there seems to have been no apology from the Scillonian side – or show of penitence let alone offer of payment – for the acts of piracy on the Dutch in the 17th century; on the other hand, it can be argued that the Scillonian population in 1651 took no part in the acts of piracy perpetrated upon Dutch merchant ships, and therefore had nothing for which to apologise. They were enduring the Royalist rebel occupation and there is no evidence that they welcomed it. In any event, the 1986 presentation by the Dutch at least showed that for their part they regarded all as forgiven.

The Victoria County History states that 'In 1650 Charles offered the Scillies to a syndicate of Dutch merchants as security for a loan of £50,000', from which it can be concluded that the danger to Scilly came less from Tromp than from Charles II. Had the Dutch accepted, and Charles II had succeeded in handing the Islands to the Dutch, and the States General had ordered Tromp to defend 'their' Islands, Blake's task of reducing them would have been much harder, if not impossible in 1651, although in the treaty of 1654 concluding the 1st Dutch War, no doubt the Islands would have been handed back. However, in March, 1651, the reported presence of Tromp off Scilly with a fleet of 12 warships demanding reparations for piracies committed by Grenville's frigates, caused still greater alarm in the Council of State in London. It was feared that matters might drift out of hand and that Grenville's rebel forces in Scilly might either be attacked by Tromp and the Islands occupied by the Dutch, or that Grenville might be driven by his shortage of supplies to accept succour and support from them, either such eventuality being most unwelcome. Moreover, if Charles was offering the Scillies to the Dutch in return for a loan, this would have been regarded as an alarming treachery. There was thus an air of uncertainty about the matter, and the Council of State had fears enough that the Dutch might resort to taking Scilly – despite Dutch protestations to the contrary – in order to stop the piracy of the Royalist rebels upon their shipping once and for all. The fear was groundless, if the States General's instructions to Tromp of March 11, 1651, which urged him to 'maintain a friendly attitude', are to be believed; but the Council of State decided that the risk was not worth taking and that the subjection of Scilly was therefore more important and more urgent than either that of the Isle of Man or of Barbados. Accordingly, on April 1st, they issued orders for Sir George Ayscue, who was at Plymouth preparing an expedition to Barbados, to place himself, his men and his ships under Blake's command, and with Blake's squadron, which had been preparing to reduce the Isle of Man, to sail to Scilly to oppose Tromp 'if his intentions were prejudicial to the Commonwealth's interests', and not to leave Scilly until the rebels there had been brought into subjection. But it is clear from the Calendar of State Papers, 1651, p. 123, that, once in Scilly, Blake was to assure Tromp that the Commonwealth did not intend to hinder the Dutch 'from righting themselves' upon the Royalists, even if he was not prepared to accept Tromp's military support in reducing them.

✴ ✴ ✴ ✴ ✴

Blake arrived in Scilly on April 13 to begin his task of planning the reduction of Scilly. In this Ayscue was especially helpful to Blake for he had been captain of the *Expedition*, a ship which had taken part in inducing the surrender of the Scillies by the Royalists after the 1st Civil War in 1646. With local knowledge thus acquired, he was able to advise Blake to concentrate on Tresco and Bryher initially because as he wrote: 'the two islands command the road as well as St Mary's, and the gaining of those islands would render St Mary's useless to the enemy ... (their) men-of-war ... will be like mice that run from a falling house, and must be forced to seek a new rendezvous: neither can St Mary's exist without them.'

The Royalist rebels had plenty of defences on St Mary's, with batteries mounted at Toll's Island, Bar Point, Carn Morval and Peninnis, as well as the earthern wall (still traceable) along the north side of the Hugh at the land's edge. But, mindful of his other tasks to perform after subduing the Royalists in Scilly – he went on to take Jersey later in 1651 – Blake decided that he could secure his objective without incurring many casualties, as might have arisen in a full-scale assault. To achieve this, he accepted Ayscue's plan, realising the force of the argument that, once Tresco had been taken, it would be possible to deny Grenville the use of his port on St Mary's, so that, without fresh supplies, Grenville could probably be induced to surrender without need of a landing on St Mary's – and this was in the event to prove the successful strategy. Moreover, as the best natural anchorages in the Scillies are between the islands within the 5 fathom contour, where the Atlantic swell is reduced and where there is shelter from the southwest prevailing winds under the lee of a large island, St Helen's Pool, if a little small, proved quite adequate. Blake also found his ships well positioned here to attack Tresco on its east side, as the west side of the island was strongly defended by the rebels, who also had two frigates there, the *St Michael* (32 guns) and the *Peter* (16 guns), to assist their troops at New Grimsby. The east coast of

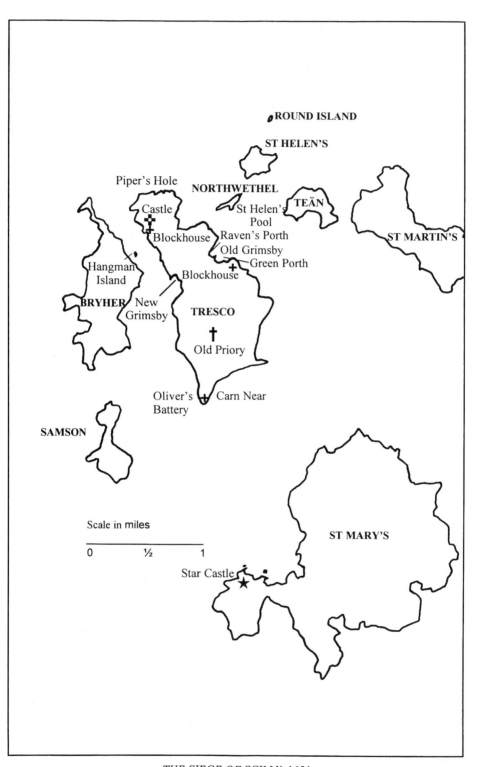

THE SIEGE OF SCILLY, 1651

The ruins of King Charles's Castle on Tresco as they appeared in pre-1st World War days before the site was tidied up and many stones replaced in what was thought to be their original positions. Much of such conservation seems to involve restoration, and can invite criticism; Betjeman used to bemoan the tidying up of the grass at Tintern Abbey so it no longer appeared as Wordsworth saw it. The castle was built 1550-54 to cover New Grimsby from attack by ships sailing down Tresco Channel from the north, but was thought to be badly sited as its guns were said to be unable to depress sufficiently. Photo: Gibson, Scilly

Tresco had an old harbour at Old Grimsby, and many sandy beaches (now called Raven's Porth, Green Porth and Cook's Porth) providing an easy landing access for his soldiers after only a short row in the ships' boats, the main Royalist defences being some earthworks and the blockhouse, whose cannon fire from such a position should have caused more problems than apparently it did.

A strong, easterly wind on April 16 delayed the attack but, by Thursday, the 17th, the wind had abated; so, at 6 a.m., forty boats under Lieut-Colonel Clarke and Lieut-Colonel Bawden set off from the fleet in misty conditions, and made their first assault on Tresco, most of the boats having in their bows a brass gun with grape-shot. However, the operation failed to go according to plan, for some boats, holding three companies of Bawden's men, were much confused by the many islands around them, and found themselves coming ashore in the wrong place; in the prevailing gloom they landed on Northwethel which, although next to Tresco, was separate from it. This happening seems understandable in the circumstances, as anyone who has rowed a boat in the dark near unfamiliar shores may testify; also familiar is the reaction of these soldiers when trying to excuse their mistake, for they blamed a local man called Nance, who had been involuntarily co-opted to help guide them. To make Nance's culpability greater – and therefore their own error more pardonable – they even suggested that he may have misled

Blake's soldiers carried muskets in the open boats when invading Tresco, and some hand-to-hand fighting on shore came to club of muskets. But pikes were used, as they are mentioned in Bishop Leslie's letter; he refers to the Royalist defenders on Tresco being overpowered 'with multitudes and strength of their pikes'.

the rowers through malice – a most common way in which soldiery, fearful of being blamed for a misdeed or mishap, have throughout history tried to evade censure. There are said to be two basic rules of successful soldiering: one is to do what you like but not to get caught, for nobody will help you if you do; the other – and one easy to recognise in the 21st century, when people seem increasingly concerned to cover their legal backs – is that when things might go wrong, always have something or someone upon which or whom to shift the blame. In this instance of landing on a mistaken shore, heaping the blame on the local pilot is a classic example of this rule in operation, whilst the notion that one unarmed Scillonian would dare deliberately to pursue a one-man campaign against hundreds of armed men is patently unlikely, unless one is persuaded that the Islanders were dedicated supporters of the Royalist rebels – a dubious belief, as is evident from Grenville's letter to Nicholas of February 23, 1649, above.

In the event no opposition to the landing of Bawden's men was encountered, so the mistake was quickly realised and the soldiers re-embarked. It is exaggerating to describe the incident as farcical, for war operations are full of such small enforced deviations from plan; moreover, we have no knowledge of Nance's political views, if any, other than the soldier's accusations that his incompetence as a pilot may have been grazed with treachery, accusations rather suspect since they appear made to help excuse their own perceived errors. Lereck's account also mentions timerity and incompetence as reasons for the error. It is doubtful if the ordinary Scillonian civilian population were given to indulging in political views, for usually, as elsewhere, they had little option on the whole but to accept whatever military or political rule was in the ascendant at any one time. There is insufficient evidence for assuming with certainty anything particularly heroic about Nance's error.

However, the mistake had consequences beyond anticipation, and if the misdirection was sabotage, it was remarkably successful. The reason is that, while Bawden's soldiers on Northwethel were all safely put back on their boats, the other boats were kept waiting for them, swaying up and down in the choppy sea for rather too long, with many of their occupants growing tired with rowing, and succumbing to debilitating seasickness. Other boats went aground with the ebbing tide, and had to be manhandled towards the open water to refloat them. The advantage of surprise was lost, and the Royalist defenders of Tresco – mainly musketeers under Colonel Wogan firing from behind the cover of rocks on the beaches – were able to mount quite a fusillade against the crowded invaders. Indeed, the occupants of many of the boats were so tightly packed that they found difficulty in aiming their own muskets to return the fire. Only one boat, that under Captain Smith, successfully effected a landing, but his men were forced back – and, with that, the assault was abandoned for the day. However, despite this initial failure in which six men were lost, one shallop was sunk and another lost its oars, the island's defences had been tested and they had proved stronger than had been anticipated; it was estimated that 70 great and small shot had been fired at the boats besides musket shot in abundance.

It is not known exactly how many men Grenville had at his disposal, but by 1651 over 1000 appears a likely figure and many of them, led by himself, he took as reinforcements from St Mary's to boost the defences on Tresco once it became clear where Blake's main assault was likely to be made. The Royalists had their headquarters in Scilly at Star Castle; but they also manned several batteries on St Mary's commanding Crow Sound, with one on Bryher, and on Tresco a battery at Crow Point (a few traces of which are claimed to be still visible). There was also Tresco Castle (now called King Charles's Castle) and two blockhouses; but Grenville's weakness was that, although the initial assault on Tresco had been repelled, he knew the attack would be resumed and he had little option but to sit tight and await it in the hope that it could also be repelled.

That night, leaving a few dozen men on Northwethel 'to alarm and arouse the enemy', most of Blake's soldiers made camp on the larger, uninhabited island of Teän, and there spent a cold and comfortless night in their tents. There was little water on Teän, and what little there was soon became unfit. Royalist guns on Tresco fired some great shot at them but a little inaccurately, knocking down a few tents but causing no casualties. Blake's commanders decided to resume the assault the next day as the weather was still reasonable and the sea calm, so much-needed supplies were rowed in to them from some of Blake's ships riding at anchor some distance from the shore, and detailed plans were drawn up for the following day's assault.

The Old Blockhouse or Dover Fort at Old Grimsby on Tresco is sited on a natural granite outcrop and seems well positioned to defend the beaches below it. It was probably constructed between 1548 and 1552 under the direction of Sir Francis Fleming and John Killigrew, Captain of Pendennis Castle, Falmouth. It had a small rectangular gun-platform, with living quarters for the gunners to the rear. Old Grimsby was then more important a port of Tresco than New Grimsby – as indeed their names may suggest – and its main function was to protect the one area of beach it apparently failed to do in 1651.

Many of Lieut-Colonel Clarke's soldiers were new recruits, raw and inexperienced; it was thought that some of them might have become demoralised by their recent repulse, so Clarke sent Captain Hatsell and Captain Smith to Blake to ask for more men. In response, and in the light of his experience defending Lyme Regis, Blake decided that this time the leading assault boats would be manned by 200 of his seamen, who were all experienced men, hardened by previous action, and would be more skilled in handling the boats. They were under Captain Lewis Morris, who was later to be given a grant of £100 for the gallantry he displayed in the action which followed.

To deceive the enemy, camp fires were left burning on Teän and Northwethel, which also created something of a smokescreen, and, in the early morning of Friday, April 18, on a flat calm sea – in gloom but without cover of the mist of the previous day to help conceal their approach – the invasion was begun, careful note having been taken the previous day of the exact places best suited for landing. Once again the Royalists mounted a hail of fire on the boats, but enough sailors in the leading boats were landed under Captain Morris to form a bridgehead long enough for the soldiers to disembark and establish themselves. Most of the following boats landed almost simultaneously and some hard fighting then took place on the beaches for about an hour. The hand-to-hand fighting came even to club of musket

44

All that can now be seen of Oliver's Battery at Carn Near, but clearly indicating its coverage of the entrance to St Mary's Harbour 1½ miles away. Denied supplies by this battery it was only a matter of time before the rebel Royalists under Grenville surrendered to Blake on the best terms they could secure.

before Blake's forces put the Royalist rebels to flight, leaving one captain and fourteen men dead. Sir John Grenville then made a rapid escape from Tresco back to Star Castle on St Mary's and withdrew his men from Bryher; but he left behind his 25 cannon and some men were left to join the garrison of Tresco Castle. This was the island's Royalist strongpoint and was commanded by William Edgcumb, the officer Grenville now placed in charge of all his forces on Tresco – although Edgcumb was even younger than Grenville himself. Meanwhile, Blake's forces penetrated inland on Tresco and set fire to the priory, burning it to the ground, while some of Blake's ships entered the channel between Bryher and Tresco and took New Grimsby, capturing both the rebel frigates there and renaming them *Bryher* and *Tresco*. But the Royalists still held their strongpoint at Tresco Castle, which today is called King Charles's Castle to distinguish it from the later Cromwell's Castle. It is best described as an artillery fort, built 1550 to 1554, with a semi-hexagonal western end to allow a wide field of fire, and with two storeys to provide for two tiers of guns. The domestic quarters for the garrison were at the rear of the fort. During the 1st Civil War, 1642-46, earthworks of the bastion type were dug inland from it to give extra strength to repel any landward attack, and these earthworks can still be traced today. Edgcumb strengthened the castle's garrison by rallying as many men as he could to its defence, calling in all units formerly holding detached posts on Tresco. But increasingly he realised his position was hopeless because he had no means of securing fresh supplies, and really his castle faced west, when Blake's forces were expected to attack from the east.

Colonel Fleetwood, a fine and courageous soldier, then directed the land attack on the castle, while some of Blake's ships, in the channel up from New Grimsby and under his personal direction, bombarded the fort from the sea. It may seem ironic that this fort, which was criticised for its difficulty in directing fire at ships in the channel, apparently did not at this time have difficulty in receiving fire from them. Under Fleetwood's attack the Royalist resistance began to crumble, but it is said that Edgcumb was determined that he would not surrender the castle intact and decided to take a dramatic course of action: unseen by the enemy, he laid a trail of gunpowder from the castle's magazine to a position where he was hidden outside the walls, and then set the trail alight. The resulting explosion blew up much of the fort killing many of both defenders and attackers, and it was assumed at the time that Edgcumb had died in the carnage, although his body was not identified. Colonel Fleetwood gave all who perished in this final act of folly, both friend and foe, an honourable soldier's burial. In addition, four captains and about 163 Royalist soldiers were taken prisoner, the remainder (between 300 and 600) fleeing to St Mary's, although about forty of these were drowned when their small craft capsized en route.

The allegation that Blake had some of the Royalists strung up on Hangmen's Island is a later Cavalier insinuation and has no foundation in fact. It was not Blake's or Fleetwood's way of doing things, as is evidenced from the subsequent negotiations; but the calumny still gets repeated, even in modern publications, with Cromwell taking the blame, even though he was not Protector until two years after the reduction of Scilly. The name of the island is from the Cornish *An Main* (meaning *The Rock*) and has nothing to do with executions, despite the representation of a gibbet thoughtfully provided near its summit by a mischievous visitor.

The tale so far is one of conflict, yet it had a romantic sequel. When hostilities ended, normal life returned to Tresco, and Colonel Fleetwood's daughter, Mildred, spent some of her time enjoying sitting on the cliffs above Piper's Hole. Here – she later revealed – she met a young man, who, although emaciated and ill-clothed, claimed to be William Edgcumb; he said he had escaped the soldiers and was hiding in the recesses of Piper's Hole. The story goes that he showed Mildred his bed, weapons and the provisions which he had stored in the cave, some of which were allegedly supplied to him by an islander. Mildred was said to have been entranced by William and did not betray him; she even helped to disguise him as a local fisherman and engineered his escape to St Mary's, eventually to join Charles on his 'travels' in France. Before going, William pressed Mildred to marry him, but she refused, feeling that she had been disloyal enough to her father; but the tale has a happy ending, for the couple kept in touch and, after the Restoration of the Monarchy in 1660, they married, and Mildred became one of the ladies at the Court of the Merry Monarch.

The most vivid contemporary account of the assault on Tresco on the April 17 and 18, 1651, is by Jos. Lereck, who was a soldier with Blake's forces. The original document is preserved in Tresco Abbey but, by kind permission of Mr Robert Dorrien Smith, it is reproduced here, followed by Jos. Lereck's narrative again, rendered in parts in more modern English, with spelling and punctuation in places updated. In addition, certain words of Lereck's have been changed to modern equivalents in order to promote better understanding; 'emulation', for example, is now almost confined to the meaning 'copy', but in the 17th century also meant 'jealous rivalry', and so the word has been changed to the meaning which Lereck surely intended. Similarly 'bestead' and 'remora' are hardly in common circulation today, and have also been changed to, respectively, 'help' and 'hindrance'. Such liberties seem justified to ensure that Lereck's account may be more clearly conveyed.

It is also worth observing that Lereck is writing for a definite and specific purpose – that of rebutting certain allegations. The account is a robust defence of the part played in the attack on Tresco by the Parliamentary soldiers, and an answer to those who were claiming that Blake's sailors played the main role in this 'service'. Some may feel that Lereck's anger somewhat spoils the account, until it is realised that we might not be fortunate enough to have such an account at all had Lereck not been driven to put right what he saw as an injustice to the reputations of the soldiers. He seems to make his point repetitively, if not in every detail convincingly, and some of his sentences may be found inordinately long for modern readers: but overall he has given a vivid eye-witness account of one of the more dramatic episodes in Scilly's history:

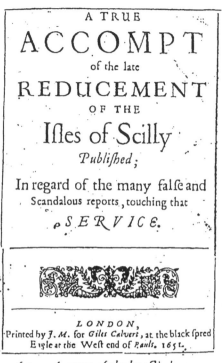

A TRUE

ACCOMPT

of the late

REDUCEMENT

OF THE

Ifles of Scilly

Publifhed;

In regard of the many falfe and
Scandalous reports, touching that

SERVICE.

LONDON,
Printed by *J. M.* for *Giles Calvert,* at the black fpred
Eagle at the Weft end of *Pauls.* 1651.

*A true Accompt of the late Reducement
of the Ifles of* Scilly, *publifhed in regard of the many falfe and fcandalous
Reports touching that Service.*

FOr as much as fome men have taken upon them to
write and report very falfly, and indeed fcandal-
oufly, traducing the unfpotted reputation of
faithful Inftruments in managing the late Reducement of the Ifles of *Scilly:* I hope 'twill be accounted no tranfgreffion, if I take leave to reprefent an honeft
and true Account of the fervice done there.

I fhall not venture, as fome have unworthily done, to
fay ought upon bare hear-fay, but fhall write upon better knowledg, being actually in the fervice from firft to
laft, and an eye witnefs of what was done.

And why I may not with more reafon expect to win
credit upon that Account, then thofe who have written
and reported fwelling words of vanity, and yet never hazarded their carkaffes within Cannon fhot of danger
in the fervice; I fee not.

'Tis to be feared, I wifh it be not fo, That greedinefs
of honour have prompted fome to prepoffefs the world
with their own worth above what was meet; and nct
only fo, but thereby, detracting from others, have, with

too much affectation, attempted to pin the Honour of
the work upon their own fleeves.

I fhall avoyd Partiality in my Relation, and follow
the unbyaffed way of Truth; I refer my felf to the *Teft,*
let any difprove me if they can.

The manner of the fervice was thus:

After we had layn at Sea, from Saturday *April* 12.
til Thurfday 17. in the morning betimes (each Officer
having received Orders over-night) we boated our Soldiers, intending to gain a landing place upon *Trifcoe,* to
that end we divided our Boats and Men into two parts,
the one to land in a fandy Bay by their Fort within old
Grimsbay Harbor, the other in a more ftony Bay, fome-
what to the Weftward of that; But the quicknefs of
the Tyde had fet our Boats fo much to the Eaftward out
of the way, and the fearful Pilots directing another
courfe among the Rocks, we were neceffitated to fet all
forwards toward Old *Grimsbay* Harbor. The Enemy
perceiving our motion, drew their chief ftrength thi-
ther-wards to oppofe us. Our Boats being all of them
exceedingly cram'd with men, and many of them very
flenderly accomplifhed for fuch a fervice, rowed exceeding heavily, & could not by any means be brough to row
up clofe one with another, and fom were fet faft upon
the Rocks for want of water: Whereupon Orders were
given, that the Boats fhould ftop under a Rock till they
came up altogether, that we might joyntly fet upon the
Work. But in the Progrefs, the Pilots, and many of the
Rowers (who were taken up in the Weft Country, very
backward to the fervice) mifguided our headmoft
Boats to a little Ifland called *Northwethel,* ftanding in
the entrance to Old *Grimsbay* Harbor, and within half
Musket fhot of *Trifcoe,* divided by the water, and fo fci-
tuate, as none, fave thofe who were acquainted, could
know whether 'twere part of *Trifcoe* or not. To this
place the timerous or treacherous Pilots directed, affirming once and again that it was *Trifcoe;* and when
Major *Bawden* replyed, he was doubtful of it, in regard
he difcovered none of the Enemy coming down to oppofe their landing, one *Nants* (accounted the moft
knowing Pilot for the place) affirmed refolutely (upon
his life) that it was *Trifcoe,* whereupon three Companies prefently landed; but the Miftake difcovered, prevented the landing of any more, yet not without fom dif-
order upon our bufinefs; Notwithftanding which, and
that the Tyde and opportunity might not be loft, Orders
were given, that the reft of the Boats fhould row on into
the Bay, where we intended to land; but our foremoft
Boats were again mifguided, and unadvifedly made, to
that part of the Iland neareft hand, occafioned the rather
as I fuppofe, for that the Enemy had there drawn down
a Body of Mufketeers, and fired much upon our Boats,
with whom our men defired to be doing, but the place
proved craggy & inacceffible, fo that we could not land:
Here was hot firing between our men and the Enemy,
(the Rocky fhore being the only Interponent;) They
had a fufficient advantage againft us, having the Rocks for
their fhelter, and our men fo very thick crowded in their
open Boats, as many of them could not make ufe of their
Arms: indeed it was a miracle of mercy that we loft
not very many men here; if any of our Boats had been
foundred, all the men muft needs have been loft; for
every Boat was fo exceeding full, that in fuch an extremity, one could not poffibly have helped another.

48

Now to be plain, when the Boats drew somewhat neer, and the great, small, and case-shot flew about to some purpose, and danger must be lookt in the face, (for I believe we endured about 70 great shot, besides muskets in abundance) many of the Boats, in stead of rowing forward into the Bay, turned the Helm, end rowed backward, and aside, from the business. And notwithstanding Lievt. Colonel *Clark* (of whom, to speak the truth in this place, I hope will be no offence) strugled all he could to draw them on, earnestly calling to one and commanding another to follow him with their Boats, yet would neither commands nor threats perswade them to observance ; but, do what he could, they rowed off. This I must affirm for truth, for that I heard and saw the gentleman above-named standing on the head of his Boat, amidst the thickest of the shot, under this performance. And I beleeve there want not sufficient testimonies ; Captain *Dover* may please to remember, that he among others was called to, yea and commanded too, upon pain of death to follow on with his Boat : What his Answer was, and how carefully observed, cannot be unknown to himself, nor yet to others; for I am sure his boat rowed off, and came no neer.

After some time spent, I think neer half an hour, in this perilous, yet successless manner, we withdrew to *Northwortbel*, the little island where our Boats were first misguided ; Our loss was not great in respect of the hazard, which I wish may be recorded upon all our hearts as a signal testimony of Gods abundant goodness and favor to us, Some four Soldiers and one or two Seamen were slain, and the like number of the Enemy, with Colonel *Wogan* wounded.

Three Companies were left upon *Northwortbel* to keep the Enemy busie, and the rest were landed upon an adjacent island, called *Tean*, from whence we had a better discovery of the Enemies shore; The place yeelded but little fresh water, which, through the number of our men, was soon troubled, and made unfit to drink, which together with the want of provisions, and the raw constitution of our men newly come on shore, made this cold nights lodging the more irksom and comfortless.

The next day, *April* 18. the enemy spent some great shot at us, which sell among some of our Tents and brake them, but did no farther harm ; We labored to get some provisions ashore (which could not be suddenly done, our ships riding at that distance) for want of which our men were indeed distressed : and some thereupon murmured even to discontent, repining at the condition of the service they were to undergo upon such faint terms ; But through a supply of victual, and careful regard of Lievt. Colonel *Clark*, all was put into an exact posture, in order to a second attempt ; To which end *Capt. Hatfel* and *Capt. Smith* were sent aboard Admiral *Blake*, to desire that the Boats, and Rowers who would stick more resolutely to their Oars, might be sent to us, which he did : And that we might be the better besteaded in our landing, he moreover appointed about 150 or 200 Seamen (who were better acquainted with Marine affairs) to attempt with us, under the conduct of *Captain Morrice*.

We thought it necessary to deal with the enemy speedily, while the weather was seasonable, for should it have proved otherwise, and our ships have been forced

off to Sea, we must either have perished, or have given our selves up to the Enemy for a morsel of bread. Upon Consultation, we resolved (it being judged best) to storm the Enemy by night, and to that end, had, in this day-time, carefully observed how to direct our course to the place we intended for landing, (which was about ⅓ of a mile, and interrupted with many rocks in the way,) for now we became our own Pilots.

We boated our men (having drawn off those three Companies from *Northwortbel* in the dark of the evening, and left there onely some 80 men to Alarum and amuse the enemy in that quarter while we fell on,) and between 11 and 12 of the clock at night set forward [the Seamens Boats being head-most,) at which time it pleased God that it was very calm ; so that the enemies Friggots, whom we doubted might injure us in our passage (being thereunto designed) and do most prejudice, could not come up to do any harm, though they spent some great shot at us. We made fires upon *Tean* as if we had continued there, the smoke wherof was blown towards the enemy, which somewhat obscured our passage ; Yet the enemy discovered us when we came about half way over, and took an Alarum, and ere we attained the shore fired many Ordnance upon us, which did no hurt.

The boats came up for the most part roundly together, and put to the shore, where the enemy disputed our landing with stout resistance, in so much as the Seamen were forced back into the water ; yet our men charged them resolutely, even to club-musket, and through the blessing of God worsted them, killed upon the place one Captain, and some 12 or 14 others, took Prisoners 167. whereof four Captains, the rest fled, none had escaped, had we been acquainted with the Island.

The Enemy opposed us at this place with about two hundred of their best men, but the Lord was pleased to make their strength as stubble, and to give the place with a greater advantage into our hands, then if we had succeeded in our first Attempt ; for the Enemy grew the more confident, and sent over another supply of their best men from Saint *Maries* Island to make this the more sure, which made up in all above 300 men, a greater strength by far then was imagined : But the Lord was our Helper, graciously answering to the Word given out amongst us, which was [*Help Lord.*]

This nakedly represents the sum of our Proceeds, which indeed is circumstantiated with so much of the manifest Providence and Power of God, as might make the most deserving Instruments (concerned in the work) humble and sober, and not to have high thoughts of themselves.

And now what reason there is for some to write and report, *That the Seamen did all the work, That they alone gained the landing place, That they did the main, the work, That the work was undertaken by,* &c. undervaluing and declaiming the service of the Souldiery, let all men judg.

Truly I would not detract a hairs bredth from their worth, nor would I write one word that might provoke emulation, or stir up animosity, I love the girdle of Amity and Unity ; the Sea-men did good service, and the Souldiers did no less. But that the main work, or gaining the landing place, was (as some have too largely written and reported) solely performed by them, I must deny as untrue. For although the Sea-men were in the second or third headmost Boats, (as, I conceive, in reason they should, in regard of their better experience for guidance of the rest through that Rocky passage in the night, and greater skill and acquaintance with Maritine service, and besides having under them the choycest and best accomplished Boats for that purpose,) yet had not the rest of the Boats been carefully kept on together with them, and, as it were, in the nick of time, put to the shoar and the Souldiers immediately grapled with the Enemy (who to give them their due, sternly opposed,) without doubt the Sea-men had come to an ill Market, and must needs have perished: For 'tis well enough known, that upon their landing they were presently beaten back into the water, even under their Boats, and were as soon relieved by the Souldiers, whose courage was no whit daunted from doing their duties: I insert not this as any blemish, the best men in the world may receive a check, but that the clear truth of the business may be fully known.

This appears no fiction; besides a Cloud of Testimonies, honest and valiant Corporal *Perry*, of Captain *Northcots* Company, carryed the mortal witness of this charge to his grave, who then received his deaths wound upon the edg of the shoar.

But if one hundred fifty, or two hundred Sea-men, (which were the utmost) thus interested in the work, be accounted such a high matter; it may be remembred that (upon Conference between the Sea and Land Commanders at *Plymouth* about this business) the Assistance of so many Sea-men was no more, nor indeed so much, as was thought requisite to the carrying off this Mariterrene service; which, give me leave to say, is another manner of business, and of another complexion, then that we usually are acquainted with at Land.

To say more: Put the case (though it be not the case here) a party of Souldiers or Sea-men should of themselves have carried that or the like Attempt against an Enemy, without the actual Assistance of the residue of the Forces orderly following to the service, should that party have so vainly blown the Trumpet before them, as that they had done the main work? the Honour of it was due to them,---&c. causlesly decrying and traducing the rest of the Forces. Truly, I conceive, so doing would not, only, be accounted a frothy vapour, but an unhandsom peece of injury to the rest.

All that can be said to this particular (as far as I can see) is, That Admiral *Blake* sent about one hundred fifty or two hundred Sea-men to assist the Land Forces in the storming of *Trißoo*: God was pleased to give a blessing to the Attempt, and thereupon we forced our Entrance, spoyled the Enemy, and gained the Island: A slender ground, methinks, for any to vent such lofty language on the one hand, and causlesly to bespatter the good service of the Souldiers on the other.

What should move *Captain Peck* to insert in his letter such false intelligence to Major General *Desborough*, as that the first days attempt failed through the timerousness of some Commanders of the Soldiers, that the Seamen did the work, &c. his own heart best knows: little reason I beleeve he had: I am sure he shot his bolt at randome, and could write nothing of his owne knowledg; for indeed neither himself, nor any other

Sea-Commander hazarded themselves in either of the Attempts; The Seamen who were with us the last day were commanded by Captain *Morrice*, a Passenger to the *Barbados*; And when *Captain Peck* was questioned about this, by some of the Officers at *Trißoo*, why he would offer to injure and disrepute the Soldiers, by writing such detracting language, without any real ground of truth, things which he indeed knew not; and withall desired that he would name some that had failed their duty; He answered, he could name none; nor knew nothing, but by hear-say, and report of some Seamen, and that he was sorry his writing should any ways prove prejudicial, and that he thought no more harm in what he wrote then he intended to his own heart. I would not have been thus particular but for the Truths sake.

No better ground, questionless, had some others, to give the like blinde Account of the business; and among the rest Captain *Pecks Brother* (as I am informed) took upon him the boldness, very unworthily to traduce the reputation of Lieut. Colonel *Clark*, and to exercise his tongue very scandalously; the Gentleman hath no need of my pen to vindicate or commend him; his merits and faithful endevors in this peece of service, will, I question not, survive the lying reports of all detractors. If any failing may be imputed to him, I think it can be no other, unless the over-much care and pains he took in prosecution of the work may be so accounted; indeed he underwent too much for his body, which was but sickly when he came from *Plymouth*, and which the Sea had much oppressed with continual distemper all the while he was on ship board, and now more weakened on shore for lack of natural rest, &c. Yet I am confident none can truly say, he either swerved from his duty at any time, or favored himself from hazard, or yet accounted his life precious for the works sake.

But 'tis more then probable, this Gentleman, as some others, who have impudently lashed with their tongues, wanted a true prospect of the business, being muffled up in the smoke of the Ordnance fired from Aboard, the ships far enough out of danger; and mistaking so much at hand, ran into grosser absurdities farther off, speeding those false reports abroad, where (for present) were none that could contradict them.

'Tis a good part of Religion to bridle the tongue; if that were observed more, we should have less strife and emulation.

Thus much I have adventured to publique view; I hope I have therein not exceeded the bounds of soberness and truth; my end is, that this peece of service may be truly understood; and the Honor and Worth of faithful Instruments vindicated. Indeed I was hitherto loth to exercise my pen upon this subject, lest I might hazard the breach of amity; and, truly, had not done it now, had not the lavish tongue and pens of some gone about to crop off the best flower in a mans garden, viz. his honor & reputation: And therforr, speaking but the truth, I hope I shall justly give no offence; *if offences come, woe be to them by whom they come.*

Let the exceeding goodness of God to this unthankful Nation, in lopping off the bough even with terror, and giving into our hands a place stufft with about 12

and but yesterday the *remora* to our Maritine affairs, a
scourge to the Merchants, thought invincible for
strength, and desperate to attempt, with so little loss,
and in so short a time; Let, I say, the eminent hand of
Gods good Providence in these particulars teach us all
to live the life of Faith, and to walk more humbly and
thankfully before him, and not to forget and undervalue
such signal mercies, or disesteem such faithful instruments, whose hearts and hands (I may confidently say)
were really fixt, and through *Gods* blessing became instrumental for the compleatment of the work, which as
it carries in it a singular high advantage to the Com·
monwealth, so let it gather from all our hearts due acknowledgments of praise and glory to the *God* of our
Salvation, who hath delivered and will yet deliver us,
if we wait and put our trust in him.

Jos. Lereck.

F I N I S.

A TRUE ACCOUNT OF THE LATE REDUCEMENT OF THE ISLES OF SCILLY, PUBLISHED IN REGARD TO THE MANY FALSE AND SCANDALOUS REPORTS TOUCHING THAT SERVICE

For as much as some men have taken upon them to write and report very falsely, and
indeed scandalously, traducing the unspotted reputation of faithful instruments in
managing the late reducement of the Isles of Scilly, I hope 'twill be accounted no
transgression if I take leave to present an honest and true account of the service done there.
I shall not venture, as some have unworthily done, to say ought upon mere hearsay, but
shall write from better knowledge, being actually in the service from first to last, and an
eyewitness to what was done.

And why I may not with more reason expect to win credit upon that account, than those
who have written and reported swelling words of vanity, and yet never hazarded their
carcasses within cannonshot of danger in the service, I see not.

It is to be feared – I wish it to be not so – that greediness of honour has prompted some to
prejudice the world with their own worth above what was meet; and not only so but,
thereby detracting from others, have, with too much affectation, attempted to pin honour
of the work upon their own selves.

I shall avoid partiality in my relation, and follow the unbiased way of truth. I refer myself
to the test, let any disprove me if they can.

* * * * *

The manner of the service was thus. After we had lain at sea from Saturday, April 12th, till Thursday, the 17th, in the morning betimes (each officer having received orders overnight), we boated our soldiers, intending to gain a landing place upon Tresco; to that end we divided our boats and men into two parts, the one to land in a sandy bay by their fort within Old Grimsby harbour, the other in a more stoney bay somewhat to the westward of that. But the quickness of the tide had set our boats so much to the eastward out of the way, and the fearful pilots directing another course upon the rocks, we were necessitated to set all forwards towards Old Grimsby harbour. The enemy, perceiving our motion, drew their chief strength thitherwards to oppose us. Our boats, being all of them exceedingly crammed with men, and many of them very slenderly accomplished for such a service, rowed exceedingly heavily, and could not by any means be brought to row up close one with another, and some were set hard upon the rocks for want of water. Whereupon, orders were given that the boats should stop under a rock till they came up together, that we might jointly set upon the work. But in the progress, the pilots and many of the rowers (who were taken up in the West Country and were backward to the service) misguided our headmost boats to a little island called Northwethel standing in the entrance to Old Grimsby harbour, and within half a musket shot of Tresco, divided by the water, and so situated that none, save those who were acquainted with the place, could know whether it was part of Tresco or not. To this place the timorous or treacherous pilots directed us, affirming once and again that it was Tresco; and when Major Bawden replied that he was doubtful of it, because he discovered none of the enemy coming down to oppose the landing, one Nance (accounted the most knowing pilot for the place) affirmed resolutely (upon his life) that it was Tresco, whereupon three companies presently landed but, the mistake discovered, prevented the landing of any more, yet not without some disorder upon our business; notwithstanding which, and that the tide and opportunity might not be lost, orders were given that the rest of the boats should row on into the bay where we intended to land. But our foremost boats were again misguided, and inadvisedly made to that part of the island nearest at hand, occasioned there rather, as I suppose, because the enemy had there drawn down a body of musketeers and fired much upon our boats, with whom our men desired to be engaging. But the place proved craggy and inaccessible so that we could not land. Here was hot firing between our men and the enemy (the rocky shore being the only interponent). They had sufficient advantage against us, having rocks for their shelter, and our men so very thick crowded in their open boats, as many of them could not make use of their arms; indeed, it was a miracle of mercy that we lost not very many men here. If any of our boats had foundered, all the men must needs have been lost, for every boat was so exceedingly full that in such an extremity one could not possibly have helped another.

Now to be plain, when the boats somewhat near the shore, and the great, small and caseshot flew about to some purpose, and danger must be looked in the face (for I believe we endured about 70 great shot besides musket shot in abundance), many of the boats, instead of rowing forward into the bay, turned the helm and rowed backwards, and aside from the business. And notwithstanding Lieut-Colonel Clarke (of whom, to speak the truth in this place, I hope will be no offence) struggled all he could to draw them on, earnestly calling to one and commanding another to follow him with their boats. Yet would neither commands nor threats persuade them to observance; but, do what he could, they rowed off. This I must affirm for truth, for that I heard and saw the gentleman above-named standing on the head of his boat, amidst the thickest of the shot under this performance. And, I believe there want not sufficient testimonies; Captain Dover may please remember that he among others was called – yea and commanded too upon pain of death – to follow on with his boat. What his answer was, and how carefully observed, cannot be unknown to himself nor yet to others, for I am sure his boat rowed off and came not near.

After some time, I think near half an hour spent in this perilous yet unsuccessful manner, we withdrew to Northwethel, the little island to which our boats were first misguided. Our loss was not great in respect of the hazard, which I wish may be recorded upon all our hearts as a signal testimony of God's abundant goodness and favour to us. Some four soldiers and one or two seamen were slain, and the like of the enemy, with Colonel Wogan wounded.

Three companies were left upon Northwethel to keep the enemy busy, and the rest were landed upon the adjacent island called Teän, from whence we had a better view of the enemy's shore. The place yielded but little fresh water, which, through the large number of our men, was soon a trouble; it became unfit to drink, which, together with the want of provisions and the raw constitution of our men newly come on shore, made this cold night's lodging the more irksome and comfortless.

The next day, April 18th, the enemy spent some great shot at us, which fell among some of our tents and broke them, but did no further harm. We laboured to get some provisions ashore (which could not be suddenly done as our ships were riding at some distance), for want of which our men were indeed distressed: and some thereupon murmured even to discontent, repining at the condition of the service they were to undergo upon such faint terms. But through a supply of victual and careful regard of Lieut-Colonel Clark, all was put into an exact posture, in order to make a second attempt. To which end Capt. Hatsel and Capt. Smith were sent to Admiral Blake to desire that boats and rowers who would stick more resolutely to their oars might be sent to us, which he did: and that we might be the better helped in our landing, we moreover appointed about 150 or 200 seaman (who were better acquainted with marine affairs) to attempt the landing with us under the conduct of Captain Morrice.

We thought it necessary to deal with the enemy speedily while the weather was reasonable, for should it have proved otherwise, and our ships have been forced off to sea, we must either have perished or have given ourselves up to the enemy for a morsel of bread. Upon consultation, we resolved (it being judged best) to storm the enemy by night, and to that ends, had, in this daytime, carefully observed how to direct our course to the place we intended for landing (which was about three quarters of a mile and interrupted with many rocks in the way), for now we became our own pilots.

We boated our men (having drawn off those three companies from Northwethel in the dark of the evening, and left there only some 80 men to alarm and amuse the enemy in that quarter while we fell on), and between 11 and 12 of the clock at night set forward (the seamen's boats being headmost), at which time it pleased God that it was very calm, so that the enemy's frigates, whom we feard might injure us in our passage (being thereunto designed) and do most damage, could not come up to do any harm, though they spent some great shot at us, we made fires upon Teän as, if we had continued there, the smoke whereof was blown towards the enemy, which somewhat obscured our passage; yet the enemy discovered us when we came about half way over, and took an alarm and, ere we attained the shore, fired many ordnance upon us, which did no hurt.

The boats came up for the most part roundly together, and put to the shore, where the enemy disputed our landing with stout resistance insomuch as the seamen were forced back into the water; yet our men charged them resolutely, even to club-musket, and, through the blessing of God, worsted them, killed upon the place one captain and some 12 or 14 others, took prisoners 167; whereof four captains and the rest fled, and none would have escaped had we been acquainted with the island.

The enemy opposed us at this place with about two hundred of their best men, but the Lord was pleased to make their strength as stubble, and to give the place with a greater advantage into our hands than if we had succeeded in our first attempt; for the enemy grew the more confident and sent over another supply of their best men from St Marys to make this the more sure, which made up in all above 300 men, a greater strength by far than was imagined. But the Lord was our helper, graciously answering to the word given out amongst us, which was 'Help us Lord'.

This nakedly represents the sum of our proceeds, which indeed is circumstantiated with so much of the Manifest Providence and Power of God, as might make the most deserving instruments (concerned in the work) humble and sober, and not to have high thoughts of themselves.

And now what reason there is for some to write and report that the seamen did all the work, that they alone gained the landing place, that they did the main work etc.... undervaluing and declaiming the service of the soldiery, let all men judge.

Truly I would not detract a hair's breadth from their worth, nor would I write one word that might provoke jealous rivalry, or stir up animosity, I love the girdle of amity and unity; the seamen did good service, and the soldiers did no less. But that the main work, or gaining the landing place, was (as some have too largely written and reported) solely performed by them, I must deny as untrue. For, although seamen were in the second or third headmost boats (as, I conceive, in reason they should be in regard to their better experience for guidance of the rest through the rocky passage in the night, and greater skill and acquaintance with maritime service, and besides having under them the choicest and best accomplished boats for that purpose), yet had not the rest of the boats been carefully kept on together with them, and, as it were, in the nick of time put to the shore and the soldiers immediately grappled with the enemy (who, to give them their due, sternly opposed), without doubt the seamen would have come to an ill fate and must needs have perished.

For, 'tis well enough known that upon their landing they were presently beaten back into the water, even under their boats, and were as soon relieved by the soldiers, whose courage was no whit daunted from doing their duties: I infer not this as any blemish, the best men in the world may receive a check, but that the clear truth of the business may be fully known.

This appears no fiction; beside a cloud of testimonies, honest and valiant Corporal Perry of Captain Northcot's company, carried the mortal witness of this charge to his grave, who then received his death's wound upon the edge of the shore.

But if one hundred and fifty or two hundred seamen (which were the utmost) thus involved in the work, be accounted such a high matter, it may be remembered that (upon conference between sea and land commanders at Plymouth about this business), the assistance of so many seamen was no more, nor indeed so much, as was thought requisite to the carrying out of this maritime service, which, give me leave to say, is another manner of business, and of another complexion, than that we usually are acquainted with at land.

To say more: put the case (though it be not the case here) that a party of soldiers and seamen should of themselves have carried that or the like attempt against an enemy, without the actual assistance of the residue of the forces orderly following to the service, should that party have so vainly blown the trumpet before them, as that they had done the main work? The honour of it was due to them etc, causelessly decrying and traducing the rest of the forces. Truly, I conceive, so doing would not only be accounted a frothy vapour but an unhandsome piece of injury to the rest.

All that can be said to this particular (as far as I can see) is that Admiral Blake sent about one hundred and fifty to two hundred seamen to assist the land forces in the storming of Tresco; God was pleased to give a blessing to the attempt, and thereupon we forced our entrance, spoiled the enemy, and gained the island – a slender ground, methinks, for any to vent such lofty language on the one hand, and causelessly to bespatter the good service of the soldiers on the other.

What should move Captain Peck to insert in his letter such false intelligence to Major General Desborough, as that the first day's attempt failed through the timorousness of some commanders of the soldiers, that the seamen did the work etc, his own heart best knows; little reason I believe he had. I am sure he shot his bolt at random, and could write nothing of his own knowledge; for indeed neither himself, nor any other sea commander, hazarded themselves in either of the attempts. The seamen who were with us the last day were commanded by Captain Morrice, a passenger to the Barbadoes; and when Captain Peck was questioned about this by some of the officers at Tresco, as to why he would offer to injure and disrepute the soldiers by writing such detracting language, without any real ground of truth, things which he indeed knew not; and withall desired that he would name some that had failed their duty, he answered he could name none, nor knew nothing but the hearsay and report of some seamen, and that he was sorry his writing should any ways prove prejudicial, and that he thought no more harm in what he wrote than he intended to his own heart. I would not have been thus particular but for the truth's sake.

No better ground without question had some others to give the like blind account of the business; and among the rest Captain Peck's brother (as I am informed) took upon him the boldness, very unworthily to traduce the reputation of Lieut-Colonel Clark, and to exercise his tongue very scandalously; the gentleman hath no need of my pen to vindicate or commend him; his merits and faithful endeavours in this piece of service will, I question not, survive the lying reports of all detractors. If any failing may be imputed to him, I think it can be no other, unless the overmuch care and pains he took in prosecution of the work may be so accounted; indeed, he underwent too much for his body, which was but sickly when he came from Plymouth, and which the sea had much oppressed with continual distemper all the while he was on board ship, and now more weakened on shore for lack of natural rest etc. Yet I am confident none can truly say he either swerved from his duty at any time or favoured himself from hazard, or yet accounted his life precious for the work's sake.

But 'tis more than probable that this gentleman, as some others who have impudently lashed with their tongues, wanted a true prospect of the business, being muffled up in the smoke of the ordnance fired from aboard the ships far enough out of danger; and, mistaking so much at hand, ran into grosser absurdities farther off, speeding those false reports abroad, where (for the present) were none that could contradict them.

'Tis a good part of religion to bridle the tongue; if that were observed more, we should have less strife and jealous rivalry.

Thus much I have ventured to public view; I hope I have therein not exceeded the bounds of soberness and truth; my end is that this piece of service may be truly understood, and the honour and worth of faithful instruments vindicated. Indeed, I was hitherto loth to exercise my pen upon this subject, lest I might hazard the breach of amity; and, truly, had not done it now, had not the lavish tongue and pens of some gone about to crop off the best flower in a man's garden, viz. his honour and reputation: and, therefore, speaking but the truth, I hope I shall justly give no offence. If offences come, woe be to them by whom they come.

Let the exceeding goodness of God to this unthankful nation, in lopping off the bough even with terror, and giving into our hands a place with about 1200 or 1300 men, a greater number by far than we were, and but yesterday a hindrance to our maritime affairs, a scourge to the merchants, thought invincible for strength; and desperate to attempt, with so little loss and in so short a time: Let, I say, the eminent hand of God's good providence in these particulars teach us all to live the life of faith, and to walk more humbly and thankfully before him, and not to forget and undervalue such signal mercies, or disesteem such faithful instruments, whose hearts and hands (I may confidently say) were really fixed, and through God's blessing became instrumental for the completion of the work, which as it carries in it a singular high advantage to the Commonwealth, so let it gather from all our hearts due acknowledgments of praise and glory to the God of our salvation, who hath delivered and will yet deliver us, if we wait and put our trust in him.

Jos. Lereck

With the fall of King Charles's Castle, Royalist resistance on Tresco ceased. It was at about this juncture that Tromp re-appeared off Scilly, with about twelve ships, and it is believed that he offered Blake assistance in subjugating the rebels, hoping perhaps to receive some recompense that way, an offer which Blake declined; so, once again, Tromp was obliged to leave Scilly without satisfaction.

On April 20th, Grenville proposed that there should be an exchange of prisoners; this was refused by Blake, who made the counter-proposal that the rebels should simply surrender. Grenville held a council of war at Star Castle, where it was pointed out to him that St Mary's would be a hard island to hold against a determined attack because there were so many sandy bays where boats could land. Commissioners were sent by both sides to the neutral ground of the uninhabited island of Samson on April 30 to pursue negotiations, Grenville being represented by Colonel Marsh, Dr Cole, Sir Fulk Hulks and Mr Morton, and Blake by Captains Morris, Hatsell, Smith and Mr Daniel Scearl. Prisoners were exchanged, with Captain Godolphin and Captain Beach of the Royalists exchanged for Captain Dover and Captain Hooper of the Parliament's forces. But these talks broke down, so all four had to be exchanged back again. It was not in the temperament of a Grenville to consider surrender before being absolutely obliged to do so.

Meanwhile, Blake had positioned one whole and two demi-culverins at Carn Near, although the first shot fired from here was disastrous. The gun blew up, killing the gunner and Ensign Jefferies, wounding Captain Wright and eight spectators, with flying fragments narrowly missing Blake and Ayscue. However, once this problem had been solved, Blake found – as had been planned – that the guns could command St Mary's Roadstead and deter Royalist ships from entering or leaving Hugh Town harbour. Borlase, writing in 1756, pays tribute to Blake's use of the old breastwork on the hillock above Carn Near – which suggests earlier defences here, as confirmed in recent excavations – and which he furnished with guns to ensure that supply ships from France attempting to enter or leave St Mary's harbour could do so only under a gauntlet of fire. Moreover, when winds were violent or tides low 'ships must come within range of the battery or risk running upon the rocks or flats'. One Royalist ship did attempt to sail into St Mary's, but was chased by the *Amity* which captured her.

The consequence of this blockade was that Grenville and his forces were soon in dire distress. Moreover, Blake's fleet entered the Roadstead and bombarded the Hugh – but not Star Castle – and elsewhere to add to the defenders' discomfiture.

Not only food but water was a problem. There were few wells in the vicinity of Star Castle other than a modest dew-pond beyond the castle walls to the south, and the main well not far from the Garrison Gate; but the shortage of water may have been exaggerated for, historically, such

An artist's drawing of what Star Castle and Hugh Town were thought to have looked like in the middle of the 18th century – from William Borlase's Observations ... . *Star Castle, although the major defensive fort for the Islands since 1593, was never stormed nor damaged by bombardment. But it did play another important role for several decades in the 17th century as a place of confinement for prominent persons whose views were contrary to the government's, and who were troublesome or, in some cases, threatened by enemies and so placed in Star Castle for their own safety. John Bastwick, Henry Burton and William Prynne were kept at Star Castle for about three years, not in the dungeons – that was for offenders of the lower orders or prisoners of the worst crimes – but in a condition where escape from the Islands would be difficult. The 1st Duke of Hamilton was sent there for a year in 1643, also John Biddle, headmaster of what became The Crypt School, Gloucester, and John Wildman and Sir John Ireton in 1662, the latter being formerly the Lord Mayor of London. Sir Harry Vane arrived in 1660, but he was beheaded on Tower Hill in 1662 because, as Charles II wrote in a letter rather revealingly: 'He was too dangerous a man to live, if we can honestly put him out of the way'. The last important prisoners were 'Seven Popish Priests', who were imprisoned in 1682 on the spurious accusations of the infamous Titus Oates.*

deprivation has served as some mitigation for the dishonour of a surrender. On April 18th, on the advice of Henry Leslie, the Bishop Down since 1635, Grenville sent a signal to Blake that he was again ready to discuss terms, and Mr Philips was despatched to the Prince, then in Holland, for orders, returning later with instructions to Grenville that in the circumstances he should surrender upon making the best terms possible.

Indeed, Grenville was in a hopeless position and his surrender was inevitable; but he seems to have delayed for a while hoping that some miracle would rescue him from his plight. The position grew worse when the two Royalist frigates, which had been under the Hugh helping to guard it against possible invasion from the sea, were both driven ashore in a storm and wrecked, at a time when most of Blake's ships had put to sea to ride out the storm. When the wind abated, Blake and his ships returned, but had to keep up the siege for another whole month before the die-hard cavaliers in Star Castle were convinced, partly by their deprivations and partly by the wise and generous terms that Blake was offering, that further resistance was no longer a viable option. Henry Leslie had been with Grenville at Star Castle some while, and did his best to convince his leader that he should surrender; when this came about and power was handed over to Blake's men, he was there to witness and record the event. Another meeting was arranged on Samson, and this time terms were agreed in the surrender document of May 23. They included acceptance of Blake's offer to provide a ship to take the Irish soldiery back to Ireland, and the English to Scotland, the handing over of all ordnance and ships to Blake, together with 50 barrels of powder and match, all estates in England belonging to the Royalist rebels to be free of sequestration, an indemnity to be issued for all past acts, and the provision that the rebels could carry away with them from Scilly all their personal belongings.

Michael Baumber comments, that this capitulation when it came was with 'far more generous terms than a man of Grenville's rapacity had any right to expect.' Delayed for one day by further bad weather, the actual surrender took place at 10 a.m. on June 3, when Sir John Grenville with his garrison marched proudly out of Star Castle 'together with their arms and horses, with beat of drums, sound of trumpets, colours displayed and matches lighted at both ends' – almost like conquering heroes rather than defeated rebels. But this was far from a unique way of surrendering. On December 12, 1645, Sir John Mallory had surrendered at Skipton 'with colours flying and trumpets sounding.' It is said that Grenville's forces at the surrender numbered about 800 men altogether, but with enough officers 'to head an army', including 13 colonels, and 9 majors. Blake provided a ship to take those of his opponents who wished (about 300 or so) to Kinsale in Ireland, from whence many of them originated. Sir John Grenville was even permitted within the following twelve months to raise a regiment of 1500 men in Ireland for service on the Continent in the cause of any foreign prince or state, provided that such service was not prejudicial to the Commonwealth of England. Royalist officers were allowed to stay in Scilly for up to nine months to settle their affairs, and a proclamation of indemnity was made pardoning them all. Blake even agreed to pay Grenville £1000 for guns Grenville had mounted at Star Castle. A copy of these terms of surrender was taken to London by three parliamentary officers, Colonel Sadler, Colonel Le Hunt and Lieut-Colonel Axtell – all of whom were released after having been confined for some time as prisoners of the Royalists at Star Castle – and a subsequent Act of Parliament endorsed Blake's magnanimous terms. Sir John Grenville and other prisoners were taken to Plymouth on June 12, 1651, and it appears that on that day Tromp, who was still apparently in the area of Scilly, sent Captain Cornelius Evertson aboard Blake's flagship and learnt of the surrender of the rebels on Scilly 'because they were forsaken by everybody', as Tromp records in his Journal. When, eighteen years later, Cosmo III, Grand Duke of Tuscany visited Scilly, he reported that Star Castle was armed with 130 'very beautiful iron culverins' and still had a circular entrenchment around the northern shore of the Hugh – which is likely to have been the line of defence works thrown up by the Royalist rebels when they were besieged in 1651. But, by 1669, the garrison in Scilly had been reduced to two hundred men, costing about £4000 a year to maintain. One side effect of the large garrison of the Civil Wars period had been an increase in Scilly's baby population caused by soldiers marrying islanders, a circumstance which helped lead to a corn shortage in the 1660s, and eventually to the military authorities forbidding garrison soldiers in Scilly from marrying local women.

* * * * *

The document of surrender of 1651 between Grenville on behalf of the Rebels, and Blake and Clarke on behalf of the Government, is preserved in the National Maritime Museum at Greenwich. It has been remarked that it resembles more an agreement between seventeenth-century gentlemen arranging a sale of land rather than an article of surrender, but few other documents concerning surrenders in the Civil War period have survived, so this one has special interest. (The inconsistencies in spellings are quite normal, including surnames; even Shakespeare spelt his name in eleven different ways.)

ARTICLES OF SURRENDER, 23rd May, 1651

Articles agreed on this XXIIIth day of May 1651 By and between Admiral Blake and Colonell Clerke Commanders in cheife of all the Forces by sea or land, in or about the Island of Triscoe and Briar, of the one parte, and Sir John Grenvile Knight, Governor of the Island of St Maryes and Agnes in Scillcy on the behalfe or His Majestie the other part, touching the rendicion of the said Islands of St Maryes and Agnes together with all the Castles forts fortresses sconces and fortifications unto them belonging to the use and behoofe of the Parliament of England, as followeth.

That the Island and Castle of St Maryes and the Island of Agnes, together with all the forts fortresses sconces and fortificacions belonging to the said Guarrizons, 50 barrells of good serviceable powder with match proporcionable, twoe third parts of the great shott now upon the said Islands, and as many pieces of Ordnance as were found in those Islands at the arrivall of Sir John Grenvile to the Government, with all their appurtenances, together with all such Ordnance as are now there (with all their appurtenances) which have been taken in English shipps or vessells, shalbe delivered unto such persons as Admirall Blake and Colonell Clerke shall appoint to receive the same for the use of the Parliament of England at or upon Monday the second day of June next ensuing by ten of the clock in the forenoone, wind and weather permitting, or at any time before it Sir John Grenvile shall thinke fitt, timely notice being thereof given to Admirall Blake and Colonel Clerke; And that on Saturday the 24th instant, 3 or 4 such persons as they shall appoint may have their lett pass from Sir John Grenvile to come into the Islands of St Maryes and Agnes or any other Islands thereto belonging, to take an Inventary of all such Ordnance shott powder match and other things agreed on to be left upon the said Islands for the use of the Parliament And that upon the mutuall signing and concluding these articles, there be a full and finall cessacion of Armes and all attempts of hostility or surprizall on either party: But all officers and soldiers on both sides to keepe their respective guards and quarters without especiall leave on both parts granted.

That all the Inhabitants and Islanders of the said Islands now under the command of Sir John Grenvile may enjoy the libertie of their persons and full benefitt of their estates leases

59

grants prviledges of fishing and fowling, with all other immunityes and customes to them now and anciently belonging without any restraint tax or imposicion whatsoever, they submitting themselves for the future to all acts and orders of Parliament: And if any of the said Inhabitants or Islanders shall desire to remove thence, effectuall passes shalbe granted to them and their familyes with full libertie without any oath or ingagement to transport themselves, their moneyes goods etc: to what place or places they shall thinke fitt at any time within nine monthes after the surrender of the said Islands; And that the Merchants residing in those Islands shall have the like libertie and time to stay or depart with their moneyes goods and merchandize; And further that such of the Owners farmers and Inhabitants of the Islands of Triscoe Briar St Martins and Sampson, as well as fishermen and others now remaining in Sir John Grenviles quarters (except all such as have borne Command under him) shall have quiett possession given them of their former habitacions and respective priviledges.

That the Governor Sir John Grenvile with all officers and soldiers by sea and land commissioned and reformd, Civill and Military, Clergie, Gentrey and others residing on the said Islands of St Maryes and Agnes with their moneyes plate merchandize together with their Armes of all sorts and their owne horses, with beate of drum and sound of trumpett, colours display'd and matches lighted at both ends, and all the rest of the powder ammunicion and utensills of Warre with the Ordnance not granted or excepted in an other article, Together with all the victualls and provisions and particularly the Corne and wine shall at or before the said day of surrender be imbarqued to be transported in the frigates shipps and vessells belonging to the said Sir John Grenvile or any under his command and in one other vessell of 300 ton to be provided by Admirall Blake and Colonell Clerke if need shall require with furniture compleate to saile her and provisions for the Marines, as alsoe with effectuall passes and proteccions for them against all persons whatsoever according to this agreement viz: That all English and strangers Officers and Soldiers together with such of Sir John Grenviles owne Ordnance armes ammunicion and provision as he shall think fitt bagg and baggage of his and theirs be transported and safely convoyed to Glascoe or any other convenient Port neare to the Kings quarters in Scotland, into which they are to be safely conducted with convenient carriages and other things necessary for their march at the charge of the said Sir John Grenvile: And that all the Irish, Officers and Soldiers, together with their Armes ammunicion provisions bagg and baggage be transported and convoyed for Galloway in Ireland: But if Sir John Grenvile or any other now under his command shall thinke fitt to leave his or their servants on the said Islands (they not exceeding the number of 8) with the charge of any householdstuff shipps provision or goods, they shalbe protected during their abode there for the space of nine months without any prejudice reproach or abuse and shall have leave and lett pass within that time to transport themselves to such place or places as Sir John Grenvile shall appoint, and that all sick and wounded persons which shalbe left in the said Islands may after the surrender of the same have due care taken for their recovery.

That noe shipp or vessell belonging to Sir John Grenvile and now abroad upon their respective employments shall molest trouble or doe violence to any or the shipps boats or goods belonging to any of the Common [wealth] of England, and that in case any shipp boate or other vessell be taken by any Man of Warre or any other vessell any wayes appertaining to the said Islands, the said shipp barque boate or other vessell so taken shalbe restored with all the goods and merchandize which were in them at their taking and the persons sett at libertie, and that noe shipp of Warre or other vessell as aforesaid shall molest or trouble any shipp barque boate or other vessell during the time they are upon their voyage or otherwise.

That upon the conclusion of these articles present Hostages on both parts be mutually return'd, and that Colonel Buller and George Grenvile Esqr, be thereupon given as Hostages for the performance of the articles on Sir John Grenviles part.

That all Prisoners on both sides, aswell those now in the custody of Sir John Grenvile and particularly Colonel Axtell Colonel Sedler and Colonel le Hunt, as alsoe all Prisoners bearing any particular relacion to the Islands of Scilley now within the custody of the Parliament wheresoever taken at Triscoe or elsewhere and not yet disposed of particularly Colonel Theodore Cavey, Colonel Freeman, Major Floyd, Captain John Wharton and Mr Arthur, be upon the rendicion of the place forthwith inlarged and sett at libertie (as belonging to these Islands) shall enjoy the benefitt of all these and the insueing articles.

That an Act of Indempnity be procured from the Parliament to all the said persons comprehended in these articles for all acts done and committed in time and place of Warre, and that to be effectuall in all the Parliament quarters and under their Command wheresoever both by sea and land: and that all and everyone of them, for the space of 12 months next ensuing the surrender of the said Islands, shalbe protected from all accions and arrests by any person or persons upon any cause, debts or pretence whatsoever: To the end that in the meane time they may uninterruptedly and quietly pursue their particular interests and affaires: And that all officers aswell reformed as commissioned and Gentlemen shall have libertie to travell about the particular busines with their respective servants horses swords and other necessaryes whither their occasions may serve in any the Parliaments quarters, they acting nothing preiudiciall to the Parliament of England.

That all and every persons aforesaid at any time within the said twelve monthes shall have libertie to repaire to their severall Countreys and estates in England Ireland or elsewhere in the Parliaments quarters and there peaceably abide (if they please) and quietly possess and reinioy their owne proper Estates without any restraint oath or ingagement during the said 12 monthes, and all sequestracions made against any of their estates shalbe forthwith declared void, without any Composicion, And it shalbe noe prejudice to the friends of any such persons to receive and entertaine them; And if any of the persons aforesaid shall desire to make sale of his or their estates, they shall have the said 12 monthes time for the effecting thereof, and passes freely to withdraw from the Parliaments quarters with their families and goods when and whither they please within that time; and particularly Sir John Grenvile who may goe to His Majestie and returne with his servants and freinds not exceeding in number seven, together with their respective horses swords and necessary estates.

That Admirall Blake and Colonel Clerke, upon friday the 30th of this instant shall well and truely pay or cause to be paid unto Sir John Grenvile or into such hands as he shall appoint the just and intire summe of One thousand pounds current English money for certaine great Ordnance (which here bought by Sir John Grenvile) and other consideracions agreed upon.

That in case His Majestie shall not otherwise dispose of Sir John Grenvile he shall at any time within the said twelve monthes have libertie by himselfe his officers and freinds to raise in Ireland a Regiment consistin of 1500 men and with the Parliaments warrant and safe lett pass transport them for the service of any forraigne Prince or state, that may not be preiudiciall to the interest of the Common wealth of England.

That Colonel Edward Roscarrock, Colonel Richard Thornhill, Lieut-Colonel Robinson, Major Madderne, Captain Thomas Amy, Captain Thomas Laus, Captain Andrew Cory, Captain John Gealard, Captain Christopher Turnour, Captain William Hebditch, Captain Canham, Mr Andrew Moore, Mr Thomas Griffin, Nicholas Jordan, James Welch and Phillip Rossiter Merchants of Wexford which are now absent and employed for the service of these Islands shall equally have and enjoy the benefit of all these articles; And in case any of them are or shalbe taken prisoners by any the Parliaments forces at sea or land within the space of 40 dayes next ensuing, they shalbe freely released without exchange; And if the Grace frigate or any other vessells belonging to Sir John Grenvile at sea or bound upon any occasion to this place shall happen within the said 40 dayes to be taken by any in [the] Parliaments service, they shalbe restored and the officers soldiers mariners merchants and passengers discharged and indemnified.

That if any officer or soldier or other person comprehended in these articles shall in any particular breake or violate the same then it shall extend onely to the Prejudice of the particular person so offending, and shall not be imputed or charged on any other of his party.

That if any person or persons comprehended within these articles shall act any thing prejudiciall to the Common wealth of England that then hee or they shall loose the benefit of all and every of these articles: anything to the Contrary in any wise notwithstanding.

That an Act of Parliament be procured by Admirall Blake and Colonel Clerke with al convenient speed for the confirmacion and ratificacion of these articles.

In testimony whereof wee have thereunto put our hands and seals

ROB BLAKE   JOHN CLARKE

* * * * *

Henry Leslie, Bishop of Down, wrote the following two letters to Sir Edward Nicholas, Secretary of State to Charles II in exile, presenting what he several times in the letters described as a 'true and impartial relation' of the surrender of the Royalists in Scilly – the actual handing over of Star Castle, the principal fort, taking place on June 3. He describes much the same events as Jos. Lereck, but from a Royalist viewpoint, making an interesting comparison. His loyal supplications at the end of his second letter bore fruit in 1661 after the Restoration of the Monarchy, when he was translated to Meath. Some of the spellings, punctuation and paragraphing in these letters have been modernised for clarity of meaning and ease of reading. The dates on the letters suggests that they were when the letters were begun rather than when they were sent.

St Mary's Castle, Scilly, May 13, 1651.

Honourable Sir,

Your zeal to the King's service at all times, your respects to Sir John Greville, and the favour you showed unto myself when I was following his business at the Hague, bind me to give your Honour an account of my diligence to return hither, and to deliver letters committed unto me, as also of what has happened since. I made great haste to return and landed here on April 13 at night.

On the 15th in the morning, there came against these isles two great fleets, the one of English consisting of 22 ships besides many shallopps [Light open boats] and long boats and bringing with them 2,500 land men, the other of Dutch consisting of 13 ships. They attempted the out islands lying on the north side, especially that called Tresco, on each end whereof there is a harbour. The best harbour our Governor secured by two of his best frigates and other helps that they could not enter; so they discharged infinite multitude of shot. The other harbour, where it was scarce known any great ship ever ventured to come in, they gained it, being of so great a breadth that it could not be defended; and so on the 17th day they launched forth many shallopps, each having a brass piece charged with case shot in the forepart, but then were so valiantly resisted that they were forced to retreat, their Admiral being shot through and through and driven to ship his cable, one of their shallopps sunk and another so paid with small shot that she went off with two oars, all the rest dropping into the water.

But on the 18th day in the silence of the night, they having the opportunity of a great calm, came on again with all their forces, and after a long debate they overpowered our men with multitudes and strength of their pikes, having the help of seamen too, both to lead them on and to drive on their rear, and so gained the place, we having there only 400 men, which were far more than the Governor could well have spared. Of these sixscore and odd came off by the help of their boats, the rest being killed and taken prisoners.

After this, their General Blake summoned this island, offering reasonable terms of peace, if they might be accepted of in time. Our Governor presented his letter at a council of war, and albeit they all acknowledged the place not to be tenable with less than 2,000 men and some horse (we having now not 500 able to do duty), in regard that there are some 16 bays of sand upon this isle where boats may land, yet did they resolve rather to die every man than to quit the place.

Here I confess that I told them that, if these islands could be preserved for the King with the loss of all our lives and be useful for his service (which now this place cannot be, they having got our best harbours and surrounded us about that we can take no more prizes), that then I should commend their resolution to die in His Majesty's service; but since the place cannot be long maintained, in regard we have no hopes of relief and that our few men will decrease daily, they being on continual duty, and that the enemy may have fresh supplies from the mainland when he pleaseth, it were better upon honourable terms to quit the place and preserve their lives to do his Majesty service in another place.

For this advice I am reputed here a coward, yet I hope all wise men will be of my opinion, and so were they themselves afterwards, for by their advice our Governor yielded unto a treaty, but upon very high terms.

Mutual hostages are sent. The Commissioners met in an isle that is not inhabited, but upon some formality it is now broken off, they excepting that the Governor had not given to his commissioners so ample power as was given to them by their commission and refusing to stay any longer than the time limited, which was but 24 hours of such foul weather that a new commission could not be sent in time.

Now whether they will treat any more or fall upon us presently we cannot tell, but I am still of the same opinion I formerly expressed, that, if the Governor can get honourable conditions, he quit the place, since it cannot be kept. We have no hopes of relief, and, though it were kept, it is already made unuseful.

Sir, if it would not make my letter swell too big, I would show unto you at large what care the Governor has taken to preserve these isles, what means he has used, or what expense he has bestowed to get supplies of men out of Ireland, out of France and Germany, all of which is now prevented by their sudden coming upon us.

And therefore I could wish, if your letters, and letters from his Highness Royal, could come unto him in time, that you could advise him by all means to save himself and those gentlemen that are with him, who are as considerable for their valour as any that ever served the King. Or, if it shall please God to deliver us into their hands before any advertisement can come, I shall entreat Your Honour to give credit unto this my impartial relation and to assure both His Majesty and the Duke of York that nothing has been lost here either by treachery, cowardice or neglect.

So, praying God for to bless both you and all that are engaged in his Majesty's service, I humbly take leave and am, Sir,
Your Honour's most affectionate servant,
Hen. Dunensis

Second letter

St Mary's, Scilly, May 29, 1651.

Honourable Sir,

I ventured lately to give you a relation of our tragedy here, and, albeit I know that letter is not yet come into your Honour's hands, I shall now presume to give you the rest of the story, that joining both letters together you may have a true and full relation of all that is past.

After the first treaty was broken off, our Governor was resolved to sacrifice himself and all here with him rather than to manifest so much fear as to desire a new treaty; but it pleased God so to dispose of things that there came from the enemy an invitation to renew the treaty, which he had great reason to accept of, and did it by the advice of the Council of War. Nor would they have passed it had they known our condition as well as ourselves, but they were afraid to venture upon this place without more forces, which they had sent for unto the Parliament, and thought it better to gain the place by a treaty than to expect the coming of these forces and to venture the hazard of a battle.

The treaty thus propounded by them was accepted, hostages mutually sent, and the commissioners met and sat for a whole week together, and at last concluded to surrender this place upon articles more honourable and advantageous for the King's service than ever yet was granted by the Parliament unto a place which they conquered; as will appear unto your Honour by the sight of the articles which I hope you shall receive herewith, but, if not, I know you will have them in print before these can come into your hands.

The greatest matter of debate was touching the place whether Sir John should go and carry his soldiers. He much desired to go into the Isle of Man and join the Earl of Derby in His Majesty's service either in England or in Scotland; but that would not be granted, in regard they have a commission as soon as they have done here to go against that place.

Jersey was moved, but rejected, I believe upon the like reason. The place offered and accepted of by our commissioners was the Shields by Newcastle, whether Sir John was to have a convoy for himself and all his soldiers, until he should go or send unto the King to know his pleasure. But after consideration Sir John, fearing that the Scots would not admit of his Irish soldiers, and seeing that the charge of carrying them thither and keeping them there would be extraordinary, and that their return from thence to another place without a convoy would not be safe, he upon the petition of his officers and soldiers took occasion of a motion made by Blake for an interview to get the articles mended, having with him the prime officers of this place, and upon their meeting got it effected very much for his advantage, namely that he should send his Irish soldiers into Ireland under the command of a person of trust, to recruit them there up to a regiment of 2,000, that he should send his English Cavaliers (a company of gallant gentlemen) with all his powder, amunition, 9 or 10 brass field pieces, besides divers pieces of cannon, unto the King with a safe conduct.

And I hope this will let the Scots see that Sir John in this treaty has not driven his own interests but His Majesty's. He himself goes to Plymouth till all the articles be confirmed by Act of Parliament, which they have undertaken, and till he hears from His Majesty whether he will accept of his Irish soldiers with such recruits as he can get in Ireland, or lay his commands for the disposing of them other ways.

Admiral Blake upon the review offered unto him to convoy them all unto Dunkirk and to maintain them there upon his own charges until such time as Sir John could make his bargain either with the King of France or Spain, provided that Sir John would engage his honour never to employ them against the Parliament; but he hath so much zeal still to serve the King, and some hopes that His Majesty will make use of him another way for his own service, that he would not accept of that proffer, so very advantageous unto him if he had respected his own interests only.

Sir, I assure your Honour this is a true and impartial relation which I shall beseech you to make known unto His Majesty and that you will give me leave in the preclose to put a word for myself. I am by the articles to have my pass to go unto the North of Ireland, that is to say, out of the frying pan into the fire; for there I shall be in more danger of the Scots than of Parliament's soldiers.

And therefore I beseech your Honour, who has always been my noble friend, to move His Majesty by your letters to write unto the Lord Montgomery for to protect me from the violence of the Scots, or else to give me leave to live in a Parliament garrison for mine own safety, where I am sure my soul shall be more vexed than ever Lott's was in Sodome. And for this I shall ever pray God to bless your Honour and all that are faithful to His Majesty; and so I humbly take leave and rest.

Your most affectionate servant,

Hen. Dunensis

* * * * *

In Whitelock's Memorials, some additional details concerning the events of 1651 in Scilly are contained in ten extracts from contemporary letters. The dates given are those of the letters, not of the events to which they are referring:

(1)   17 April 1651: 'Lieutenant-Colonel Clarke with nine companies of foot set sail from Plymouth for the Scilly Islands.'

This extract suggests that Lieutenant-Colonel Clarke commanded fewer than 1,000 foot soldiers.

(2)   17 April 1651: 'Van Tromp came to Pendennis and related that he had been to Scilly to demand reparation for the Dutch ships and goods taken by them; and receiving no satisfactory answer, he had, according to his Commission, declared war on them.'

In this letter is the possible origin of the 'declaring war' legend. Tromp had no 'Commission' from his government to declare war on the rebels in Scilly; but he did come to try – by a show of force, threats and even by violence perhaps, although this never happened – to seek reparation for Royalist piracies, but short of resorting to any action which might offend the Commonwealth.

(3)   21 April 1651: 'Van Tromp lay before Scilly and declared that he would assist the English against it.'

Tromp offered to assist Blake in the reduction of Scilly but was refused. In both (2) and (3) the intrusion of the 'Van' in Tromp's name indicates that the error was also a contemporary one.

(4)   24 April 1651: 'Of the Fleet's arrival at Scilly and of the guns heard from thence.'

(5)   26 April 1651: '2,000 of the Parliament's soldiers and seamen were landed in the little Isles on the West of Scilly, and that the Ordnance were

65

heard thundering there many hours together.'

The figure of '2,000' sounds like an exaggeration to the next round number, and includes Blake's sailors as well as soldiers, some of whom, but not all, played a significant role in the invasion of Tresco; most are likely to have stayed on their ships.

(6)   2 May 1651:   'That the Parliament's Fleet at Scilly had taken New Grimsby after 3 times being beaten off, and that they had taken 2 Irish Frigates, one of 30 and the other of 24 guns.'

(7)   3 May 1651:   'That the Parliamentary soldiers had taken all the Islands except St Mary's and had taken 3 of their Frigates, killed 14 of their men, and taken 120 prisoners. That of the Parliamentary Forces, 8 were killed and 20 wounded; that they intended to send a summons to St Mary's Island, and if they refused, then attempt it.'

It is doubtful if Blake planned an assault on St Mary's, but the Royalists anticipated one. After the breakdown of the first round of talks on Samson, Blake's ships bombarded the Hugh – although not Star Castle – to help encourage a resumption. His tactic of blockade was to be effective and more economical than assault, although it took a little time for his persistence to prove stronger than Grenville's obduracy.

(8)   8 May 1651:   'That General Blake and Sir George Ayscue with the Fleet at Scilly intend to fall upon St Mary's Island, that the Governor thereof, Sir John Grenville, sent to them for a Treaty, which was agreed, but took no effect, and thereupon the great guns played upon St Mary's.'

(9)   12 May 1651:   'Letters from Sir George Ayscue of the action at Scilly, that Captain Morris behaved himself most gallantly in the storming of the Island. That the Scilly Islands are a key that opens a passage to several Nations.'

(10)   30 May 1651:   'That the Foot of Scilly entered at St Mary's Island, and those in the Castle were in great want of water.' This can be taken to mean that they landed under terms of surrender rather than by armed assault.

* * * * *

Thus the siege of Scilly ended and, with it, the last Cavalier resistance in England, and it was said at the time that 'a curse on our maritime affairs was lifted'. But there does not seem to have been much of great value in the military acquisitions consequent upon the surrender of the Royalist rebels. Lieutenant-Colonel J. Hunkin, who was appointed Governor of Scilly, reported to Cromwell that by 1658 only 77 powder barrels were left in Scilly and were unfit for use, with only two shots a piece for the guns.

Sir Francis Godolphin – grandson and namesake of the Godolphin who had built Star Castle in 1593 – resumed the lease and took over from Hunkin as Governor after the Restoration in 1660. By the time Cosmo visited Scilly in

1668, Colonel Janovick was the executive Lieutenant-Governor, but the Godolphins continued to lease the Islands – increasingly as non-residents – until 1785,when the male line became extinct. The Osbornes married into the Godolphin family and took the lease until their descendant, the Duke of Leeds, seemed relieved to surrender it back to the Duchy of Cornwall in 1831.

* * * * *

After he had arranged transport for the Irish soldiery to Kinsale, Blake reached Plymouth on June 28th, Ayscue having already sailed for Barbados on the 27th. In assessing the triumph of Blake over the rebels in Scilly in 1651, it is notable that it had been achieved in under 2 months, and that once Tresco and Bryher had been taken, only 7 men lost their lives and no ships were damaged, with the seas around at last made safe for shipping, with no likelihood any longer of Dutch interference. Moreover, apart from requiring more supplies, his fleet was complete and his men in good heart, ready for the voyage to the Channel Islands, where, although the population there was largely Parliamentarian in their sympathies, the islands were held by Royalist rebels secure in three castles, a situation which Blake was set to reverse in September.

It was not just that Blake had won in Scilly, but the competent and efficient manner in which he had done so that was impressive and admired, together with the honourable and magnanimous peace terms which made it easier for the rebels to give in, so completing by negotiation what began by force. In a memorandum of 1600, Godolphin had observed: 'If the Spaniards once took the Scillies, they would not be driven out with a force ten times greater'. Even allowing for the fact that Godolphin was arguing the case for more military forces to be sent to him – and therefore liable to stress the Spanish peril – his comment underlines the skill of Blake's reduction of Scilly only half a century later, especially as this was accomplished without a great preponderance of force or undue 'effusion of blood'. It was a good example of what was often said about Blake, that he always kept his overriding objective in mind and placed time and the level of bloodspill high in his considerations. Yet, in some accounts, the tendency has been to see Grenville, the young Royalist commander, as the hero of events in Scilly in 1651, even though, apart from his staunchness to the Stuarts, there seems little in his conduct of affairs in Scilly of particularly great distinction. The explanation is possibly that the events of 1651 were overshadowed by the subsequent outcome in 1660, and may be an instance of Rolf Hochhuth's remark that 'Truth is with the victor – who, as you know, also controls the historians'. After the Restoration of the Monarchy in 1660, in which arrangements Grenville, to his credit, took a leading role – he was Monk's cousin – he finally gained reward for his loyalty to the Crown by being made Earl of Bath (in memory of the Battle of Lansdown where his father had been killed), and he became prominent in Charles II's reign (1660-85) in West Country affairs. Moreover, Sir John had achieved the very best terms possible before surrendering in Scilly, as Charles had required, and could at least take comfort in this. Among other fitting rewards for his loyalty, he was later awarded or acquired a plethora of titles or appointments, including Lord Grenville of Kilkhampton and Bytheford, Viscount Grenville of Lansdown, High Steward of the Duchy of Cornwall, Lord Warden of the Stannaries, Groom of the Stole to His Majesty, First Gentleman of the Bedchamber and was appointed a Lord of the Priory Council; in Normandy he was Earl of Carbol and Lord of Thoringy and Granville. These honours for Sir John Grenville were the nearest Scilly got to receiving any thanks.

As for the civilian population of the Scillies, it was not so much the Civil Wars which produced exceptionally hard conditions for them, but the continued occupation of the islands by rebel Cavaliers during the years between 1648 and 1651. There had been a virtual cessation of all hostilities on the mainland after the Battle of Preston in 1648 and until the brief re-opening of hostilities leading to the Battle of Worcester in 1651; but on the Scillies, Grenville's occupation, accompanied by numerous hardline Royalists and soldiers, is estimated to have increased the population by up to 1,500 persons. At first the civilians had to attempt to feed them, but eventually Grenville was obliged to take desperate measures, sending out his frigates to attack and plunder – and acting like a pirate. The burden of this situation upon civilian Scillonians cannot be measured but may be imagined. It must have been their worst period in the century, although, of course, even their best of times would have been little above scraping a living. By 1651, there were no more than two small holdings on St Martin's being farmed, both at Lower Town. Apart from this, only St Mary's and Tresco are thought to have been continuously inhabited in the 17th century, and, by the time of Grenville's surrender, the civilian population was only about 650, according to a Parliamentary survey. By the time of Cosmo's visit in 1669, his estimate was that it had recovered to between 800 and 1000. A large number of the Cavalier soldiers in Scilly were Irish, and it is well documented elsewhere that Irish soldiers were much disliked even by the Royalist forces they were supposed to supplement. The beginning of the end of such extreme privations for the islanders came with Grenville's surrender, Blake's return of the Irish soldiery to their homeland, the removal of most of the Royalist rebels from Scilly, and the return of settled government under the rule of the Commonwealth. As Troutbeck records (p. 198): 'These islands will be a shelter to merchants, which before were their ruin'.

The war over, the Scillies began to return to a condition approaching normality. The Council of State, after consulting with Major-General

Desborrow for names of suitable candidates, appointed a Cornishman, Lieutenant-Colonel Joseph Hunkin, as Governor of Scilly and, from July, 1651, they authorised the payment of money to him for building mills, buying shallops and purchasing a vessel to supply the islands. They even arranged that the pay of the garrison on St Mary's should be shipped over up to three months in advance to ensure that prolonged adverse weather conditions did not result in late payments – something that had posed a problem in the past and had led to dissatisfaction among the soldiery. The building of Cromwell's Castle on Tresco after the Reduction provided some welcome employment, although its name is a much later attachment to distinguish it from the earlier Tresco Castle, now called King Charles's Castle, on the summit of the nearby hill. It seems likely that Cromwell's Castle was at first called Castle Bryher, Bryher being the island it faced, and Duke Cosmo referred to it by that name in 1669.

In this connection it is worth noting that Blake, who may have first ordered its construction, did not stay in Scilly long enough to see the completion of the building which is on the site of an old blockhouse, and that Oliver Cromwell never visited the Scillies. Moreover, although he assumed some of the reigns of power beforehand, Cromwell was not installed as Lord Protector until near the end of the year 1653 on Friday, December 16, when, in the words of the historian Thomas Carlyle (1795-1881), he appeared 'a man of strong, solid stature, and dignified, now partly military carriage: the expression of him valour and devout intelligence – energy and delicacy on a basis of simplicity ... on the whole, a right noble lion-face and hero-face'. In the event, Cromwell's Castle on Tresco was never tested. It was not attacked by the Dutch, who, in the three wars between 1652 and 1674, did not attempt to take the Scillies; the nearest they came to it was the interception of the packet ship to the Islands during the 1st Dutch War, and stealing some sheep from an off-island on August 12, 1677.

One alleged effect in Scilly, associated with this 17th century period, concerns the language. The high quality of spoken English, which was said to be discernible in the speech even of twentieth century Scillonians, has been attributed, rather dubiously, yet by no less a person than Arthur Quiller-Couch, to units of the Bedfordshire Regiment having been stationed in Scilly after 1651, some of whom married local girls and settled in the Islands. A few of the former Royalists serving under Grenville are also thought to have settled in the Islands, but no other grounds exist for assuming that these had much noticeable effect on the quality of spoken English. However, Dr Borlase, writing in 1756, comments that the islanders 'are remarkable for speaking good English', and the settlement in Scilly of former military personnel who had been stationed in Scilly during war periods has certainly continued since the Civil War, and occurred after the 1st and 2nd World Wars. There has also been quite an influx of civilian non-Scillonians into the

Islands over the last half-century, who have done much to improve the lives of the inhabitants. It is noticeable that, from about 1985, the majority of the 21 members of the Isles of Scilly Council have been people who could only call themselves Scillonians by adoption.

* * * * *

In 1651, after his success in June in quelling the Royalist resistance in Scilly, Blake sailed away with his ships to Jersey, and, by September, had ended the Royalist occupation there. In December, Blake was appointed to the Admiralty Committee and to the 41-member Council of State in London but, in the following May, the 1st Dutch War was impending, and Blake left to take command of the fleet.

The war began with what seem like mutual misunderstandings: the Dutch held that they had saluted English warships in the English Channel as required, and that their ships were proceeding peacefully when they were attacked; the English claimed that the Dutch had failed to salute their warships and had been arrogant and uncivil. In fact, the Dutch were furious at the Navigation Act of 1651, which laid down that only English ships could bring goods to English shores – thus cutting out the Dutch carriers, who were then the world's greatest traders; and the English were still smarting from the Massacre of Amboyna of 1623, when English traders were killed by Dutch traders in the East Indies.

The first action took place in 1652 off Dover, where Ayscue had 14 ships defending the port. With Blake were 15 ships, but Tromp had 42, plus the advantage of the weather gauge. Nevertheless, on May 19, Blake in the *James* obliged Tromp in the *Brederode* to retire with the loss of two of his ships. Blake sank another two Dutch ships on September 28 but, as his own ship, the *James*, had been dismasted in the earlier action, he was in the 68-gun *Resolution*. Blake also had the help of Penn in the mighty *Sovereign*, formerly called The *Sovereign of the Seas*, and the largest warship in either fleet. Size is not always the most important consideration when comparing the fighting abilities of warships, but in this case the presence of her 102 guns was overawing. The battles which followed between the rival fleets were just as hard fought and interesting as those at the time of Drake in the 16th century or Nelson in the later 18th and early 19th, but somehow seem less memorable today. This may in part be owing to the fact that the Dutch wars were based largely on economic rivalry – there was even a protestant identity between the two belligerents – and partly because, in 1689, the Dutch William became the English king, and the English and Dutch have for the most part been allies ever since. The connection between the English Stuarts and the Dutch leaders can be seen in the following chart. After his defeat at Dover, Tromp was briefly replaced as the Dutch fleet commander by De With

Top and middle: *Warships of the 17th century, and an artist's impression of one of the ding-dong sea battles between the English and the Dutch in the 1st Dutch War, 1652-54.*

Bottom: *The* Prince Royal *of 1610, with elaborate carving and a length about four times her beam. Painted by the Dutchman, Hendrick Vroom, it may be difficult to distinguish but she had 3 tiers of guns.*

71

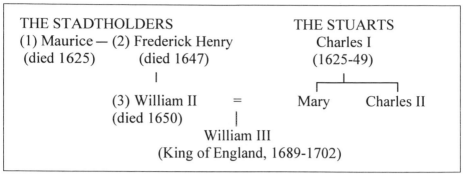

THE STADTHOLDERS
(1) Maurice — (2) Frederick Henry
(died 1625)   (died 1647)
                        |
                (3) William II   =
                (died 1650) |
                        William III
                (King of England, 1689-1702)

THE STUARTS
Charles I
(1625-49)
                Mary   Charles II

– not by De Witt, who was Grand Pensionary of Holland, and with whom he is sometimes confused – and Blake in the *Resolution* defeated him on September 28, 1652. But Tromp was soon back and, on November 30, having 87 ships against Blake's 37, he repulsed an attack by Blake on a Dutch convoy off Dungeness, and drove Blake in the *Triumph*, together with the other English ships, to seek sanctuary in the Thames Estuary. Legend has it that, for some time after, Tromp carried a provocative broom at the masthead of his flagship *Brederode* to show that he had swept the seas clean of the English fleet – a famous, if possibly fictitious, instance of triumphalism. Blake felt humiliated having to retreat into the Thames, and wrote to Cromwell confessing to what he called 'my sense of my own insufficiency'.

Within a year, however, the tables had turned and Blake was said to have replied to Tromp's challenge by hoisting a horsewhip on the masthead of his flagship, the *Triumph*, when he won a 3-days battle over Tromp in a war which was comprised of many such ding-dong sea battles – and the pennant flown today at the masthead of Royal Navy ships is believed by some to have originated from Blake's whip. Both sides fought hard in the battles, the Dutch ships usually aiming their guns to demast the English vessels, while the English more often aimed their guns at the waterline of the Dutch hulls in attempts to sink them, with both sides seeking to grapple opposing ships in the hope of boarding and capturing them. Eventually, Tromp was obliged to withdraw his battered fleet, with over 1000 Dutchmen dead and 12 of his warships sunk, along with many of the merchantmen they had been escorting. Blake lost the 32-gun *Samson* and had as many men killed and wounded as in the Dutch ships, and was himself wounded in the thigh. Thus much was lost in the battle by both sides and little gained, but Blake was soon at sea again seeking further action against the Dutch, but this exhausted him and he had to take time off to recuperate at Southwold. Thus he missed the great victory of the English fleet led by Monk at the Battle of Scheveningen on July 31, where Monk, in the *Resolution*, anticipated Nelson's tactic at Trafalgar by breaking the enemy's line from leeward and cutting the enemy's fleet in half; and it was this battle which saw the death of Tromp, who, along with De Ruyter, 1607-76, were the greatest adversaries at sea Britain ever

Top *The* Amelia *was Tromp's flagship at his greatest triumph when he almost annihilated a much larger Spanish fleet in the English Channel on October 21, 1639.*

Bottom *Maarten Tromp – the weather-beaten face of a professional, lifelong sailor and Blake's worthy opponent in the 1st Dutch War, 1652-54. Blake won their battle off Dover on May 19, 1652, with 12 ships against Tromp's 42, but Tromp won off Dungeness in November, 1652, when he had 95 ships against Blake's 37, and during the engagement Blake was wounded in the thigh.*

faced since Alfred the Great first founded a navy to fight the Norsemen in the 9th century.

* * * * *

Maarten Harpertszoon Tromp – he was never 'van' as is sometimes mistakenly included by English writers – was born at Briel near Rotterdam in 1597 and was very different from his adversary Blake – the two giants who fought seven great sea battles against each other from May 1652 to August, 1653, in the 1st Dutch War, 1652-54. Blake was a wealthy squire who had taken over his father's merchant business and was known as a stern, scholarly, somewhat dour but upright man, who joined the army in 1642 and rose to be an infantry officer with the rank of lieutenant-colonel Tromp by contrast was an ordinary seaman – a tarpaulin – who worked his way up the ranks by his ability. What they had in common was that they were both in their 50s when they were the commanders opposing each other – rather late in life for seafaring in those times; yet, between them, they may be said to have redefined the art of sea warfare.

Tromp's father was an officer in a Dutch warship but was killed when the merchant ship, on which he was travelling with his 12-year-old son Maarten, was captured by an English privateer. Maarten was obliged to become a cabin boy on an English ship, but, after a couple of years, escaped home to Rotterdam, where he took a job in a shipyard to help support his three sisters and his mother, who had been scraping a living apparently by taking in sailors' washing.

At the age of 19 Maarten went to sea again and was captured once more – this time by Barbary pirates – and was kept as a slave by the Dey of Tunis; but he seems so to have impressed his captor with his gunnery and navigational skills that, at the age of 24, he managed to gain his release and restart his career as a seaman on Dutch warships. Here, he so impressed his superiors that at 26 Maarten was made a captain, at 31 a flag captain, and at 39 lieutenant-admiral. He established a dashing reputation with his greatest victory on October 21, 1638, when, in his flagship *Amelia* and with 30 ships, he almost annihilated a Spanish fleet of 73 ships in the English Channel. But to catch some Spanish ships trying to evade him, he entered English coastal waters; this led to some dispute with Charles I, but the matter was settled amicably and involved the marriage of Charles I's daughter Mary to the son of the Stadtholder of Holland, a union which had unforeseen consequences: in 1687 their son, William, and his wife, Mary, became joint sovereigns of England when James II fled to France and Parliament declared the throne 'vacant'.

At the age of 24, one dubious honour was given to Maarten in the form of a knighthood bestowed on him by Charles I for escorting Queen Henrietta Maria and the Crown Jewels to Holland. The jewels were then promptly sold to help pay for the King to make war upon his Parliament.

It was during the 1st Dutch War that the Articles and Orders of War of December, 1652, inspired by Blake, were drawn up setting down for the English navy for the first time exactly what was expected of every naval officer. Blake's *Sailing Instructions* and *Fighting Instructions* followed, and these included the line-ahead formation for battle, which maximised the gun power directed at an opponent's ships; Blake also divided his fleet into three squadrons – red, blue and white – with himself leading the red. The blue and white were allocated in rotation to his vice-admirals, including to William Penn – the father of the founder of Pennsylvania – who is credited with having obtained the idea of a line-ahead formation from discussions he had earlier had with Maarten Tromp, and then with having passed the idea on to Blake. In any event, when the 13-hour Battle of Scheveningen (which is a place on the coast near the Hague) took place on July 30, 1653, both fleets were in line-ahead formation, each of about 120 ships stretching some 16 miles, firing broadsides at each other. Tromp in his flagship *Brederode* was, like Nelson at Trafalgar in the *Victory* in 1805, hit by a sharpshooter's musket ball fired from the *Tulip* and from which he died; the news, once it became known, is said to have taken the spirit out of the Dutch. A few month's later both countries were glad to make peace at the Treaty of Westminster – as one Dutch observer put it: 'the country was full of beggars, grass grew in the streets, and in Amsterdam 1,500 houses were untenanted'. Tromp had died at the age of 55, 'killed as he walked upon the deck with his sword drawn' (Ludlow), and the ball is said to have gone straight through his heart.

* * * * *

In contrast to Maarten Tromp's lifetime at sea, Blake's naval career lasted only nine years; yet, during that short time, he did much to advance the art of sea warfare. It was probably inevitable that 'line-ahead' should replace 'line -abreast', for a ship's armament fired broadside, not forward as with a line of musketeers in a land battle. From this came the phrase 'ship-of-the-line', meaning a ship which, by virtue usually of the number of guns carried, could take its place in the line of battle. But Blake's long-term blockading of an enemy – something he did successfully twice in his career – was quite new. Nelson did it when ships were copper-bottomed; but Blake did it at a time when ships needed frequent careening. His fleet remained at sea blockading the Spanish in 1656-7 not just in summer but also in the winter months, something no other admiral had ever before succeeded in doing. He also did something to alleviate the poor living conditions of his sailors, and their pay of 19 shillings a month in 1642 was raised to 24 shillings by 1651. It was not until 1857 that naval seamen gained a regulation uniform, and their conditions generally remained hard, with the press gang frequently used to acquire recruits, and bonuses paid for enlistments. The ships were all smelly by present-day standards, and to modern eyes would have looked proportionately short in length, broad in the beam, and high out of the water – a recipe for rolling sickeningly. There were no special quarters for the crew – except for the officers – the men living where they worked. It was not until 1683 that the Victualling Board was established to fix the ration scales considered appropriate for sailors on warships. But in Blake's time the weekly food allowance per sailor, although not fixed, generally included the following items:

    7 pounds of biscuit
    7 gallons of beer
    4 pounds of beef
    2 pounds of port

1 quart of peas

3 pints of oatmeal

6 ounces of butter

12 ounces of cheese

plus, of course, any fresh fish the crew caught. But such a limited diet was monotonous and unhealthy over longer voyages, unless it was supplemented regularly at ports of call.

There was no real concept of a modern 'balanced diet' in this list. Medievalists had talked of such a thing, but not one concerned with modern ideas about protein, fats, fibre and carbohydrates; their thinking was of the Aristotelian body humours of blood, phlegm and bile, to which various foods were linked – beef to bile, fish to phlegm, milk to blood and so forth. These notions were largely superseded in the 17th century by von Hohenheim's elements of fluids, oils and solids which replaced the humours, one incidental consequence being that sweetness was placed at the end of a meal, where it has remained to this day and is called dessert. His promotion of green salads with oil and vinegar dressings has also survived, but such dietary fads were then an indulgence of the well-to-do rather than the everyday gruel of the likes of common sailors.

Together with yellow fever, the killer on long sea voyages was scurvy, which was associated with a monotonous diet lacking in adequate fruit and vegetables. It was not until James Lind (1716-94), ship's surgeon on board HMS *Salisbury* in 1747, carried out controlled experiments which showed that a diet including lemons and oranges could cure scurvy and, in 1753, published his findings, that the problem was in sight of solution; but it was not until 1795 that the Admiralty made citrus juice part of their sailors' diet. Lemons proved too expensive, but lime, a vitamin C substitute, was issued and proved to be the answer. In 1760 the Royal Naval Hospital at Hasler at Gosport, founded in 1753 to nurse sick seamen as there was a shortage of trained sailors, admitted 1754 cases of scurvy; in 1806 they admitted only one case. Even so, it was not until 1844 that lime juice was issued regularly on merchant ships making long voyages, and helps explain the origin of the word 'limeys', standing for UK seamen.

Of punishments at sea the two best-known are keel-hauling and flogging. Keel-hauling was a severe punishment and not finally ended until early in the 18th century; the offender was tied securely to a line and dropped from a yardarm into the sea, where he would be dragged under the keel and hoisted to the opposite yardarm. Not all survived the infliction.

Flogging with the cat-o'-nine-tails also occurred, and was not finally ended in the Royal Navy until 1879. Such corrective treatment was not as resented as might be imagined because, for instance, a sailor drunk on duty might be endangering the entire ship's crew; moreover, this was how life was, no other had been known and there is a sense of security in what is familiar, accepted, and believed to be effective. A dozen strokes was the regulation limit, but counting was not always precise. A few strokes were a common punishment for offences such as being drunk on duty, but for an unusual but serious offence, such as striking an officer, it might mean receiving up to 100 lashes, which few men could survive; indeed, the inflictors would sometimes be flogging a dead body by its conclusion. Sadism was also sometimes a factor in these punishments, and Jacky Fisher, when a boy serving on a warship in the 19th century, remembered an occasion when his captain decided to flog every seaman on his ship out of some misplaced enjoyment of the cruelty.

One way a victim was believed to stand a chance of reducing the severity of the lashes was to have a crucifix tattooed on his back. This was supposed to inhibit some of those who wielded the scourge from striking too hard. But the cat was an instrument expressly designed to inflict pain, a whip with 3, 6, or 9 tails, each about 18 inches long; even when lightly applied, it was bound to hurt horribly. John Lilburne (1615-57) was scourged in 1637 with one having 3 tails, but as there were 20 knots in each tail, and as he received a lash at every 3 paces between the Fleet and Old Palace Yard in London, that was claimed to amount to something like 60,000 stripes, which, even allowing for much exaggeration, is severe. However, even this punishment did not deter him from writing pamphlets advocating reforms, including toleration in religion, freedom of speech and press, annual parliaments, the rule of law, reform of the .franchise and – worst of all to Charles I – republicanism. Titus Oates was similarly scourged in James II's reign along the road from Newgate to Tyburn with a cat having 6 lashes, from which it is therefore claimed that he received the equivalent of nearly 17,000 lashes. Although also used in the army, it is believed the cat was first used on ships, where ropes were handy, and where ropes which braced the shrouds were known to have been called 'cats'. The French used something similar called a martinet, which had 12 thongs.

The cat was still in use as a humiliating and feared punishment in some British prisons, at least until the 2nd World War. This is revealed by an incident which became public knowledge at Dartmoor Prison in September, 1941, when some inmates ganged up on some unpopular and less experienced warders and induced them to issue sicknotes certifying that the convicts were medically unfit for such severe physical beatings. That flogging was felt necessary in the navy and the army is said to have been so that the sailors – and soldiers – should fear their superiors more than the enemy, and was commonly practised in the 17th century and even into the 19th. Even as late as the 1960s corporal punishment was regularly administered in boarding schools in Britain as part of the system of discipline and, like flogging in the armed forces, the reason the practice lingered for so long was less because it was really required than because it was traditional, accepted by its victims, self-perpetuating, and genuinely, if fallaciously, considered essential; indeed, any widely-held belief such as this can become self-fulfilling. There was also the fact that most senior officers in the navy before the 20th century secured their position and promotion more through family or influence than by showing qualities of leadership or outstanding talent, and this could lead to discipline having to be harsh or their crews might rebel against their incompetence. Yet, if treatment was thought to be too harsh, it might occasionally also lead to mutiny, as happened in 1789 on the *Bounty* to the Cornish Captain, William Bligh. Apart from Nelson, the son of a Norfolk parson, who became a peer, Hood, 1792-1816, and Vincent, who all came from unaristocratic backgrounds, one of the few other senior officers who rose in the late 17th and 18th century entirely by merit was Cloudesley Shovell, who is best known, not for his capture of Gibraltar with Admiral Rooke in 1704, but his dying in Scilly in his flagship *Association* on the Gilstone in the Western Rocks in 1707. Four ships of his fleet were sunk with about 1,400 being drowned; and this led to the Board of Longitude being set up by the government in 1714, offering a £20,000 award to the designer of an accurate ship's clock – a prize won by John Harrison – which enabled a ship's longitude to be calculated accurately for the first time, and would, it was hoped, prevent a repeat of Shovell's disaster.

Mention of Bligh is nowadays connected with survival at sea in an open boat for long periods – an unusual accomplishment, for men cast adrift in such boats as a punishment have invariably died. But Bligh and eighteen seamen loyal to him, sailed nearly 4,000 miles taking 41 days, and Bligh still had 12 men with him when he returned to England. Later, he became a rather stern Governor of New South Wales and, later still, was promoted Admiral. His epic voyage, although longer, was not dissimilar to one in 1923, when the 5,000 ton Cornish cargo ship *Trevessa* sank in the Indian Ocean on June 4, and the 44 crew took to the two lifeboats. Captain Foster sailed 1,700 miles to Rodiquez in 23 days, but First Officer Charles Smith's boat, sailed 2,100 miles to reach Mauritius in 25 days. Each lifeboat had room for 20 men, but 9 died in Smith's, where the rations were one biscuit plus 1/3 of a tin of water each day. The record for the longest period of survival by a solitary seaman in an open boat at sea seems to be held by Poon Lim, a merchant seaman of the UK, who, after his ship was sunk in 1943, survived alone on a raft off Brazil for over 133 days. Casting adrift or abandonment on a deserted island was rare as a punishment, although abandonment on a rock was a punishment in the Middle Ages in Scilly. In 1301, the Assize Rolls mention a Scillonian woman, convicted of felony, left marooned on the Bishop Rock.

When considering civilian punishments of the 17th century, the evidence of a contemporary, given below, provides some comparison. It comes from the diary of John Buflon, who lived in the village of Coggeshall in Essex:

'1680, April 23:   A new pillory was put up ...'
'1680, Feb. 1:   There was a man, a stranger, whipt up Church Street at the carts tale.'
'1682, July 6:   There was a ducking stool set up in a Church pond.'
'1699, July 24:   The widow Comon was tried a third time by putting her into the river, and she swam and did not sink.'
'1699, Dec. 27:   The widow Comon, that was counted a witch, was buried.'

The last execution in the Navy – by hanging from the yardarm – was of John Dalliger on HMS *Leven* on July 13th, 1860; but such punishments at sea may be compared with equally harsh corrections ashore. In the Middle Ages drowning was an alternative to hanging, and many feudal grants in England referred to 'the right to pit and gallows', the pit being for drowning women. This was mild compared with hanging, drawing and quartering or burning at the stake, the last execution by drawing or burning in Scotland being in 1685 and in England in 1556 when Thomas Cranmer was burnt at the stake – his heart believed now to be buried under the plaque over which traffic rumbles today in the centre of Broad Street, Oxford.

In the 17th century most seamen accepted the hard life as this was the only life they knew. At sea they ate and slept and lived between the guns, with kegs and sea-chests their only seating. Some changes came with the Articles of War drawn up by Blake and others under the Commonwealth, which became the basis of subsequent naval law and discipline; but the punishments laid down were often severe, with nearly a third of the 39 Articles of War stipulating the death penalty for their transgression. Drink was often a handy solace, especially in the taverns back on shore; but the sailor's service was intermittent, and at the end of the voyage he was likely to be paid off and left to find other work – or just to beg in the streets – until required again. Yet, during the Commonwealth Period, such seamen were paid regularly and not in arrears on the whole; they fought their ships with zest and their hard life was accepted by them as normal; and their morale generally seems to have been higher than that of crews in most of the Dutch ships. This may seem strange when crews were recruited partly by press gangs, partly by an Elizabethan Vagrancy Act, which permitted the prisons to be used as a source of labour for ships, and partly by stopping merchant ships and obliging some of their skilled sailors to join; but the navy also included volunteers, and a fine ship's spirit was often created. Impressment had practically ceased by the end of the Napoleonic Wars (1815), and was outlawed in 1833 and succeeded by a service system.

The sufferings of sailors can be overstated. Their lives seemed hard, but compared with modern day comforts and conveniences rather than with the lives of men who lived and worked ashore. The majority of sailors were volunteers, and when the press gang searched the ports it was usually for experienced seamen not for landsmen. What seamen had and landsmen lacked was the chance of good profits from the distribution of prize-money, and even the most lowly seaman would benefit from this. The officers were not necessarily brutal either; the best of them were concerned about the health and welfare of their crewmen that discipline and morale might be good in order that they could fight harder; for similar reasons they usually saw to it that food was adequate with fresh meat in port and salted meat at sea. Flogging was accepted by seamen and fewer than one in twenty crewmen were ever so punished. Some occasions showed even an element of compassion. Henry Teonge, 1620-90, who was for a time a chaplain on a warship, records in his diary one sailor's punishment:

> 1675, September 28: This morning, one of our men, viz. Skinner, a known cuckold, for going on shore without leave had his legs tied together, his hands tied to a great rope, and stood on the side of the ship to be hoisted up to the yard arm, and from thence to drop down into the water 3 times: but he looking so very pitifully, and also by the gentlemen's entreaties to the Captain for him, who alleged that he had injuries enough already at home ... was spared.

The majority of deaths at sea were not the result of ill-treatment or even of conflict with the enemy, but owing to accident and, even more, to disease. The health problem was mainly on long voyages, and here it was not just the inadequacy of the diet's range, but its poor quality. Although still strictly edible, after a lengthy voyage food often became not particularly eatable owing to long storage in the bowels of a ship. Much the same could be said of the drinking water contained in wooden casks, especially if these had not been properly matured or sealed, as the poor men of the Spanish Armada discovered to their cost on their long voyage home in 1588. One perk in the British Navy to keep the sailors' spirits high was the issue of a ration of rum, called 'grog', which, in 1740, Admiral Vernon ordered to be watered down to the proportion of one pint of water to every half pint of rum, in order to reduce the 'ill effects to health and morale'. This was issued at half-a-pint a day, but by 1824 had been halved by the cancellation of the evening distribution, although still continuing in reduced amounts until 1970, when it had become only 1/8 of a pint and was finally abolished.

On the question of discipline at sea, the senior officers could themselves be severely punished in ways which sometimes seem today to be out of proportion to the offences committed. Well-known 18th century instances of this are the execution on July 19, 1745, of Lieutenant Phillips, senior officer left on the *Princess Royal*, for having the temerity to surrender his ship to the French after sixty of his crew had been killed, including the Captain and 1st Lieutenant. Even more famous was the execution on March 14, 1757, of Admiral Byng for failing to save Minorca from a French fleet – what was called 'dereliction of duty'. It led to Voltaire's famous satirical and oft-quoted remark that in England it is necessary to kill an admiral or two 'to encourage the others'. Byng died with some dignity, kneeling on a cushion on the deck of the *Monarch*, with one handkerchief over his eyes and another in his hand; when prepared, he dropped the latter, which was the signal for six marines to fire at him, five of whom found their mark.

In the 20th century such tremendous ignominy was heaped on commanders who hit the public eye as a result of some well publicised failure, that execution seemed scarcely needed. Rear-Admiral Troubridge, commanding a British squadron of ships in the Mediterranean in 1914, failed to prevent the German battlecruiser *Goeben* and the German cruiser *Breslau* from reaching Constantinople (Istanbul), where their presence is said to have influenced Turkey to enter the war on the side of Germany in the 1st World War. But his force was outgunned by the German ships and his assessment of the situation was that, if he confronted the enemy, he would simply lose some of his ships and not be able to stop the enemy anyway.

One deplorable result of his court-martial was that when, in the Pacific later in the same year, Admiral Craddock with 4 ships, including two armoured cruisers, met Admiral von Spee with 4 ships, including two armoured cruisers, he knew that to avoid disgrace he had no option but to engage in what came to be known as the Battle of the Coronel. Only on paper were the two squadrons anywhere near equal and, although he knew his ships would be sunk, Craddock had to engage and lose both his armoured cruisers, the lives of his crews and his own life – for no purpose and all for the sake of what was conceived as duty and honour.

However, in one way life at sea was limited. Even more than in ordinary existence ashore, life at sea seems in the past to have been attended by innumerable and restrictive superstitions. For instance, it was considered unlucky to name a ship after a reptile and, indeed, few are so named even today; a clergyman on board was considered unlucky, as were readings from the bible other than those required for a burial at sea; one sailor, reputed to have been hanged from the yardarm of the *Association* in 1707, was said to have horrified his executioners by shouting the words of the 109th psalm, so that when the *Association* and three other great ships were lost a little while later that year on the Western Rocks of Scilly, this was seen as evidence in support of the superstition. The story seems to have little foundation in fact, but does illustrate how belief in a superstition can easily be reinforced by chance events. Whistling at sea was also considered unlucky, but there could be a rational reason for this as sound can carry some distance over water and might apprise an enemy at night; but it must have been the effects of enforced and prolonged isolation that is said to have persuaded the first lighthouse keepers on the Bishop Rock to waste money by throwing their coins into the sea to avert storms.

Superstitions may sometimes have their origins in similar circumstances to some legends, that is in periods of great grief, particularly at the passing of some great person. For instance, when Francis Drake died in the West Indies in 1596, many sought solace in the rumour that he had promised to return and save his country if it were ever in danger, and would respond to a summons upon his drum, which was later returned to his former home at Buckland Abbey in Devon. It has been claimed to have sounded by itself at times of national relief or great stress, for instance, when Napoleon was brought into Plymouth Sound after the Battle of Waterloo in 1815, and at the start of the lst World War in 1914 and, again, at the time of the evacuation from Dunkirk in 1940. It was also reported as heard on the battleship *Royal Oak* when she was escorting units of the German High Seas fleet into surrender at Scapa Flow after the 1st World War. But this, like the 1815 occasion, was more a moment of triumph than of danger; it was not heard when the *Royal Oak* was torpedoed and sunk by U-47, when she was at anchor in harbour at Scapa Flow on October 14, 1939 – the occasion when she most needed help. She lost most of her crew who had gone below and were trapped as they wrongly believed they were being subjected to air attack. The site on the seabed of the *Royal Oak* is a war grave, but she still makes her presence felt by leaking oil – estimated at 1½ tons a week during the year 2000.

Groucho Marx, like comedians everywhere, did his best to dispel superstition by means of humour when, for example, he declared that 'When a person's nose itches, it's a sign that it needs scratching' and that 'Thirteen seated at a table is unlucky when there are only twelve chops'. But superstition is not so easily overcome: there is no surprise that church bells were rung in the Middle Ages to disperse plague, but it is eyebrow-raising to read that they were rung at Dawlish in the middle of the 19th century to ward off a great storm. Still more remarkable is to learn that among the limited food and water that Alcock and Brown carried on their epic transatlantic flight, Brown found room for 'a lucky toy', a black cat called *Twinkletoes*; and there seems something sad today when GCSE candidates, even in science exams, try to smuggle lucky charms into the exam room.

* * * * *

In contrast, Blake was not a man given to superstitions, but a practical person governed by a staunch religious faith and convinced of the righteousness of his cause. This was the spirit which informed all he did and contributed much to his success.

His achievements were not confined to victories on land and sea, important though these were. Arguably, equally important were his contributions to naval tactics and law. He helped draw up the Articles of War of 1652 under the Commonwealth, which among other matters mentioned above, clarified numerous uncertainties; for instance, prize money was in future regulated at the rate of ten shillings per ton of the ship captured and ten pounds per gun of a ship sunk, and the precise meaning of flag signals and gun discharges was also first established. Moreover, judicial authority in the fleet was given to the Captain-General, who was henceforth known as 'admiral'. In 1653, he also drew up the Fighting Instructions which became the basis for future battle tactics at sea and by which an admiral could signal precise manoeuvres to his ships. Blake's biographer, D.C. Curtiss (in *Blake: General-at-Sea,* p. 169), says of Blake that he divided his fleet 'into squadrons for the first time, and the line-ahead formation was first used off Dover on May 12, 1652 – a formation which has been used in most important naval battles since', including by Jellicoe at the Battle of Jutland in 1916.

In his appreciation of Blake as an innovator, Clarendon (1608-74) wrote in his *History of the Great Rebellion*: 'He betook himself wholly to the sea, and quickly made himself signal there, and was the first man that declined the old tack, and made it manifest that the science might be attained in less time than was imagined, and despised those rules which had been long in practice, to keep his ship and men out of danger, which had been held in former times a point of great ability and circumspection, as if the principal art requisite in the captain of a ship had been to be sure to come home safe again. He was the first man who brought the ships to contemn castles on shore, which had only been thought ever very formidable, and were discovered by him only to make a noise and to fright those who could rarely be hurt by them.'

After the 1st Dutch War, Blake recovered to lead the fleet to the Mediterranean in what was to be the highwater mark of this country's naval power in that region. He took 20 ships to punish the Barbary pirates in 1654, and destroyed the Dey's Tunisian fleet in Porto Farina on April 14, 1655. The French were also punished, the Pope and the Grand Duke of Tuscany forced to pay £60,000 compensation for having supported Prince Rupert, an indemnity of £50,000 extracted from the King of Portugal for accepting captured English merchant ships, and the Dey of Tunis further humbled and forced to release English slaves. Blake followed this with the interception on September 8, 1656, of the Spanish Treasure Fleet and the taking from it of £½ million in silver coin – an achievement that had eluded even Drake. His fleet had the *Naseby* of 80 guns, and included many of the ships which had helped him in the reduction of Scilly in 1651, including the *Phoenix* (38 guns), the *Rainbow* (40 guns), and the *Amity* (30 guns). Then came Blake's greatest victory on April 20, 1657, at Tenerife, when his ships entered the harbour and disposed of almost the entire Spanish fleet which was composed of greater ships than his. In all, he had 23 ships with him this time, and located the Spanish galleons at Santa Cruz, which was the chief port of the Canary Islands. Geography seemed to have done much to ease the defence of this port; there was a funnel-like passage at its entrance under the Peak of Tenerife, and the prevailing on-shore breeze made it easy to enter but hard to exit, a trap for any hostile intruder. Moreover, Spain had built a great fort near the entrance, together with no less than seven smaller forts around the harbour, each mounting heavy artillery; in addition, there were breastworks between the seven, from behind which musketeers could pour fire into any enemy foolish enough to attempt to enter the harbour. The commander, Don Diego Diagues, felt sure his defences were secure, the more so as he had the fleet from Mexico in the harbour, which included six great galleons each of 1600 tons, well-armed and drawn up in line near the harbour entrance, and ten smaller galleons arranged in a semi-circle near the shore. As Clarendon wrote: 'All men who knew the place concluded that no sober men ... would ever undertake it'.

But Blake was always a sober man, his puritan spirit made sure of that; and, although quite aware of the Spanish strength at the port, he was also acute enough to observe its weaknesses. The ordnance of the Great Fort was pointing seawards towards his fleet, and he calculated that if he sent a squadron under Staynor consisting of 10 ships with some of his most experienced crews, running before the wind close to the shore under the Great Fort and on a rising tide, they would be able to make it through the funnel-like passage and into the harbour before the big guns of the fort could be re-positioned; moreover, as sited, these guns would be likely to have difficulty depressing their trajectories sufficiently to fire accurately upon his ships. In the event this is exactly what happened, with Blake transferring from his flagship, the *George*, to the smaller *Swiftsure* and, with others, following Staynor in the *Speaker* and his ten ships into the harbour, and acting as guard to the extremity of Staynor's ships. Once in the harbour, Staynor's ships anchored within close gunshot range of the six great Spanish galleons and opened fire, and all six were mastered, some being taken after boarding only in the most desperate hand-to-hand fighting. Most of the forts on shore could not fire upon Blake's ships, most obviously because of the semi-circle of ten Spanish galleons blocking their line of fire, and the line of six great galleons also presented an obstacle, preventing many of the guns of the ten smaller Spanish galleons from being able to fire upon the English, the scene variously obscured by the pall created by the cannonade. But, when the six great galleons had been taken and the guns fell almost silent, the pall began to clear; so Blake ordered some of the captured vessels to be set on fire and the dense smoke drifted with the north-east breeze, once more obscuring many of the English ships, and enabling them, before the turn of the flowing tide, to descend upon the smaller Spanish galleons while continuing almost invisible from the shore. Many of the Spanish shore defenders still remained convinced of their own impregnability, Don Diego Diagues being confident that the English in the harbour must now be trapped. Yet only from one side of the harbour did the English have to endure considerable raking fire from the shore batteries, losing 50 to 60 men killed and 120 to 150 wounded; for this price, 16 of the enemy ships were eventually boarded, fired, blown up or sunk, with not an English ship lost. Their task of destruction completed, the

English ships all exited the harbour, including Staynor in the badly-crippled *Speaker*, floating out with the tide now on the ebb, and aided by a fortunate shift in the breeze to the southwest, the wind change obviating the necessity for what would have been difficult warping, and the departure effected without much further damage from shore batteries. Clarendon wrote that the English sailors 'could hardly persuade themselves to believe what they had done', for it was the greatest success ever achieved against the Spanish in a single battle. Andrew Marvel wrote:

> All the Foes ships destroy'd. by sea or fire,
> Victorious Blake, does from the Bay retire.
> His Siege of Spain he then again pursues,
> And there first brings of his success the news,
> The saddest news that ere to Spain was brought,
> Their rich Fleet sunk, and ours with Lawrel fraught.

A letter to Blake from Oliver Cromwell, the Lord Protector – expressed typically in language of religious fervour – congratulates Blake on what Earl Jellicoe later called the action of Santa Cruz, the 'wonderful finale' to Blake's career:

To General Blake, at sea.
From Whitehall, 10th June, 1657.

Sir,
I have received yours of the 20th of April last, and thereby account of the good success it hath pleased God to give you at the Canaries, in your attempt upon the King of Spain's ships in the bay of Santa Cruz.

The mercy therein, to us and this Commonwealth, is very signal; both in the loss the enemy hath received, and also in the preservation of our own ships and men; which indeed was very wonderful; and according to the goodness and loving kindness of the Lord, wherewith His People hath been followed in all these late revolutions; and doth call on our part. That we should fear before Him, and still hope in His mercy.

We cannot but take notice also how eminently it hath pleased God to make use of you in this service; assisting you with wisdom in the conduct, and courage in the execution thereof; and have sent you a small Jewel, as a testimony of our own and the Parliament's good acceptance of your carriage in this action. We are also informed that the officers of the Fleet, and the seamen, carried themselves with much honesty and courage, and we are considering of a way to show our acceptance thereof. In the meantime we desire you to return our hearty thanks and acknowledgements to them.

Thus beseeching the Lord to continue His presence with you, I remain,
Your very affectionate friend,
Oliver, P.

(The jewel mentioned in the letter cost £565, and was a portrait of Cromwell set in gold and crystal amid 46 diamonds – according to the Calendar of State Papers, Domestic, October 13th, 1657.)

This letter shows Cromwell's generous nature, but he was also tolerant for his times. When people today label him 'a dictator' during the 5 year period of his protectorate, 1653-58, there are misleading 20th century overtones in the word; Cromwell was no Hitler – indeed, rather the opposite in some ways, as for instance his permitting the Jews to return to settle in England after their long expulsion from this country since 1233.

Sir Dingle Foot pointed out that Oliver Cromwell was one of those rare humans who did not seem to do anything corrupt. 'He was a much more tolerant character than is generally recognised, and so was society under his rule. No reprisals were taken against defeated Royalist leaders, unlike those made against the Puritans after the Restoration. The law courts acted freely and made their own decisions – even if the government didn't like them – and actresses were allowed on the stage for the first time. Cromwell was not a man who deliberately sought power. He was a great military leader and that, rather than political ambition, took him to prominence ... His personality was far removed from the dour, priggish image of the school textbook ... He was a devoted family man with a great sense of humour ... Every aspiring politician should study the Cromwellian era. It was the most important political period in our history.'

Cromwell recognised in Blake someone who shared his views on life, but also someone who was successful. The Age of Blake marked the beginnings of the British maritime empire which the Elizabethan Age had presaged, and by his watch over sea coasts, Blake had demonstrated not just that enemy fleets but also governments could be dominated by English sea power. He was once asked what his task had been; he replied disappointingly straightforwardly '... to keep foreigners from fooling us' – the sort of reply that Cromwell might have made in similar circumstances.

It was on the voyage home with 11 ships from his great victory at Santa Cruz – the victory that was said to have 'startled the world more than any since Gustavus Adolphus' – that Blake became seriously ill, said to have arisen from a longstanding tendency to dropsy. He died just as his flagship, the *George*, was nearing the entrance to Plymouth Sound on the evening air of August 7, 1657, a huge crowd assembled on the Hoe to welcome him, and a grateful nation preparing to honour him.

Sir Henry Newbolt, 1862-1938, poet and official Naval Historian from 1923, who lived in the Quantocks at Aisholt close to where Blake's mother had lived in her later years, wrote the following lines of Blake's sad last homecoming:

> Only to look once more on the land of the memories of childhood,
> Forgetting weary winds and barren foam;
> Only to bid farewell to the combe and the orchard and the moorland,
> And sleep at last among the fields of home.
> Here lay the Sound and the Island with green leaves down beside the water,

The town, the Hoe, the masts with sunset fired,
Dreams! Ay, dreams of the dead! For the great heart faltered on the threshold,
And darkness took the land his soul revered.

Blake's body lay for a while at Greenwich before being carried by a river procession up the Thames for a state funeral on August 17, 1657. He was then buried in Henry VII's chapel in Westminster Abbey, only to have his body (like Cromwell's) humiliated after the Restoration in 1660. In an ungracious act, it was dug up and thrown into an unmarked pit in St Mary's churchyard. In any event, as a puritan, Blake would have been unlikely to have relished the pomp and ceremony which had attended his funeral and, as a republican, he would most likely have resented being laid to rest in the hall of Kings. However, he would have appreciated the recognition of his military and naval successes and, most of all, of what he conceived as his services to God; but, as William, his namesake, wrote in *The Everlasting Gospel*:

> The Vision of Christ that thou dost see
> Is my vision's greatest enemy
> Thine has a great hook nose like thine,
> Mine has a snub nose like to mine.

However, he would have understood the following lines in a way not all accept readily today:

> Joy and woe are woven fine,
> A clothing for the soul divine;
> Under every grief and pine
> Runs a joy with silken twine.
> It is right it should be so;
> Man was made for joy and woe;
> And when this we rightly know,
> Thro' the world we safely go.

> from *Auguries of Innocence* by William Blake

To understand the dedication of Blake, it may be helpful to consider the thinking of his friend and superior, Oliver Cromwell, and of other leading Roundheads. The puritan John Bunyan in the first paragraph of *Pilgrim's Progress*, shows, in G.M. Trevelyan's words, the 'motive force of it all ... the poor man seeking salvation with tears, with no guide save the Bible in his hand ... the force by which Oliver Cromwell and George Fox and John Wesley wrought their wonders' (*English Social History*, p. 236). Many of them would not have appreciated or welcomed any thought that they stood for anything 'democratical' – indeed, the term was then used as one of abuse; but with history's perspective, and allowing for much variation of definition, democracy seems to have been a logical consequence of what they sought when faced with continuing intransigent dictatorship. While elements such as

An artist portrays the death of Robert Blake on his flagship as it neared the entrance to Plymouth Sound on the evening of August 7, 1657, the tragedy unknown to the crowds on the Hoe, who were jubilantly expecting to celebrate his glorious homecoming. Gathered around Blake and awaiting his end, his officers appear crestfallen and disconsolate, sharing in his suffering but unable to stem the inevitable outcome.

hereditary right, hierarchical structures and great personal wealth and influence – such as newspaper proprietors possess today – still characterise power within society, democratic development has a long way to go in the 21st century; but it can be traced back to ancient Greece and its spirit was clearly manifest in the New Model Army's debates at Putney in 1648-9. Lilburne and the Levellers campaigned for manhood suffrage but not a redistribution of wealth; only Winstanley and the Diggers foresaw social revolution. The democratic spirit is not something that can be built in a decade, as Cromwell quickly discovered and never advocated; it needs an informed electorate, but the good news would seem to be that the development of information technology – although not perhaps the press – may be the means of attaining it.

The spirit of democracy and its political forms cannot solve everything; moreover, as Churchill, in a typical pithy phrase remarked, it is only 'the least worst political system'. Men like Cromwell had a hazy vision of a better political system, but could not find how to gain unified assent for it. Cromwell was mindful of the prime duty of government, which was to maintain law and order, and it led him to suppress radical groups such as Levellers, Ranters, Diggers, 5th Monarchists and others who seemed to threaten disorder, at a time when his championship of toleration – broad for his day, if limited by today's standards – would otherwise have protected them. Then, with the republicans failing to find a new system of government to which all could subscribe, the Long Parliament resorted in 1660 to the tried system of monarchy, but one which no longer possessed the means of unbridled despotism. But the previous experiments in government were not forgotten, and from them issued ideas which over time and much discussion and many a struggle are credited with helping to create the political and constitutional democracy still developing today – and, perhaps, tomorrow.

As with his leader, Oliver Cromwell, Blake's reputation suffered from Royalist propaganda at the Restoration, a further example of how history tends to be written from the standpoint of the victorious. John Buchan, in his biography of Oliver Cromwell, assessed Blake more generously when he wrote of him as 'patient, hardy, masterful, merciful and chivalrous; there is no nobler figure in the sea story of England'. Nobody knows today exactly where the remains of Blake's body are located, and it is of little consequence. As for Cromwell, there are no less than three extant skulls which claim to be his; one is held by the Master of Balliol College, Oxford, but does not quite match Cromwell's death mask; another was buried on March 25, 1960, in Sydney Sussex College, Cambridge, and possesses a groove in it consistent with a spike which was stuck in the head to display it in Westminster Hall in 1660 – after the rest of Cromwell's disinterred body had been thrown into a ditch over which today Regent Street is said to run; the third skull was in the keeping of the Ashmolean Museum until 1911 ... but then mysteriously vanished.

The Interregnum, between the death of Charles I on the scaffold in 1649 and the accession of Charles II in 1660, saw one of the most interesting periods in English history, and many of the issues of government raised in the debates within the New Model Army at Putney in 1648 are still being worked out in the 21st century. During the 5 years of rule of Oliver Cromwell as Lord Protector in 1653 – he refused to become King – he tried to find a parliament with which he could rule, in contrast to Charles I who tried to rule without parliament. He permitted a measure of religious toleration, limited only by the overriding need to maintain law and order. Cromwell explained that he was 'only playing parish constable in a large and disturbed parish', but abroad, the country's foreign policy was its most successful in the century. After Cromwell's death on September 3rd, 1658, the country failed to find a settled form of government and anarchy seemed to threaten. This was averted by Monk (1608-70), who had been one of Cromwell's major-generals, and who, in 1659, stepped in – as Cromwell had done in 1653 – to keep order. He did so by marching to London with his Coldstream Guard Regiment – the sole surviving regiment of the New Model Army, which had taken part in Cromwell's victory at Dunbar – and by recalling the Long Parliament which decided to restore the monarchy on terms. Monk then personally welcomed Charles II on the beach at Dover in 1660, and metaphorically handed him 'the keys of the Kingdom'.

Monk was a Devonian and Sir John Grenville's cousin. He was born in 1608 and noted for his honesty. He was one of those rare, great men who are not ambitious for power for themselves but, once having had it thrust upon them, use it briefly for the good of all before retiring from it – rather like Garibaldi in Italy. For a landsman he showed considerable ability commanding the fleet in Charles II's reign, although he never mastered the language of the sea by all accounts. 'Starboard or larboard, Sir?' he was once asked; to which he is said to have replied: 'Certainly – board the enemy'. He once told his helmsman 'wheel to the right', and his fleet he ordered to 'charge' – but it is likely these stories were somewhat embroidered in the telling.

Charles II seems to have had a special regard for Monk, treating him a little like a father-figure; after all, in a sense, he owed his kingdom to him. But it was Edward Montagu who was sent with a flotilla of ships to collect Charles from Holland; Montagu had been one of Cromwell's Generals-at-Sea, and was a kinsman of Pepys and was later to be his patron, securing for him the post of Clerk of the Acts. But the ship in which Charles sailed was the *Naseby*, so a tactful renaming ceremony was held by Montagu – the vessel becoming the *Royal Charles* – before Charles stepped on board. Montagu was afterwards created 1st Earl of Sandwich by Charles II, but was drowned going down with his ship in the 3rd Dutch War, 1672-74. He was not the inventor of the sandwich; that was a subsequent earl in the 18th century (in the time of Walpole), who designed the snack to satisfy his hunger while not interrupting his gaming.

17th century accounts can also be a source of confusion because of the differing meanings of some words. For instance, 'admiral' usually referred to what is now called 'the flagship', while the officer in charge of the ships was called 'the General-at-Sea'.

Under Blake and Monk, instead of the army's 'Right, Centre and Left', the fleet was divided into the Red, being the senior section and flying the red ensign, and in the Dutch War, led in the *Triumph* by Blake or by Deane, who had handled the army's right wing superbly at the Battle of Preston in 1648; the White, later led by Monk in the *Vanguard* (56 guns); and the Blue led by Penn in the *Speaker* (64 guns). Today, all naval ships fly the white ensign, while the red ensign is the flag of the merchant navy, and the blue is that of the naval reserve.

Monk could be said to have married beneath him for his wife was a sewing teacher called Nan Clarges, described by Pepys as 'ever a plain homely dowdy'; but she became Duchess of Albermarle when her husband received his well-deserved dukedom from Charles II, and she is buried near her husband in St George's Chapel, Westminster Abbey, with Clarges Street off Piccadilly today named after her family.

Monk's greatest defeat came in 1667 at the end of the 2nd Dutch War

(1665-7) when the Navy suffered its greatest-ever humiliation. The Dutch Admiral de Ruyter sailed up the Medway, broke the chain defences of Chatham and captured the English flagship, the *Royal Charles*, the great ship launched in 1633, and towed her away after ravaging the dockyards of Chatham. The English sailors, so poorly paid by Charles II, ran away. Some English turned traitor, Colonel Thomas Dolmen even leading in the Dutch transport ships. The population of Gravesend fled, the garrison of Sheerness deserted, and only Albemarle tried to rally some resistance; but he was hampered by a painful bullet wound in his posterior received the year before, or as Andrew Marvell indelicately put it:

> When the rude bullet a large collop tore
> out of that buttock never turn'd before.

Monk found he could not prevent the English crew abandoning the *Royal Charles*. 'The courage of the Dutch crews seemed in inverse proportion to the cowardice of the English, who abandoned every ship or position as the Dutch reached them' (G. Regan, p. 142, *The Guinness Book of Blunders*, 1993). Pepys wrote in his diary that a run on the bankers followed, with people fearing London was about to be taken, although, actually and fortunately, the Dutch were by then only anxious to conclude peace. It was the third disaster of Charles II's reign after the Plague of 1664-5[1] and the Fire of London of 1666, and the one for which Charles II was mainly responsible by his running down of the navy and leaving its crews unpaid; the lesson was, however, learnt, and ever since then there has always been sufficient money found to keep ships of the navy at sea.

It is sometimes overlooked that the Restoration in 1600 was of the Stuart family but not of the former King's powers, and it needed both King and Parliament to agree to provide money for the navy. In 1660, arbitrary rule was made illegal, none of the prerogative courts were restored, and the King

NOTE

1 A graphic picture of the plague's effect on London is provided in John Evelyn's diary, of which the following is an extract:

1665, July 16: There died of the plague in London this week 1100, and in the week following 2000.

1665, August 8: I waited on the Duke of Albemarle, who was resolved to stay at the cockpit in St James's Park. Died this week in London 4000.

1665, August 15: There perished this week 5000.

1665, August 28: The contagion still increasing and growing now all about us, i sent my wife and whole family (two or three necessary servants excepted) to my brother's at Wotton, being resolved to stay at my house myself and to look to my charge, trusting in the providence and goodness of God.

1665, September 7: Came home, there perishing near 10,000 poor creatures weekly; however I went all along the City and suburbs from Kent Street to St James's, a dismal passage, and dangerous to see so many coffins exposed in the streets, now thin of people, the shops shut up, and all in mournful silence, as not knowing whose turn might be next.

had henceforth to rule with Parliament, and he could no longer impose taxes at his will, such as ship money. An Act of Indemnity and Oblivion (forgiving and forgetting) attempted to heal wounds, but regicides – those 41 still alive of the 45 who had signed Charles I's death warrant (and four others) – were excluded. Fifteen of these fled abroad, but the first of thoseremaining to suffer the awful punishment – of half-hanging, disembowelling and quartering while still partly alive – was the 5th Monarchist, Thomas Harrison, who went to his death with equanimity and a courage which much impressed the crowd who witnessed it. Pepys records the execution in his Diary, but apparently the sight did nothing to curb his appetite: 'I went out to Charing Cross to see Major-General Harrison hanged, drawn and quartered ... he looking as cheerfully as any man could do in that condition. He was presently cut down and his head and his heart shown to the people ... From thence took Captain Cuttance and Mr Sheply to the Sun Tavern and did give them some oysters'. Pepys as a schoolboy had applauded when he watched Charles I lose his head – but that was not something he would have cared to remember in the 1660s.

Apart from such acts of revenge, there was no great attempt to reverse the beneficial consequences of the victory of the Roundheads over the Royalists in the Civil War, and many of these survived the political Restoration of the Monarchy in 1660. They included the continued expansion of the power of the merchant classes in England, to the great benefit of England's wealth and fortunes generally. London grew by immigration and became the world's most populated city for almost the next three centuries, despite each year during that time, more people dying than were born, as they succumbed to hunger or disease. Most important of all, in terms of the development of English society and thought, was the affirmation – as Edward Coke, England's greatest lawyer, had championed – of the supremacy of the common law over other law; this meant that law in England was separate and above government, and led to such things as political opponents of the government being more fairly treated when brought to trial than they were in other countries, and to torture being abolished in England long before it was in other countries.

A generation later, at the so-called Glorious Revolution in 1689, the monarch's powers were further limited, thus taking still further the gains for which the Civil War had primarily been fought. Cromwell's Protectorate of 1653-58 failed to last: but it had been relatively efficient and free from corruption; Charles II's rule was to be rather the reverse – but that is another story.

II

THE FIRST WORLD WAR, 1914-18
AND DEVELOPMENTS IN THE AIR BETWEEN THE WARS, 1918-39

'There are few who die well
that die in a battle' Henry V, Act IV, Scene 1

In the Middle Ages, the distinction between war and peace was somewhat academic in the Scillies because piratical attacks could and did occur at any time. The population was relatively poverty-stricken, scraping a living mainly from the soil and by fishing. Even ostensibly friendly visitors could be a menace, as happened in 1342, when six hundred Welsh soldiers on passage to Brittany to fight for Edward III in the Hundred Years' War against France, were becalmed (some accounts mention strong adverse winds) near Scilly for about three weeks. They were unpaid and starving on their ships, so they landed on St Mary's in uncaring mood and helped themselves to anything they wanted. Later, these troops are said to have served in the English Army which won the Battle of Crecy in 1346. At that time the Scillonians are thought to have had few means of defending themselves, although proprietors who held Scilly in medieval times were supposed to maintain a dozen armed soldiers at the strong point of Ennor Castle, which is above Old Town, then the principal settlement on St Mary's. However, signs of earlier defences date from the Iron Age, and there are traces of at least three cliff castles, the most obvious being that called Giant's Castle on St Mary's. But it is in Tudor times that the more substantial defences visible today in Scilly were first built, including the incomplete Harry's Walls in 1551 and Star Castle in 1593, this latter a consequence of the fear that another Spanish Armada, similar to the one in 1588, might this time attempt to occupy the Islands. Three other armadas were planned by Philip II but none invaded Scilly or the mainland, except for the brief attack on Mousehole, Newlyn and Penzance in 1595.

In the 17th century, the so-called Cromwell's Castle was built on the site of an earlier block-house in case of a possible Dutch attack. Defences in later centuries included the substantial wall which today extends most of the way around the Hugh, and there were other defences erected in the period of the seven French Wars between 1793 and 1815. There were also naval engagements off Scilly; on May 2, 1694, for instance, the French privateer *Diligente* was captured only about four miles from St Mary's, and, in 1796, the 44-gun French warship *Virginie* was similarly captured by the 38-gun

Indefatigable near Scilly. But, apart from attention being paid to improving the defences, such as Captain Edward Pellew's redoubt on Toll's Island and a signal station on St Martin's, Scilly was not as directly involved in the wars as happened in the 1st and 2nd World Wars of the 20th century.

Between the building of such defences, there were periods of neglect – during which the building works tended to become ruinous – until, in 1900, there was drawn up a great plan to make Scilly a naval base. Three gun-forts were built on the Hugh, now more usually called The Garrison; but these plans were cancelled as too costly after much money had already been spent, and a period of dilapidation set in. These plans had envisaged Scilly being a naval base, with breakwaters, docks and shore facilities, but Jacky Fisher realised that the depth of water in St Mary's Sound at low tide would be insufficient for his new dreadnoughts safely to navigate the channels because of their deep draught, so he developed Scapa Flow instead.

No serious attempt has ever been made to invade the Islands since 1651. But, in 1914, there began a conflict which, although it did not offer any immediate threat to the Islands, enabled Scilly from 1917 to play a part in prosecuting the war through serving as a base for seaplanes. However, the First World War is nowadays increasingly seen as something that happened far back in the past, with hardly anybody now who remembers it. How the conflict arose and why it did are matters left to history books, which may be largely unread; so some outline of how the war affected Britain generally may be appropriate and help set the scene for events within the Islands.

* * * * *

The shot that precipitated the 1st World War was fired by Gavrilo Princip, a Bosnian student who wanted Bosnia-Herzegovina to unify with Serbia and be independent of Austro-Hungary. He was one of seven would-be assassins, who were all 'fired-up' by the growing spirit of nationalism, a force, destined in the next few years to break-up the Austro-Hungarian Empire, which in 1914 contained 17 separate nationalities.

On June 28, 1914, Princip found himself and his pistol only five feet away from a stopped car in a street in Sarajevo. The vehicle was carrying the Archduke Francis Ferdinand, heir to the Austro-Hungarian throne, together with his wife Sophie, and it had come to a standstill because the driver had taken a wrong turning. Princip fired two shots and Sophie died first, the Archduke dying after he had repeated several times his last but rather inappropriate words 'Es ist nicht' ('It is nothing'). Neither the Kaiser nor the Emperor, although appalled, saw the event as likely to lead to the wide and drawn-out conflict it subsequently became. The following four years of war can only be explained in terms of the complicated contractual obligations entered by states beforehand, and by the determination of political leaders not

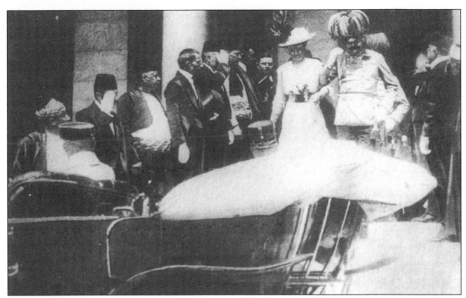

The photograph shows Archduke Franz Ferdinand, heir to the Austro-Hungarian throne, and his wife, leaving the town hall in Sarajevo to enter their open cab a few minutes before being shot dead by Gavrilo Princip, a Serbian national supporter. This was the shot which they said 'rang around the world' and started the chain of events which culminated in war between two alliances of powers – the Triple Entente of France, Russia and Britain versus the Triple Alliance of Austria, Germany and Italy (although Italy was in 1915 to support the Allies). These hostile alliances were fully formed by 1907 and produced a balance, which can be said either to have been a cause of war or a cause of peace for 7 years – or both.

to lose face or influence. It also had something to do with a war plan drawn up originally in 1905-6 by Schlieffen, the Chief of the German General Staff, detailing what Germany should do to win if the fatherland should ever find itself involved in a war on two fronts. This plan although subsequently disastrously modified by Moltke, was based on railway timetables, and required a successful attack on France in the West before Germany had to deal with Russian hordes in the East. Schlieffen was dead by 1914, but his modified war plan was adopted, as it was the best one which was available and worked out in some detail. Schlieffen's reputed dying words had been 'Keep the right wing strong', but Moltke weakened it by 30%, which in the event enabled the British and French armies to survive the German attack, Paris to be saved, and the war to settle on the Western Front into a long stalemate of static trench warfare.

The Schlieffen plan involved the attack on 'gallant little Belgium', for which Kaiser Wilhelm II was personally blamed in Britain, where he was portrayed as a hard and evil man, an appearance weak men may sometimes seem almost to encourage in order to hide their weakness. He had a withered left arm about which he was acutely conscious, to the extent that senior German officers, when in his company, would invariably obscure one of their own arms – in a pocket, behind their backs, or otherwise unobtrusively hidden – in deference to the King's sensibilities so that he should not feel conspicuous, a practice clearly detectable in photographs. To Britons, if one man can take the blame for starting the war, the Kaiser was the leading candidate, if only by default rather than through a monstrous nature with which he was attributed. The Queen Mother, Alexandra, had a particular dislike of the Kaiser, seeing him as some sort of reincarnation of his grandfather, William I, whom she held responsible for the 19th century brutal German attack on Denmark. When a young man in 1889, the Kaiser had attended the review of the Royal Navy at Spithead with his uncle, Prince Edward (later Edward VII), and was made an honorary Admiral of the Fleet in the Royal Navy, even wearing the admiral's uniform for the occasion; but his remark at the time that he was 'proud to wear the uniform that Nelson had worn', was a little off the mark historically, and is perhaps indicative of his glamorous and unrealistic view of war, an incompetent posturing as a warlord. In return, George V wore a German uniform, including a spiked helmet, at Kaiser Wilhelm's daughter's wedding in 1913. The Kaiser died on June 4, 1941, aged 81, at Doorn in the Netherlands – which had been overrun by Hitler's army – after quite a happy number of years in retirement, hunting, entertaining and the like.

Niall Ferguson, in his book *The Pity of War*, points out that Britain cannot place all the blame on Continental Europeans, and that there was considerable jubilation among the public in Britain when the news came that George V (in privy council with just two officials and Lord Beauchamp) had declared that the war would start at 11 pm on August 4, 1914. Neither the Cabinet nor Parliament actually authorised the declaration, and Grey sent his 'note' without consulting the Dominions or probably anyone other than the Prime Minister, although the Cabinet had previously decided that Britain must help defend Belgium, if it were ever attacked, something that Britain had undertaken to do in the Treaty of London, 1839, and thus, in that general sense, authorising the declaration of war by Britain on Germany.

Once the war had begun, it then became a matter of prosecuting it successfully, and volunteers were called for and responded in such large numbers that recruiting offices were almost overwhelmed. Most young men wanted to 'put some service in' – as their fathers had done before them – and were anxious to take part quickly because it was believed that the war would all be over by Christmas. Even the Kaiser announced that the fighting would stop 'before the leaves had fallen off the trees'. It was easy to believe this in the summer of 1914, for it was difficult to point to any great cause over which the Great Powers would endure such a long and bitter conflict as in fact occurred. In Britain, with so many volunteers, there was no need to introduce conscription before 1916, and at first the British public saw the conflict mainly as sending troops abroad to do great deeds and win honours, as in the

Lord Kitchener's famous recruiting poster at the start of the 1st World War that is said to have been a deciding factor in persuading so many young men to volunteer to join the armed services. He was commander-in chief from 1900 of the army in the Boer War in South Africa and was mainly responsible for the use of British concentration camps into which were rounded up Boer women and children, nearly half of whom died from disease, starvation or neglect. Popular with the public, as Minister for War he was blamed by others in the government for the shell shortage of 1915, a problem left to Lloyd George to solve.

Boer War, 1899-1902, and in the Crimean War, 1854-56, with little to disturb civilian life at home. By issuing posters, the Government in 1914 was urging fit young men between the ages of 19 and 30 to come forward and enlist in the armed forces. The wording of one such poster today decorates the bar of the Turk's Head on St Agnes, and reads as follows:

A Call to Arms
Lord Kitchener is confident that this appeal will be at once responded to by all those who have the safety of our Empire at Heart. Your King and Country need you for General Service for a period of 3 years or until the war is concluded

In the above the use of the word 'concluded' in place of 'won' seems to confirm that an early negotiated peace was anticipated rather than the long, bitter struggle that ensued. On the other hand the mention of '3 years' conveys an impression of something more drawn out.

Britain's declaration of war upon Germany was greeted by cheering crowds in London streets, with thousands singing patriotic songs outside Buckingham Palace. Less demonstrably, but equally heartfelt, was the war's welcome throughout the rest of the country, and similar large, excited crowds to those in London welcomed it in Paris, Berlin and Moscow in a display of what, in retrospect and with the benefit of hindsight, seems like mutual madness. Everyone believed God was on their side and His aid was invoked in every country; as J.C. Squire expressed it:

God heard the embattled nations sing and shout
'Gott strafe England' and 'God save the King!'
God this, God that, and God the other thing –
'Good God', said God,
'I've got my work cut out'.

The first few days of the war saw some panic buying of food – and of ammunition for privately-owned guns – in case the enemy should come or, possibly, because there might be civil unrest in these disturbed times. Contrary to some contemporary belief, people in the UK in the 21st century live in a relatively safe and peaceful society. In 1900, the likelihood of being killed by another person was five times (and in 1600, twenty times) what it was in 2000. Even earlier, Court Records of the Middle Ages show high levels of violence, not just after dark in the unlit streets of towns, but in the countryside, and especially to travellers. With the growth of travelling in the 17th and 18th centuries, the risk increased, and coaches were often defended by a blunderbuss; this was a weapon which sprayed shot – in a manner likely to hit a moving target even with a slightly inaccurate aim – and was thus calculated to make any highwayman hesitate before approaching. Until the

Servicemen awaiting embarkation in the 1st World War, standing with their friends and families at the Bank – the area outside what is now the chemist shop on St Mary's.

19th century, violence was present in all classes, with many people opting to carry a weapon before they ventured far from their homes, the most popular defensive implement being a simple stick such as a quarterstaff. Its descendant, although now rarely used, may still be carried in the 21st century by patrolling policemen in the form of a modern truncheon or baton. With the outbreak of war in 1914, a firearm did not seem an inappropriate defensive weapon for a householder to possess in case of unknown dangers – for these were unsettled times. For similar reasons, many customers wanted to withdraw gold and deposits from the banks and cash their shares, so the Stock Exchange was closed for a time and the August Bank Holiday extended. Arrangements were made for gold sovereigns to be called in and replaced by paper money – the first one-pound and ten-shilling notes – and, on August 8, after only a few minutes' debate, the Defence of the Realm Act was passed by the House of Commons, giving the Government enormous potential powers, including control of shipping and railways, the detention of suspects without trial, and the requisitioning, if required, of land and goods, including boats and vehicles, to an extent that even Charles I had not possessed. In 1916, all wool and leather was directed for the use of the services – for uniforms and so forth – and even some non-essential activities such as painting houses, could be prohibited, if seen as wasting scarce resources.

Hurried plans were put into effect involving the sending over to France of a British Expeditionary Force of seven regular divisions, plus a few aircraft of the small Royal Flying Corps, followed a little later by Territorials, all of whom paradoxically took pride in calling themselves *Old Contemptibles* under – as it turned out – the mistaken belief that this insult to them had actually been uttered by the Kaiser. Prime Minister Asquith argued that Britain had a bounden duty to declare war by reminding the House of Commons of Britain's guarantee of Belgian independence; but at the same time he spoke of the war as a 'purification freeing the country from luxury and sloth', an incredible statement in the light of the poverty of over half the population and the long hours of work of most of them, but conditions at the time judged normal and inevitable. 'For the poor always ye have with you' (John 12 v.8) was as commonplace a remark then as 'spare the rod and spoil the child'.

The general mood of the country seemed to be one of exaltation and of rampant nationalism, to the extent that some simple folk are said even to have thrown stones at pet dachshunds, while others, more refined but just as silly, were quoted as refraining from listening to the music of German composers such as Beethoven. The king reflected this xenophobia in his hobby of stamp-collecting, confining his collection strictly to the products of Britain and the Empire. But George V managed later in his reign and long after the war – and to his surprise and delight – gradually to win the affection of most of his subjects. Until that time came, monarchs had been revered and respected, but never loved; it was his pioneering Christmas Day wireless broadcasts starting in 1932 which seemed to change all that. His subjects enjoyed the novelty of hearing their Sovereign speak in his gravelly, classless, reassuring tones, when he read a script prepared for him by Rudyard Kipling.

* * * * *

In the first two years of the war, there were alarmist fears in Britain of a projected invasion by Germany; these were quite unfounded, but a few tip-and-run bombardments were made on English east coast towns by German battlecruisers – the first one on November 3, 1914 – something never expected or experienced before, and they caused considerable civilian panic. Refugees fled from the East Coast with their most precious belongings to safe inland areas; but, as they went, they passed on the roads going the other way, streams of sightseers intent on viewing the damage at the coast. Whitby, Scarborough, and the Hartlepools suffered most, with 137 people killed in the first raid on those particular towns on December 16. It was the first time British citizens had experienced real war, and so answering the call to the colours seemed the natural response and the manly thing to do, especially when posters appeared on billboards in towns urging men to join the services, the one of Lord Kitchener, with his pointing accusatory finger, being the best known. The raid on Lowestoft on April 25, 1916, began suddenly without warning at 4.30a.m. when German battlecruisers appeared offshore and began shelling the town. They destroyed 40 houses and damaged hundreds more – two men, one woman and a child being killed. They then went on to bombard Yarmouth. An earlier raid on Scarborough had been in broad daylight and had involved a direct hit on the town's magnificent Victorian Grand Hotel, one shell going through the lighthouse at the end of the pier.

Public opinion was incensed by the news of these terror attacks and, there were frequent playings of the National Anthem to help promote the patriotic mood. In the first two years of the war, over two million men came forward, a remarkable achievement, making Britain the only country which fought half the war almost entirely with volunteers.

Air raids by airships began in 1915, the 650 feet long zeppelins each carrying 27 tons of bombs lodged beneath a bag containing two million cubic feet of inflammable hydrogen. In January, four young people died from their bombs dropped on Great Yarmouth and King's Lynn, and it was London's turn in October, when the zeppelins killed thirty-eight people. The shock of these first aerial bombardments on the capital was far greater than the extent of the damage caused and the sadness occasioned by the lives lost; but calls for reprisals went unanswered, for Britain at the time lacked any long-range bombers or large airships. But, on the home front, many changes were made, one of the first affected aliens between the ages of 17 and 45 living in the UK – even some whose only claim to be regarded as foreigners was a German-sounding name – most being sent to be interned either in Alexandra Palace or on the Isle of Man. The awful Horatio Bottomley, editor of the magazine *John Bull*, even went so far as to recommend to his readers that if they were served in a restaurant by a waiter with a German-sounding name or voice, they should throw the soup in his face. Bottomley made £27,000 selling jingoistic speeches to anyone who would buy them but, later in the war, ended up in prison for 7 years for selling fraudulent war bonds. Prince Louis of Battenberg, a naturalised Briton, was forced to resign his office as First Sea Lord and to change his name to Mountbatten, despite his former good work in helping to prepare the fleet for war, which included founding the Royal Naval Air Service on July 1, 1914; and the Lord Chancellor, Haldane, whose reforms had prepared the BEF, was dismissed, partly, it is said, because of his inordinate interest in German art and literature. Others prudently anglicised their German-sounding names, with 'Preuss' becoming 'Price', 'Teck' becoming 'Cambridge', 'Steineke' becoming 'Stanley' and 'Rosenheim' becoming 'Rose'. Even the Royal Family changed its family name on July 17, 1917, from 'Saxe-Coburg-Gotha', and adopted the plain, English-sounding 'Windsor'. The Bryce Report of 1915 seemed to confirm alleged German atrocities in Belgium, but was written with the aim of winning over American public opinion; it included horrific tales of children having their hands cut off when clinging in terror to their parents, of a Canadian prisoner found nailed to a door, and of bodies melted down for their useful fats – most of these later discounted but, at the time, found useful as war propaganda to stir a reluctant and formerly mainly peace-loving population to military ardour. As Rudyard Kipling wrote in his poem:

> For all we have and are,
> For all our children's fate,
> Stand up and meet the war,
> The Hun is at the gate!

* * * * *

The biggest battle involving the British army in the war was the Battle of the Somme which began on July 1, 1916, but was preceded by the firing of 1½ million shells over the previous week to try to clear enough of the enemy's defensive barbed-wire for British soldiers to penetrate through it after they had emerged from their trenches and 'gone over the top' into No-Man's-Land. In practice, however, as soon as the shelling stopped, all too often German gunners emerged from their deep dugouts, fixed their machine-guns and mowed down British attackers as they were searching for a gap in the barbed-wire. There were 60,000 British casualties on the first day of the battle and half a million by the time it ended in November. Newspaper correspondents were allowed up to the front for the first time and gratefully reported a victory, although in fact little was gained and much was lost. As the war progressed the mood changed and it was not uncommon in Britain to hear bitter remarks, such as 'the only good German is a dead German', as was also heard in the 2nd World War; but, at the start in 1914, soldier-poets were reflecting the optimistic public mood by writing quantities of what now seem rather sentimental verses, the best of them being by Rupert Brooke, who was later to die in the ill-planned Gallipoli Campaign of 1915. At the same time, artists made up for the lack of war photographers by inspiring drawings of heroic soldierly deeds performed by Tommy Atkins and his comrades in confrontations with the enemy which, like old Hollywood films, lacked much of the blood-and-gore of reality. War to most civilians in 1914 was not young men being wantonly blown to pieces, but was still seen as a glamorous, romantic, chivalrous opportunity, with the sordid aspects of the emerging trench life on the Western Front sanitised; and this representation only gradually changed with the publication of lengthening casualty lists in local newspapers, but took a little time to take full effect. In 1914, *The Times* was urging English girls to avoid the company of any man of military age who could not show good cause for not being in uniform, and white feathers were sent to so-called 'cowards' to shame them. Baroness Orczy, author of *The Scarlet Pimpernel*, formed an Active Service league of about 20,000 women who, by means of incessant propaganda, pledged to persuade men 'to go to the Front and fight'; and popular, music-hall songs such as Phyllis Dane's:

How the war on the Western Front was imagined by people in England – a glorious charge into the German trenches south of Ypres on March 27, 1916, by Northumberland and Royal Fusiliers. It was often the same in such illustrations: no British casualties, some inconvenient enemy barbed wire, and a German with his hands up.

Oh, we don't want to lose you
But we think you ought to go

made it very hard for any young man to resist the call to arms and 'do his bit for his Country and for his loved ones'. A National Register of everyone between the ages of 15 and 65 was compiled, all carried Registration Cards, and men aged 18 to 41 were asked to attest that they would volunteer to serve in the forces when wanted. Men in reserved occupations, such as munition-making or coal-mining, were given armbands to save them from humiliation in the streets; while Special Constables were recruited for evening duties from men who had already done a full day's work. The most serious hiccup to the war effort was not any lack of men or diminution of will, but a shortage of shells. Seven hundred shells a day were manufactured in 1915, compared with Germany's quarter of a million a day. Lloyd George saved the situation when he was appointed Minister of Munitions, and by 1916 the factories were making more shells in a week than they previously produced in a year. The consumption of shells by both sides was enormous: one rather useless statistic that someone felt worth collating is that in the 1st World War, for every soldier killed on the Western Front, 1,400 shells had been fired – whereas relatively few soldiers were killed by the bayonet. Lloyd George also successfully persuaded the Army council to develop three new and ultimately successful weapons of war – the machine-gun, the Stokes mortar and the tank. His Munitions Act of 1915 outlawed strikes in munition factories and stopped workers moving into other jobs unless they had been given a leaving certificate. He also suspended all trade union practices judged to be 'restrictive', and set up special Munitions Courts to settle factory disputes. The leaving certificate was withdrawn in 1917, but mainly because the threat of conscription was by then enough to keep most workers at their benches and refrain from striking. Unemployment almost disappeared by 1915, drinking hours were made shorter with no morning opening in licensed premises, and beer reduced in strength and increased in price so that drunkenness decreased, with convictions falling from around 156,000 in 1913 to under 77,000 in 1916. This also helped to reduce the amount of absenteeism from work associated with inebriation. King George V gave a lead in this by publicly taking the pledge to abstain from alcohol for the duration of the war.

The suffragettes, led by Emmeline Pankhurst, had been most active in the decade or two before the 1st World War demanding that women should have the right to vote, but looking to many more rights in the longer term. Some of their agitation dated back to a great book published in 1792 entitled *A Vindication of the Rights of Women* by Mary Wollstonecraft, 1759-97, who died at the age of 38, but not before she had given birth to Mary Godwin Shelley 11 days earlier, who was later, incidentally, to create in her writings the Frankenstein monster. As soon as the 1st World War broke out the suffragettes more or less ceased their agitation and turned their energies to helping the war effort, including encouraging women to take jobs in banks, factories and offices. Women were particularly welcomed in munition-making, and by 1918 there were three women to every man in the armament factories, although women's pay for similar work was only half the men's rate. Conscription of men meant more opportunities for women to find work to fill the gaps, and they became land girls, tram conductresses and the like, and adopted trousers and short or bobbed hair. They began using make-up, smoking cigarettes, and wearing silk-stockings and skirts which came almost up to the knee; in factories, washrooms were built and medical services were provided in the larger ones, together with some recreational facilities, canteens and nurseries for the young children of employees. Lloyd George noted 'the irony that the making of weapons of destruction should afford the occasion to humanise industry' – one of the 'good' effects of the war.

The *Daily Mail*, among other newspapers, deplored these signs of growing independence of women, and described hems which were more than six inches from the ground as 'extravagantly short', even though skirts at such a length would actually be saving material and could be cheaper to buy – more economical in fact, the very opposite of extravagance. However, by 'extravagant' they probably meant in fashion rather than in finance.

In January, 1916, conscription was introduced for single men aged between

18 and 41, if not already in reserved occupations; in May, married men of these ages were added, but conscientious objectors were provided for, if they could convince a local Tribunal – they began in March, 1916, and were usually chaired by a senior military figure – of the genuineness of their beliefs. The first question put to objectors was usually a variant of 'What would you do if a German attacked your mother, sister or wife?' Alternative work, such as forestry, road building or the ambulance service, was often agreed with such objectors, but about six thousand were imprisoned in the war, including intellectuals such as the philosopher Bertrand Russell. In 1916, in an article in *The Tribunal*, Russell advocated acceptance of a German peace offer, for which he was given 6 months sentence in Brixton gaol. As Davidson wrote in his play *Bruce*: 'great courage goes to make an open coward'. Apropos of Bertrand Russell, T.S. Eliot used to recount knowing a taxi driver who prided himself on recognising famous people. One of his fares was Russell, and he asked the philosopher, 'What's it all about? And do you know,' added the taxi driver, 'he couldn't tell me'.

Wilfred Tregenza, the son of the Mayor of Penzance, also held pacifist views, but the Local Tribunal did not accept his pleas; he was taken to Flanders and could well have been shot, and was perhaps lucky to receive a reprieve. Such pacifist views were anathema to most people during the war, as Sylvia Pankhurst, Emmeline's daughter, found when writing for the *Workers' Dreadnought*; such pacifists were called 'Conchies' or cowards – or 'Cuthberts', if they were thought to have avoided the fighting by getting themselves into a reserved occupation such as a job in the Civil Service. These were names given to them by people who were incensed by the fact that such people were escaping danger when others were prepared to give up their lives for their country. Sylvia Pankhurst noted particularly the attitude of many of the women of London's East End towards the enemy, for many of those she spoke to were demanding revenge, even calling for the elimination of the entire German population. For them it was much easier and simpler to blame the deaths of their sons on the enemy, who was, after all, directly responsible, rather than to entertain complex thoughts of what level of responsibility might lie with generals, governments, or on the other factors which were supposed to have led to war, such as the greed of armament manufacturers, favourite scapegoats in the inter-war years. It did not seem to occur to the women Sylvia interviewed that women on the other side were suffering in the same way when their sons were killed; but, if that were put to them, they would reply that this was the enemy's just deserts for causing the war. Such views can be understood because the women wanted to be loyal to their side and to their country, and to believe in whatever was written in the newspapers and what their 'betters' told them and what their neighbours and friends thought. For this reason they would have been unlikely to have welcomed John F. Kennedy's later observation that 'war will exist until ... the conscientious objector enjoys the same reputation and prestige that the warrior does today'. Thomas Hardy used to visit German prisoners-of-war at Dorchester during the 1st World War to give them books; he wrote that what struck him was that 'men lie helpless here from wounds: in the hospital, a hundred yards off, other men, English, lie helpless from the same wounds, each scene of suffering caused by the other.' The 4th verse of Lawrence Binyon's poem *For the Fallen* has become the key wording in the Service of Remembrance every November:

> They shall grow not old, as we that are left grow old:
> Age shall not weary them, nor the years condemn
> At the going down of the sun and in the morning
> We will remember them.

But, because the poem was written in 1914, when there still seemed the possibility of 'music in the midst of desolation', and death was 'august and royal' – to quote other verses in the poem – only the British fallen are mourned. Paul Fussell in his excellent book *The Great War and Modern Memory* (OUP, 1975) writes that Quiller-Couch's *Oxford Book of English Verse* 'presided over the Great War in a way that has never been sufficiently appreciated'. It can be judged to have been the source of the soldier's song *The Bells of Hell*, and there was an edition printed on Indian paper, which, even if not in every knapsack, seems to have been well known.

* * * * *

It has often been observed that truth is one of the first casualties in modern war, and that much wartime news consists largely of propaganda written to enthuse those on one's own side. At the same time myths, which extol one's own side or condemn the enemy, can often be encouraged for the same reason. One widely believed myth in the First World War concerned the enemy's alleged human atrocities; while looting and vandalism were common practices by soldiers of nearly all armies in all wars, what was alleged of the Germans – often called 'the Hun' to sound worse – were exceptional crimes such as human mutilations and the murdering of children with bayonets, allegedly worse than the 'rapine and slaughter' of Britain's Viking invaders.

People brought up in the 1st World War, such as Elizabeth, the Queen Mother, for instance, 100 years old in the year 2000, were inclined from habit to call the Germans 'the Hun' even late in life, and Attila the Hun has long been a byeword for barbarity, allegedly creating terror and destruction from the Steppes of Russia to the Gates of Rome; but in Hungary he is remembered more for wise and benevolent leadership, who spent a year at the Court of Rome and hated its corruption. He was as cruel to his enemies as most leaders of his time, but there may be found something tragic in the story of his dying in 453A.D. on the night of his wedding to Hilda – from a nosebleed – however much the adverse criticism of him may be deserved.

The crimes of the Germans of the 1st World War listed in the Bryce Report added that some outrages were so barbaric that they were 'believed possible only of the Kurds', a people regarded in the West by the 21st century as more sinned against than sinning. Most – not all – incidents later investigated were found either to have been exaggerated, unfounded or could not be proven; but, in 1914, when Germany invaded Belgium, the spreading of the stories had a purpose, in that they served to rouse the British public to the justness of Britain's making war on Germany, and were instrumental in stimulating army and navy recruitment and in gaining the public's full support for the war. There was also something rather satisfying about going to the aid of a little neighbouring country being so ill-treated by a big bully, it being a view the British have always imagined for themselves, that some of their best history consists of episodes when they have defended the good but weak against the evil but strong. The Government censored the press but allowed the circulation of stories about German mistreatment of Belgian civilians, especially when about 100,000 refugees arrived in the UK from Belgium in 1914, many with firsthand accounts of German atrocities. Most people on becoming refugees, deserve sympathy and help, and one cannot blame them, in their often pitiful condition, for some slight licence in some of their tales. In fleeing their homes from an invading army, there was often quite enough of genuine horror. The refugee influx in 1914 certainly served to rouse an ire in Britain, which led Bertrand Russell to pose the question: 'Why is propaganda so much more successful when it stirs up hatred than when it tries to stir up friendly feelings?' Few people in 1914 would have agreed with Ernest Hemmingway's later remark: 'Never think that war, no matter how necessary, nor how justified, is not a crime; or with John Foster Dulles, who, after yet another world war, commented: 'The world will never have lasting peace so long as men reserve for war the finest human qualities'. 1914 was the era when the concept of 'the just war' was accepted, when military service was regarded as the highest form of service, and when the struggle was seen as 'the war to end war', a phrase invented by H.G. Wells who later regretted it, calling it 'not the least of my crimes'. Even the ten commandments at some period underwent a small but significant amendment from 'Thou shalt not kill' to 'Thou shalt do no murder', thus rather conveniently lifting the restriction on compassing the death of the enemy.

* * * * *

While the stories of German atrocities in Belgium did more than any other single factor to stir up the British people to military ardour, the lack of adequate verification for the horror stories does not establish that they did not occur, only that the gathering of sufficient evidence for many of them proved too difficult after the war. Indeed, it is clear that brutalities by German forces did occur, largely as a consequence of their trying to follow the Schlieffen Plan, which may explain but does not excuse them. This plan was based on the fact that the French armies could mobilise relatively quickly, while those of Russia were slow; therefore, to avoid a war on two fronts at the same time, the plan laid down the means of defeating France first before transferring forces to the east to meet the Russians. It was a question of numbers; the German army was thought to be the best in the world, but Germany felt insecure rather than confident because both French and Russian armies seemed to be improving in quality, and German superiority was thus a diminishing factor and insufficient to outweigh the more numerous Russian and French. The common German / French frontier was well defended by the French, so Schlieffen planned that, if war came, the Germans would attack through relatively undefended Belgium, outflanking the French armies and surrounding Paris in six weeks. All was worked out in meticulous detail, including the times of trains required to transport German men and materials westward. Schlieffen anticipated little resistance from Belgium, which had only a tiny army; but, in fact, the Belgians put up a most spirited defence, so that, instead of the German armies crossing Belgium in 48 hours it took 10 days. This led to much exasperation by the German commanders, who were ordered to push through quickly at all costs, yet were being held up – needlessly as they saw it – by Belgium forces which were bound eventually to be overcome, but which, unknowingly, were jeopardising the success of the whole German war plan. It was this exasperation which seems to have led to some, at least, of the most savage German assaults and slaughter to clear the way and try to keep up with the timetable, and this led also to Belgian civilians suffering and to atrocities. For example, 639 civilians were shot by the Germans at Dinant between August 21 and 23; and armed snipers in civilian dress were a constant problem for the advancing Germans, with mistakes occurring when innocent civilians were shot at when suspected of being snipers – even when the evidence was flimsy – on the grounds that it was better to be safe than sorry. Moreover, Schlieffen had not envisaged that the attack on Belgium would bring Britain into the war – in August, 1914, the Germans were saying that Britain went to war merely 'for a scrap of paper', a reference to the Treaty of London of 1839 guaranteeing Belgium independence. The Germans failed to realise that their determination to pass quickly through Belgium, at the cost of brutal treatment to Belgium civilians, would provoke an outcry in Britain and almost universal public backing for the British Government's decision to stand by its treaty obligations and support the 1907 Triple Entente of Britain with France and Russia. The Germans ignored historical evidence which indicated that British policy had always been to keep the Low Countries in the hands of small countries, not let big ones take them over.

* * * * *

Rumour, although duly deplored and often scotched, was sometimes found of value in the war. One widely-circulated rumour was that Russian troops were being secretly sent by train through Britain to the Western Front, a false story later embellished with unlikely details such as that the soldiers had been seen with snow on their boots. One explanation of the story's origin is that some Lovat Scouts, who wore unusual but distinctive headgear, had been transferred by train from Scotland to Huntingdon, and could have been mistaken for Russians; enquiries would have elicited from them that they came from 'Ross-shire' which, if delivered in a broad Highland accent, could have sounded to an Anglo-Saxon ear like 'Roscha'. It is said that, when the rumour came to the attention of the British authorities, they may have seen advantages in assisting its spread, if it should serve to limit German military pressure on the Eastern Front.

Undoubtedly the most widely believed yet most preposterous myth of the 1st World War was that, when the British Expeditionary Force was retreating from Mons in 1914, some English bowmen – similar to those who had won the Battle of Crecy in 1346 and the Battle of Agincourt in 1415, but in spectral form – appeared on the Flanders battlefield and their intervention forced the German attack to halt. The story first appeared in the *Evening News* on September 29, 1914, written by Arthur Macken, who always claimed that what he had written was pure fiction. But his account was widely believed as factual, although in later versions the bowmen became a cavalry squadron, and then archangels – the angels of Mons. As with the rumour about Russian troops, eye-witnesses were not plentiful, but people who claimed they knew eye-witnesses were innumerable, and many soldiers claimed to have seen what they took to be arrow wounds on the bodies of dead German soldiers, which – at least to them – proved that the event happened. An affidavit was sworn by Private Robert Cleaver of the 1st Cheshire Regiment in August, 1915, in which he declared 'I personally was at Mons and saw the vision of Angels with my own eyes'. One possible explanation of this was provided by Friedrich Herzenwirth, who was believed to be in German Military Intelligence, and who revealed to a New York newspaper in 1930 that German aviators at Mons had projected movie images onto banks of clouds to try and convince Allied troops that God was on the side of Germany. But this story has since been alleged to have been a hoax. To arrive at the truth of what British soldiers saw at Mons – or thought they saw – may never be fully explained; but it is fair to add that it was probably not angels.

111

Horace Smith-Dorrien, younger brother of Algernon Dorrien Smith of Tresco Abbey, and the man who saved the Allies in the German advance in 1914.

However, as it happened, there was one man who, through his decisions when operating independently for a whole week at the height of the battle, actually saved the military situation for the Allies, and – though he would have been the first to denounce the label – was the real angel of Mons. This was General Sir Horace Smith-Dorrien, the commander of the British forces which stemmed the German attack. He was born on May 26, 1858, the eleventh of a family of six boys and nine girls, their father being an army colonel. His brothers – except for one who became vicar of Crediton and another who died young – all had distinguished army or naval careers and some, like Horace, went to Harrow and Sandhurst and served in the South African War, 1899-1902. Horace's eldest brother, Algernon, was for some years in the 10th Hussars, but his army career was cut short when his childless uncle, Augustus Smith, died in 1874, and Algernon inherited the lease of the Isles of Scilly. He went to live on Tresco until he died at the age of 72 in 1918, adding 'Smith' to his name – as his uncle had insisted – and dropping the first 'Smith' in everyday use, confining it to legal documents. The reasoning seems to have been that Augustus had a younger brother called Robert, who had married an heiress and took the name Dorrien, his wife's maiden name, becoming Smith-Dorrien; on his (Robert's) death, his estate was inherited by his nephew, Thomas Smith-Dorrien, who added 'Smith' to his name, becoming Smith-Dorrien Smith and dropping the first 'Smith' in normal usage. Thus the family divided into the Smith-Dorrien's and the Dorrien Smith's, and Augustus favoured the latter. At the same time, Augustus had insisted that to inherit the lease of Scilly, Algernon must reside in Scilly and not be a non-resident proprietor, this latter being a condition from which Scilly had suffered for many years when ruled by the later Godolphins. So, Algernon had to abandon his promising military career, and

112

leave to his younger brother the honour of outshining militarily all the other brothers. This Horace did outstandingly well, and was described as 'potentially Britain's best general of the 1st World War' (*The World War One Source Book*, P.J. Haythornthwaite, 1992, p. 346). Horace first saw active service in the Zulu war of 1879 and took part in the Battle of Ulundi which destroyed King Cetewayo's army. Later, he served in Egypt and India and was in command at Aldershot 1907-12, where he abolished the night pickets, putting all his men on their honour to be of good behaviour in the town – and this worked.

At the start of the 1st World War, Horace was in command of the Second Corps and fought his way against an enemy four times as numerous. He had to face the main German onslaught at Mons whilst cut off from communication with high command. On his own initiative he saved the Allies from disaster – and the war from being lost – by halting the retreat at Le Cateau, earning fulsome praise for his actions; even his opponent, the commander of the German First Army, General von Kluck, recognised this, and later wrote: 'The way the retreat was carried out was remarkable. I tried very hard to outflank them, but I could not do so. If I had succeeded, the war would have been won'. (Quoted in *Memories of Forty-Eight Years' Service*, General Sir Horace Smith-Dorrien, John Murray, 1925, p. 415)

However, upon promotion to command the Second Army (half of The Old Contemptibles), Horace was driven to disagree with the less competent but more senior Sir John French. If Horace had been permitted to retire his men to more defensible positions, he could have greatly reduced the huge number of casualties the British army suffered around Ypres. Eventually, Horace felt bound to protest at the tactics of Sir John French, who reacted peevishly by summarily relieving Horace of his command; if only Horace had been allowed to stay and been given his way, it is fairly clear that much of the dreadful and unnecessary slaughter of 1916-17 on the Western Front would also have been avoided. (See *The Man who Disobeyed: Sir Horace Smith-Dorrien and his enemies*, A.J. Smithers, 1970, and *Smith-Dorrien*, Brigadier-General C. Ballard, 1831.) Haig succeeded French in 1915 and ungenerously, if perhaps accurately, he remarked that 'French was quite unfit for high command in a time of crisis'. But what happened to Horace was not unique, for even the able von Kluck suffered interference from the much less talented but higher-ranking Moltke, who ordered a retreat at the very moment when von Kluck seemed to have victory within his grasp. In 1918, Horace was appointed Governor of Gibraltar until his retirement in 1923; he died in 1930 after a road accident.

Haig's biggest offensive started on July 1st, 1916, at the Battle of the Somme, with 60,000 British casualties on that first day, of whom about 20,000 were killed, horrendous figures, but still fewer than those of the French offensive of April, 1917, which had 90,000 casualties on the first day.

113

Of possibly most interest are not illustrations made principally for propaganda purposes, but those drawn by soldiers on the battlefield as a recording of the scene. The following four drawings are by Colonel John (Jock) Walford, made while he was serving in the Royal Field Artillery on the Western Front, 1914-18.

Above: *shows a worn field-gun being replaced during a quiet spell.*

Below: *shows a snow-covered battlefield, the field-guns harnessed-up awaiting orders. Remarkably, the officer lighting his pipe in the foreground is identifiable, and was later to live in Scilly.*

These four drawings are published for the first time, having been stored in a trunk for over 80 years, part of that time in the loft of a house on St Mary's. Twelve other similar drawings by Walford – one representing the battery during each month of the year – are now in the Imperial War Museum.

114

Above: *shows a field-gun being moved out under fire, an unexploded shell in the foreground suggesting either that enemy fire is uncomfortably close, or that the evacuation is unduly hurried leaving behind a shell or its discarded case.*

In the left foreground is the roll of telephone wire of much importance to the battery. When firing, an officer with field glasses would crawl forward to some higher ground, and observe where his field-guns shells were landing; he would then telephone back to the battery telling them what adjustment was needed to their aim.

Below: *entitled* Moving Warfare *by Walford. Coupling, moving out, then uncoupling the guns in a better position – as the action shifted – was hard work for men and for horses.*

Haig was a hard-working and dedicated man and cared about high casualties, but was convinced they were a necessary price to pay to win; his weaknesses were a failure to listen to others and a dislike of anybody who advanced a different opinion to his own. The British offensive ended in November with only a few miles of muddy ground won and no sign of the breakthrough of the German lines which Haig had envisaged; on the other hand, if the British had not attacked and undertaken the attrition, the French might not have been able to hold the German advance, and the war could have been lost. Edmund Blunden remembered that for a week or more in June, 1916, as the British artillery bombarded the enemy trenches in Flanders trying to clear the German barbed wire in preparation for the Somme offensive on July 1, there was an incessant rattling of the windows of his school near the coast of Kent, referred to also by Thomas Hardy in his poem *Channel Firing*.

The biggest battle of the war, involving the British Army on the Western Front after 1916, occurred in 1917, when, on July 31, Haig began an offensive to try to break the German lines in the 3rd Battle of Ypres. Its object was partly to capture the Messines and Passchendale Ridges – both successfully accomplished with the aid of massive tunnelling and mining – partly to wear down the enemy by means of attrition, partly to give some support to the French – whose living conditions in the trenches were even worse than the British and German, and had suffered mutinies until Petain took over at the end of May. The mutinies began when the French infantry were ordered to advance. They made loud 'baa-ing' noises, in imitation of lambs being led to the slaughter, and their officers could not stop them. The historian R.H. Tawney remembered a not dissimilar incident in the British trenches when there were heavy casualties; one of his men buried his head in the ground and cried, and only got up when Tawney drew his revolver and threatened to shoot him if he didn't. Haig's attack was also partly to capture the nearby German rail junction, and partly, if a breakthrough was made, to capture the German U-boat harbours in Belgium ports; but, through a massive artillery bombardment of 4½ million shells, what it mainly achieved, in a particularly rainy summer, was the wrecking of the field drainage systems, transforming the battlefield into a quagmire of mud. A 4-mile advance was made in 4 months of fighting with 324,000 Allied casualties, some of them drowned, as in Siegfried Sassoon's realistic poem:

> And Trunks, face downward, in the sucking mud
> Wallowed like trodden sand-bags loosely filled:

– a stark contrast to the optimistic romanticism of the poets of 1914. Yet the will to win at all costs still dominated public thinking despite legless, sightless, armless, nerve-shattered, young men becoming an increasingly common sight in Britain, something which was replicated in every war-making country. As Philip Gibbs in his book *Realities of War* has put it: 'There was no large-hearted common-sense in any combatant nation in Europe. Like wolves they had their teeth in each other's throats, and would not let go, though all bloody and exhausted'.

One curious aspect of the war on the Western Front was that the soldiers rarely actually saw the enemy alive. Weeks might be spent peering over a parapet into *No Man's Land*, knowing that the Bosch were only a few hundred yards away – perhaps less – and hearing the machine-gun shots from invisible firers 'out there'. However, sometimes a dead German would be encountered, perhaps still wearing his *picklehaube* (spiked helmet); this headware was like a coal-skuttle over the head, and made the enemy, even in death, appear all alike and menacing.

A breakthrough of sorts was at last achieved at the Battle of Cambrai in 1917, and was even temporarily welcomed in Britain by the ringing of church bells, though these were officially banned. The advance was achieved by the use of the new weapon of tanks, but they were poorly supported by infantry and their success is now held to have been somewhat exaggerated. Then came the withdrawal of Russia from the war in 1917, which allowed the Germans to reinforce their forces on the Western Front and mount the offensive led by Ludendorff beginning on March 20, 1918; Haig issued an alarming 'back to the wall, fight to the end' order, but there were by then just sufficient fresh American troops on the Western Front to back up the tired British and French armies and hold this last major German onslaught.

* * * * *

As the war progressed, streets in British towns had increasing numbers of homes with windows where the blinds were kept permanently drawn, indicating that a member of the family once living there had been killed. Street shrines also appeared, to be replaced or supplemented after the war by about 50,000 war memorials all over Britain, of which the Cenotaph in Whitehall is perhaps the best known. 'Cenotaph' is a word meaning 'empty tomb'; it was designed by Edwin Lutyens and placed in Whitehall in 1920. It has no religious symbol on it. Until the 1930s, it was the custom for people to raise their hats as they passed it, as indeed people used to do when a funeral cortege passed them in the street; but the wearing of hats suitable for doffing went out of fashion and the pace of life increased, so that funeral hearses today try not to hold up busy traffic.

As the war went on, militia units were formed in the UK for home defence, composed of volunteers below 60 years of age, and monster petitions were organised to persuade the Government to intern all remaining aliens; at the same time, German street names – a legacy of Prince Albert's – were altered suitably. Conscientious objectors were denied voting rights until after the

117

war; miners, and even munition workers, were called up 'to fill the gaps in our troops', and the Military Service Act of April, 1918, led to conscription for all men up to the age of 51 who were fit enough and not exempt – although the war was over before any of these were 'sent to the Front'. Most of these older men were given some basic training, but for others it consisted of scarcely more than learning how to salute properly – that strange hand movement which is believed to have derived originally from the motion of lifting the visor when a medieval knight in full armour needed to identify himself to his own side.

The delivery of a War Office telegram, informing the next-of-kin of tragic news, became a sad but all too common an occurrence. Because of air raids, street lamps in London were dimmed by means of blue paint, and curtains were installed in trams and buses to make their lights less visible from the air. Car headlamps were supposed to be turned off and some black material placed over lighted windows. Signs of the effects of war could be seen also in the clothing people wore, many demonstrating that they were 'doing their bit' and 'not squandering precious resources' by wearing coats which looked a bit worn, and top hats went completely out of fashion as unsuitable for wartime. Statues in London were sandbagged to protect them from bombs, valuable stained-glass windows were removed to safe quarters, and many museums and art galleries were closed, their exhibits often stored in basements. For some reason Big Ben was stopped from striking but, by contrast, London theatres and music-halls flourished. George Robey's song, 'If you were the only girl in the world' was 'top of the pops' in 1915, and crowds went to *Chu Chin Chow* at His Majesty's Theatre, while shows at the Alhambra in Leicester Square were always a sell-out. Helen Porter Mitchell – stage name Nellie Melba, a name derived from her home town of Melbourne – was a great favourite. By 1916, there were about 3000 picture-houses (cinemas) throughout the country showing silent films, the most popular being of escapist humour such as Charlie Chaplin's *Shoulder Arms*; but there were also patriotic films featuring British soldiers, sometimes with captions such as 'the noblest manhood of our race responding to the divine impulse'; whatever his motivations were – divine or otherwise – it was incredible what awful conditions and tribulations the ordinary soldier was prepared to put up with in the war – although, it can be added, that he had little choice in the matter. Asquith's son wrote of his 'inspiring memory of the steadfastness and fortitude of the British private soldier, combined with his queer ironic humour, in days of deep privation and extreme adversity'. By the last part of 1916, there were some short silent films shown in UK picture palaces of the early days of the Battle of the Somme; although these were censored, they were a small start in acquainting the British public with what was really going on in Flanders, and almost as significant as Russell's despatches to *The Times* had been in the Crimean War, 1854-56. Jazz bands played the new pop music – ragtime – which became fashionable just before the war, its syncopated rhythms so different from the 'sweet' melodies of Edwardian days; but, by 1918, the jingoistic, sentimental, patriotic songs of 1914 had disappeared from Music Halls because the war had become too grim. In April and May, 1917, there had occurred some strikes which lost 1½ million working days. These were caused mainly by wartime restrictions and exasperation, by food shortages, long hours of work, dissatisfaction with the way the war went on and on, and the obvious profiteering of many well-to-do people, who seemed to share few of the wartime hardships of 'ordinary' working people; even some London police struck in August, but the strikers were soon dealt with and gained nothing.

In the 1st World War, Scilly was not attacked but the inhabitants were advised that, should an enemy warship appear and open fire on Hugh Town, then everyone should make either for the Garrison or to Moor Well, whichever was nearer. Humby's hand-bell, used extensively between the wars by Wilfred Tonkin, St Mary's town crier, was kept in reserve in the 1st World War, and in the 2nd World War kept ready to sound the All Clear if a gas attack should be made on the islands. One of Tonkin's last cries in Hugh Town's streets in 1939 was: 'All able-bodied men aged between 18 and 45 please report to the Town Hall'. During the war, in place of the bell, he used a whistle to announce the holding of a local dance or other forthcoming function. However, no gas attack ever occurred in Scilly in either war. In the 1st World War there were no air raids by Zeppelins or Gotha bombers on Scilly either; these were confined to London and the East Coast of England. On October 1, 1916, the German zeppelin leader, Commander Mathy, in a super-zeppelin, was hit by gunfire when flying on a bombing mission over Woodford Green in north London, and he landed in flames at Potters Bar. The dead crew were buried with full military honours, but the event marked almost the end of raids by the vulnerable zeppelins, and their replacement by Gotha bombers. 1,413 civilians in the UK were killed in the zeppelin air raids before the Gothas finally replaced them.

These latter were mainly directed to London, their first air raid being on November 28, 1916, when a Gotha dropped six bombs. The greatest air raid of the war on the capital happened on June 13, 1917, when Gotha bombers dropped 72 bombs killing 162 people and wounding 432. The Gothas returned on July 7, 1917, flying in V-formation over St Paul's Cathedral, and they accounted for the lives of another 50 people. This led to more anti-German violence in London, but Britain still possessed no large bombers with which to retaliate. General Smuts – who had fought for the Boers as Britain's enemy in the Boer War, 1899-1902 – was put in charge of the city's defences. He ringed London with guns, fighter planes and barrage balloons with streamers trailing from then, and placed observers with large ear-trumpets at coastal sites to help give warning of the enemy's approach. Police

A German zeppelin flying above ships of the High Seas Fleet in the First World War. In 1914, the German navy only had one airship and the army six. But three commercial zeppelins were converted for military use and there were 3 small airships but, in the first month of war, 3 airships were shot down, their bulk proving a good target and their vulnerability obvious. Other airships built later for the navy proved useful for reporting on Allied shipping movements. Larger airships look part in 51 air raids on Britain between January 19, 1915, and August 5, 1918, dropping altogether 5,806 bombs; the greatest of these zeppelins was LZ-70, 225 metres long with a range of 12,000 kilometres. This was long enough for its commander, Strasser, actually to plan (with two other zeppelins) an air raid on New York after the USA came into the war in 1917; but, fortunately for the Americans, LZ-70, with Strasser on board, was shot down before it could take place.

were given 'Take cover' placards and were told to blow their whistles when the bombers were approaching, and maroons were made available at police stations. In September, 1917, air raids on London occurred by day and night causing some panic, and some food kitchens were set up and shelters dug out, and some underground stations became packed with people during the raids. The blackout had become almost complete over the capital by the time the raids ceased altogether in May, 1918. In all there had been 20 bomber raids on London causing 836 deaths and wounding 1,982 people.

Because of the adoption by the Germans for a short time in 1915 of unrestricted U-boat warfare, 500,000 tons of extra shipping was sunk in that year resulting in price rises in shops, long queues and food shortages. Lloyd George, who took over from Asquith as Prime Minister of a coalition Government on December 7, 1916, and formed an inner cabinet of five ministers to direct the war, had created the Ministry of Food earlier in 1916

General Jan Christian Smuts (above), *was Botha's second-in-command in the Boer War, 1899-1902, but in the 1st World War commanded the British forces in East Africa and then became a member of the Imperial War Cabinet, organising the defences of London against German bombing. He was Prime Minister of South Africa, 1919-1924, had an influence on the founding of the league of Nations, and was again Prime Minister, 1939-48. In 1926 he published his philosophical work* Holism and Evolution.

David Lloyd George (below) *went from being almost the most unpopular man in Britain at the start of the 20th century – because of his opposition to the Boer War – to being perhaps its most popular in 1918, hailed as 'the man who won the war'.*

Lloyd George was born in Manchester in 1863, became a solicitor and MP for Caernarvon for 55 years. As Chancellor of the Exchequer from 1908 in the Liberal Government under Asquith, he started Old Age Pensions, curbed the powers of veto of the House of Lords when they rejected his budget, and began National Insurance in the Act of 1911.

As Prime Minister of a coalition government after the war, he achieved the founding of the Irish Free State in 1921. By some he is acknowledged as 'Britain's greatest Prime Minister', by others he is 'the Welsh Wizard whose eloquence could charm a bird off a tree'; but he could not prevent the partition of the 6 counties in the North of Ireland from the 26 counties in the south, a source of much trouble since.

121

Din-din !" One especially delightful moment in the delightful day. Dinner at a dear little table, in dear little chairs, all just the right height for dear little people. Being photographed was interesting, but not so exciting as the actual sight of dinner coming.

A magazine photograph from the 1st World War of children of nursery age awaiting their lunch. The caption accompanying it is representative of the adult patronage of the young, which was normal at the time, when the maxim 'children should be seen but not heard' was considered most sensible. The caption reads:

'Din-din. One especially delightful moment in the delightful day. Dinner at a dear little table, in dear little chairs, all just the right height for dear little pupils. Being photographed was interesting, but not as exciting as the actual sight of dinner coming.'

and had instituted a voluntary food-rationing scheme, but this failed to work satisfactorily. One reason for this was that poor people, who usually had hardly enough to eat anyway, resented being urged by better-off, well-fed speakers, to eat less. Rationing of food therefore started in 1918 with sugar being the first commodity on ration on January 1st, extended soon after to butter, marmalade, jam, tea, bacon and meat, the weekly ration per person including 2½lb of meat and ¾lb of sugar. Rationing was progressively lessened after the armistice, but not entirely ended until 1921.

For sugar to be the first item of food rationed in the UK may appear a little surprising but, as with so many apparent quirks, there is an historical reason. Briefly stated, the making of sugar from cane was known in India nearly 5,000 years ago and spread slowly to Europe, the Arabic-held regions of southern Spain growing the cane by the 8th century. Christopher Columbus took some cane to the New World on his second voyage in 1493 – the start of its cultivation in the West Indies. Refining of sugar in Europe was carried out mainly in Venice and then Antwerp, but the product was used more as a sedative until the 17th century rather than as a sweetener, sugar beet at the time serving as cattle fodder. The first factory to extract the 15% of sugar from beet was established in Breslau in 1799, and Germany became almost the world leader in sugar production from beet by 1914. In Britain, the first factory to extract sugar from beet was not set up until 1912 at Cantley in Norfolk, so the cessation of supplies from Germany in 1914, from whence Britain had formerly obtained large quantities of the beet-originated sugar, explains the crisis and early rationing.

Other food-related regulations and recommendations were also introduced by the Government. Restaurants were urged to serve meatless and potatoless menus on some days, and regulations forbade the selling or use of sugar-icing and crumpets. The Ministry of Food recommended cooking potatoes in their jackets, as it was said that 1/5 of their value lay in their skins. This dietary advice should still be appropriate but, unfortunately, with pesticides much used in farming today, much else – it is suspected – may also now reside in their jackets. In 1915, there were half a million allotments in Britain and over 3 million additional acres of farmland were bought under cultivation, and the Womens Land Army of over a ¼ million contributed much of the increased manual labour required. But food shortages became appreciably worse in 1917 when unrestricted U-boat warfare recommenced. Forty million ration cards were issued in April, 1918, covering meat (15ozs), bacon (5ozs), and margarine and butter (4ozs), to be replaced by books of coupons in July, 1918, with only tea, cheese and bread, of the so-called staple foods, remaining unrationed at the end of the war. The King and Queen were said to be keeping to the rations, and the King had arranged that a plot be dug within Buckingham Palace grounds to grow vegetables for the Royal table; and it became acceptable, indeed welcomed in some polite circles, when an invited guest brought as a gift to his hostess in place of a bunch of flowers, a bag of potatoes.

The 2nd World War with its wider spread of food rationing, and prices of essential foods held low, achieved a greater improvement in the health of the nation than the 1st World War. But, even so, something was achieved; a Medical Officer's report of 1918 revealed that the proportion of children judged to be in a poorly-fed condition was less than half that of 1913. Children were urged to do their bit for the war effort and, as well as being generally better fed, the war prosperity, resulting from the increasing number of jobs available, meant that they were also better clothed. It is estimated that half a million children under the age of fourteen were in full or part-time work illegally during the war, and this meant that they had a better living than ever before. On Scilly, ration books were issued in 1918 to heads of families on presentation of birth certificates and marriage lines, a notary coming over from the mainland to cover the paperwork for those people not churched.

The already large number of restrictions on personal liberty of the early war years were further increased in 1917 when citizens of the UK were prohibited from talking in public about matters pertaining to the armed services (in case enemy spies overheard them); they were also forbidden to trespass on railway tracks, light fires out of doors, set off fireworks, fly kites, purchase field-glass (binoculars), melt down any gold or silver, feed bread to dogs, horses or fowl, trespass on allotments (fines were heavy if caught pinching produce), speak or write anything detrimental concerning the British army or navy (D.H. Lawrence's novel *The Rainbow* was banned during the war because of this), and, if suspected of any infringement, their houses could be entered and searched by the police.

The abolition of bank holidays was understandable, but some regulations appeared to some people as unnecessarily restrictive. For instance, rice was forbidden to be thrown at weddings, stale food could not legally be put out for the birds, and price controls on some items simply meant that they disappeared entirely from the shops or led to long queues for them. Coal was rationed in October, but the ration amount depended on the number of grates (not persons) in a house, so the poor did relatively badly. One of the unexpected consequences of the war was a shortage of dyes, which led to increasing numbers of people wearing dark-coloured clothing.

Some babies born during the war were given strange, topical names, 'Verdun' being quite popular for girls for a time and 'Mons' for boys. But these names were of short duration. In contrast the most popular name given to baby boys in 1947 was John (nearly twice as popular as the next two favourites, which were Michael and Richard). The most popular name for a baby girl that year was Ann or Anne (half as popular again as the next favourites which were Elizabeth, Mary and Jane) – from a letter to *The Times*, January 9, 1948. These names may be compared with the year 1973, when for boys, James beat John, and were followed by Alexander, Edward and William; for girls, Jane and Elizabeth were followed by Louise and Mary. Juvenile crime increased greatly during the 1st World War, possibly connected with the inevitable splitting of families, and the absence (often death) of many fathers, and this despite almost full employment, better wages and an improvement in the standard of living for many children of the poorer half of the nation.

To save daylight, a Summer Time Act was introduced in 1916, extended during the 2nd World War to double summer time. Lloyd George was also concerned to look to the future, and he appointed H.A.L. Fisher to draw up educational reforms which were enacted in 1918; the school leaving age was made 14, fees were abolished at state schools and the Burnham Committee was set up to recommend the levels of teacher's salaries and pensions throughout Britain, and provide for nursery schools.

The part that women were playing in the war effort probably did as much for the campaign to give women the vote as the previous agitation of the suffragettes. In 1916, the House of Commons gave their first approval in principle to the idea of giving votes to women (as part of the post-war 'Better World' promised by politicians), and this was achieved in 1918 by women

'Women – bless'em – taking the place of men on the factory floor, making shells for the heroes fighting at the front'– such were the sort of patronising comments to accompany photographs or illustrations in newspapers and periodicals of women factory workers in the 1st World War. It came as a profound shock when it was discovered that women were, if anything, rather more proficient at this job than the men they had replaced, and at much less pay.

over the age of 30 – except for various categories, such as prisoners – and it produced 6 million women voters. One of the reasons expressed for not giving women the vote on the same terms as men was that, because women at the time outnumbered men in population – the census figures for Cornwall in 1881 were 153,779 males and 175,705 females – it might lead to 'petticoat government'. In November, 1918, there was a further development in that women were allowed for the first time to stand for election to the House of Commons. Britain was not the first European country to enfranchise women, but neither was it the last; one Swiss canton did not give women the right to vote until 1991.

Despite the tremendous part played by women towards the war effort, there were significant conservative forces opposing any attempt to give women the vote. F E. Smith, speaking in the House of Lords in 1928, described what he called 'the slippery slope' which led to women over 30 gaining the right to vote in 1918. He revealed that it was not proposed at that time that women should get the vote at all, until one MP pointed out that 'our brave soldiers' who had fought in the war deserved the vote, to which another added, amid the applause for the army, that 'our brave munition workers' also deserved it. This was also agreed with applause, but after that it became difficult logically to exclude 'brave munition workers' who were also women, particularly as they considerably outnumbered men in the armament factories. These rights for women were extended in 1928 by Ellen Wilkinson's Equal Franchise Bill, which gave the vote to another 1½ million women in their twenties and was sometimes called, rather inaccurately, the Flapper Vote Act. But she had an even harder job to win for women M.P.s the right to take meals in the Strangers Dining-Room, quite as big a task as persuading elderly M.P.s in the 21st century that more social hours might improve Parliamentary debates, and encourage more women with children to stand for Parliament. R. Viner in his book *A History in Fragments* gives another and most convincing reason why women gained the right to vote; it was to prevent the rise of popular radical movements, and was based on the belief that women would be a conservative force and act as a useful counterweight to emerging parties representing the more radical male proletariat.

* * * * *

Train fares increased by about 50% in the war, but the war was financed largely through spending the proceeds of the years of Victorian and Edwardian prosperity, by means of increases on income tax, by a super tax levied on the wealthy, by the sale of War Bonds, the issue of War Savings Certificates paying interest at 5%, and even by a 'tank-bank' campaign, by which a town which contributed enough could have its name painted on a tank. But there were also voluntary subscriptions which raised £600,000, and *Feed the Guns* week resulted in an additional £31 million. By 1918, it was calculated that the war effort was costing about £7 million a day, partly financed also by the sale of investments overseas, special taxes, and loans from the USA.

The end of the war on November 11, 1918, was signalled by Church bells breaking their long silence, and by cheering crowds assembling outside Buckingham Palace – indeed, just as joyfully as when the war was declared in 1914. A popular and cheerful postwar song was:

> The bells are ringing
> For me and my girl.

But the relief was overshadowed somewhat by the so-called Spanish Influenza outbreak from June, 1918, to May, 1919, which resulted in schools, cinemas, and theatres closing in Britain, and some people wearing masks in crowded streets, and even forbearing from shaking hands, which became for a time socially unacceptable in some circles. Of the 42 million population of the UK, about three-quarters suffered from the virulent virus, with about 150,000 dying as a result of it; but, by comparison, nearly 745,000 British soldiers and sailors had died as a result of the war. However, worldwide, and possibly made worse by the lowered health of the populations of the belligerent countries owing to war conditions, the epidemic killed between 20 and 27 million people between May, 1918, and June, 1919, a greater number than all those who had died on all sides fighting in the war, the estimate for which is about 15 million. But these figures do not include the estimated 20 million people who died between 1914 and 1918 world-wide as a result of typhus and related diseases, spread largely by body lice. It is arguable that disease has had more effect on history than war, and certainly contaminated water supplies have had (and still have) horrid effects. The consequences of population decimation by disease are sometimes regarded as incidental in human history, but have frequently been crucial to it. The bubonic plague of 1348-9, known as the Black Death, was spread by fleas from black rats, with up to three million people estimated to have died from the disease in England in that year, that is between one third and one half of the population. This caused an immediate shortage of labour, so that the peasants at last were able to demand higher wages – a most important factor in undermining feudalism in England. The Black Death was only one of many visitations of the plague in the Middle Ages, an ailment which caused great pain, coughing blood and often death within days. London lost about 100,000 people in 1348, but the whole British Isles suffered from outbreaks, Dublin, for instance, lost around 14,000 people in1349. One difficulty with dealing with the plague was the inability of the authorities at the time to determine its cause; people supposed it might have something to do with putrefaction, and consequently hung bunches of lavender and other sweet-smelling items on interior house walls. There was even a suggestion that lascivious dancing might be connected with it and, in so far as such activity facilitated the hopping of fleas from one individual to another, it had a basis of truth, especially as the only effective remedy to the disease at the time seemed to be to contain it by isolation – most famously practised by the inhabitants of the village of Eyam in Derbyshire at the time of the last great plague in 1665.

For another example of the influence of disease on history, measles is said to have helped to break up the Roman Empire and, even more striking, is the story of European invasions of the American continent. In 1504, and in subsequent years, Cortez and a few hundred Spaniards – assisted by superior weapons, horses and policies of duplicity and cruelty – conquered a large population of Aztecs in the New World; but what in the long term secured this defeat of the indigenous Mexicans was not war but disease. Europeans had the advantage that their animals such as cattle were domesticated, serving as beasts of burden and power machines, and not just as a source of food, unlike animals of North and South America, Africa and Australasia, such as buffalo, wildebeest and zebra, which were wild, and where the people were still partly hunter-gatherers. Europeans, through close associations with their domesticated animals, had acquired a degree of resistance to the diseases they carried such as influenza and smallpox; but the populations of other parts of the world succumbed in large numbers upon contact, not only with human European diseases – particularly venereal disease – but with those of European domestic animals introduced to their lands. Europeans have been successful in history and exported their culture world-wide – and for a time imposed their political rule – largely because they harnessed nature rather than just tried to live in harmony with it. Such diverse persons as Adam Smith and Karl Marx both regarded the conquests of the Conquistadores in North and South America as 'the greatest event in human history', a claim understood in the light of subsequent events, even if it can be shown to be overstated.

However, great advances in medical treatment in the 20th Century prevented the wholesale spread of diseases expected from the increase in travel, and the Second World War became the first great conflict in which more people seem to have died from enemy action rather than from disease.

Another important determining factor, whose part is sometimes not fully appreciated in tracing the history of events, is climate, which can change unpredictably and crucially. In 1657 there was a frost over England in May, and snow lay on the ground in southern England for 102 days in that year, with the River Thames freezing over and people walking and playing on it. Yet, less than a decade later in 1665-66, there were two inordinately hot summers, one result being the Great Fire, which burnt part of the City of London in 1666.

A third factor which is hard to comprehend in the 21st century, when democracy is the ideal in social spirit as well as in political government, is the notion of rank and class. Historical dramas in the cinema and on television often still show only the 'baddies' as dismissive of servants, without realising that all 'people of quality', including the 'goodies', treated servants in a way that would now be considered abominable. In the armed forces the insidious place of rank and class can still be seen in the separate messes provided for officers, NCOs and ordinary men – justified in the name of 'good discipline', but absent, for example, in the Chinese army, where good discipline does not suffer. A revealing instance of it in 1914, and in no way untypical, was that of Admiral Berkeley Milne, nicknamed 'Arky-Barky' among junior officers, against whom an ordinary seaman happened one day accidentally to stumble, slightly grazing the Admiral's coat. Milne quickly brushed the point of contact with his crisp white handkerchief, and then ostentatiously threw away the soiled item.

However, in some defence of Milne, disease does not recognise class distinctions; so that, until the growth of democracy and its following consequence of greater equality, there was some justification on health grounds – and nothing to do with snobbery – for his aversion to a brush with one of the lower orders, for dirt, and all that was attendant upon it, was an ordinary seaman's constant companion.

As class divisions seem gradually to be easing in the 21st century, that they still existed so rigidly in the 1st World War can make them seem surprising. For instance, officers in London were not allowed to carry a parcel or ride on a bus; they were to behave, even when wearing 'mufti', as gentlemen. Many little practices reinforced the division between officers and other ranks; for example, when marching in column up the roads to the Front Lines, it was customary for ten-minute breaks to be taken en route; invariably, the officers fell out on the left hand side of the road, and other ranks on the right hand side – to the comfort of both. In this connection, it is worth mentioning an unexpected obstacle to egalitarianism which arose when one of the red brick universities opened after the 2nd World War. It was proposed that the eating quarters should cater equally for all members of the university, staff, students and everybody, without distinction; but the scheme had to be partially abandoned when it was rejected by the ground staff, who wanted to eat uninhibitedly in their shed.

Class distinctions in the 1st World War could lead to amusing incidents. Lady Cynthia Asquith recorded in her diary for April 26, 1917, that Lady Wolverton, in a gesture of economy which was being urged on people, decided to go by bus one morning instead of in her usual mode of travel in her chauffeur-driven car. In the bus she sat next to a woman who kept sniffing loudly; so, in her authoritarian voice, Lady Wolverton asked her pointedly if she hadn't got a handkerchief: 'Yes', the woman replied, 'but I never lends it on a bus'.

* * * * *

The first census in Britain was in 1801 and has been taken every 10 years since, except in wartime. Therefore, figures previous to 1801 are estimates, but it is thought that the population of England and Wales was about 2.2 million in 1520, 4.5 million in 1600, 6.5 million in 1750, and rose to nearly 9 million by 1801. Registration of births and deaths did not start until 1837, but, even so, the cause in the rise of the population figures could be the rise in the birth rate but seems more likely to have been the fall in the death rate or both, especially over the period of the fastest rise in population between 1801 and 1971. Numerous factors are cited as facilitating this rise including vaccination, better sanitation, medicinal developments, immigration (but lessened by emigration), industrial and agricultural developments, etc. The 1st World War is said to have lost a generation, but the crude census figures are not by themselves evidence of this. According to census figures, the UK population in 1911 was 45,268,000; in 1921 it was 47,168,000. However, during both world wars, there was in the UK a noticeable scarcity of eligible young men in civilian life, as was to be expected; but, after the wars, returning servicemen coincided with what was called a 'baby boom', a factor which affected almost every area of the country, including Scilly.

* * * * *

At the start of the First World War, there was a tendency to see submarines as mainly defensive weapons – to ward off invasion and for suchlike purposes. The Wolf Pack did not appear until the Second World War, as Admiral Doenitz says in his *Memoirs* (p. 19) 'the First World War did not furnish a single occasion upon which even two U-boats operated in unison'. This was not quite accurate as, on one occasion at least, 9 U-boats attempted to act together in May, 1918, but found difficulty in communicating with one another. They were strung out west of Scilly in the path of convoys, but only succeeded in sinking 3 merchant ships, losing 2 U-boats in the process. The British Admiralty in 1914 dismissed the importance of the submarine as a weapon of war, Admiral Lord Beresford declaring that 'the submarine can only operate by day and in clear weather'. Even in 1915, if a warship was lost to torpedo attack by a U-boat, it was still considered likely that someone was to blame, indeed negligent, for allowing it to happen. HMS *Formidable* was struck on her starboard side by a torpedo from U-24 on January 1st off Start Point, and soon after on the port side by a torpedo from the same U-boat, causing *Formidable* to sink with 547 men drowned out of a complement of 780. As a consequence, Admiral Bailey was relieved of his post – a necessary scapegoat for what was still not fully realised as a likely hazard of war, especially in what was regarded as 'the submarine-infested English Channel'. In 1914, the controller of the Admiralty had declared confidently that submarines 'would never be any use in war'. However, in the interests of balance, it should be mentioned that, only a few years before the war, similar remarks were being made about aircraft and war. Taking turns, Orville and Wilbur Wright, the American air pioneers, made four sustained flights with a powered machine on December 17, 1903, and the occasion went largely unreported, and many came to regard it as 'an overblown claim'. In October, 1905, their *Flyer III* flew over 24 miles in about 38 minutes, yet the American War Department still could not see any value in the 'plane.

An Admiralty letter of 1907 to the Wright Brothers, who had freely offered them some of their patents, referred to aircraft as follows: 'Their Lordships are of the opinion that they would not be of any practical use to the Naval Service'. But the War Office, together with the French and American Governments, also turned down the Wright's offer on much the same grounds; however, £35,000 was included in the Naval Estimates for 1909-10 for constructing a rigid airship, rather insensitively named *Mayfly*, with Captain M.F. Sueter (a torpedo specialist) appointed to supervise, and he can therefore be called one of the founding fathers of the RNAS, later to be the Fleet Air Arm.

It may be fair to temper criticism of the Admiralty and War Office by mentioning that innumerable new inventions were being offered to them in both world wars, and it was hard sometimes to distinguish between those which had a future and the many which were unworkable or just crackpot. The famous Hollywood film star, Hedy Lamarr, born Hedwig Kiesler in Austria, and her companion, the concert pianist George Anthiel, together devised a way of hiding secret messages in musical chords, which could be transmitted by wireless in such a way that torpedoes could be fired from a distance without the wireless trigger being detected. They filed a patent for the invention in 1941, and it sounds eminently possible today, but then was regarded as unlikely to be helpful. Similarly, another 2nd World War invention, which sounds promising but turned out not to work well, consisted of a searchlight fitted to a twin-engined Douglas Havoc aircraft. The idea was that it should be turned on to illuminate raiding enemy bombers so that Hurricane fighters alongside could more easily shoot the raiders down. However, when tried out it had the opposite effect, for the Hurricane pilots lost their night-sight in the blinding light and, by the time they had recovered, the enemy bombers had made off into the surrounding gloom.

Aircraft, however quickly showed their worth in war. The RNAS early on showed how useful aircraft could be, when a German cruiser, the *Königsberg*, after sinking the Royal Navy cruiser *Pegasus*, then went into hiding, but remained as a potential menace to Allied shipping. The task was to find and destroy this raider and it was in helping to accomplish this that the RNAS first showed its use, the circumstances being as follows.

Captain Sydney Drury-Lowe, of the *Chatham* had been sent with 3 Short seaplanes aboard the liner *Laconia* with orders 'to find the German light cruiser *Königsberg*', but all intelligence reports could tell him was that the German raider had hidden herself in Tanganyika (German East Africa) 'at a place spelt with six letters'. Drury-Lowe was a resourceful chap and went ashore in the German territory in disguise to find more clues; actually, Captain Loof of the *Königsberg* had hidden his ship seven miles up the Refugi River, painting her green, covering her with shrubs and installing her lighter guns behind breastworks in case a land attack should be made on her. In the event it was naval seaplanes which located her – thus proving their worth – and on Christmas Eve one seaplane dropped a note near the *Königsberg* which read:

Konig we wish you the best of good cheer
But blame you for stopping our Christmas beer.

Captain Loof sent a runner with a white towel with the reply:
Thanks. The same to you. If you want to see me I'm always at home.
Looff, *Königsberg*

131

If this exchange sounds bizarre, it is worth remembering that some British and German army units on the Western Front stopped fighting each other and fraternised in No Man's Land at Christmas, 1914, swapping smokes, playing impromptu football, and wearing each other's headgear – all unknown to the General Staffs and officers, of course. When eventually they found out, there were severe reprimands all round for showing such seasonal cheer when they should have been intent on killing each other. The fraternisation was not repeated.

Once *Königsberg*'s location had been found, the Admiralty was at first at a loss how this potential menace to Allied shipping could be dealt with, until two monitors, the *Mersey* and the *Severn* were sent out to Africa, each of 1,260 tons, drawing only 4 feet and 9 inches, and armed with 6-inch guns. They sailed up the River Refugi and, on July 6, opened fire on the *Königsberg* from 4½ miles, but the *Königsberg* scored the first hit, knocking out the *Mersey*'s forward 6-inch gun. This accuracy was thought to be due to a concealed observation post the Germans had built in the trees, so fire was concentrated on it until it was destroyed. In all, 635 shells were fired that day by the two monitors, with the seaplanes reporting six hits or near-misses on the *Königsberg*, but causing disappointingly little damage.

On July 11, after repairs, the two monitors returned to within 100 yards of the German raider, and Lieutenant J.T. Cull and his observer in a seaplane were able to help direct their fire; the seaplane was struck by German ground fire, and forced to land, but not before many hits from the monitors had this time virtually disabled the German cruiser, and had persuaded Captain Loof, himself twice wounded, to order scuttling charges to be set which blew up his ship. Loof and his crew then marched away to join Colonel von Lettow-Vorbeck's small East African army, but the potential danger from this raider was past and the crucial role played by seaplanes was at last recognised by the Admiralty.

* * * * *

More important than aircraft in the 1st World War were the submarines. Their development can be traced back to a British mathematician, carpenter and gunmaker, William Bourne, who drew up plans in 1578 for the first craft which, in theory, would have been capable of travelling underwater. However, he died before it was built, and it was Cornelius Drebbel, 1572-1634, a Dutch physician living in England, who was also tutor to the boy who later reigned as Charles I, who built the first submarine in the 1620s. It was propelled by 12 men, whose oars poked through fabric sleeves, and its wooden frame relied on a greased leather covering to keep the water out. Sailing a short way up the River Thames at a depth of 12 feet – with, it is said, James I as a passenger – the craft proved it could be done; but it was not until

132

the 18th century that skinbags were incorporated in the hull in such a way that they could be filled and emptied of water by twisting a rod on them, thus submerging and raising the vessel – the origin of the ballast tank. But Drebbel was much in advance of his time – some credit him with inventing the telescope, the microscope and the thermometer as well – and few were aware of the potential of the submarine. Napoleon saw the *Nautilus*, built by the American, Robert Fulton, 1765-1815, and, even though it could convey a torpedo, dismissed it as 'an amusing toy'. It took the invention of the internal combustion engine and the electric storage battery in the 1890s to create the modern submarine, the first British one being in 1901, the *Holland I*. She sank near the Eddystone Lighthouse in 1913, while being towed to the breaker's yard. She had only 7 crew, was 60 feet long, and could do 7 knots on the surface and 5 knots when submerged, and could dive to nearly 100 feet and remain there for a few hours. Raised from the deep in the 1970s, she was placed in a museum at Gosport.

A submarine was first used as a weapon of war at the time of the American War of Independence, 1776-83. It was called the *Turtle* but only consisted of a one-man crew who fixed an explosive device to the hull of HMS *Eagle* in New York harbour – and then retired quickly as the explosion damaged the British warship. But nobody seemed to take submarines very seriously, even in 1900 one British admiral described them as 'underhand, underwater and un-English'. The Admiralty saw them as no more than an auxiliary weapon to deploy with the fleet. Some thought of the submarine as 'an invisible and inaudible weapon', but that was only its theoretical potential, and by 1914, it had not yet proved itself. Germany's first submarine, U-1, joined the German navy on December 14, 1906, but only the U-boats ordered after 1910 with diesel engines (U-19 onwards) were considered really effective.

The first U-boat operation, in August, 1914, saw 10 of them leave Wilhelmhaven, but U-9 turned back with engine trouble, U-15 fired a torpedo at the British battleship *Monarch* but missed, and then her engines broke down and she was rammed and sunk by the light cruiser *Birmingham*, and U-13 is believed to have blown up on a mine – a disastrous start. On January 1st, 1915, Germany had lost 5 U-boats and only had another 29 in operational condition, which raises the question of why Germany did not construct more. It is easily answered, for the Germans did not expect the war to last long, and believed it would be won long before 1916, the earliest that large numbers could be built and be operational; moreover, U-boats were still seen mainly as fleet auxiliaries; and, even though the invasion of Belgium had gained Germany the port of Zeebrugge as a U-boat base, the efforts of German war factories were still geared principally to the demands of the army, not to a speculative and minor arm of the navy. But then the British light cruiser *Pathfinder* of 2,940 tons, although steaming at speed, was hit and sunk by one torpedo from U-21 on September 5, with the loss of 259 of her 360 crew;

this incident should have alerted the British Admirals to the danger from the U-boat, but they failed to realise it. The sinking of *Pathfinder* was the first sinking of a warship by a U-boat in the 1st World War, and possibly the first sinking by a submarine of an enemy warship in history. U-21 went on to achieve two more warship sinkings by torpedo, both in 1915 – the *Triumph* near the Dardanelles on May 25 and the *Majestic* off Cape Helles near the entrance to the Dardanelles on May 27, and was also credited with sinking 7 ships not far from Scilly on February 22, 1917, but this may have been carried out by U-3, or possibly by a British submarine as later described.

The slowness of admirals and politicians on both sides to appreciate the importance of new developments in warfare in 1914 was no new phenomenon; Melville, 1st Lord of the Admiralty in 1828, memorably remarked that 'The introduction of steam is calculated to strike a fatal blow at the naval supremacy of the Empire'. But, in defence of such attitudes, it must be pointed out that the great majority of war inventions and new weapons were never developed and would not have been effective if they had been, and that a sceptical view of new ideas has at least the merit of being economical with resources.

Another incident which contained warning signals of the importance of submarines occurred on October 20, 1914, when U-17, commanded by Feldkirchner, sighted the British merchant-ship *Glitra* of 866 tons, which he stopped and his men boarded and sank by means of scuttling charges. International Cruiser Rules were adhered to, the crew being allowed to take to their boats safely and these even being towed towards the English coast; but it was the first sinking of a merchant-ship by a submarine, and, although it now sounds incredible, Feldkirchner even received a mild rebuke from his superiors when he returned to Germany. Cruiser rules were for both sides, not just for the U-boats. They laid down that a challenged merchant-ship of a country at war was not allowed to use false colours by flying the flag of a neutral country, and was not allowed to act in a hostile manner, such as aiming a gun at the U-boat, and must stop and not attempt to ram the U-boat, such as happened when the cargo-ship *Phrygia*, of 3,350 tons and capable of only 9 knots, rammed and sank a challenging U-boat not far from where *Lusitania* was later sunk. The sinking of the *Glitra* was followed by Schneider in U-24 sinking the French steamer *Ganteaume*, this time without issuing a warning and with the loss of 40 French lives. From then on the submarine war was continued within international rules, but not very vigorously, until on February 4, 1915, Germany announced a volte-face in policy, in that from February 18 onwards every ship in British waters was liable to be sunk without warning, a situation which lasted only until the attack on the *Lusitania*.

The sinking of the liner *Lusitania* on May 7, 1915, off the old Head of Kinsale when on passage from New York to Liverpool, is probably the best known of all U-boat sinkings in the Western Approaches in the 1st World War; but this is more because of the tragic loss of human life, the political rows that followed and the propaganda value of the event, than for its more important consequence of cancelling all-out U-boat warfare by Germany in 1915 and delaying its full resumption until 1917. The importance of this is revealed in the figures for April, 1917, when 395 ships were sunk, totalling 881,027 tons, a rate of loss which, if it had continued, Britain would not have been able to sustain.

The *Lusitania* was a 4-funnelled, 195 feet long liner which had made her maiden voyage in 1907, and was then hailed by her owners, Cunard, as the fastest ship in the world. She was regarded in 1907 as the world's most luxurious liner and had flush toilets, but only in the 1st and 2nd class accommodation. In the 3rd class accommodation, the shipbuilders believed the majority of passengers there would never have seen flush toilets before and would not know how to operate them, being more familiar with outside earth closets; so they arranged that the toilets serving the 3rd class passengers flushed continuously, but only while such passengers sat on the seats, thus obviating any need to pull chains – a sidelight on the class divisions endemic in Edwardian society.

Her speed of 25 knots had enabled her to win the Blue Riband of the Atlantic in 1907 from Germany, until losing it to her slightly faster sister-ship *Mauretania* in 1909, a record which *Mauretania* then retained until 1929, a longer time than any other liner had held it previously.

Because of *Lusitania*'s fast speed, which was twice that of any submarine, Captain Turner believed she was safe from attack, especially as she had not experienced any trouble on any of her 201 previous transatlantic voyages; but, in 1915, Germany had decided to intensify its U-boat warfare, as by May 1, 1915, only 51 of about 15,000 ships sailing in British waters had been sunk since August 4, 1914, for the loss of 8 U-boats – not a very effective blockade. In line with this new policy, warnings were given on February 4, 1915, that waters around Britain would be declared a war zone after February 18, and clear notice was placed in the *New York Times* that travelling on the *Lusitania* was dangerous, and advice given not to sail in her – a warning seen, but almost entirely ignored, by *Lusitania*'s intending passengers. Exemptions were supposedly given to ships of neutrals, hospital ships and Belgian Relief ships, but such exemptions, by demanding investigation of every ship's identity, made U-boats vulnerable, and so were not a guarantee. Meanwhile, Germany had been receiving reports that the Heligoland Bight was about to be attacked by British forces – a plan which the British had contemplated but had long since abandoned – and in response Germany sent out U-30, U-27, and U-20 (Schweiger) to search and destroy the transport vessels carrying the troops for the expedition. Some of these were believed about to embark at Liverpool on ships which were actually scheduled to sail later for the

Dardenelles not the Bight.

Of the top 30 most successful U-boat commanders was 30 year-old Walther Schwieger, ranked 7th in ships sunk. He left Emden in U-20 on April 20, 1915, with a crew of 42 in a submarine equipped with 6 torpedo tubes. By May 7th, Schwieger, having already sunk three merchant ships during the voyage, was off the south of Ireland when he spotted through his periscope off the Head of Kinsale on a fine day in good visibility, a particularly large vessel steaming towards him on the flat calm sea and unescorted; he took the vessel to be an armed merchant-cruiser – it was listed as such in Jane's Fighting Ships – but it was not following a zigzag course, as recommended by the Admiralty to their ships in submarine-infested waters, and only later did he learn that the vessel was the *Lusitania*. Moreover, it was only going at ¾ speed as commanded by the Company's directions to save fuel costs. He submerged U-20 to about 44 feet and, when the 785 feet long *Lusitania* had come within close range, fired one torpedo at 2.12 p.m. which hit the starboard side. The passengers on board had just finished lunch when it struck; a second explosion a minute afterwards was then heard, which was said at the time to have been a boiler explosion caused by the inrush of sea water, the doors of the boiler-room having been left open, but was more likely the 193 containers holding 46 tons of aluminium bronze powder exploding, an item which had been deleted from the manifest. The liner quickly developed a 15 degree list to starboard. There were also over four million Remington rifle cartridges which were 'live', but tests have shown that these cartridges would not detonate en masse even in a fire. The hand-written 28-page Manifest for the *Lusitania* lists about 200 different goods carried in her holds, some of which could have played a part in the explosion, but Schwieger in his log noted an extraordinary explosion under the liner's bridge, which mystified even him, and which was not the very small-scale affairs that most of the 200 items might have occasioned. By the 1950s, the exploding ammunition theory to account for the second explosion seemed less likely because the 52 tons of 3.3 inch shrapnel shells on board the *Lusitania* had been shown to be unfilled. With regard to the theory concerning *Lusitania*'s boilers, the ship consumed up to a thousand tons of coal daily on a voyage and had to be able to carry enough coal both for the outward and return voyages, and had nearly 200 firemen quartered in the bow area to stoke the 25 boilers. It was suggested that the inrush of seawater could have produced an explosion, but this now seems increasingly a less likely explanation. *Lusitania* had carried munitions on previous voyages, usually ones supplied by the Bethlehem Steel Corporation in the USA. These were desperately required by Britain because in 1915 the UK's shell production was only 22,000 units a day, compared with France's 100,000 and Germany's 250,000. The shortfall was owing to trade union intransigent practices, a scarcity of skilled labour and strikes, but most of all to alcoholism. Lloyd

George, when he was Chancellor of the Exchequer, even remarked that Britain had three main enemies, namely 'Germany, Austria and drink'; and a law was promulgated in October, 1914, which tried to curb the taking of alcohol, so serious was its adverse effect on war production. Whatever its cause, the second explosion was the reason the ship sank so quickly.

Lifeboats were released but Schweiger, in his report, mentions the considerable confusion visible on board the *Lusitania*, with 'lifeboat tackles released so unequally that every now and then a boat full of people would hit the water stern or bow first and sink at once'. Schweiger also wrote in his log for May 7: 'It is inexplicable that the *Lusitania* was not routed via the North Channel'. Only 6 of the 48 lifeboats carried eventually reached Queenstown safely, one reason being that *Lusitania* went down in only 18 minutes, which did not give time to launch all the lifeboats safely and resulted in high casualties; of 1,959 passengers and crew, 1,198 died, of whom 291 were women, 94 (out of 134) were children, and 128 were citizens of the USA. The ship sank by the head, still making some slight forward motion, and settled on the ocean floor, 315 feet down on her starboard side concealing the torpedo hole.

There was an outcry of horror from the USA, Theodore Rooscveldt describing it as an 'atrocity' and President Wilson declaring that Americans had the right to travel the seas without fear; so, on June 1st, the Kaiser ordered that neutral vessels must not be attacked, and declared an immediate cessation of the unrestricted U-boat campaign, lest the USA should declare war. Thus, until 1917, except for one short period, there was a return to international law, under which U-boats must give warning before sinking a merchant-ship by torpedo or gunfire, and must give time for all on board to take to their lifeboats before commencing the sinking. The British press made much of the *Lusitania* sinking as a demonstration of the iniquity of Germany, and it served as useful propaganda to inflame public opinion at home and abroad; moreover, there were pathetic photographs in the press of bodies washed ashore on the coast of Ireland, with mass graves being arranged for those corpses which could no longer be identified because of the length of time they had been in the sea. People who took up a body from the sea were paid £1 for their service or £2 if it were the body of an American, but nearly ¾ of the bodies were never recovered.

A famous cartoon in a British magazine showed callous members of the German U-boat crew on their deck watching unmoved as passengers from the *Lusitania* struggled in the water, one of them astride an upturned lifeboat defiantly – and heroically, of course – shaking his fist at the brutal Germans. It was a successful propaganda picture, although, in actual fact, U-20 never surfaced at all after submerging on the approach of the 4-funnel ship.

Many people, including Churchill, criticised Turner for the tragedy and he was accused of disobedience for not zigzagging, a manoeuvre only of naval ships at that time. The Admiralty wreck commissioner was Lord Mersey, who chaired both the *Titanic* and *Lusitania* enquiries, both of which were whitewashes. Turner, who had survived nearly 3 hours in the water before he was rescued, was largely exonerated, and he was actually to survive another attack by a U-boat when captaining the Cunard liner *Ivernia*, which was torpedoed and sunk off Greece on January 1st, 1917 – unlike Schwieger who died in his U-boat in 1917, but not before he had sunk two other unarmed liners in the war, the *Hesperian* and the *Lymric*. The Admiralty claimed that two torpedoes struck the *Lusitania*, but this was an error – possibly a cover-up – to explain the second explosion. Orders said to have been issued by the Admiralty to take the *Lusitania* into Queenstown were denied by the Admiralty and 'lost' in 1922. As to whether the attack was legitimate, although Schwieger did not know all of it, there were grounds for arguing that it was. For example, *Lusitania* was listed as an armed merchant-cruiser, and had 12 gun-mountings on her decks, if not the guns; although Cunard disapproved, Captain Turner had flown the neutral USA flag in British waters, which was a contravention of international law; Turner said that no passenger had received a warning telegram; and the *Lusitania*'s manifest revealed that the liner was carrying 4,200 cases of cartridges, and also cases of unloaded shrapnel shells and fuses for artillery shells, all military equipment along with her other cargo of foodstuffs and so forth. An American journalist wrote: 'Britannia not only ruled the waves but also waived the rules'. One aspect of the unrestricted submarine warfare was secretly welcomed by the British Admiralty, in that it might induce neutral countries, particularly the USA, to enter the war on Britain's side; this was eventually to occur in 1917, and it was the American involvement on the Western Front – fresh troops helping the tired British and French – which led to the defeat of Germany in 1918. In May, 1915, Room 40 (the Intelligence Department) at the Admiralty knew that U-20 was at sea and operating in the area, but no warning of this was issued to neutral vessels or to Captain Turner. One signal from the Admiralty to Captain Turner refused his request to sail to his destination of Liverpool via the north of Ireland and this obliged him to sail to the south. It may have been sent because of the numerous mines laid off Donegal by the German ex-liner and armed merchant-cruiser *Berlin*. In 1914, on October 27, the freighter *Manchester Commerce* had been sunk by one of them, followed, on the following day, by the destruction of the dreadnought *Audacious*. Five other signals were sent to Captain Turner, the last ones just before the *Lusitania* was torpedoed; but the content of these communications are missing from their files at the Admiralty, being replaced by blank sheets. The tribunal appointed to investigate the circumstances of the *Lusitania*'s sinking asked Captain Turner what the signals he received had contained; he replied that he was not allowed to answer that question. It is not thought that the mislaid messages are connected with the well-known poor relations which existed between the Operations Division of the Admiralty and the civilians of Room 40, although there were certainly occasions when information from the latter was not passed by the former in full to the ships at sea; and there is no evidence that Churchill was responsible for allowing *Lusitania* to steam to her doom so as to inflame American opinion against Germany. And although a particularly sad occurrence, it had useful propaganda value, as the 1st Lord of the Admiralty, Winston Churchill, realised and exploited to his country's benefit. Indeed, if Churchill and the Admiralty did play any part in luring the Lusitania into U-boat infested waters in order that her sinking might result in the loss of lives of prominent citizens of the USA, it was remarkably successful. There was such an outcry in the USA against the sinking by the U-boat that the Kaiser gave immediate instructions to halt unrestricted submarine warfare, and it was not fully resumed until 1917. Moreover, Germany took responsibility for the loss of American lives, and was still paying compensation to the families in 1925.

When unrestricted U-boat warfare was resumed in 1917, the situation in April of that year was so dangerous that defeat of Britain looked a distinct possibility, and was only avoided by Lloyd George's insistence on the adoption of the convoy system. Thus there is the possibility that had the *Lusitania* not been sunk, and unrestricted submarine warfare had continued in 1915, then Britain might have had to consider making peace earlier. It could possibly be claimed, therefore, that the sinking of the *Lusitania* enabled Britain to continue the war and helped in the process of bringing in the USA. Just as Churchill had rejected the idea of Britain seeking peace with Germany in the 2nd World War after the crushing defeat in 1940 at Dunkirk – when nearly half the cabinet were urging him to do so – so, in the 1st World War, it is just possible – horrendous though what happened to the *Lusitania* was – that its sinking also saved Britain from seeking terms with Germany – Churchill thus in the 2nd, and just possibly the 1st, playing a key role at a crucial moment in enabling Britain to survive in both conflicts. An informed discussion of the issues concerning the *Lusitania*'s sinking is contained in Patrick O'Sullivan's interesting work *The Lusitania: Unravelling the Mysteries*, which also mentions the findings of John Light, the first man to dive on the wreck of the liner, who died in 1922.

It is tempting to compare the sinking in 1915 of the *Lusitania*, which went down in 18 minutes, with that of the *Titanic* in 1912, which took nearly 3 hours to founder. They both experienced trouble with launching the lifeboats, partly owing, it has been said, to inadequate crew training, and partly owing to both vessels developing lists; moreover, with *Titanic*, many of the boats rowed away only half full – they could take about 65 passengers in each – and decided not to return to try to save others, boats 6, 7 and 8 having fewer than 29 people in each. The torpedo was not observed on the *Lusitania* in time to take evasive action before it struck, but on the *Titanic* the iceberg was seen beforehand. That it was not seen sooner was because on the night of the collision the sea was flat calm, and some wave motion against an iceberg is required for its outline at water level to be clearly observed at any useful distance. Moreover, the iceberg had turned over – as many of them do – so it would not appear a conspicuous snowy white but rather an indeterminate glassy hue. Also, on the night in question, the lookouts, because of rota changes, did not have the use of field-glasses (binoculars), as they were not aware where they had been stowed. However, the collision might still have been avoided if the officer on duty on the bridge had not given two orders which sound sensible but actually, in combination, may have led to the collision.

The *Titanic*'s captain, E.J. Smith, aged 62, of 43 years experience, and most popular with passengers – including the 12 millionaires on board – was on his last voyage before retirement, and perhaps, considering the icy conditions, he was taking an unjustifiable risk going so fast (21 knots) to make his last voyage a memorable one. Certainly, by arriving on time, he would please the Managing Director of White Star, Bruce Ismay, who was on board and was to survive the accident and face much personal criticism afterwards, and inevitable censure for the Company's 'insufficient attention to safety'. This last criticism has a little of 'being wise after the event' about it, because if everything is within legal requirements – as the *Titanic* appears to have been – how do you know how much additional attention it is reasonable to give to safety? Smith also certainly knew of the near presence of icebergs; the evening grew rapidly and noticeably colder, a recognised phenomenon indicating that icebergs were in the vicinity, for they chill the water which, in turn, chills the air above – and radio reports and warnings, including one from the *Baltic*, had confirmed their presence. One warning from the *Mesaba* reported ice in *Titanic*'s path, but the message failed to be delivered to the bridge because, it was alleged, the two wireless operators were too busy with messages being sent to and from 1st class passengers. Smith was well experienced, but his career was not without mishaps, and only a few weeks before, as captain of the *Olympic*, he had been involved in a collision.

At 22.00 the watch changed and First Officer Murdock, formerly of the *Olympic*, and one of those who did not survive the *Titanic*'s sinking, took over on the bridge, with seamen Flint and Lee in the crow's nest. When these two telephoned 'iceberg right ahead', Murdock ordered the helmsman, Robert Hichens from Newlyn, 'hard-a-starboard'. At that period this meant the ship would turn to port, for it was assumed, in seaman's parlance, that the steering-wheel was still a tiller; but he also ordered 'full speed astern', which slowed disastrously the effect of the first order. In fact, if the *Titanic* had not tried to go astern, she might conceivably have passed safely by the iceberg. Unfortunately, in the belief that *Titanic* had cleared the edge of the iceberg,

Murdock soon after ordered 'hard-a-port', hoping that *Titanic*'s stern would swing away from the iceberg; but, in fact, it was too late and the starboard bow struck. Yet the blow was felt as little more than a shudder, rather like a vessel making a somewhat hard contact with a jetty when berthing. Some pieces from the iceberg landed on the promenade deck, and some passengers used them to snowball each other. Perversely, *Titanic* would probably have survived a head-on collision, for that would only have flooded perhaps one or two of her holds. Unfortunately, it was damage along the starboard side below the waterline which was crucial, although more a series of holes than a gigantic gash as thought at the time. *Titanic*'s plates were riveted – plates were overlapped and triple riveted, for there was no welding at that time – and many of the rivet heads were sliced off in the impact. Murdock closed all watertight doors and, since the ship was designed to withstand as many as the first four holds flooding without sinking, he was, together with Smith who had been hastily summoned from his cabin, not unduly alarmed. But the ship's designer, Thomas Andrews, then told Smith that he had inspected the holds and No's 1 and 2 were full, No 3 was filling and, as the bulkheads only extended to D or E decks, when full they would lop over into No 4, which would itself fill and lop over into No 5, and so on. He estimated that the ship would stay afloat for only 1½ hours. Smith, anxious to avoid panic, failed to tell passengers or most of the crew that the ship was sinking, but he did send distress messages out on *Titanic*'s powerful transmitter which were picked up by at least six ships. Yet only one, the *Carpathia*, 58 miles distant, answered the call – but only because her wireless operator happened by chance to stay at his post longer than he needed – and she altered course to help *Titanic* and eventually picked up about 675 people from 13 lifeboats.

One ship, the *Californian* was about 5 miles away almost in sight of the *Titanic* and saw her 8 distress rockets, but took them at first to be shooting stars and then thought they were evidence only of partying on the *Titanic*. Lifeboats on the *Titanic* were lowered, but Murdock on the starboard side with lifeboat No 7 had great difficulty in persuading passengers to get into it as they felt safer staying on board the *Titanic*. 2nd Officer Lightoller, one of only 4 officers who survived, had the same difficulty with his passenger allocation and managed to fill his lifeboat with only 24 passengers and 2 crew, although it could have taken 65. To many passengers, staying in the luxury on the 'unsinkable' *Titanic* seemed infinitely preferable to tossing about in the dark in a cold and comfortless open boat. The matter is complicated because it is not generally realised that despite being on her well-hyped maiden voyage, *Titanic* was only about two-thirds full. There were 2,235 people on board, whereas there was accommodation for about 3,500. Moreover, even if all the lifeboats had been full, this would have saved only about another 200 people, a small proportion of the 1,522 who lost their lives. All told, *Titanic* carried 16 lifeboats and 4 collapsibles, which, even allowing for a maximum of 65 in each, was only accommodation for 1,300 – quite inadequate for a total capacity of 3,500; but this amount satisfied Board of Trade regulations at the time, because there were also 3,560 lifebelts and 48 lifebuoys, Another contentious but rather minor and irrelevant area concerns the last hours of the *Titanic*'s music. There were two bands on the liner – one of 5 pieces, the other of 3 – and one of them is said to have played on gallantly, the musicians not fully realising that the ship was sinking – even though she was listing – and content to keep people's morale up; but that they played the hymn 'Nearer My God to thee' or 'Autumn' as their final piece is now thought unlikely. The bands usually played waltzes, ragtime and tunes from musicals, and Bride, one of the two wireless-operators, said it was a ragtime tune he last heard. (*Abide With Me*, composed by the former curate at Marazion, was the hymn at the mass funeral at Queenstown Cemetery for those who had drowned in the *Lusitania*). Bride also reported that a stoker attempted to wrench the lifebelt from off the back of his brave fellow wireless-operator, Jack Phillips, who was still transmitting distress signals; and Bride had to knock the stoker unconscious to the floor to stop him.

William Thomas Stead had been editor of the *Pall Mall Gazette* and was, in 1912, the editor of the *Review of Reviews*. He had espoused many good causes in his 64 years, from outright opposition to the Boer War, 1899-1902, to the desirability of establishing public libraries. One of his most successful campaigns was his exposure of child prostitution, particularly in London's fashionable and hypocritical West End; he bought a 13-year-old girl there, Eliza Armstrong, for £5, so raising a moral storm, the result of which was the raising of the age of sexual consent to its present level of 16. Stead was travelling on the *Titanic*, on his way to address an audience at Carnegie Hall in New York at the invitation of Howard Taft, and did little to save himself from drowning. Indeed, it was said that he had been seen still working on the speech as the ship sank; it was on the subject *Combating Militarism*.

About 700 of the 900 crew did not survive. Among those who died was Joseph Nicholls from St Ives who helped his mother and 9-year-old stepbrother John into lifeboat No 3, but did not follow; Sam Rule from Hayle, a steward, who helped 65 passengers into lifeboat No 15; and Harry Cottrell, Percy Bailey and George Hocking, all from Penzance. There were altogether 64 people from Cornwall aboard the *Titanic*, either as passengers or crew, and only one Cornish passenger survived. This was William Canter who subsequently made a near-fortune in the USA and was in collapsible lifeboat No 3 with Bruce Ismay, who was later criticised for boarding it when most, but not all, the women and children had got away. The body of the St Ives young man, William Carbines, was later taken up from the sea by the *Mackay Bennett* – a ship chartered by White Star to recover floating bodies – and it was brought back to St Ives to be buried in Barnoon Cemetery, where it was attended by over 500 mourners. His name is carved at the base of the family's headstone overlooking Porthmeor Beach.

The quartermaster on the *Titanic* was Archie Jewell, a Cornishman who did duty in the crow's nest, and was coxswain of one of the lifeboats. He was also on the *Lusitania* when that liner was torpedoed in 1915, and later was on the hospital ship *Donegal* bringing home wounded soldiers from the Western Front across the English Channel in 1918. The *Donegal* hit a mine and sank with proportionately greater loss of life than either the *Titanic* or *Lusitania* – and this time the death toll included Archie Jewell. A naval architect, William Garzke, wrote in 1998 that no lives should have been lost on the *Titanic*, if the cracks in the starboard hull had been plugged with clothing, as the holes were mostly less than an inch long and, in total, the openings represented less than 12½ square feet. Plugs, he alleged, would have kept the ship afloat until *Carpathia* arrived; but it seems unlikely that a crew could have been assembled to do the plugging once holds Nos 1 and 2 had flooded. A metallurgist from Maryland, Timothy Foecke, has blamed the tragedy on brittle rivets, which, he says, popped apart when the iceberg was hit, because they contained over 8% slag when the proportion should be less than 3%; however, techniques to analyse metal quality in this way had not been developed in 1912.

The helmsman, Robert Hichens from Newlyn, had been allocated to take charge of lifeboat No 6, and he got it away with 32 people on board. He was later criticised at the enquiry for having 'a surly disposition' and little maritime knowledge, and it was Mollie Brown, a wealthy passenger, who organised the women in the lifeboat to row, but could not persuade Hichens to allow the lifeboat to return to pick up survivors struggling in the water, presumably because, despite the calm sea, he thought the boat might be overturned in the press of desperate people in the sea trying to climb aboard. Hichens was subsequently helmsman on other liners but, to avoid needless anxiety, passengers were never informed that the man steering the ship was the seaman who had been at the helm of the *Titanic* when she hit an iceberg. Later in his career, Hichens received a five-year jail sentence at Exeter for threatening another man with a gun in an argument over a boat; but the length of the sentence was said to have been rather less than expected because the judge was believed – somewhat strangely and irrelevantly – to have taken Hichens's *Titanic* experience into account.

One of the 711 survivors from the *Titanic* was Maud Sucock, aged 22 and from St Ives, who was on one of the last lifeboats to leave *Titanic*. She was thrown into the lifeboat wearing only her night-dress and boots, and endured 6 hours like this until picked up by the *Carpathia*. She was emigrating to the USA, where she eventually married Arling Roberts and became a telephonist in Michigan, dying in 1984 aged 94. Her report on the *Titanic* sinking made agonising reading because, from the lifeboat and across the calm sea, she described listening to the screams of the men remaining on the liner as they rushed in panic from the plunging bow towards the rising stern, just as the *Titanic* began to founder, followed by an awful silence as they were all swept away into the icy sea.

Titanic was an unlucky ship, but an example of a particularly lucky liner was *Aquitania*, the world's last 4-funnelled liner, and perhaps the most successful of all Cunarders. She was designed to operate with the smaller *Lusitania* and *Mauretania* as a refined version of the earlier *Olympic / Titanic* liners, although bigger and taller, and made her maiden transatlantic voyage on May 30, 1914. She continued mostly to ply these waters – often passing within sight of Scilly – for 36 years until scrapped in 1950. She served constantly in two World Wars and escaped all serious damage, the number of her transatlantic crossings, in peace and war, scarcely rivalled, and estimated to have taken her about 3 million miles.

It was not only liners and battleships – such as the *Warspite* – which were considered unlucky or lucky, sailors, also, could be so labelled. Statistically, there are likely to have been a number of seamen in the World Wars who served on several ships which were sunk by enemy action. But, when this happened, there were some crews who became convinced that such a seaman was an unlucky person, and they would sometimes refuse to sail with him. One such instance was the fireman, John Priest, who was serving on *Titanic*'s sister-ship *Olympic* when that liner collided with the Royal Navy warship *Hawke*; then he survived the loss of the *Titanic* and the loss of *Titanic*'s other sister-ship *Britannic*, sunk in the Aegean in 1916. He also was on the *Alcantara* and on the *Donegal*, both of which were sunk during the 1st World War; after which his retirement was involuntary but long – he died in bed from pneumonia in 1935.

Similarly, with so many novels on the subject of war published, it is not altogether surprising that some of them may have seemed to predict the future. Morgan Robertson's novel of 1898 entitled *The Wreck of the Titan* is a case in point; another is that of William T. Stead's, who sailed on the *Titanic* and had previously written a story about a liner which had sunk after hitting an iceberg; and he had also another story about passengers on a stricken liner drowning because there were not enough lifeboats. Perhaps stranger than these items of fiction was that 55 people cancelled their bookings for *Titanic*'s maiden voyage – an unusually large number – which raised the question of premonition, although those investigated all seemed to have mundane reasons for their cancellations.

One obvious difference between the sinkings of the *Titanic* and *Lusitania* was that the former was in peacetime and the latter in wartime. The significant difference here is that much more newspaper coverage – and therefore of public knowledge – was given to the former. Lady Cynthia Asquith acknowledged this in her diary entry for May 6, 1915, when she wrote: 'how one's standards have altered – in fact, how out of drawing

Laid probably by a U-boat, the photograph is of a German mine which drifted ashore on Bryher at Stinking Porth during the 1st World War on December 12, 1917. It did not explode and was quickly diffused by an electrician and then taken to the Valhalla as an exhibit; but someone must have had a change of mind, for it was later thrown away on Tresco's refuse dump.

On February 18, 1918, there was a huge explosion on the Crim Rocks, west of Scilly. As there were no ships around, it was thought to have been a drifting mine detonating upon colliding with the granite rocks. Another mine came ashore on St Mary's on March 6, 1918, but failed to explode, and this time a service disposal team made it safe. Because all three mines came ashore within weeks of each other, the surmise is that they were laid by the same U-boat.

everything is. Very nearly as big a disaster as the *Titanic*, which loomed so large in one's life for months, and this is merely an incident, so full has one supped of horrors'.

* * * * *

The invention of the torpedo had led to the development of the submarine, but also to that of the torpedo-boat from which the weapon could also be launched. This, in turn, led to the development of the torpedo-boat destroyer – the first one in the Royal Navy being the *Havoc* in 1884 – larger, faster and with bigger guns than the torpedo-boat, and able to protect the line of capital ships from a torpedo-boat attack. The name was shortened to 'destroyer', and the new class of warship grew bigger, faster and increasingly versatile as development continued and the destroyer was given more tasks. *Havoc* could do 26 knots, but life on board was dreadful because, to achieve that speed, the vessel was unduly narrow, and, even at slow speeds, was inclined to pitch, roll and yaw abominably. Of course, the development of the submarine meant that the torpedo could be fired from a vessel hidden under the water, and the destroyer was therefore given the means to counter this menace, including

Most people have never seen a torpedo and perhaps do not realise quite how large they can be; but, having seen one, it is easier to appreciate why U-boats preferred to surface and sink merchant-ships with gunfire at the start of the 1st World War, rather than waste one of the few torpedoes they could carry.

The name 'torpedo' originated from the torpedo fish, an electric ray which could deliver a stunning shock to its prey, and this name was first used by the American David Bushwill in the 1770s. The particular quality of the torpedo is that it is an underwater explosive weapon which is self- propelled; if static, it is termed a 'mine'. In 1876 the torpedo, as then developed, had a diameter of 14 inches, a speed of 18 knots and 26lbs of dynamite in it. The more modern Mark 8 torpedo, running on diesel fuel and compressed air, was used by the Royal Navy in the Falklands War in 1982 to sink the former British heavy cruiser, General Belgrano, and one of these torpedoes is photographed above, with the National Trust's engine-house of the former tin mine at Poole near Camborne seen in the right background. Could the torpedo fired in 1982 be the last ever to be fired in anger by the Royal Navy?

depth-charges and listening devices. If the destroyer captain spotted a torpedo coming from a submerged submarine, one tactic was to run parallel back along the torpedo's track, and depth-charge the track's end. In 1914, Britain had 78 destroyers and Germany 61, and Scheer at the Battle of Jutland used his destroyers to launch a torpedo attack at 7,500 yards on the battle-line of the Grand Fleet to cover his ships when his own battle-line reversed direction – an attack which served successfully to deter Jellicoe from following Scheer. The German battlefleet thus found itself being led home by its last and oldest battleship, the *Pommern*, which was sunk by a torpedo from a British destroyer the following night. In this way the destroyer came to be regarded by all navies as an essential constituent, and the United States had well over two hundred by the end of the 1st World War – all with 4 funnels – and most were mothballed and used again in the 2nd World War.

Nevertheless, destroyers, like submarines, were still seen by 1914 as subsidiary weapons, not prime ones, because admirals on both sides assumed that, soon after the war had started, there would be a great naval battle between the capital ships – a modern equivalent of the 1805 Battle of

David Beatty, the quintessential British admiral who succeeded the cautious Jellicoe as First Sea Lord. Three of his battlecruisers blew up at Jutland, leading him to make his oft-quoted, much in character remark: 'There's something wrong with our bloody ships today'. Photographs reveal that he never learnt to wear his cap with full dignity, but it may have been deliberate in order to appear rakish or jaunty.

Trafalgar – and that this would probably decide the outcome of the war. In fact, only one such big battle took place – at Jutland in 1916 – and, despite the participation of 240 warships, the battle decided little except the preservation of the status quo, with the Grand Fleet from Scapa Flow still, at the close of the engagement, effectively continuing to blockade the High Seas fleet for the duration.

The problem for the Germans was that, in the pre-war naval building race, the Grand Fleet had kept its numbers ahead of the High Seas Fleet, and so Britain was able to maintain a four-year blockade of Germany which, by 1918, was playing a significant part in securing the German collapse. If Scheer had been able at Jutland to redress the balance of his capital ships with Jellicoe's, the war would have been won for Germany. But he failed, and Germany had only momentary consolation in that during the battle the Grand Fleet lost 14 ships and 6,097 men, while the High Seas Fleet lost 11 ships and 2,545 men. The Germans had begun the action by emerging in strength into the North Sea hoping to encourage at least part of the Grand Fleet to leave port, their projected path having mines and U-boats lying in wait, the hope

147

being that U-boat torpedoes might help to redress the Royal Navy's numerical advantage in capital ships. But none of the U-boats sighted Jellicoe's battleships or Beatty's battlecruisers, and the German Admirals, Hipper and Scheer, found themselves heading straight at Jellicoe's line of battle, their 'T' having been crossed. Scheer then executed a marvellous manoeuvre to escape, each ship reversing its heading one after the other, so that, in effect, the German ships turned tail and headed for port. Jellicoe took no risk and did not follow, for which he was much criticised, but also by others applauded. These latter judged his famed caution the right policy for the day, because, as Churchill wrote: 'He was the only man on either side who could have lost the war in an afternoon', and made the preservation of the Grand fleet rather than the destruction of the High Seas Fleet his prime consideration.

Like Jellicoe, Jacky Fisher also can be given praise and blame, praise for his steam turbine, all-big-gun Dreadnought battleship, which could outfight any ship it could not outrun, and blame for his battlecruiser design which concentrated too much on speed and guns at the expense of armour. Britain lost 3 battlecruisers at Jutland (*Queen Mary*, *Invincible* and *Indefatigable*), while the German battlecruisers had more armour, more watertight compartments and more turret safety and, despite heavier attacks, had only one (the *Lützow*) sunk at Jutland. The matter is complicated, however, by the fact that British shells tended to explode immediately upon impact, causing less damage than German shells which penetrated before exploding. The battleship *Tiger* typified Jacky Fisher's faults on warship design, her gunnery proving deplorable at both Jutland and Dogger Bank. But, in Fisher's defence, *Invincible* had already proved that she had a proper war role, when, accompanied by *Inflexible*, their twin assets – 12-inch guns and a speed of 27 knots – had enabled them to catch and to overwhelm Spee's crack armoured cruisers *Scharnhorst* and *Gueisenau* at the Battle of the Falkland Islands on December 8, 1914, and probably no other type of warship at the time could have accomplished that.

Fisher was right in regard to that battle because the extra speed of the British ships enabled them to catch and destroy 4 of the 5 ships of von Spee's squadron, although the cruiser *Kent* seems to have achieved enough speed only by mustering almost her entire crew to stand on her stern. This detail from the 1914 engagement is a vague reminder of something that occurs in Scilly today, when pleasure launches attempt to navigate the Tresco Channel at slow speed at lower tides; on these occasions there is sometimes an order from the skipper for all passengers to congregate in the bow, to give the screws in the stern more room between them and the sandy sea bottom – a procedure which invariably enlivens the trip.

* * * * *

The mistake at Jutland, which caused losses, was to deploy battlecruisers against battleships and against other battlecruisers with heavy guns, something for which they were not designed – and a lesson reinforced in the 2nd World War by the loss of the battlecruiser *Hood*, overwhelmed by the German battleship *Bismarck*. Another, less striking example was the loss of the outgunned, but better-protected battlecruiser *Scharnhorst*, overwhelmed on Boxing Day, 1943, by the battleship *Duke of York* and by cruisers and destroyers, although it took at least thirteen 14-inch shells, twelve 8-inch shells and eleven torpedoes to accomplish the sinking.

From the Battle of Jutland, the Grand Fleet appeared to do very little for the rest of the war, and to those at the time unfamiliar with naval strategy, it seemed wasteful. Nowadays, people are better informed and realise that the possession of, for instance, a nuclear weapon, is also important – i.e. its potential use rather than its actual use – and so it was with the Grand Fleet.

From 1916 its units lay inactive and at anchor at Scapa Flow, Moray Firth and Rosyth, but actually contributing greatly to winning the war just by being there – the strategy of 'the fleet-in-being', a phrase said to have been first used by the Earl of Torrington in 1690. But the U-boats were the exception, as they could journey unseen and could not be blocked in as were the German battleships; however, submarine warfare was seen by many in 1914 in most countries as 'underhand fighting', Churchill, for instance, once voicing the opinion that 'submarine warfare was not suitable for civilised countries to indulge in'. Germany came to adopt U-boat warfare because they could find no other practical way of prosecuting the war at sea. At first they followed the international rules and sank only British merchant ships, and then only after the merchant ship crews had been given warning and time to escape safely in their ships' boats; but, with the failure of the High Seas Fleet at Jutland in 1916, unrestricted U-boat warfare was resorted to, with almost calamitous results for Britain in 1917. It was a case of trying harder to beat Britain below water when they had failed to do so on the surface. In the circumstances it was perhaps inevitable that the U-boat would become Germany's main weapon at sea against Britain, and came by 1917 to be regarded as such by both Germany and Britain. As a consequence, the geographical position of Scilly in the Western Approaches took on an importance it had not previously possessed. There had been only 63 aircraft of all sorts available to the Royal Flying Corps and the Royal Naval Air Service in July, 1914, and it took a couple of years before the full extent of the U-boat menace to Britain came to be appreciated; yet the decision to establish a seaplane base in Scilly was taken a while before unrestricted submarine warfare had been started by Germany – other than for the brief period in 1915 – and before the convoy system had been adopted by Britain. Indeed, it was the adoption of the convoy system which enabled seaplanes to help with escort and spotter activities more systematically and effectively than when merchant ships ran the gauntlet on their own; and it is, therefore, the story of the work of these seaplanes in 1917 and 1918 which forms the major part of Scilly's role in the 1st World War.

* * * * *

The first war incident near Scilly took place on August 5, 1914, the day after war was declared, when two German ships, the 3-masted schooner *Bolivar*, with a cargo of hides, and the *Roland*, carrying coffee and tobacco from New Orleans, were captured by the Royal Navy's cruisers *Doris* and *Isis*. The German crews were blissfully unaware that hostilities had commenced; but when this had been explained to them, four of the crew of the *Bolivar* made a dash for it in one of the ship's boats, and escaped. They were later picked up by the steamer *Pioneer* in the Bristol Channel, completely lost and all suffering from exhaustion from lack of food and water.

In the first months of the war, one of the most successful U-boats was U-9, commanded by Kapitänleutnant Otto Weddigen, a noted tennis player and half-Danish, who used to holiday in pre-war days in the Isle of Wight and spoke perfect English. His greatest success occurred on September 22, 1914, when U-9 intercepted the British cruisers *Aboukir*, *Cressy* and *Hogue* and sank all three in under half-an-hour. These were on guard against German torpedo-boat attacks on British shipping, but were ambling along at only 10 knots and not even taking the precaution of zigzagging. The first two cruisers were torpedoed, *Aboukir*'s captain believing that his ship had hit a mine; *Aboukir* sank so quickly no lifeboats could be lowered, but *Hogue*, foolishly but understandably and, in 'the best traditions of the Royal Navy' turned and came immediately to rescue *Aboukir*'s crew struggling in the water, only to be torpedoed and sunk herself – and all this without the U-boat shifting position from a depth of only six feet below the surface. Thus, a relatively tiny submarine of between 500 and 600 tons, with only between 28 and 40 crew and out-of-date even in 1914, with only 4 torpedo tubes and one 2-inch gun, had scored an easy hat-trick of sinkings, in which 1,459 British sailors drowned and 36,000 tons of British warships had sunk. There was considerable confusion: *Cressy* which was the last of the three ships actually to sink, fired her guns at floating debris and claimed a 'kill' of a submarine, and then fired unsuccessfully at a nearby Dutch trawler in the mistaken belief that it was a spy-ship directing the attack. The three captains deserve some blame for the disaster, together with the Admiralty as no destroyers were escorting the cruisers, no life jackets had been issued to the ships, and such vulnerable old ships ought not to have been in that position. Few immediate lessons seem to have been learnt, for U-9 ambushed and sank the cruiser *Hawke* in similar circumstances only two weeks later.

Weddigen later commanded U-29 and sank 3 steamers in one day off Scilly without any loss of life: on March 12, 1915, the *Headlands*, of 2,982 tons, was torpedoed and sunk off the Bishop Rock; the *Indian City*, of 4,645 tons, carrying cotton, caught fire and sank after her Chinese crew donned their best clothes before consenting to take their boats and make for St Mary's; and the *Andalusian*, of 2,349 tons, whose captain at first attempted to out-run the U-boat by steaming at full speed for St Mary's, but was caught and boarded and his crew forced into their boats, the Germans helping themselves to *Andalusian*'s charts, instruments and some cutlery before opening her valve cocks. The end came for U-29 on March 18, 1915, when Weddigen encountered a number of ships of the Grand Fleet on an exercise; undaunted, he attempted unsuccessfully to torpedo the battleship *Neptune*, only to be run down by the battleship *Dreadnought* approaching at her top speed of 21.6 knots from the opposite direction, the U-boat becoming the only enemy vessel the *Dreadnought* ever sank. Curiously, *Dreadnought* was old-fashioned enough to be the last British battleship built with a ram on her bow, and it was the impact of this ram (helped by the dropping of depth-charges) and not her famous ten 12-inch guns, which proved important. However, although not used on this occasion, it was her armament of all big guns, combined with steam turbine engines, that had, at her launch in 1906, made all other battleships in the world obsolescent, and from that time onwards had defined battleships as 'dreadnoughts' or 'pre-dreadnoughts'. Jacky Fisher was 1st Sea Lord, 1904 to 1915, and this vessel was the finest creation of his inventive mind, and gave Britain a lead over all other battlefleets and enabled her in the 1st World War to maintain the 4 year blockade of Germany which – some claim – won the war. It was what *Dreadnought* was capable of doing, not what she did that was important.

Yet it was also *Dreadnought*'s bad luck to be the victim of a group of practical jokers, who convincingly duped her crew in the most humiliating hoax ever perpetrated on the Royal Navy. Some well-heeled young persons – dilettantes is one description of them – led by man-about-town Horace Cole, and including Leslie Stephens's daughter, better known as Virginia Woolf, forged a Foreign Office telegram and sent it to the Vice-Admiral of the Home Fleet at Weymouth. It informed him that there was to be an impending and important visit to his flagship, HMS *Dreadnought*, of the Prince of Abyssinia and his entourage. The pranksters then arrived dressed in outlandish garbs and speaking a quite incomprehensible babble, but accompanied by a so-called Foreign Office official, who did the interpreting. The party were welcomed aboard *Dreadnought* with full honours and a band playing a national anthem, not that of Abyssinia as nobody knew the music – but that of Zanzibar, well pleasing to the hoaxers who were, of course, unacquainted with either.

A tour of the ship was followed by a reception, with all the ship's officers

A 19th century view of Lloyd's signal tower at the corner of the sports field on the Garrison, St Mary's. From here information from Tresco air station was relayed to the mainland in the 1st World War.

The old mill on Peninnis, built about 1726, was used as a windmill until 1821, when it was superseded by one on Buzza Hill; the Peninnis mill then became a signal station until about 1870, when it, in turn, was replaced by Lloyd's tower on the Garrison. This tower was originally built to receive signals from passing ships and to send replies to them. An undersea cable to the mainland was laid from October 23, 1869, although not used until December 12, owing to what was called 'a kink in the cable' had been straightened out. Lloyd's tower later became known as Bailey's tower, but in the 21st century is part of a private dwelling.

present in full dress uniform, but conversation was inevitably limited. Eventually, the 'man from the ministry' explained that the Prince and his entourage needed to leave for evening devotions, and they all departed with due pomp and ceremony. The ruse had been so successful, given that so little planning had gone into it, that the pranksters enjoyed themselves by continuing to act their parts on the train all the way back to London, and even insisted on being served dinner on the train only by waiters wearing white gloves. The consequence was that the train was held up at Reading Station, while the train's head waiter went shopping to purchase several pairs.

A few days later, the *Daily Mirror* was apprised of the hoax by Cole, and made it front page news. In a subsequent edition the paper reported that sailors from the *Dreadnought*, who had gone ashore on leave, had been pursued by taunting street kids crying 'Bunga-bunga', the alleged nonsense utterance made by the Prince and his entourage as a sort of appreciation mumble when touring the ship.

The revelations in the national press led to innumerable music-hall jokes, to questions in Parliament and to red faces in Whitehall; nothing was done, however, to the pranksters, the episode being described as 'a lark', a word commonly used at the time to excuse the young of the well-to-do and influential for committing offences which by lesser mortals would have been denounced as illegal and for which punishment would have been demanded.

* * * * *

As for U-29, there were no survivors from *Dreadnought*'s ramming. It is conjectured that Weddigen failed to see *Dreadnought* bearing down upon him because his attention and periscope were directed exclusively at the battleship *Neptune* which he was proposing to torpedo, and thus he had no intimation that his periscope had been spotted or of the danger he was in.

Although the Admiralty was slow to learn the lessons of the early U-boat successes, their long-term effects were considerable, for they showed the submarine to be the most formidable new weapon of sea warfare. This was further demonstrated by the British submarine E9 commanded by Max Horton, who, anxious to avenge the loss of the *Pathfinder*, sank the German light cruiser *Hela* on September 13 between Heligoland and the German shore, an area formerly regarded by the Germans as their safe home waters. These events so alarmed the admirals on both sides that most of the British Grand Fleet were sent temporarily from their unprotected anchorages at Scapa Flow to the safety of Loch Ewe on the Scottish west coast, and the German High Seas Fleet retreated in similar fashion through the Kiel Canal to the comparative safety of the Baltic. It also led the Germans to come to regard the U-boat as the answer to the Royal Navy's battleship preponderance.

Some of the U-boat commanders came close to Scilly in the early years of the war, which they tended to avoid after the seaplane base had been established. In June, 1915, for instance, one German submarine – believed to have been U-34 – had the temerity to adopt the disguise of an innocent sailing-vessel, complete with false mast and sails, in order to approach closer on the surface to targeted merchant-ships without alarming them. This disguised submarine lurked off Scilly, but was spotted from Bryher by that island's inhabitants who are not easily fooled, and her ruse was quickly reported. There were two phones on Bryher used to report all sightings to Lloyds Signal Tower on the Garrison, the messages being then relayed to the mainland enabling the Admiralty to take appropriate action.

The resort of a U-boat to hoisting sails in order to disguise its presence on the surface was not uncommon; U-74 was 'under sail' on May 27, 1916, laying mines in preparation for the High Seas Fleet to emerge into the North Sea and tempt Beatty's battlecruisers out of Rosyth. Four British trawlers spotted the U-boat and saw through the ruse; they attacked and one of them, the *Kimberley*, holed the U-boat before it could escape; there were no survivors. Beatty's battlecruisers did then emerge from Rosyth and engage the High Seas Fleet at the Battle of Jutland, but somehow their course took them past the mines U-74 had laid. Another instance of the use of sail concerns U-44 which, on August 12, 1917, was tying to return to Germany in a damaged condition and unable to submerge, a hoisted sail being a gesture of disguise; but the destroyer *Oracle* spotted the U-boat and rammed and depth-charged the disabled craft. There were no survivors from the 44 crew, although, as proof of her success, *Oracle* was able to bring home some cork insulation debris which had floated to the surface.

All sorts of other forms of disguise were adopted by naval craft of all sides during the war, the addition of an extra funnel being a favourite one. This was most famously practised by the German light cruiser *Emden*, raiding merchant ships in the Indian Ocean in 1914, and fooled some merchant captains into thinking that she was a 4-funnelled British cruiser. From April 6, 1915, many Royal Navy ships had false bow-waves painted on them, which at a distance could mislead an enemy into exaggerating the vessel's speed; others were given a dazzle camouflage, which made them less easy to identify in a choppy sea.

The first couple of years of the war at sea showed a degree of conformity with the codes of war by both sides – and also respect for the enemy. Indeed, despite all the propaganda to the contrary, after the war only one case was proved in which either side had clearly broken the rules and behaved inhumanly without cause. Inevitably, the war produced incredible suffering, crews on surface ships and in submarines dying horrible deaths; but an example of a different spirit occurred when a U-boat surfaced and shelled the 4,656 ton, merchant ship *Caucasian* off Scilly on July 1, 1915. Seventeen shells had hit the ship, which was soon in a leaking condition and liable to sink, when Betty, the *Caucasian's* 10-month-old, Pomeranian dog, jumped into the sea and swam towards the U-boat. Captain Robinson of the *Caucasian* – his wife was actually the dog's owner – immediately jumped into the sea and caught up with Betty, returning to the *Caucasian* with the dog on his shoulders. The U-boat commander later reported that he refrained from further firing because he was impressed by the captain's concern for his pet and admired his bravery in rescuing her. Another instance, almost of camaraderie, occurred when the submarine commander Forstmann sank the Norwegian barque *Fiery Cross* on July 3, 1915; he insisted upon giving Captain Gedde a receipt acknowledging the sinking – to some amusement. But this was most unusual; mostly the war was fought desperately by both sides, unarmed merchant-ships putting up a spirited opposition, as for instance, in March, 1915, when the *Vosges* met with a U-boat on the surface off Scilly. The weather was rough so that, although shell after shell was fired by Captain G. von Forstrer's U-28 at the *Vosges*, all found their target only above the waterline as heavy seas were running; Captain J.R. Green countered this attack by attempting to ram the submarine, which resulted in a hard-fought contest lasting nearly 4 hours before *Vosges* finally sank. Green survived with most of his crew, but all his other officers died.

Similarly impressive was the duel fought at dawn on October 19, 1917, between U-62 and the American ship *J.L. Luckenbach*, which was bound for Le Havre. The ship was damaged by torpedoes and gunfire but remained afloat, dodging shells and torpedoes all that day until the American destroyer *Nicholson* sped to the scene. Upon the destroyer's arrival, the U-boat hastily broke off the engagement and disappeared. On the *J.L. Luckenbach* some of the crew had suffered injuries, but not one of them fatally, despite the length of time they had had to endure shelling while unable to return fire. Some ships under attack sank quickly, others obstinately stayed afloat and this usually depended upon where the torpedoes or shells struck. On June 3, 1915, U-34 sank the Belgian trawler *Marie José* by gunfire after ordering all the crew into their boats; but it took the U-boat 35 shots before the trawler sank, the crew later being picked up from their boats off Scilly by the armed trawler *Samphire*. Most of the attacks by U-boats allowed merchant seamen to leave their ships in their lifeboats before being sunk by gunfire – shelling being a more economical method of sinking a ship than torpedoing, especially as U-boats only had room to carry a relatively small number of torpedoes. But the liner *Falaba*, sunk in the Western Approaches in March, 1915, was an exception; the U- boat flew the British flag and only changed to a German one just before opening fire with torpedoes at fairly close range, which resulted in the drowning of 112 people on the liner. Some U-boats, having ensured that a merchant ship's crew had taken to their boats, would board the merchant ship, replenish the U-boat's supplies by raiding the ship's stores, and then sink the merchant ship in the most economical and effective way by opening her stop-cocks.

To counter these surface attacks by U-boats, the British used decoy vessels, and these were often successful in waters around the Scillies in the 1st World War. They began as a consequence of the large number of fishing-boats destroyed by U-boats in the North Sea; so, in 1915, the Admiralty put a hidden gun on some of the fishing trawlers and had a submarine following the trawler as escort. This tactic destroyed U-40 which surfaced to attack the trawler *Taraniki* and was sunk by the Royal Navy submarine C-40. Three officers in the conning-tower of the U-boat survived and became prisoners-of-war, but they criticised the tactic as 'a dirty trick'. The Germans eventually learnt about the possibility of Royal Navy submarines escorting trawlers from beneath the waves through German prisoners-of-war passing information to German civilian internees, who were better able to apprise German spies. But this was not before the trawler *Princess Louise* was able to telephone the submarine C-27, astern of her and in cable communication, which resulted in U-23 being destroyed on July 20, 1915. To gain time for C-27 to slip her cable and get into position to torpedo U-23, a 'panic party' on the trawler pretended to be abandoning ship. However, after two British submarines had hit mines, the escorting submarine idea was abandoned in favour of disguised merchant ships, armed but pretending to be hapless potential victims, what came to be called Q-ships. The first successful one of these was the *Prince Charles* which sank U-36 in July, 1915. This new tactic was both more economical and more effective than having a submarine trailing behind. Sometimes deception went too far, as when the schooner Q-ship *Cymric* on October 15, 1918, spotted what it thought was the German submarine U-6, but which, owing to something dangling from its conning

An innocent-looking coal-carrier which was actually a deadly Q-ship in the 1st World War. The schooner Mary B. Mitchell, *serving in the Royal Navy as Q9, lured several U-boats to within range of her hidden guns and so to destruction.*

tower and interfering with the line of sight, was actually the British submarine J6. Overlooking the white ensign on the submarine's flagpole (which had on occasion been a deliberate error by the enemy), the Q-ship's crew dropped their gun-covers, fired their guns and reduced the submarine to a sinking condition. Only when the 15 survivors swam to the Q-ship, some still wearing hatbands displaying the words 'H.M. Submarines', did the awful truth dawn. The court of enquiry absolved all from blame; it transpired that the submarine crew at first believed that *Cymric* was a German Q-ship.

One of the most successful of the British Q-ships in the 1st World War was Q9, the 3-masted barque *Mary B. Mitchell*, which before the war had carried coal from South Wales to Scilly and to mainland Cornwall. In 1916, the Royal Navy commandeered her, manned her with volunteers from the Royal Naval Reserve and equipped her with a hidden 12-pounder gun and two 6-pounders, but at first without an engine, so that she relied for power entirely on her sails. She was off the Scillies on December 2, and about 15 miles from the Wolf, when she was approached by U-26, and her crew were ordered by the Germans to abandon ship prior to being sunk; at that the action bell was sounded, the guns were revealed and opened fire, and the U-boat was destroyed. An additional 4-inch gun was subsequently fitted together with two engines; thus equipped, the second encounter with a U-boat occurred in June, 1917, 200 miles southwest of the Lizard. A ship's lifeboat was spotted and it proved to be a decoy from a German U-boat hoping to lure a British ship into coming to investigate it. As the *Mary B. Mitchell* approached the lifeboat, the U-boat opened fire from 3 miles distant; 7 crewmen from the *Mary B. Mitchell* appeared to abandon ship in response, and the U-boat was fooled by this and approached to within 50 yards, at which moment the screens on the *Mary B. Mitchell* were dropped once again, and in a hail of fire the U-boat blew up. On the return journey another U-boat was seen ahead, and once more some of the crew ostentatiously appeared to abandon ship as the German submarine shot one of the Q-ship's masts over the side; but, when the enemy was only 200 yards away, the screens were lowered and 30 rounds fired, which secured 11 direct hits causing the U-boat to sink in a cloud of smoke. The next action against a U-boat was on August 16, 1917, off Start Point; once again fire from the U-boat was accompanied by some of the Q-ship's crew abandoning ship, although on this occasion there were two

156

British casualties; but, the screens were lowered and British guns returned fire from the U-boat for 10 minutes until the U-boat rolled over and sank – the 4th and last action by HMS *Mary B. Mitchell*. On her return to Falmouth, the ship was opened to the public for a small charge to boost War Bonds, but after the war was decommissioned and returned to her pre-war role of carrying Welsh coal to Scilly and mainland Cornwall.

One of many ploys used by Q-ships to fool U-boat captains into believing that the merchant-ship crew were abandoning their ship, was for a seaman to dress up in the captain's uniform and hold a stuffed parrot in a cage as he hastily stepped into the lifeboat. This was meant to confirm that the evacuation of the ship was real and is said to have convinced and amused one German U-boat captain, lulling him into approaching too close; but it sounds a bit like over-acting and was unlikely to have occurred often.

Another stratagem employed by Q-ships was to follow a convoy pretending to be an unprotected straggler and therefore easy meat for a pursuing U-boat, and this would be more convincing as engine trouble would sometimes oblige a ship to follow behind when she was unable to maintain station. Between July, 1915 and December, 1917, – the time when Q-ships were mainly in service – 11 U-boats were sunk by Q-ships, and another 60 damaged to varying extents. U-boat losses from all causes in the 4 years of the 1st World War are estimated to have been as follows:

1914 – 5 U-boats lost by Allied action
1915 – 19 U-boats lost by Allied action
1917 – 66 U-boats lost by Allied action
1918 – 74 U-boats lost by Allied action

plus some by mines and others in accidents and so forth. This table, even though only approximate, indicates clearly the increasing losses of U-boats as the war progressed. By the last months of the war, the average life expectancy of a U-boat had been reduced to only about 4 trips. The short answer to the question why the U-boats did not win in 1917 was not only Lloyd George's adoption of the convoy system, but also because there were just not enough U-boats.

It was as a result of a Q-ship incident 80 miles off the Scillies that a degree of viciousness is said to have entered the U-boat conflict in the 1st World War. It involved the Royal Navy's Q-ship *Baralong*, a converted merchant-ship and one deliberately looking rather rundown – but equipped with two hidden guns and a hold packed with buoyant material, such as cork and timber, to help her stay afloat if disabled by a U-boat, and also to look as if she was carrying cargo. The circumstances were as follows: on August 16, 1915, *Baralong* sighted the 6,369 ton ex-liner *Nicosian* – which was carrying about 800 mules, much fodder, and also about 80 American muleteers –

sailing to Britain from the USA. Commander Bernhardt Wegener in U-27 had intercepted the *Nicosian*, whose captain Chester Manning, made desperate attempts to escape by zigzagging at speed away from the U-boat, but eventually, outpaced and under a hail of shells from U-27's deck gun, was obliged to heave-to. *Nicosian*'s last wireless message seeking help read: 'Captured by enemy submarine. Crew ready to leave. Latitude 50° 22'N, Longitude 8° 12'W. Help! Help! For God's sake Help!'

Responding to the call, *Baralong,* with little sign of urgency, approached the *Nicosian*, now under way but proceeding slowly with U-27 astern of her. Captain Chester Manning signalled to *Baralong* that his ship had been captured and that the U-boat was astern. Wegener, for his part, would have been able to make out through his binoculars some of *Baralong*'s crew relaxing at the rails, on the bridge the unprepossessing figure of the captain with long straggly hair, the American flag flying at her stern, and even the ship's name *Baralong* painted on the rusty bow – clearly an intruding neutral vessel which needed warning off, but of no danger to the submarine. *Baralong* approached with *Nicosian*'s great hull interposed in the line of sight from U-27, and was overtaking *Nicosian* on her port side. Wegener also started to overtake the slowly-moving *Nicosian* on her starboard side, intending to fire a warning shot at *Baralong* as soon as the interfering merchant ship appeared ahead of *Nicosian*'s bow. But, while obscured from view behind *Nicosian*, a transformation took place on *Baralong*; the bedraggled captain cast off his unkempt wig and old jacket, revealing his smart naval uniform, a sheep-pen on the poop collapsed revealing a 12-pounder gun, a brown lifeboat-locker amidships also fell apart revealing another 12-pounder and the American flag was run down and replaced by the Royal Navy's white ensign.

As the two vessels sighted each other simultaneously when they emerged ahead of the *Nicosian*, the U-boat only got one shell away – and that fell short – before the U-boat's conning tower was shot away and the deck gun knocked out by a hail of 34 shells from *Baralong*'s two 12-pounders. Holes also appeared in the U-boat's hull and, in a sinking condition, many of the German crew dived into the sea.

Meanwhile, those on the *Nicosian* were taking to their lifeboats and making towards the *Baralong*, with Commander Godfrey Herbert happily welcoming them on board. It was while this was happening that he became aware that many of the German sailors were swimming to the *Nicosian* and climbing up the rope falls left dangling by the *Nicosian*'s crew and passengers, who were now making their way in lifeboats towards the *Baralong*. Moreover, although *Nicosian* still had some small fires burning on her, caused by the original action with the U-boat, the German sailors were putting them out and taking control of the ship prior to making a bid to escape in her. This was at a time when the U-boat had been riddled with holes from the *Baralong*'s gunfire, was sinking and had virtually surrendered; in the view of the British, the Germans should simply have been waiting to be picked up by the *Baralong* as prisoners-of-war, and certainly should not have been trying to take over the *Nicosian* to make an escape. Neither Herbert nor his men were prepared to be lenient with the Germans, having absorbed the bitterness generated in Britain by the sinking of the *Lusitania* three months previously, and having heard that very day of the sinking of the *Arabic* with the loss of many passengers. The *Baralong* therefore sailed alongside the *Nicosian* and a boarding party of armed marines leapt aboard, engaging in angry combat with the unarmed U-boat sailors. The end result was a wholesale shooting or bayoneting of the Germans on the *Nicosian*, while Commander Bernhard Wegener was shot as he swam in the water, a savagery which the marines are alleged to have boasted about on shore afterwards, and which Berlin heard about and to which it reacted angrily. The *Nicosian* managed to limp to a British port, where heavy censorship was imposed in Britain on all aspects of the event. But the 80 American muleteers could not be silenced, and some of them gave full and graphic accounts to American newspapers of what had happened. After which there were protestations about the illegal use of the American flag, which seemed to put US ships in greater danger of attack by submarines, and the secret role of the Q-ship was now clearly revealed. The outcry in Germany led to reprisals, with one U-boat machine-gunning the lifeboats from the torpedoed collier *Ruel*, killing the captain and injuring others, and to two German destroyers machine-gunning the crew of the British submarine E-13, which was stranded helpless on the Danish coast, with fifteen of the crew being killed before Danish boats came to the rescue. *Baralong* also sank U-27 on August 19, 1915, and had another battle with a U-boat on September 24, 1915, when the Q-ship, again flying the American flag, came upon U-41 which had just sunk the steamer *Urbino* off the Isles of Scilly. *Baralong*, looking innocent and harmless, was able to approach quite close to the U-boat as its commander, K. Hansen, was quite unaware of any danger until too late. Two officers only were rescued by the *Baralong* from the 37-man submarine crew.

British, French and American opinion was further incensed in October when Edith Cavell (1865-1915), a British nurse in Belgium, was accused of helping Allied soldiers to escape, and was executed. She was shot at dawn on October 12, 1915, her last words – indeed the epitaph on her grave – contained the famous words 'patriotism is not enough. I must have no hatred or bitterness for anyone' – a mild rebuke to the excesses of nationalism, embodying some of the Christian message, and less strident than Samuel Johnson's 'Patriotism is the last refuge of the scoundrel' and Oscar Wilde's 'Patriotism is the virtue of the vicious'. Dean Inge wrote: 'A nation is a society united by a delusion about its ancestry and by a common hatred of its neighbours'. Probably no other factor in the last thousand years, not even

Nurse Edith Cavell was charged specifically with helping to smuggle Belgian men over the frontier; she was found guilty by a German court and shot on October 12, 1915, although not perhaps quite in as brutal a way as depicted in the propaganda drawing. In Britain a Who'll Avenge Nurse Cavell *recruiting campaign was begun with many rallies; it is estimated that over 10,000 Britons enlisted in the armed forces in response. In wartime, Spinoza's dictum that 'intolerance should never be tolerated' is hard to accept when propaganda fans hatred.*

religion, can have figured so prominently in wars as has the clash of national egotisms sanctified by the name of patriotism.

Yet many U-boat commanders, even in 1917, continued the older, more humane practices, and showed their concern to avoid unnecessary casualties; but it is hardly surprising to find that, during the war, stories of German chivalry towards prisoners-of-war went largely unreported. Captain Hans Rose of U-53, for example, sank the 3,000 ton American freighter *Housatonic*, a vessel on passage to Britain with a cargo of wheat, just as she was approaching the Scillies on Saturday, February 3rd. He invited Captain Ensor aboard the U-boat and explained why he had had to sink his ship, and then insisted upon towing the *Housatonic*'s two lifeboats, holding Ensor's 37 crewmen, past the Scillies and to within sight of Penzance. There Rose attracted the attention of a Royal Navy patrol-boat by firing a shot in its direction, ordered Ensor to let go the two tow-ropes from the lifeboats, then quickly submerged his U-boat and disappeared. He could hardly have done more to preserve the letter and the spirit of international law.

Some U-boats suffered damage from Q-ships yet succeeded in reaching their home ports. U-93, for instance, under Kapitanleutnant Frieherr von Spiegel, had sunk 27,000 tons of Allied shipping when the U-boat approached a defenceless-looking schooner, which turned out to be the Q-ship *Prize*. U-93 surfaced and was then hit nine times by shells from *Prize*'s guns, knocking Spiegel off his conning-tower and into the sea, from which he was picked up by the *Prize* and became a prisoner-of-war. But U-93 was not destroyed by the bombardment and quickly submerged and slipped away, although having lost fuel. When this ran out completely, a German trawler came to the rescue and towed the U-boat to Wilhelmshaven. On this occasion

Ramming was often very effective against U-boats. On December 9, 1917, the trawler Ben Lawer, *when escorting colliers across the English Channel to France, rammed U-18 with no survivors from the submarine crew, but with considerable damage to the trawler's bow – and she only just reached port. On January 7, 1918, the steamer* Braenil *rammed U-95 in fog between Scilly and the Lizard, and the steamer's master collected the usual reward from the British Government for the destruction. On May 12, 1918, the White Star liner* Olympic, *while transporting American troops to Southampton, was intercepted at the entrance to the English Channel by U- 103, which lay on the surface awaiting just such a supposedly easy target; but* Olympic *was making 24 knots and altered course straight towards the enemy, and drove clean through the centre of the U-boat before its commander, C. Rucker, had time to dive. There were ten casualties on the U-boat, but the rest of the crew were picked up by the USS* Davis *and taken to Queenstown as prisoners-of-war. Such episodes were reported in the Allied press as victories of great heroism but were given the opposite interpretation in the German press; their illustrated papers produced the same drawing above, purporting to show 'the cowardly ramming by a British trawler of one of their heroic submarines'. Thus propaganda used the same event to stir contradictory spirits - with people on both sides tending to believe what the newspapers relayed to them as 'correct' opinion.*

the Q-ship was simply not successful in destroying the U-boat, but occasionally it was the Q-ship which was the victim; the following August, *Prize* was sunk by one torpedo from U-48, before the Q-ship had any opportunity to open fire, and she went down with no survivors. A similar fate was suffered by the Q-ship *Bergamot*, sunk by U-84 on August 13, 1917.

But most Q-ships survived, the *Farnborough* being one that was successful. Disguised as a collier, she was intercepted by U-68 on March 22, 1916, west of Scilly and to the southwest of Ireland; but after putting a 'panic' party into her boats, the U-boat was tempted to approach her and was quickly disposed of by the Q-ship's guns, there being no survivors from the 38 U-boat crew. In a similar area, on February 17, 1917, *Farnborough* (Q5) intercepted U-83 off southwest Ireland, the submarine commander, Bruno

Hoppe, acted warily, firing one torpedo which struck *Farnborough*'s engine-room and watching carefully at periscope depth while the steamer's crew appeared to abandon ship; only then did he surface about 100 yards away and emerge out of his U-boat and on to his conning-tower. As he did so, the White Ensign unfurled on the *Farnborough*, the gun shields descended, and the guns opened up firing 45 rounds, the majority hitting the U-boat, and one decapitating its captain. Only two crew survived by swimming to the *Farnborough*. Bruno Hoppe seems to have been unfortunate in his errors; he had been commander of U-22 which, on January 21, 1915, torpedoed and sunk what he took to be a British submarine, only to discover from the one survivor that it was U-7.

On March 24, 1916, U-29 under Herbert Pustkucher torpedoed and sank the cross-channel steamer *Sussex*, which had 25 citizens of the USA on board. The resulting anger in America was so great that Germany abandoned once again an even shorter spell of unrestricted U-boat warfare. Pustkucher later commanded U-66 which, on June 12, 1917, fell victim not to a Q-ship but to a British trawler off the Lizard – what to Pustkucher may have appeared an easy prey. This was the *Sea King*, one of several trawlers the Royal Navy had fitted with hydrophones to operate as a group against U-boats in the Western Approaches. Pustkucher surfaced near the trawler, but the trawler rushed at him and, as Pustkucher attempted to dive out of the way, dropped depth-charges right on top of him. The submerging U-boat then succumbed to a further half-dozen violent explosions of the mines it was carrying, and from which there could be no survivors.

Q-ship crews were expected to maintain their false identities even in their home ports, in case German spies were watching them. White feathers from members of the public were sometimes delivered to crew members, who usually wore civilian clothes, even quite tatty ones. They kept up their innocent, merchant seamen roles by lounging about on deck when in port, looking as if they were rather an indisciplined bunch; while, below decks, the strictest discipline was maintained in practice. It required some acting ability and even a sense of gamesmanship to serve successfully on a Q-ship, as demonstrated perhaps in one of the most illustrious if disappointing actions of the war, when the Q-ship *Dunraven* met UC-71 on August 10, 1917. This involved the Q-ship's gun crews having to lie prone on the deck and absolutely still near their guns and ammunition, while under prolonged fire from the U-boat. If they had stirred, this would have revealed their presence, while the U-boat was still too far away for them to reply to its gunfire. In the event, they never did manage to sail the *Dunraven* near enough to the U-boat for them to be able to spring into action and open fire. Instead, the U-boat sank the *Dunraven* and escaped, but so great had been the crew's dedication to duty that 4 Victoria crosses were won, and an unprecedented number of awards given for bravery.

The *Penshurst* (Q7) was yet another successful Q-ship, sinking U-37 on January 14, 1916, and UB-19 on November 30, 1916. This latter sinking was in the Western Approaches, when UB-19, after firing a warning shot, was injudicious enough to come close under the *Penshurst*'s stern to try to read the decoy's name. A hail of fire at about 250 yards soon disposed of the U-boat, which never seemed to suspect either why the *Penshurst* had no name, or why an otherwise innocent-looking merchant ship should be painted in battleship grey. There were 16 survivors and 8 casualties including Niemeyer, the commander, who never seemed to explain why he was so taken in by the crew pretending to 'abandon ship'. Others were also tricked; U-81 came to the surface to sink a merchant ship on March 12, 1917, only to be overwhelmed by the Q-ship *Privet*; earlier, on February 19, in the English Channel, U-18 stopped the steamer *Lady Olive* with a torpedo and passed close under her quarter to try to read her name before sinking her; but *Lady Olive* was also a Q-ship and opened fire destroying the submarine in a matter of minutes, although *Lady Olive* was herself so badly holed by the torpedo that she, too, sank a while later.

While laying mines off the French coast, U-72 survived an action with the Q-ship *Penshurst* on August 19, 1917, the *Penshurst* later being torpedoed and sunk by U-120 in the Bristol Channel on Christmas Day, 1917. But, on August 20, 1917, U-72 encountered the Q-ship *Acton*. *Acton*'s crew pretended to abandon ship in the normal way, but, in addition, left small fires burning on board *Acton* tended by a hidden crew; this so fooled Oberleutnant E. Voigt as he watched through his periscope that he surfaced and was quickly overwhelmed by *Acton*'s hidden guns. This was one of the last U-boats sunk by a Q-ship, one reason being that unrestricted submarine warfare meant that U-boats had little need any more to surface and run the risk of being shelled.

Another reason for the ending of this type of warfare was that Q-ships and their stratagems could only be successful while German U-boat captains remained in ignorance of what tricks were being practised upon them. This ignorance came to an end partly through the enterprise of a German spy, Jules Silber, a linguist with flawless English, who was employed in the censorship department of the Post Office. He happened to come upon a letter written by the sister of a naval officer, in which she wrote that her brother was working on a weapon to deal with U-boats. In his job capacity as sensor, Silber visited the sister ostensibly to reprimand her for putting secret information in a letter, but at the same time he took the opportunity to find out from her about Q-ships and their tricks, and conveyed that information to Berlin. It resulted in more torpedoes being fired at merchant ships without warning, as U-boat captains felt they could no longer risk the safety of their submarines by surfacing, and one Scillonian, Malcolm McFarland, serving on the Q-ship *Cowslip*, lost his life when it was sunk by a U-boat's torpedo in this way.

There was also another reason why U-boats decided to torpedo merchant ships in preference to surfacing and using gun fire; this was because by 1917 most merchantmen had been equipped with a gun on their sterns, often not of very high calibre, but something with which to return fire, with the distinct possibility of breaching the attacking U-boat's hull if it was on the surface and within range.

Doenitz, who was to command the U-boats in the 2nd World War and became German Fuehrer after Hitler had committed suicide in 1945, had commanded U-68 in the 1st World War and sank the 3,883 ton freighter *Oopack* when he attacked a convoy on October 4, 1918. But, after going ahead with the intention of attacking the convoy a second time, his U-boat developed malfunctions, including broaching (veering uncontrollably). These defects obliged Doenitz to surface, only to find himself in the middle of the convoy, with all the escorts opening fire on him at close range. After scuttling his craft by opening the vents, Doenitz had little option but to surrender, and he spent the rest of the war – and some time after – as a prisoner-of-war in a camp in Britain. There were 33 survivors picked up from U-68, and only one fatal casualty, the engineer Jeschen; Jeschen seems to have blamed himself for the malfunctions, as he deliberately remained below and chose to go down with the U-boat.

But there were other more subtle ways to dispose of a U-boat than by Q-ships; one of these was to get the Germans to do it themselves. Unlikely as this sounds, this is what British Naval Intelligence succeeded in accomplishing on August 4, 1917, resulting in the loss of UC-44, commanded by Kapitanleutnant Kurt Tebbenjohanns. It happened in the following way: Rear-Admiral Hall, the talented Director of Naval Intelligence in Room 40 at the Admiralty who devised the cunning plan, knew that the Germans had obtained the code the British used whenever they had cleared a German minefield and wirelessed the information; he therefore ordered that, when the next German minefield was discovered, it should be reported as cleared in the normal way, although actually left alone. His intention was to lure the Germans into sending a submarine to re-lay mines in the area of sea which they would believe had been swept, and thus they would fall victim to their own mines – and this is exactly what occurred. UC-42 laid mines in an area of sea off Southern Ireland in June, 1917; this was reported by Rear Admiral Sir Lewis Bayley as having been swept; UC-44 was then sent out by the Germans to re-lay mines in the same area, but inevitably blew herself up on one of UC-42's original mines. 28 crew died and only Tebbenjohanns escaped from the conning-tower and became a prisoner-of-war. In September, 1917, UC-44 was recovered from the ocean floor and her papers provided useful information, including instructions on how to sail through the Straits of Dover to avoid British minefields – leading the British to make a number of adjustments. Room 40 at the Admiralty had another success in 1916, when, on September 16, they leaked a story to the *Daily Mail* about British troop concentrations at Dover and Harwich. The Germans hastily and needlessly moved troops to the Belgium coast to meet the expected invasion, with a commensurate decrease of pressure on the British sector of the Western Front, so attaining the original objective. One device used successfully to mislead the enemy was to transform a few merchant ships to look like warships. The 11,621-ton *Merion*, for example, was given wooden guns in plywood turrets and pretended to be a battlecruiser being given the name of HMS *Tiger*.

In the war against the U-boat the mine was a principal weapon, even though hardly considered as such before 1914. The figures show that it was one of the most successful. During the war, gunfire destroyed about 20 U- boats around British coasts, depth-charges about 30, but mines over 40. In 1914, the Royal Navy laid 4,390 mines around the Straits of Dover – between Dunkirk and the mouth of the River Thames – and 16 miles of nets, and these not only deterred but destroyed a number of U-boats; and, by obliging U-boats – who thought the defences more extensive than they were – to exit the North Sea via the north of Scotland, added over a thousand miles to each U-boat voyage from Germany.

The toll of ship losses from U-boat activities around the Scillies was increased by losses resulting from navigational errors – victims of the elements rather than the enemy – the rocks of Scilly maintaining their evil reputation regardless of the war.

The Germans also had surface raiders during the early part of the 1st World War, usually fast German liners armed with guns. The *Kaiser Wilhem der Grosse*, built 1897 and, except for Brunel's *Great Eastern*, the first 4-funnel liner, was sunk by the British warship *Highflyer* off the African coast on August 26, 1914. One raider was the *Kronprinz Wilhelm* captained by Paul Thierfelder who, in a 250-day cruise, sank 15 ships totalling 58,000 tons, nearly all by the economical method of ramming them. This saved ammunition but was hard on the raider's bows.

One unique encounter between armed liners in the 1st World War occurred in 1914. Captain Langerhanz of the new 3-funnel liner *Cap Trafalgar*, pride of the German liner fleet, on hearing of the outbreak of war, sailed from Buenos Aires leaving all passengers ashore, and met up with the German supply ship *Eber*. Ten guns and much ammunition were then transferred to the *Cap Trafalgar* and, thus converted, she sailed as a potential armed raider. On September 14, she met up with the British armed merchant-cruiser *Carmania* an ex-Cunard liner, which had been armed by August 14 and sent to the South Atlantic.

Both ships, being liners, were huge targets and proceeded to exchange murderous fire. Incongruously, stewards in white coats served the gunners with drinks from silver trays, despite the terrible damage being suffered on both vessels. On the German liner, a winter garden of palms and hundreds of potted plants was set alight and burned like a forest fire; on the British liner masts, lifeboats, derricks, and part of the bridge were destroyed and fires were started everywhere. But the *Carmania*'s gunners concentrated their fire on the *Cap Trafalgar*'s waterline, a tactic which paid off when the German liner began to list and the German crew rapidly abandoned ship before their liner rolled on its side and sank. *Carmania* limped to Gibraltar, but it was two years before she returned to service.

* * * * *

In the 21st century, it is sometimes assumed that navigational aids are now so accurate that shipwrecks are a thing of the past; unfortunately, however good the equipment, human error or slackness in seamanship can result in tragedies just the same. The fishing vessel *Rachel Harvey* on October 1, 1999, ran on to rocks off Peninnis Head, even though a new track control navigation system was in use on board and despite global positioning equipment; the vessel sank in 3 minutes and one of the crew lost his life, all because a visual lookout was not also being adequately maintained. A comprehensive list of shipwrecks in and near Scilly over the last few centuries is recorded in Richard Larn's excellent *Shipwrecks of the Isles of Scilly*, second edition, published by Thomas and Lochar, 1993.

One somewhat confusing aspect of searching for shipwrecks is the number of vessels bearing the same name. 4 ships with the name of *Eagle* have been wrecked in waters around the Scillies and West Cornwall, but other names appear in 5 or 6 wrecks, and one in no less than 8 wrecks. The reasons are that so many wrecks have occurred in these waters over the last 500 years owing to their location athwart the world's busiest sealanes, that, until recently, navigational techniques were rough and ready and even maps could be inaccurate, and because there were fashions in naming ships just as there are in the forenames of people.

It was fortunate that during the 1st World War Admiralty tugs were usually stationed in Scilly and were available to tow damaged vessels to the mainland for repair. One example of this, occurring just before the war began, was the 7,000 ton *Gothland* which, on June 23, 1914, carrying a general cargo, plus 38 ordinary passengers and a group of 48 'undesirable' Belgian refugees from Montreal – this was before the German invasion of 'gallant little Belgium' – struck Zantman's Rock on the Crim in dense fog. The *Lyonnesse* took off the passengers, while tugs took the stricken vessel in tow to Southampton for repair. By coincidence the Captain of the *Gothland*, and the coxswain of the St Mary's lifeboat which came to assist him, discovered that they had once served together as shipmates on the *Picton*.

Other ships sunk or damaged around the Scillies, 1915 to 1918, include the following: on March 29-30, 1915, the 3,500 ton steamer *Flaminian* and the 4,505 ton merchant ship *Crown of Castle* were both sunk by U-28, the commander of the submarine informing Round Island lighthouse of the happening so that rescuers would be sent. One month later the steamer *Minterne* was torpedoed by U-28 at almost the same spot, and a Greek fireman called Caliphas was in one of the torpedoed merchant ships on each occasion – another remarkable coincidence. On May 1, 1915, the steamers *Edale, Europe* and *Gulflight* were attacked off Scilly. *Edale* and *Europe* were hard to sink, the 3,110 ton *Edale* surviving nine shells and two torpedoes before sinking, and the 2,026 ton *Europe*, carrying coal and only 3 miles northwest of the Bishop Rock, receiving some twenty shells before the U-boat commander used one of his relatively-precious torpedoes finally to dispatch the French collier. The 5,189 ton *Gulflight* on passage from Texas to Rouen, was torpedoed by mistake 23 miles west of Scilly but ran on to Guthers and was eventually salvaged. She was an American oil tanker with 38 American crew who, except for three who drowned and Captain Gunther, who died later from a heart attack, were brought safely into St Mary's. On June 5, the German authorities apologised to the USA; apparently the U-boat had fired a torpedo at a British patrol boat, but the torpedo had passed under the shallow-draught patrol boat and run into the *Gulflight*'s bow. Drifters helped tow her into St Mary's, and eventually some Scillonians sailed her to her owners in Le Havre, each receiving £25 for their trouble. On July 31, 1915, the 486 ton *Turquoise* and the 405 ton *Nugget*, bound from Glasgow for the ill-fated Dardanelles Campaign, were sunk by a U-boat's shellfire off Scilly. The crews alleged that they were fired upon when getting into their boats, with 8 men wounded and one man killed, but the Nugget had attempted to ram the U-boat. The remainder rowed away and were later brought safely into Scilly by the patrol boat *Anthony Hope* and the Dutch sailing-ship *Annetta*. *Turquoise* did not sink immediately, but drifted unmanned for several days before disappearing beneath the waves. The stern of one of the lifeboats from this dual sinking is now preserved in the Valhalla on Tresco. Another vessel sunk near Scilly while bound for the Dardanelles was the *Ben Vrakie*, a 3,000 ton lighter, sunk on August 21, 1915.

In 1916 the *Guen* was wrecked in fog, but a boat from St Agnes saved the 13 crew. On August 15, 1916, the 4,277 ton *Eastgate* was torpedoed and sunk off Nut Rock while carrying a cargo of lingerie including silk stockings, medical items and perfumes. Eau de Cologne was much sought after by Scillonians when it drifted ashore in quart bottles on Samson and Tresco. The scent from this permeated the Scilly air for days. But, later, the 6,999 ton steamer *Great City* was also torpedoed and sunk in Scilly, her cargo of rotting grain producing an altogether different aroma, 4 of the crew dying from the 'gas' while trying to free the pumps. Later still, the *Fusilier*, a naval patrol boat, was sunk off Crebawethan, and the *Carbineer*, another naval patrol boat, struck the Crim Rocks on May 18, but was fortunate in having a Scillonian on board, W. Trenear, who directed her captain on to Crebawethan, where she grounded with her crew all safe, but became a total loss. In 1916, on November 11, the 3,567 ton, steel-hulled *Brodfield* was wrecked in dense fog on rocks below Blue Carn near Giants Castle, St Mary's. Large numbers of vessels attempted together to tow her off the rocks, but she ended up broadside to the shore and broke in two. Today, some of her rusty parts are still discernible from the coastal path below the airport at very low tides.

In 1917, on February 3, the *Housatonic* was sunk off the Bishop Rock lighthouse by U-53 after the crew had taken to their boats, and the 3,593 ton *Lady Charlotte*, with a cargo of coal, ran on the rocks at Porth Hellick in fog and became a total loss on May 11, but all the crew were saved. On May 10-11 also, the *Blue Carn* was wrecked on St Mary's at nearly the same time as the Italian steamer *Italia*, bound from Cardiff to Naples laden with coal, struck Great Wingletang on St Agnes. A young St Agnes girl witnessed the *Italia* tragedy, but few believed her as the ship had sunk by the time they checked her story, and the sinking had not been seen by any of the many Scillonians who acted as volunteer coast watchers during the war years. A 40mm gun was recovered from this wreck in 1965 by a party of Fleet Air Arm divers who were taking a busman's holiday in Scilly.

On December 6, 1917, the 4-funnel, American destroyer *Jacob Jones* was torpedoed by U-53 when returning from convoy duty off Brest with six other US destroyers heading for their base at Queenstown in Ireland. The *Jacob Jones* sank about 25 miles off the Bishop Rock. 64 crew died, some because there were depth-charges on the destroyer's deck, primed for action, which exploded when the destroyer rolled over. Two wounded men were landed by U-53's commander, Hans Rose, for medical attention at Heligoland. The action of U-53 in taking on 7 destroyers was a brave act, matched by a humane one when Land's End radio was informed of the sinking by U-53's Commander, Hans Rose, who later refrained altogether from sinking one French sailing-ship when he discovered that the ship's lifeboats were unseaworthy. British propaganda suggested U-boat commanders left merchant-ship survivors to perish, but more often they picked them up and looked after them. But sometimes ships were sunk with little trace of them remaining, only a few pieces of deck cargo drifting ashore as sad evidence of their former existence; one example occurred in 1917, when one empty lifeboat came ashore in Scilly. Much other smaller, shipwrecked goods were washed ashore in Scilly not only during the war but for many years afterwards; but most were items unmarked and therefore their origin was unknown. On one day in 1917, dead horses and human bodies were washed ashore on Bryher, on another day it was juicy oranges on Pelistry; usually it was items described by Scillonians who collected them as useful but 'not worth bothering the Customs with'.

168

On July 24, 1918, the 975 ton destroyer *Pincher* ran on the Seven Stones in fog, but all her crew were saved; in September, the *San Mondego*, carrying wines, was lost on St Mary's, but all her crew were saved, if not all her cargo. Two other vessels were torpedoed and sunk near Scilly in 1918, the *Delphic* on September 8, and the *Montfort* on October 3. On November 11, the last day of the war, the 283 ton tug *Blazer*, returning from Penzance, struck Steval Point in fine weather and on a calm sea, but all her crew – many somewhat the worse for wear as a result of injudicious celebrating – were saved. The Captain was exonerated at the subsequent enquiry, but divers later found live ammunition close to where the tug lay on Conger Ledge.

One multiple sinking in the year 1917 has raised controversy. It was during a period when shipping losses around the Scillies and in the Western Approaches were at their greatest; on February 23, 7 Dutch ships and one Norwegian, which had left Falmouth together on the previous day, were attacked west of the Bishop Rock lighthouse by a submarine in broad daylight and on a calm sea. Three were sunk by torpedoes and two others were boarded and scuttled. The St Agnes lifeboat (37 feet long with 12 oars) went out and, with other boats from St Agnes, guided 27 of the ships' boats into St Mary's. One, with 10 survivors, was located and escorted in by the gig *Czar* from Bryher. For the rescues, which were carried out without a single life being lost, the crew of the St Agnes lifeboat all received medals from the Netherlands section of the League of Neutral Nations.

The ships sunk were the *Noorderdjik* of 7,166 tons, the *Jacatra* of 5,373 tons, the *Zaadijk* of 4,189 tons, the *Gaasterland* of 3,917 tons, the *Eemland* of 3,770 tons and the *Bandoeng* of 5,851 tons, plus the Norwegian *Normanna* of 2,900 tons. Two other Dutch ships escaped, the *Medado* of 5,874 tons, which eventually arrived back at Falmouth, and the *Ambon* of 3,598 tons which went to Plymouth. The episode looks fairly clear-cut, but a question mark hangs over it; U-21 is sometimes named as the U-boat responsible for the sinkings, and it is said that the Dutch ships were relying upon their neutral status to keep them safe from attack; but there has been the allegation – by Howard Pender writing on February 20, 1979 – that the submarine involved was not German but British and on a clandestine mission; and that the Dutch ships were in fact running the British blockade, intending to bring food and equipment from across the Atlantic and sell it on to Germany. If this is correct, it might explain why the eighth ship, a Norwegian vessel, was not sunk, because presumably she was not running the blockade; but the story raises the question why the *Normanna* was sunk and a further question as to how the German Government was fooled into paying compensation to the Dutch for the sinking of their ships. On the other hand the Isles of Scilly Museum Publication No 3 on *Shipwrecks around the Isles of Scilly*, when reporting this event adds the comment that the weather was 'fine and the crews landed in their best clothes' – which does make it sound as if they were

SHIPS SUNK OFF SCILLY – 22 FEBRUARY 1917
Table kindly supplied by M.J. Ingham, May 2000

Name of Ship & country of origin	Tonnage	Position sunk	Alleged U-Boat	Method of sinking
Bandoeng Netherlands	5,851 steamship	50.10N 07.05SW 30 miles NW Bishop Rock	*U-21	torpedoed after crew took to boats
Eemland Netherlands	3,770 steamship	49.52N 07W 30 Miles NW Bishop Rock	U-21	sunk by demolition charges
Gaasterland Netherlands	3,917 steamship	50.10N 07.05W 30 miles NW Bishop Rock	U-21	sunk by demolition charges
Jacatra Netherlands	5,373 steamship	50.10N 07.05W 30 miles NW Bishop Rock	U-21	torpedoed after crew took to boats
Noorderdijk Netherlands	7,166 steamship	50.10N 07.05W 30 miles NW Bishop Rock	U-21	torpedoed after crew took to boats
Zaandyk Netherlands	4,189 steamship	49.52N 07W 30 miles NW Bishop Rock	U-21	sunk by demolition charges
plus				
Normanna Norway	2,900 steamship	49.49N 06.45W 17 miles west of Bishop Rock	U-21	sunk by demolition charges
	tonnages are GRT		*it may have been U-3 or it may have been a British submarine acting on secret orders to prevent blockade running	

sunk by a friendly submarine rather than a hostile one, and Lewis Hicks has written that the account of the rescue on the board at St Agnes is inaccurate.

U-boats were also used in the 1st World War to try to stir up rebellion within British dominions. Many in Ireland resented British rule – and with good reason – and felt that 'Britain's difficulty was Ireland's opportunity'; so, on April 21, 1916, Sir Roger Casement was landed at Tralee by a U-boat for the planned rebellion in Dublin which took place on Easter Sunday, April 23; and the steamer *Libau*, from Germany, with 20,000 rifles and other military equipment aboard, bound for the rebels, reached Tralee on April 20. However, unknown to the Germans, messages between Washington and Berlin were being intercepted by British Intelligence, who were therefore able to arrest Casement on April 22 – he was hanged on August 3 – and to capture the *Libau* before she unloaded, and escort her to Queenstown, where her captain, Karl Spindler, blew her up off Daunt's Rock. The German involvement was a failure and the Easter Rising of 1916 in Ireland was soon suppressed.

The majority of the people in the south of Ireland are Roman Catholics and Roman Catholicism is hierarchical in structure, which means that such people are not natural rebels against authority. Yet, by hard struggle, they won their independence eventually in the 20th century, and the marked prosperity of Eire in the 21st century, compared with their poverty over the centuries, has been one of the results.

* * * * *

The Germans also had many successes with mines: U-75 laid mines off Marwick Head, Orkney, on May 28-29, 1916, and one of them sank the cruiser *Hampshire* carrying Lord Kitchener – he was not among the 12 survivors. In his book, *The Crisis of the Naval War*, Jellicoe estimated that in February, 1917, Germany had 130 submarines available for use around British shores, and that about half of them were capable of laying mines. In that month 513 German mines were swept up by British minesweepers, but it was a hazardous procedure and Britain lost nearly one minesweeper a day during that month. Over 1917 as a whole, 63 U-boats were sunk one way or another around Britain, and about half of these were equipped with and capable of laying mines. Over the 4 years of the First World War, mines sank more ships than gunfire. One advantage the British had in the war was that they could intercept and read German naval signals, their codes having been broken. The secrets of the codes were obtained in three ways: one was through divers who were sent down to break into sunken U-boats and recover the codes; another was that Britain's ally, Russia, had recovered the German codes when they sank the cruiser *Magdeburg*, and they obligingly handed them to the British; and a third was that on November 30, 1914, a British trawler had a box dragged up in her fishing net, which was found to contain some of the German codes. The Germans were quite ignorant that British Naval Intelligence had their codes, and only found out that their signals were being read after the war was over.

One service the Scillies performed in both 1st and 2nd World Wars was to provide immediate shelter and aid to the crews of sunken or damaged ships, the busiest time being March to June, 1917. On March 12, the crew of a Portuguese steamer sunk by a U-boat were landed in Scilly, followed the next day by 2 lifeboats with the American crew of the *Algonguin*. The 4,115 ton *Vigilancia*'s crew were brought ashore on April 1, and eighteen crew were later landed from the *Argentine* and the *Hunstanton*, plus the crew of a fishing boat on April 25, forty crew from a steamer on April 27 and the crew of another one on May 8, and from the 6,827 ton Australian *Limerick* a day or two later. In addition, by June 2, there were in St Mary's crews from lifeboats from the 3,045 ton *Bagdale*, the 2,821 ton *Bathurst*, and from the *Jeanne Cordonnier*. Two damaged ships and their crews, the 6,382 ton *Kathlamba* and the 6,999 ton *Great City* were towed in to St Mary's on June 18, and later in the month the crew of the 1,292 ton *Kelso* were landed and the German crew of the U-boat oil-supply ship *Sherman*, caught and escorted in by an armed trawler. While the crews remained in Scilly, quite a strain was placed on accommodation and medical services in the Islands.

* * * * *

Many premises were requisitioned on St Mary's in the 1st World War for the use of service personnel. Lemon Hall, for instance, taken over by the navy, became a temporary hospital for wounded or sick merchant seamen, where Dorothy, Malcolm McFarland's wife, worked as a nurse. Service officers used Master Gunner Tovey's 18th Century White House on the Garrison for their headquarters and Tregarthen's Hotel as their wardroom, while Holgate's Hotel served as the military sick bay, and the Church Hall became the Army and Navy Club. Telegraph Hotel and the Atlantic Hotel were also used. Some aircraft servicing crews were at first billeted in Holgates and in Old Town.

About 50 soldiers of the 3rd Devonshire Regiment, convalescing from illness or wounds, were sent over to Scilly from the mainland to provide a guard for the wireless station at Telegraph, the Quay and the Garrison, and also to man Kite balloons (one of which was at Holy Vale), the searchlights at Bant's Carn, Steval and Woolpack, the artillery posts on the Garrison, and also to provide a soldier with a rifle to stand guard on Great Arthur whenever the packet-boat *Lyonnesse* (and her successors) was expected.

The reason for the Great Arthur sentry was that it was feared that a U-boat might lie in wait for the packet-boat, and the armed soldier on coastguard duty could give the alarm if he spotted any signs of one; but the *Lyonnesse* was not attacked and was sold by Mr Banfield in 1917, when he received about £18,000 – nearly twice as much as he had paid for the vessel new some 30 years before – when her original purpose seems to have been to carry fish from Scilly to Penzance. After the sale, the Ministry of Shipping used trawlers and drifters to supply the Islands, plus a coaster, the *Artificer*, but the Government gave notice that they would withdraw their supply ships at the end of the war, and did so once the air station on Tresco had closed. It was because of that announcement that many Islanders proposed that they should form a steamship company and run a supply-ship themselves, and this led to the formation of the Isles of Scilly Steamship Company in 1920 and the purchase of the *Lapwing*, replaced in 1921 by the 224 ton ex-naval patrol-vessel *Argon*, bought for £8,000 and re-named *Peninnis*, which plied the route until the 1st Scillonian replaced her in 1926.

* * * * *

During the 1st World War, in order to deter U-boats from approaching too close to Scilly, armed trawlers laid netting at the entrance to some of the channels into Scilly. Netting laid in a similar fashion off Falmouth did catch one U-boat which was then depth-charged to destruction; but, off Scilly, the nets caught nothing – except a turtle.

Some billets had also to be found for some dockyard workers – usually put up by Scillonians who had a spare room, and in local boarding-houses, Colletts, for instance, which had been established in 1909, or in hotels in Hugh Town, such as Telegraph in Hugh Street, or Bluett's or Gahan's. One of the two cottages just inside the Garrison Gateway served as a supply depot and the other as the garrison's guardroom, including for those who did duty at the Wireless Station at Telegraph, the highest point on the island. Admiralty trawlers and other craft obtained their supplies from the store at the landward end of the quay (now the Mermaid Inn), and workshops on Rat Island did minor ship repairs. For part of the time in the later years of the war, the depot ship *Ark Royal* was stationed at St Mary's to help with these tasks. Fresh water was obtained from Moor Well and pumped to a tank on the Garrison and to the Quay to replenish the ships. A free newsroom and reading-room was opened for all service personnel in Well Lane, and accommodation was arranged for female secretaries at Bank House, who attended at Tregarthen's and operated telephones at the White House. The Defence of the Realm Act required all civilians to comply with military requirements, one of which was that one beach was allocated for the exclusive use of female service personnel.

It was a time also of what appears today as excessive nationalism and patriotism. Just as D.H. Lawrence and his wife, Frieda von Richthoven, were suspected of being spies – and in their case were actually made by the authorities to leave Cornwall from their home at Zennor – in Scilly, the rector, because he came from Alsace, was regarded by some Scillonians as a possible spy and watched closely; particularly suspicious to locals were his lamps of varying types which he repositioned in the chaplaincy windows. As with D.H. Lawrence, who carelessly allowed his curtains to flap while reading in bed late at night, the rector's lamps were seen as possibly some sort of signalling to U-boats. It is perhaps not surprising that, as soon as the war ended, the rector left Scilly.

It may seem reprehensible that a decent man of the cloth should be so regarded, but such criticism is to overlook the times in which it occurred, for in the 1st World War there was an obsession everywhere with spies. In all the

European belligerent countries, and not only in Britain, people were asked to report suspicious behaviour – it was part of civic duty – for it was widely believed that spies were operating everywhere and trying to undermine one's country. Partly this may have been a result of Marconi's inventions, for it was now easier through the use of wireless to convey messages to a foreign country; but mainly this was because the 1st World War was different from all previous conflicts in that it was a war of propaganda, in which there were deliberate moves to rouse people's feelings against the enemy – a national hate campaign to sustain the war effort. Patriotism demanded that everyone should help identify and frustrate possible enemy agents, it was something ordinary citizens could do on the home front, and was a response to the enemy and 'his evil wickedness'.

Reports of German atrocities in the newspapers could arouse extreme feelings which sought outlets. When the liner *Lusitania* was sunk by a U-boat in 1915, Quentin Bell recalled how a Swiss banker, with a German-sounding name who lived near him, had all his windows smashed by a 'patriotic' English crowd. This was a case of people venting their frustration and anger; it was not that the banker lived in a particularly large house – nothing like Versailles Palace with its 2,143 windows – and it was not an expression of resentment at his presumed wealth, but because, as a foreigner, he was suspect, and the nearest the crowd could get to the enemy. Even that most English of Englishmen, the onetime Poet Laureate, John Betjeman, suffered at school because his name made others suspect him and his family of being enemy spies, even though the family origin was not German but Dutch. The atmosphere of suspicion and hate which found expression and release particularly against anyone who might conceivably be an enemy agent, is perhaps most poignantly revealed in the best known and least just of 1st World War spy cases. This concerned the Dutch woman, Margaretha Geertruida Zelle, who was not, as sometimes described, oriental, talented or an enemy spy but, in later life, a somewhat stout woman, mistaken in Britain in November, 1917, for the German agent Clara Penedix. She was eventually executed in order – some said – to cover up French military failures, the prosecution supporting their case with lurid revelations of her supposed tawdry lifestyle. Secret files, released in 1963, show her to have been an innocent scapegoat, but her adopted name, Mata Hari, still carries stigma. The revelation of truth has done little to rehabilitate her blighted reputation.

She was born in 1876 in the Netherlands, the daughter of a shopkeeper who sold hats. By the age of 13 both her parents had died, and in her late teens she trained briefly as a Kindergarten teacher before, in 1895, she made an unsuitable marriage at the age of 18 to Rudolph MacLeod, an army officer twice her age, who became a drunkard and abused her violently. He was posted to Java in the Dutch East Indies, where their son died of poison, and where eventually, in 1902, after 11 years of abused marriage, she escaped

Mata Hari, the exotic Indonesian dancer and master spy – as everyone imagined her – gaining secrets in pillow talk from all those of high ranking with whom she slept. Sir Basil Thomson interviewed her on behalf of British Intelligence, but found that 'of all the people that I examined during the War, she was the quickest on the uptake'. Her execution created a sensation.

back to the Netherlands, filed for divorce and by 1905 was successful (which was unusual), but had to give up the custody of her beloved daughter, Nan, to her husband, and never saw her again.

At the age of 29 in 1905, she went to Paris, unskilled and penniless; so she changed her identity and reinvented herself as Mata Hari, calling herself either a Javanese princess or a Hindu dancer, at a time when orientalism was much in fashion. She abandoned all feelings for family and domesticity in an age when most people still believed 'a woman's place was in the home'. She was not a prostitute in the accepted sense, more a courtesan, seeking only the company of the rich and powerful such as the American Rothschild and the German Crown Prince, from the likes of whom, she said, she claimed a fee of 30,000 marks. She moved in high circles and performed in Paris theatres and music-halls, inventing striptease by partially unveiling herself seductively and scandalously as she danced erotically, but at a time when even the revelation of a naked ankle could be censured as wanton – although this can be exaggerated; it is sometimes said, for instance, that Victorians covered their piano legs for reasons of modesty, but this was done to prevent marking of the wood carving from maids clumsy with cleaning brushes – an action of prudence rather than prudery.

Mata performed in many European capitals before the 1st World War, including Berlin and Madrid, and was feted for her fascinating stories of her supposed previous life in the Dutch East Indies, a region of which polite society knew little. Eventually she became rather too stout for top billing, and was once sacked from a role she was to play as Cleopatra. When the 1st World War broke out, her connections and travelling – and she spoke four languages – made her seem a likely candidate for spying. She may have accepted offers, and certainly she became an agent for the French Counter-Espionage Service. She may even have taken posts as a double or even triple agent, but she only did it for money; there is no evidence that she ever revealed anything secret to anybody. In November, 1916, she was first arrested off a ship in Falmouth and interrogated by Sir Basil Thomson of Special Branch, until the British learnt that she was an agent of their ally France; but, when she returned to France, she was accused of spying for the enemy, although without any real evidence, and the Russian aviator living in Paris with whom she had fallen in love, abandoned her. She was arrested on February 13, 1917, and maintained that money given her was for services not spying; but the French armies were suffering mutinies, and she was convicted, and executed without benefit of a blindfold on October 15, 1917, at Vincennes by a firing squad of 12 expert French marksmen, 9 of whom contrived to make their shots miss her, 2 struck her where injury was slight, but one shot went straight through her and killed her instantly. No one claimed the body and it went to a medical school, where an anatomy class dissected her heart. However, posterity has not entirely neglected her; in 1964, a film of her life was made, and in 1976 a statue of her was erected in Leauwarden, her birthplace in Holland.

In contrast to the rector, one popular person in Scilly in the 1st World War was the hardworking doctor, W.B. Addison, who worked the practice from 1912 to 1927. During the war years he was medical officer to the hundreds of men in drifters and trawlers who came to Scilly, and also to the men of the RNAS (later RAF) on Tresco and St Mary's, and to the Air Balloon Section, also to about 50 convalescent soldiers of the 3rd Devonshire Regiment who composed the guard on the Islands and, of course, to all the civilians in Scilly – 2,097 in 1911, 1,749 in 1921 – huge numbers of potential patients for one doctor, which were periodically swollen further when crews from sunken ships were brought in. During the 2nd World War, Dr Addison placed himself 'on call' in Scilly for the duration of the war, but he was in his late 70s in 1939. He died in 1947 at the age of 85.

* * * * *

The most important role that Scilly played in the war was from 1917, when Britain was facing the greatest crisis in the whole war, April, 1917, being the time when surrender to Germany was actually being contemplated in private by some of the more despondent British admirals. The circumstances, often forgotten now, were as follows: in August, 1914, Germany had only 28 operational submarines, but by 1917 their number had vastly increased. In

176

February, 1917, they sank 26 merchant ships, in March 103 and in April 155. To protect the merchant fleet the Royal Navy deployed nearly 3,000 warships, many of them actively hunting U-boats; but, during the last six months of 1916, they managed to destroy only 15. The admirals, including Jellicoe, the First Sea Lord, resisted demands from politicians that they adopt the convoy system, arguing that the convoy system was 'too defensive-minded', and that convoys merely concentrated merchant ships together and made them easier targets; moreover, as such an accumulation of ships would limit a convoy to the speed of its slowest member, the U-boats would more easily catch the convoys. In addition, the Admiralty declared that it was quite unrealistic to expect merchant-ship captains to be able to keep station in convoys during a long voyage; poor visibility would lead to collisions, and Jellicoe wrote of 'unmanageable organisational problems' being created. He produced a report demonstrating that there were too many ship movements around Britain to convoy them all. Actually, these figures were misleading because they included all the short ferry journeys around the UK coast, whereas only about 130 merchant ships on long hauls arrived and departed from Britain each week – and in April, 1917, 40 of these were sunk.

The annual figures of British merchant ships lost in the 1st World War were approximately as follows:

1914 — 64
1915 — 278
1916 — 396
1917 — 1,197
1918 — 544

Comparing these losses with U-boat losses, about 178 U-boats were destroyed by Allied action in the 1st World War (784 in the 2nd World War), with about 5,400 of their crews killed, which is about 30 per cent of them. (In the 2nd World War the number of U-boat crewmen who died is about 27,491.) Many U-boats were lost as a result of hitting mines; U-15 was rammed on August 9, 1914, U-13 hit a mine on August 12, U-11 on December 9, U-5 on December 18, and U-31 in January 1915. U-7 was itself torpedoed, U-8 on March 4, 1915, was caught in a net, U-12 was rammed on March 10, U-37 hit a mine, UB-3 was destroyed in an accident, and U-14 and U-40 fell victims to decoy ships, as did U-23 on July 20, and U-36 on July 24. If a table is compiled of how U-boats were destroyed by 1918, it would look something like this, although these numbers in each category are only approximate:

By ramming — 19
By gunfire — 20
By depth-charges — 30
By torpedo — 20
By mines — 58

To give a picture of how U-boat losses occurred, the following selection from 1915 to 1917 is probably representative. U-27 was destroyed on August 19, 1915, off Scilly, U-6 was torpedoed, U-41 was sunk by a Q-ship's gunfire, as was U-68 on March 22, 1916. U-74 was sunk by 4 trawlers, U-51 by the submarine H5, U-20 on November 4, 1916, after grounding, UB-19 by the Q-ship *Penshurst*, U-83 by the Q-ship *Farnborough* on February 12, 1917, U-85 by the Q-ship *Privet* off Start Point on March 12, 1917, and UC-29 by Q-ship *Pargust* on June 7, 1917.

In 1917, UC-66 was sunk off the Lizard by the trawler *Sea King*, UB-37 by the gunfire from a decoy, U-76 by being rammed by a trawler, and UC-48 by being rammed by a destroyer, U-83 by gunfire from a decoy, and U-68 was destroyed in the same area by her own mines. Later, U-81 was torpedoed and U-26 rammed and mined. However, depth-charges were sometimes used in addition, so that it may not always be strictly accurate to ascribe a destruction only to one sort of attack such as ramming or gunfire.

An Admiralty Memorandum of January, 1917, stated: 'The system of several ships sailing together in a convoy is not recommended in any area where submarine attack is a possibility'. The naval historian, John Winton, commented that the Memorandum: 'pigheadedly ignored all the lessons of past naval history'. Had losses continued at the high April rate, Britain would have been obliged to sue for peace within months, and the Admiralty could see no way of stopping this happening. Jellicoe was deeply pessimistic; his cautious, conservative temperament saved Britain in 1916, when he commanded the Grand Fleet against the German High Seas Fleet at the Battle of Jutland. He was criticised then by some members of a bellicose public for not bringing the German High Seas Fleet to close action when he had the opportunity, and he was blamed for the Royal Navy suffering higher losses in the battle than the enemy; but he won the action in strategic terms because the German fleet never again emerged in such force to challenge the dominance of the Grand Fleet. The nearest Scheer came to a repeat was in 1918, from 22nd to the 25th of April, when a portion of the German fleet sailed into the North Sea intending to intercept and destroy a British convoy bound from Scotland to Norway – but they had to turn back when it was discovered that the convoy had sailed at an earlier date. Thus the blockade of Germany was maintained over the four years, and slowly but inexorably began to have an effect on the German economy; the first obvious cracks in German morale were to occur, not among frontline troops, but among naval crews largely confined to inactivity within port. Actually, there was one more attempt at action when, on October 29, 1918, the High Seas Fleet was ordered out to the North Sea, presumably for one last desperate attempt at a showdown with the Grand Fleet; but the crews had had enough and mutinied, refusing to sail their warships; and so, on the next day, the order was cancelled. After the armistice on November 11, most of the German fleet was escorted across the North Sea to Britain and into 'captivity'.

It was mainly the relative weakness in numbers of the surface fleet which persuaded the Germans to intensify their U-boat campaign, a method of sea warfare which could be pursued irrespective of the superiority of Britain's 43 capital ships over Germany's 24. Therefore, in January, 1917, the Germans adopted unrestricted U-boat warfare, warning that all vessels approaching British shores would be liable to attack and this was done regardless of the offence this would cause to the USA.

The success of the policy can be seen in the losses of British, Allied and Neutral shipping in the early months of 1917 before the convoy system was adopted on May 10:

Ships Sunk		Tonnage (approx.)
January	181	298,000
February	259	468,000
March	325	500,000
April	423	849,000

To counter this form of warfare, Jellicoe's temperament was inappropriate, and, indeed, it can be claimed that he was the one man who nearly lost the war for Britain in one month after April, 1917. The trouble with so many admirals – and generals – is that their long service and training may have qualified them ideally for warfare in a way they have previously experienced, but not necessarily to unlearn this and adopt new tactics to suit changed circumstances. Another possible reason for this may have been that the average age of admirals was quite advanced – even though nowhere near as bad as the situation in 1840, when the Royal Navy had 33 admirals aged over 70 and only one under 65. Moreover, elderly commanders were a feature of many units in the 1st World War; the German general deploying forces against the French-held Verdun, Field Marshal Gottlieb von Haeseler, was eighty years old, and the supreme French army commander, Joffre, was 62 but behaved as an older man, going to bed at 10.00p.m. with nobody allowed to disturb him thereafter before morning. The situation was hardly better at first in the 2nd World War. Gamlin, the French commander was 68 in 1940 and rarely left his headquarters at Vincennes – where Mata Hari had been executed – and which was not even equipped with radio. He announced that 'to attack is to lose' and was replaced by the 73-year-old Weygand. With the British admirals, their dated professionalism seemed to inhibit their vision, and the Prime Minister, Lloyd George, became so concerned, indeed exasperated, by the short-sightedness of these experts that, conscious of Briand's and Clemenceau's remark that 'war is too important to be left to the generals', he intervened on May 10, 1917, and overruled the admirals, virtually threatening to replace them unless they immediately adopted the convoy system. For this dramatic act of leadership alone he deserves the title

(Above) *The seaplane base at Tresco as it appeared after the 1st World War. Some of the buildings did good service between the wars as bulb sheds.*

(Below) *The launching ramp for the seaplanes at New Grimsby, Tresco, with the old hangar buildings in the background. During the 1st World War the derelict 554 ton* Sophie *lay on the beach alongside the slipway; but all that remains of this former 'Marie Celeste of Scilly' are her sideboards, which adorn the Valhalla in Tresco Gardens, and her anchor set in cement on New Grimsby's harbour wall.*

1) *Short Cromarty 120 seaplanes were stationed at Tresco from 1917 in the 1st World War. Smaller Short 184 seaplanes were also there, and one of these (No. 8359) is preserved at the Imperial War Museum. This aircraft was a 2-seater biplane, the first British aircraft to carry a torpedo and to sink a ship with it. Felixstowe F3 seaplanes also served at Tresco.* Photo: Gibson, Scilly

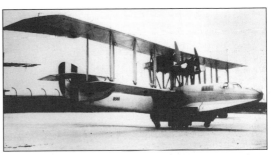

2) *Curtis H12 (Large America) at rest on the concrete standing.*

3) *Short 184 lifted by a crane and with a torpedo slung beneath.*

'the man who won the war' because the change of policy had an almost immediate beneficial effect; in July and August, 1917, only 5 out of about 800 ships sailing in convoy to and from Britain were sunk by U-boats and, by October, 1917, only 10 ships had been lost out of 1,502 sailing to and from Britain in 99 convoys. By the end of 1917, 98% of ships were getting through. Another way of presenting the figures is to state that U-boats sank 5,000 ships during the 1st World War, but after convoys were introduced in May, 1917, only 250 Allied ships were sunk during the rest of the war. Even so, Jellicoe, a conservative to his fingertips, was still reluctant to abandon his views, and he tried to limit convoying to homeward-bound shipping – and this obstinacy is not unconnected with his replacement as First Sea Lord by the more flamboyant Beatty in December, 1917.

* * * * *

The adoption of the convoy system meant that seaplanes could now be more effective in helping to defend merchant ships, and could watch out for U-boats which might be waiting in their paths. A seaplane patrolling along the convoy route ahead of a convoy might not sink or even sight a hostile submarine, but its presence could be a deterrent. The situation may be roughly compared to a policeman on his beat; he may never arrest or even see a criminal engaged in a nefarious act in his whole career, but his presence may deter all sorts of crime without his being conscious of it. A seaplane – a term which embraces float-planes and flying-boats – made its first flight in March, 1910, near Marseilles, but one of the most dramatic episodes involving seaplanes in the 1st World War was on September 15, 1916, when two Austrian flying-boats sank the French submarine *Foucault*, landing on the sea and taking all the submarine crew as prisoners. Britain used H-12 Curtiss and Felixstowe 2A flying-boats from 1916 against zeppelins; but they could not outclimb zeppelins even when the planes carried no bombs and were equipped only with guns to make them lighter. However on May 14, 1917, a Curtiss shot down Zeppelin L22 into the sea, and Zeppelin L43 a month later. In the West Country, seaplanes were based at Plymouth, Falmouth and Pembroke, as well as on Tresco from 1917, and by 1918 the GRW wheel-float attachment allowed floatplanes to taxi on land to and from the sea, but was not used in Scilly.

It was the need to give maximum help to individual merchant ships (and later to the convoys) which led to a seaplane base being established in Scilly. The idea of seaplanes coming to Scilly was to base them as far out in the Atlantic as possible. Their range was limited, so the Scillies represented the most westerly place from which they could fly to be of most use in searching for U-boats. They arrived in Scilly in January and were housed in a wooden hangar above the beach at Porthmellon, and on a concrete standing area which is still to be seen today. Two solid-wheeled lorries were brought over to Scilly late in 1916 to help build the hard standings and slipways – the first motor vehicles in Scilly. But their work on St Mary's proved useless, as it was quickly discovered that the waves breaking on the beach at Porthmellon were proving too much for the planes to be launched safely; so, by February 26, all the equipment and lorries had been transferred to near New Grimsby on the west side of Tresco, where at a later date were built hangars and a concrete stand – also still in existence – and where the waters of the channel between Tresco and Bryher are much calmer than at Porthmellon. The first aircraft at Porthmellon – which had proved unsatisfactory there – were sent back to the mainland; they were Curtiss H12 (large America) flying-boats, designated waterplanes before the 1st World War, and designed and built in the USA, but with two 250 horsepower Rolls Royce Eagle engines giving a maximum air speed of 85 mph and a landing speed on the water of around 55 mph The first one (8656), which came over to Scilly to start up the new base on Tresco, was piloted by the newly-appointed commanding officer of the Tresco Air

A British airship helping to escort an Allied convoy to Britain in the 1st World War.

The seaplanes on Tresco co-operated with British airships to provide protection for convoys and, in particular, to spot U-boats which might be lurking in the path of a convoy. In bad weather the Tresco seaplanes sometimes substituted for the mainland-based airships. Airships were occasionally moored approximately where Tresco heliport is now located. This provided a useful

halt for fresh fuel or supplies from the Air Station, particularly if bad weather had kept the airships aloft overlong in their patrols of the Western Approaches.

After the war, Britain built 17 rigid airships of the R series, but their future as passenger-travelling aircraft ended somewhat abruptly when the R101, in stormy weather, crashed in France on October 5, 1930, as a result of engine failure. It hit the ground, went up in flames and 48 lives were lost.

Station, Squadron Commander Hope-Vere, who flew in from the seaplane base at Plymouth on February 28, 1917, together with Flight Sub-Lieutenant W.L. Anderson and Air Mechanic McKenzie. A second Curtiss H12 (8652), piloted by Flight Sub-Lieutenants Railton and Hoare and with Leading Mechanic Birse, arrived shortly after, and made the first anti-U-boat operational patrol on February 28, and were soon joined by three crated Short 184 seaplanes shipped over and ready for assembly on Tresco. Short 184s were the most numerous of all RNAS aircraft in the 1st World War and even versatile enough to carry a torpedo instead of bombs, if required. Felixstowe flying-boats were to arrive a little later but, soon after establishment, the base was enabled in suitable weather to keep at least one seaplane permanently on patrol looking for U-boats during daylight hours – and eventually there were to be up to 22 aircraft of all three types at Tresco keeping several patrols daily. Included later were Felixstowe F2A and F3 flying-boats, which were stronger than the H12s and with more powerful Rolls Royce engines, and could carry a crew of five and four 230lb bombs, twice the load of the H12s. F2A and F3 flying-boats were made by Short Brothers in the Isle of Sheppey, were armed with two Lewis machine-guns, and had a maximum speed of about 95 mph. Britain was the first country in Europe fully to realise the value of flying-boats for reconnaissance and anti-submarine duties, and the 'F' series were the first to go into service in large numbers. The Germans had nothing equivalent, only float planes such as the FF33, the Gotha WD-14, and Brandenburg GWs – although these last had the ability also to drop torpedoes. From the start a report was written each evening setting out the day's flying activities at Tresco and sent to the Royal Navy Air Department's headquarters, which, in 1917, was at the Hotel Cecil in London. A practice

183

and training programme was devised which included dropping bombs on White Island off Samson as if it were a U-boat, and this has left a number of small pits on the island. To assist landing on the water and taxiing in poor light, especially at dawn and dusk, a gas light was installed on a beacon on Hulman rock – the beacon stand is still there – and search-lights were positioned at Woolpack, Steval and Bant's Carn. A floating-dock for the flying-boats was designed by E.J. Burling, traces of its remains could still be seen in August, 1982, at Green Par on Bryher.

Before the construction of the permanent air base buildings at New Grimsby, the crews were in bell tents, and a Bessonnean Tent, 200 feet long and 120 feet wide, was erected as a hangar for the planes and their equipment; but they had at first to use an old slipway and, although more and proper hangars were requested, they were not immediately granted, perhaps because the authorities wanted to see how the base performed before more resources were committed. On this score they need not have worried because, when the USA entered the war in 1917, there were immediately many more merchant ships vulnerable to U-boats approaching Britain and France, so the seaplane base in the Scillies was found increasingly useful in its anti-submarine role. Curiously, news of the USA's entry into the war in 1917 actually occupied less American newspaper columns than Lindbergh's rapturous ticker-tape reception from two million New Yorkers a decade later in 1927 on his return in May from his epic-making 33½ hour solo transatlantic flight of 3,500 miles to Paris.

On March 13, 1917, Flight Commander R.B. Maycock took over command of the station, and on his appointment was given extra aircraft to make up a complement of 12 of the large Curtiss H12 flying-boats – all coming from the seaplane experimental base at Felixstowe, together with 6 of the smaller Short 184 seaplanes, and 4 which were held in reserve on the mainland. With this number, it is hardly surprising that Maycock asked for extra hangarage as well. Many of his men on Tresco slept under canvas at first, and others were accommodated on St Mary's and ferried up to Tresco each day. A big steel and asbestos hangar was not built until 1918, the smaller original Bessoneaux ones only capable of taking the H12 when it took its wings off. When the slipway was at last constructed it had a rail- track of wooden beams on which a two-ton trolley carried the seaplanes down to the sea.

From 1917, the aircraft at Tresco were supplemented in their task of U-boat spotting and hunting by seaplanes at Newlyn, Bude, Laira, and Torquay, and by airships based at Mullion. But none of the First World War aircraft, airships or seaplanes, were fast fliers, and so, although attacks were pressed home on U-boats – thirteen by the seaplanes and flying-boats of Tresco – it was only rarely that a U-boat on the surface could be spotted without the aircraft also being detected by the U-boat. The result was that by the time the aircraft had flown to a position above the U-boat where it could drop a bomb

The Hulman as it was in the year 2000. In 1917, with a beacon on top, it marked the entrance to Tresco Channel for the seaplanesof the 1st World War. In the background are the familiar twin hills of the uninhabited island of Samson.

on it, the U-boat had crash-dived, and there might only be a few traces of an oil slick left to serve as a target. In such circumstances it was often difficult to know how much damage, if any, the bomb had done. On May 9th, 1917, one of the flying-boats (FB 8664) came down in the sea between St Mary's and St Agnes with the loss of three crew (Flt. Sub Lt. Railton. Flt. Sub Lt. Whigham and Leading Mechanic Birse). But, a few days later, came a great success, although involving a hazardous flight home; in his Flying Log Book, Sub-Lieutenant W.L. Anderson describes this, the first definite sinking on May 27, 1917, of a U-boat by an H12 flying-boat (8656) from the Royal Naval Air Station on Tresco. The seaplane took off on submarine patrol at 10.05 and was in the air for 45 minutes, flying at first at 1000 feet, looking for a U-boat which had been reported as having been seen to the north of the islands. At 10.20 they sighted it on the surface on their starboard bow, so they immediately altered course to attack. However, the U-boat also spotted them, for it opened fire with machine-guns, but in the seaplane they carried on and were able to drop four 100lb bombs, scoring two direct hits forward of the U-boat's conning tower. They saw the submarine sink by the bow, its stern coming right out of the water at an angle of 60°, and they observed bubbles, foam and a considerable quantity of oil appearing on the surface, at which they altered course and headed for home. But then they noticed that the submarine's machine-gun fire had caused a serious leak in the starboard radiator affecting the cooling system; Chief Petty Officer Tadman climbed out on to the wing and plugged the hole with rags and his handkerchief, which lessened the flow sufficiently for the seaplane to make the return flight. The visibility was excellent, and the destroyer *Medina* was sighted and was sent signals at 10.50; but the seaplane was losing height all the way back to base from the effects of what were subsequently discovered to have been eight hits from the machine-gun fire of the U-boat. All four crew received decorations for this success: Flight Sub-Lieutenant Anderson, D.S.C.; the pilot, Flight Sub-Lieutenant Hoare, D.S.C.; Chief Petty Officer Tadman, C.G.M.; and Wireless Telegraphist Chapman, D.S.M. Since 1997 the museum on St Mary's has had on display the Distinguished Service Medal awarded to Anderson for his sinking of this U-boat.

On another similar flight on October 14, 1917, Sub-Lieutenant Anderson in H12 (8680), with a crew consisting of McGill, Atkinson and Pike, dropped another four 100lb bombs near a U-boat, but this time failed to gain a direct hit and there was little sign of resulting damage. In the same seaplane they had dropped three 100lb bombs on a U-boat on August 21, but with a similar frustrating lack of any confirmation of any damage. Exactly the same situation occurred to 8665 which dropped 3 bombs on a submerged U-boat on June 25; but, without at least a sign of oil, a negative result had always to be recorded. On May 10, 1918, U-103 was hit by a bomb from N4341, but was not sunk; however, later, after U-103 had been sunk by the Olympic, its commander actually produced some fragments of the bombs which had damaged his vessel in the original air attack on June 25, which was unexpected and unusual confirmation from the enemy of how near the attack had come to being successful.

It was not only enemy action that accounted for the somewhat heavy losses of aircraft and of some men from the Tresco station. Two men, Air Mechanics William Creasey of Framlingham, and Charles Alfred Ellingworth of London, were killed when a shed on Tresco, a one-time potato-store but in 1917 used as a bomb store, exploded without warning on June 6, 1917, as a result, it was rumoured, of one of them having been trying to loosen a recalcitrant nut using a hammer; another accident scenario is that they were inserting a stiff fuse in a bomb and hammering it home with a piece of wood. Either way, it exploded and both died, a petty officer walking nearby lost an eye, and another airman received cuts. The two mechanics today lie buried in the churchyard on Tresco, where there is a memorial to them erected by the RAF. Another accident occurred on June 14, 1918; a pilot called Pike was drowned when his aircraft suddenly plummeted into the sea near the Bishop Rock lighthouse, the cause apparently being sudden engine failure. A similar cause may have been responsible for the seaplane which crashed on Peninnis Head on May 9, 1917, killing all 4 crew members.

On the plus side, the planes were able to provide much useful information, as, for instance, in May, 1918, when a number of U-boats were spotted off Scilly in the path of convoys, thus enabling Royal Navy surface warships to be directed to the area to deal with them.

But the seaplanes also had technical problems; there were difficulties experienced in operating the bomb-release gear, the Bowden cable-release being liable to corrode. On two occasions bombs became detached from a seaplane when it was landing on the water, resulting in explosions loud enough to be heard all over Scilly and, on both occasions, with some injury to the crews and damage to the aircraft. On May 29, 1917, an H12 had dropped four 100lb bombs on a U-boat and had seen an oil slick; but when they tried to drop some more bombs on another U-boat later on the same day, the bomb-release gear jammed, and the seaplane had to return to Tresco.

A modification was designed and made by the local blacksmith on St Mary's, and the fault seems to have been remedied. The pilots were also dissatisfied with the bomb-aiming equipment, and a modification was designed by Flight Sub-Lieutenant Anderson and fitted. This bomb aimer was tested successfully on a water tank on Bryher, and after the war was placed in the Fleet Air Arm Museum at Yeovilton. The weather could also cause problems for the seaplanes even when they were not flying; 3 seaplanes (8665, 8680, and 8686) were badly damaged in a gale, which sprung up on December 16, 1917, and lifted the parked planes off the ground and onto their sides. Later, Flight Sub-Lieutenant Anderson in F3 N 4000 had trouble upon landing his seaplane on August 7, 1918, but managed to beach the damaged aircraft on Samson without further mishap. A trouble of another kind was when some of the 230lb bombs, released properly and aimed accurately, nevertheless failed to explode; but on Tresco there was little they could do to rectify that manufacturing or design fault.

July, 1918, saw more U-boat activity in the Western Approaches, but high winds prevented airships based at Mullion on the mainland from escorting convoys, so Tresco seaplanes took over this role. The Curtiss H12B seaplane (N-4341), piloted by Captain V.B. Scriven and Lieutenant L.A. Rees, was patrolling above a convoy of 29 ships approaching UK waters, when they spotted mines laid by U-boats in the path of the convoy. The Tresco seaplanes quickly destroyed them with gunfire, for which the base received congratulations from the C. in C. Plymouth. Between March and October, 1918, N-4341 made 85 patrols, which was the record for aircraft based at Tresco.

Casualties occurred on July 5, 1918, when a Short seaplane (N-2963), piloted by Second Lieutenant J.C. Hendry, accompanied by his observer Lieutenant C.W. Capes, sent a wireless message that they had some flying problem and might have to land on the sea. They did not return, and a search was instituted the next day in Short (N-2955) piloted by Captain C.R. Morrish and his observer, Lieutenant W.R.L. Jenkins, and also by a Felixstowe F3 (N-4234), piloted by Captain C.R.H. Stewart and Lieutenant F.H. Prime, but no trace was ever found of N-2963; but one body, believed to have been Flying Officer Hendry's from this plane, was washed ashore near Ushant some time later; moreover, the searching Felixstowe N-4234 itself suffered from engine trouble and was forced to land on the sea, fortunately near to a hospital ship, the former liner *Braemar Castle*, which took the two airmen on board, the aircraft having to be abandoned.

A report to the war cabinet of August 17, 1917, written by General Smuts of South Africa, recommended the formation of the RAF to comprise all heavier than air flying machines. He wrote: 'aerial operations with their destruction of industrial and populous centres on a vast scale (could) become the principal operations of war to which the older forms of military and naval operations may become secondary and subordinate'. These far-sighted ideas proved to be at best premature, but the cabinet was convinced, and so the RAF was formed on April 1, 1918, despite opposition from Field Marshal Haig and others. One sartorial result of the amalgamation was The Royal Flying Corps' predominant influence on the RAF; it meant that many of its officers in the early years tended to wear white shirts, riding boots and carry a stick.

The RAF thus took over the air station at Tresco, and for the rest of the war operated the Short seaplanes as part of what was in August, 1918, called 234 Squadron RAF. Maycock was succeeded as the station commander on Tresco by Squadron Leader Cox, formerly of the Royal Flying Corps. In the 2nd World War, Richard Maycock became Britain's Air Attaché to Sweden.

A steel and asbestos hangar was eventually built at Tresco by the RAF in 1918, together with a slipway which had a new railtrack for ease in handling the aircraft; but there was felt to be some danger that a party from a U-boat might land at night and attack the base, so dogs were retained at the station to give the alarm if the enemy arrived by stealth.

On August 30, Captain Stewart and Lieutenant Fairhurst in a Felixstowe (N4238) spotted in the distance the conning tower of a U-boat which was crash-diving; Stewart dropped two 230lb bombs on the spot where the U-boat had submerged, but it had by then disappeared. However, on September 7 in the same seaplane, Captain Stewart spotted another U-boat in the act of torpedoing the Allied military transport ship, *Persic*, and observed another Felixstowe drop two 230lb bombs on the U-boat from which Stewart was able to confirm that the submarine had been sunk. The damaged *Persic* was then towed under escort from destroyers and from the seaplanes of Tresco; she was a former White Star liner of 8,273 tons, which had a crew of 56 and was transporting 2,108 American soldiers from New York to the Western Front. She was torpedoed about 50 miles west of Scilly, while she was the rear ship of a two column convoy, the second torpedo fired by a U-boat scoring a hit which created a hole 72 feet by 22 feet in the hull and caused a port list. *Persic* was sister ship of the *Delphic*, which had been torpedoed and sunk off Scilly only a few weeks previously on August 10, 1917, and this latest torpedoing could have become a repeat event; but no lives were lost, the troops being hastily transferred to destroyers and landed at Plymouth. The *Persic* was then brought slowly into Scilly on September 8, her supplies of bread, baked originally for the troops, were landed on St Mary's quay for the Islanders to help themselves, and found to contain delicious white flour, which would even take rebaking after getting a little wet in the drizzle.

Surplus meat and biscuits were also landed – a great bonanza lasting until the *Persic* left for more major repairs at Falmouth on September 24, with Captain Harvey eventually reimbarking his troops and able to deliver all of them safely to France to serve at The Front.

The last recorded attack on a U-boat in which a Tresco seaplane was involved was on October 11, 1918, when a Curtiss seaplane (4341) spotted the wake of a partially-submerged U-boat about 4 miles ahead of convoy HH71, which was sailing straight towards it. The seaplane dived down and bombed the area of sea where the by now submerged U-boat was estimated to be, and where there was a small tell-tale patch of oil; however, it is not known whether the U-boat was damaged, but the positive result was that the convoy reached port without being attacked.

* * * * *

The huge expansion of the RNAS during the war can best be demonstrated by numbers. At the outbreak the RNAS had 128 officers and about 700 ratings operating 40 aeroplanes, 31 seaplanes and 7 airships. By early 1918 there were about 650 seaplanes, 150 flying boats, 103 airships and 170 kite-balloons. Officer rank titles in the RNAS from July 1, 1914, were as follows:

RNAS	Naval Equivalent	RFC Equivalent, 1912-18
Wing Captain	Captain	Colonel
Wing Commander	Commander	Lieutenant-Colonel
Squadron Commander	Lieutenant-Commander	Major
Flight Commander	Lieutenant	Captain
Flight Lieutenant	Lieutenant	Lieutenant
Flight Sub-Lieutenant	Sub-Lieutenant	2nd Lieutenant

A two-inch gilt badge of an eagle was worn on the left sleeve (allegedly modelled on a brooch bought in Berlin by the wife of Captain Sueter), the forerunner of the wings worn subsequently on Fleet Air Arm sleeves.

Throughout the last years of the 1st World War, when the Tresco Station was operating, the seaplane aircrews showed great bravery and dedication in flying such craft and tackling the U-boats. However, that is not to claim that the service on Tresco compared in terms of danger and hardships with that suffered at that time by many soldiers in the trenches; the fact that some British soldiers on the Western Front – six of them only 16-years-old – were shot for cowardice by British firing squads suggests the contrary, especially as it now seems likely that many of these young men were more shell-shocked than fearful – a condition which would now be called 'post traumatic stress disorder', and first so-named in the USA in 1980.

The Germans, with an army many times the size of the British, shot fewer than 50 of their men in the 1st World War, but this was probably connected with the fact that the German army was largely a conscript army while the British were either 'regulars' or mainly volunteers until 1916. By 1916, official 'shell shock' casualties were 16,000, but this 'condition' was afterwards no longer recognised, it is said because the pension bill was rising sharply.

The first British soldier shot for desertion was Thomas Highgate, aged 19, from Shoreham near Sevenoaks in Kent, who had been a farm labourer. After two weeks with the West Kent Regiment in the front line at Mons, he ran away from the battlefield, telling his companions that he could not take it any longer. He was later discovered hiding in a barn, dressed in civilian clothes which he had pilfered from a scarecrow; he was found guilty by court martial and shot at dawn on September 6, 1914, the first of 286 British soldiers executed for desertion between 1914 and 1918. In 2000 a campaign was waged to have his name added to the war memorial in Shoreham village, where are inscribed the names of 51 others of the village who lost their lives through enemy action. The majority of villagers in 2000 voted in favour of the addition, whereas had the vote been taken at any time over a decade previously, it is dubious whether it would have been positive. It is one of those cases where both sides of the question are clear and evoke strong sympathies; but what is now increasingly appreciated is the enormous amount of fright Highgate must have endured to 'let down' his colleagues so badly. Mountesquieu wrote that 'a rational army would run away', so, when men are ordered 'over the top' into a hail of machine-gun fire, it is hardly surprising if the odd one opts for rationality. Gradual but important changes have taken place in armies since the 1st World War, especially has the belief diminished in war as a glorious opportunity to test manhood, although there still exists the glorification of elite organisations such as the SAS. Executing young men in the 1st World War may be judged wrong now, but it was then entirely in accordance with law. Moreover, it is worth pointing out that the boys of 16 who were shot must have claimed to be of higher age when they enlisted, and none of them is thought to have admitted being under age when brought to court. Moreover, Haig refused to confirm death sentences on some 90% of those placed before him, always trying to give a second chance where any doubt could possibly exist. In all the British services only 306 men out of about 5 million were executed – not a high proportion; most of them could not be said to have been shell-shocked, over 200 were accused of 'aggravated desertion', and others of offences such as deserting an important post, striking an officer, or flagrantly disobeying orders – with only 18 tried for actual cowardice. These figures can be compared with the average number of 400 servicemen who each day gave their lives over 4 years doing their duty. Moreover, there was no army on either side in the 1st World War which did not possess the death penalty for similar offences.

The ordinary modern soldier finds himself employed on many more and different tasks to frontline fighting; he feels himself sometimes more in the role of a policeman or social worker, sorting out a situation as a peacekeeper, not one expecting to kill, let alone be killed. His changing role is recognised at West Point Military Academy in the USA, where the word 'kill' is avoided as much as possible in the 21st century military training programme. However, the increase of danger and discomfort of infantrymen over airmen in the 1st World War can be exaggerated; casualties to airmen could also be high, and the life expectancy of a pilot in the Royal Flying Corps in Flanders was down to not much more than four weeks by April, 1917, and it was similarly short for their opponents..

The public knew about the German air ace, Baron von Richthofen, because Germany made a point of publicising his successes. Richthofen had an unparalleled successful career, with a score of 80 'planes downed', the next highest being Udet with 62; this compares with Mannock's and Bishop's 70 each. Richthofen's end came in 1918; Lieutenant Wilfred May, a relatively novice pilot in a Sopwith Camel, dived on Baron von Richthofen's red Fokker tri-plane, but was chased and tried to escape by hedge-hopping. The experienced Canadian pilot, Roy Brown, immediately dived down on Richthofen and opened fire to try and save May from the consequences of his somewhat foolhardy attack; at the same time Australian troops on the ground joined in and fired at the red Fokker. Richthofen received a bullet nearly through the heart; he managed to land safely behind German lines, but died in his cockpit, and whether the bullet was Canadian or Australian is still a matter of some controversy.

After the war the Tresco base was used for experimental work, and a prototype Short Cromarty came to Scilly but was damaged beyond repair when it taxied onto a reef. It is said that this accident directed Oswald Short's attention to building improved metal hulls on all his seaplanes.

* * * * *

The 1st World War ended formally at the eleventh hour of the eleventh day of the eleventh month of 1918 in calm, sunny weather. By then, all fit men in Scilly, up to the age of 45, were in the Services or in reserved occupations, and some of these went on to take part in the Afghan War, 1918-20, while others were taken back into pre-war occupations by former employers, if still in business. 45 Scillonians gave their lives fighting in the armed services in the 1st World War, their names recorded on the War Memorial in Old Town Churchyard; but this does not record service personnel posted to the Islands, who died in Scilly. 234 Squadron RAF was finally disbanded at Plymouth in May, 1919, when under the command of Wing Commander (later Air Commodore) Gerrard. An RAF Seaplane Development Flight was briefly re-established in Scilly in August, 1922, under Squadron Leader R.B. Maycock, who had been at Tresco in the RNAS in 1917. The purpose of the exercise was to practise operating flying-boats away from their home base, but the establishment lasted only just under three weeks; it included four aircraft – two Felixstowe's, a Phoenix and a Short Cromarty N120 – but heavy seas made use of their accompanying floating-dock difficult, and St Mary's Roadstead proved a little too exposed for an anchorage. Moreover, the need for economies in expenditure brought about the final closure of the Tresco Air Station.

The Roll of Honour, in the parish church of St Mary's, was the gift of Mrs Addison, and also gives the names of 45 Scillonians who gave their lives in the 1st World War. The design was by Professor Richardson, architect to the Duchy of Cornwall, and has a cross at the top, a bay-leaf at the bottom, and the 14th century lamp in front of it was also the gift of Mrs Addison, wife of Dr W.B. Addison, Scilly's hardworking doctor from 1912 to 1927. The wooden roll in 1926 replaced a former cardboard one that was thought less than suitable for the purpose. In St Martin's churchyard are the graves of four seamen whose ship was sunk by a U-boat, and there is also a War Memorial Cross commemorating three men from St Martin's – all surnamed Ashford – who died on active service in the 1st World War.

As for the surrender of German arms in 1919, German U-boats, 176 in number, were held at Harwich, but 74 German surface warships were brought over the North Sea and interned together at Scapa Flow, with many of their German crews still on board but not allowed ashore; on June 24, the British Fleet at the Flow (the 1st Battle Squadron under Admiral Fremantle) – other than a few destroyers left on guard – all put to sea for 'an exercise', despite the fact that the war was over. The Germans then took this opportunity to relieve their humiliation and salvage some of their honour; at a signal at 11.20a.m. from Admiral von Reuter, nearly all the German warships ran up the German ensign, opened their seacocks and watertight doors and gradually sank to the sea bottom, their crews all taking to their boats safely. One British destroyer, in a display of frustration, opened fire to try to stop them, only succeeding in killing the captain of the German battleship *Markgraf* and nine of his crew. Such reaction, though perfectly understandable, was remarkably ill-conceived; if it had succeeded in sinking German ships, it would in effect, have been helping the Germans to do what they were already intent on doing anyway. 48 German ships sank, including 11 of the 12 battleships – the *Baden* was beached in shallow water – all five battlecruisers, four of the eight cruisers – the others being beached – and about 36 of the 50 destroyers, with some of these still lying on the Flow's seabed even in the 21st century, a rusting memorial to the former High Seas Fleet. The mass scuttling created a scene of unique and remarkable confusion, reported with scorn in British newspapers but greeted as a triumph in the German press.

* * * * *

Between the wars there was little military preparedness in Scilly because what was called 'the war to end all wars' had just been fought. But there were a few visits from big warships on exercises, which had the unintended effect of widening the marriage opportunities of Scillonian girls at a time when women still considerably outnumbered men in the population. Marian Hicks of St Agnes, for example, daughter of Obadiah Hicks (he who gave his name to the barrow on Gugh) met her future husband, Warrant Officer Camp, when the 33,000 ton battleship *Rodney* paid a 5-day visit to the Islands from July 6th to 10th in 1930, during which much entertainment was organised for and by the 1,400 members of the crew.

After the war, the first plane to land in Scilly was a de Havilland Gipsy Moth in 1929, which had been flown from Cornwall by Lord Sempill, then president of the Aeronautical Society. He came again in 1931 on a seaplane – a de Havilland Puss Moth – which he parked in Hugh Town Harbour. On Friday, March 30, 1930, another Gipsy Moth flew over to Scilly; it was owned by the Prince of Wales. This was only the second land plane to come to Scilly, and it brought Major MacCormack, the Secretary to the Duchy of Cornwall, the 'plane landing on the Garrison sports field. After depositing Major MacCormack, the pilot took off and 'looped the loop' over Hugh Town for the entertainment of the islanders who crowded the streets to watch him – in the 1930s an aeroplane was still an unfamiliar sight and people would rush to the windows just to see one pass over. After this aerobatic display the pilot landed on the golf links, from whence he picked up Major MacCormack in the afternoon and flew him back to the mainland, an unremarkable event today but quite an occasion at the time.

In 1913 the furthest any aircraft had flown was 630 miles over land. Then the *Daily Mail* offered £10,000 to anyone who managed to fly non-stop across the Atlantic. In response, Harry Hawker took off from St John's in Newfoundland on May 18, 1919, in a single-engined biplane, with his colleague K. Mackenzie Grieve as navigator, intending to land at Connemara in Ireland. But engine trouble and bad weather brought them down in the sea, where they had the good fortune to be rescued by a passing ship. Another vessel came upon their biplane which was brought home and later exhibited at Selfridges store in London. Glenn Curtiss also took up the challenge in 1919 using 4 flying-boats and impressive organisation. He arranged for a fleet of 5 battleships, 5 cruisers, 27 destroyers and 2 tankers to be placed across the Atlantic at suitable intervals below the intended flight path. Despite this planning, success evaded him: flying-boat NC-1 force-landed near the Azores and sank; NC-2 caught fire even before becoming airborne; NC-3 lost its way, came down on the sea and had to taxi to the Azores; only NC-4 managed eventually to reach Plymouth, but after several stops during a journey of 11 days.

One successful pair of fliers over the intervening ocean were Boyd and

Captain Boyd's Columbia *awaiting refuelling on Pentle Beach, Tresco, after its epic transatlantic flight.* Photo: Gibson, Scilly

Connor. Captain J. Erral Boyd, accompanied by Lieutenant R.P. Connor as his navigator, were two transatlantic fliers who made an epic journey across the Atlantic in 1930. Their aircraft was called *Columbia*, also named *The Maple Leaf*, and was a single-engined Wright-Bellanca monoplane with a Wright Whirlwind engine. They set off from St Hubert Airport, Montreal, on September 22 and landed at Harbour Grace in Newfoundland, taking off from there to begin their transatlantic flight on October 9. 23½ hours later and short of fuel, they landed without mishap on Pentle Beach, Tresco, having experienced oil pressure trouble. They discovered that a blocked oil pipe was the cause of the trouble, and this may have persuaded them during their flight to jettison a petrol tank as a precaution, so diminishing their fuel supply. RAF Mount Batten supplied them with more fuel, and the fuel used was brought over to Scilly by a flying-boat and then taken up to Pentle Bay in the fishing boat *Violet* owned by Matt Lethbridge (senior) and his brother, whose father, once a sailor on the *Cutty Sark*, had performed a similar task during the 1st World War supplying fuel to the air base on Tresco. After this, the aircraft took off from the beach safely and arrived on October 11, 1930, at Croydon airport to a tumultuous welcome. The same two airmen in the same aircraft later flew from New York to Haiti. Actually, they were not the only aviators to land on Pentle Beach; on February 24, 1932, Colonel Paynter, Master of Sempill, flew from Boskenna near Penzance and landed there to have lunch at Tresco Abbey.

Neither were they the first Britons to make the transatlantic flight. That had already been achieved by Captain John Alcock and Lieutenant Arthur Whitten Brown, a flight which is often claimed to have been the launch of transatlantic air travel. Their Vickers Vimy bomber is now hanging from the

194

roof in the Science Museum in London. But if Boyd and Connor, running short of petrol and having to land on Pentle Beach, Tresco, sounds risky, it was not so hair-raising as Alcock and Brown's flight, for not only were they the first two to fly the Atlantic successfully, but they did so in open cockpits.

Arthur Whitten-Brown was a Glasgow-born, 33-year-old former navigator with the Royal Flying Corps who had been shot down in the war, damaged his leg and walked with a stick. Despite this handicap, he got a job with Vickers Aircraft Factory which involved flying with Captain John Alcock – a war ace, who had made a reputation by dropping the first bomb on Constantinople (Istanbul) in September, 1917 – to make an attempt to win the £10,000 prize put up by the *Daily Mail* for the first plane to fly the Atlantic.

Loaded with extra tanks, in which were 870 gallons of fuel, the plane took off from Newfoundland on June 14, 1919. After 5 hours at about 90 mph, flames from the starboard engine melted an exhaust pipe. They carried on, but a thunderstorm forced the plane down from 5,000 feet to below 500 – but again they carried on. Then, the air intakes to the engine carburettors began to freeze with snow. Brown had to struggle out along each wing in turn while Alcock kept the plane absolutely level; holding on to the struts with one hand, Brown opened his penknife with his teeth and proceeded to cut away the frozen snow from the intakes. It took him six trips altogether out along the wings, but once he was safely back in the cockpit, Alcock was able to fly the plane up to 11,000 feet above the snowstorm. However, the cold at that height produced ice on the wings and the controls became increasingly stiff, so they flew down to find warmer air, spotted land and what they thought was a flat field, and landed on it to discover it was actually a Galway bog. They came to a halt nose down and tail up but unharmed, after a flight of nearly 16½ hours. They won the £10,000 prize and received knighthoods, but months later Alcock was killed in an air crash and Brown never left the ground again. A statue of Alcock and Brown today stands at Heathrow commemorating their epic journey.

The first person to make the flight solo across the Atlantic and non-stop was Charles Lindbergh (1902-74) – nicknamed the Lone Eagle – and in 1927 the 79th person to make a transatlantic flight. He flew from New York landing at Le Bourget at Paris on May 21, 1927, covering a distance of 3,610 miles in 33½ hours. Lindbergh took meticulous preparations over the flight and reported that, as he could not allow himself to sleep on the journey, he kept awake by flying low 'where the sight of waves would make the way more interesting'. Almost forgotten is that Lindbergh flew combat missions against the Japanese during the Second World War and that he did important work towards the development of the artificial human heart; more people remember his supposed admiration of Hitler and the Luftwaffe in the 1930s – a view shared by many others at that time on both sides of the Atlantic, who later preferred to forget it.

Sir John William Alcock (1892-1919) and Sir Arthur Whitten-Brown (1886-1948) were British airmen and became the first non-stop fliers to cross the Atlantic, and so won the Daily Mail's *£10,000 prize. They flew from Newfoundland to Ireland in a Vickers-Vimy bomber, stripped of all unnecessary fittings to allow for the extra weight of additional fuel tanks, and arrived in June, 1919, having made the journey at an average speed of just over 120 m.p.h. A few months after their epic flight the British Airship R34 also crossed the Atlantic in 108 hours, rather overshadowing their achievement. Alcock was killed a few months later on a journey by air to France.*

(below) shows the Vickers-Vimy bomber after it had landed in a boggy Irish field in 1919. Armed guards stand around to repel souvenir seekers.

Charles Lindbergh made the first solo crossing of the Atlantic in the knowledge that six pilots had died in previous attempts. He had no wireless or sextant, but made sure he would not run out of fuel by giving his plane, *The Spirit of St Louis* (a 46 feet wingspan Ryan monoplane), several extra fuel tanks. He spent 2 nights in the air, reaching Le Bourget airfield 33½ hours after setting off, thus travelling at an average speed of 107.5 mph. His aircraft was never flown by anybody else and now hangs in the Air Museum in Washington DC, and Lindbergh won the 25,000 dollar prize for his achievement.

In the course of time, however, the Lone Eagle, as Lindbergh was called, became unpopular with the Jews because he warned of what he called 'undue influence of Jews in the American media' (*Sunday Times*, 6.9.98). It was also later remembered and held against him that he had accepted an invitation from Goering to visit the Luftwaffe, although his connection with the Nazi was owing mainly to a shared interest as ace fliers, for Goering, for all his faults, had been a respected pilot (he scored 22 victories in air combat) and had been Baron von Richthofen's successor as leader of 'the circus' on Richthofen's death in 1918. He qualified as a German air ace, but national differences were displayed in the qualifications needed to be called an air 'ace'. In France, a pilot had to have shot down over 5 enemy planes or balloons – their greatest ace being Fouck who scored 75; in Germany, a pilot had to have shot down ten enemy aircraft, and Manfred von Richthoven had 80, mostly in his red Fokker triplane. In Britain, there was no official score, partly because Haig felt that much publicity for airmen might be at the expense of the work of his ground troops. As a result, although the Britons, Mannock and Bishop, both had scores over 70, they are not exactly household names today.

Thus it was principally a common interest in air matters that drew Lindbergh to Goering and the Luftwaffe, more than an especial interest in Nazi ideology. His reported remarks, although judged politically incorrect today and 'right-wing', were really reflecting part of the racism which was commonplace in many countries in the 1930s. For example, there was then a fairly widespread belief that African people, although considered brawnier generally than white people, were not regarded as brainy. It can be seen how this idea may have arisen because at the time those people of African origin generally found themselves limited to manual and less intellectually-demanding labour. Moreover, there were many other people, even more distinguished than Lindbergh, who also visited Nazi Germany and were urging peace; the ex-King Edward VIII, later Duke of Windsor, made a wireless broadcast after visiting Hitler (even pleasing his hosts by making an attempt to give the Nazi salute), imploring political leaders 'to save humanity from the terrible fate which threatens it today'; but the BBC decided not to broadcast the speech in this country, and, in any case, European politicians

The Hindenburg *descends in flames. In 1900 Count Zeppelin (1838-1917) made his first airship, with an aluminium frame and powered by two engines. His first travel company was formed in 1909, but it is for his wartime zeppelins that he is best remembered in Britain because of their use as bombers.*

However, it was in their use after the war as passenger-carrying craft across the Atlantic that they were to prove most successful. From the first passenger flights in 1910, no German passenger airship had ever crashed; then, on May 6, 1937, after crossing the Atlantic, and just after passing over New York's Empire State Building – opened in 1931, and at 1,472 feet the world's tallest building for 40 years and a treat for the passengers to see it from above – the giant airship Hindenburg *was approaching its mooring mast at Lakehurst when its 7,000,000 cubic feet of hydrogen burst suddenly into flames; 37 of the 97 passengers and crew died in such a horrific manner that the sister airship,* Graf Zeppelin, *which had sometimes flown over Scilly on its transatlantic trips, was withdrawn from service in 1938, so marking the end of German passenger-airship travel in the 20th century.*

Recent research suggests that the inflagration of the hydrogen was the result of a fire not the cause of it, and that the Graf Zeppelin, *in similar circumstances, would not have caught fire. It is believed that, for some unknown reason during manufacture, the covering of the* Hindenburg *was given a mixture containing iron oxide and powdered aluminium – this latter to reflect the sun's rays — and that this only needed an electrostatic charge to ignite. This may have been provided by nearby thunderstorms, which had already delayed the arrival time of the airship; in other words, the* Hindenburg *could have met with disaster, whether filled with hydrogen or not.*

The Graf Zeppelin *first flew across the Atlantic in October, 1928, at a cruising speed of 70 mph and propelled by five engines. She carried up to 20 passengers in comfort, and had a crew of twice that number.*

An airship passes over Tresco on July 11, 1936. Photo: Gibson, Scilly

were by that time mostly too committed to their policies to respond positively.

Some of the German leaders in the 1930s seem to have been misled concerning the British attitude towards Germany owing to their contacts with so-called 'top people'; Ribbentrop, for example, the German foreign minister, was always welcome at the 'Clivedon set', the guests of the Astors, where he seems to have gathered the opinion – and passed this on to the German government – that Britain would not fight Germany as they had no fundamental quarrel with each other. The influential Mitford sisters, on the other hand, possessed widely differing political views; but Unity Mitford was quite enamoured of Hitler – even sitting for hours waiting for a sight of him in the Osteria Restaurant in Munich in his earlier days – and was in Germany when war broke out. With Hitler's permission and connivance she returned to England from Germany via Switzerland after Christmas in 1939, still an admirer of Hitler but forced by war to choose her own country. Lindbergh had not been an uncritical admirer, so it may seem a little unfair to criticise him alone for expressing opinions widely shared by others at that time, and his anti-Semitism was never as pronounced as that of some other prominent people who still remain venerated for little obvious reason – the film actor Errol Flynn, for instance. Anti-Semitism is not prejudice just against the Jews, but against Arabs, Assyrians, Phoenicians as well as Jews – all those races supposed to be descended from Shem, the son of Noah.

Still more people probably remember Lindbergh for the kidnapping on March 1st, 1932 – from out of his 2nd floor nursery window reached by means of a ladder – of Lindbergh's blond, curly-haired, dimple-chinned, blue-eyed, 20-month-old baby son, which he nicknamed 'Little It'. Lindbergh paid out a huge ransom to the kidnappers ($50,000 in numbered dollar bills), only to discover 2 months later that the baby had already been killed, the body being found in a shallow grave in woodland 5 miles from home. The murder was called 'the crime of the century' and the sad sight of Lindbergh cutting one tiny, fair curl from his son's body lingered in the mind.

(Top) *De Havilland Dragon G-ACPY of* Channel Air Ferries, *with its wings folded back prior to parking in the hangar at Land's End Aerodrome. G-ACPY was first registered with* Olley Air Services *in 1934, but was sold in 1935 to a new company,* Aer Lingus, *and became that company's first aeroplane. It flew a regular service between Dublin and Bristol, with occasional flights to the Isle of Man. The plane became Olley's again in 1936, his airline then merging with* Great Western and Southern Air Lines. *The service to Scilly opened from St Just on September 15, 1937, and was operating under Olley's subsidiary,* Channel Air Ferries, *when G-ACPY was shot down by a Heinkel on June 3, 1941, with the loss of all 6 people on board. There were about 70 Dragons operating throughout the UK in the late 1930s, and G-ACPY was replaced by a similar aircraft, G-AECZ, which had been used by the RAF since October 11, 1939, and from 1941 served on the route to Scilly for many years.*

(Middle) *G-AECZ, registered as EI-AFK, ended its operational flying days in Ireland in 1959, having been used since 1950 to take people for short pleasure trips over Ireland.* Aer Lingus, *its owners, realised the aircraft's historical importance and then painted it in the original manner they had operated G-ACPY, known as the first IOLAR, and suspended this new IOLAR in 1976 from the roof of Dublin Airport, making it airworthy again in 1986 to celebrate the 50th birthday of* Aer Lingus.

(Bottom) *shows G-AECZ in its* British European Airways *livery in the late 1940s on the Scilly route.*

Also sad was the arrest of Bruno Hauptmann, a German carpenter and immigrant, who was tried and convicted for the crime – allegedly mainly on faked police evidence – such as a planted ransom note in his pocket together with Lindbergh's numbered dollar bills – and Hauptmann was executed in an electric chair on April 4, 1936. The harassed Superintendent of the New Jersey State Police at the time was H. Norman Schwarzkopf, father of the commander of the later 'Operation Desert Storm' in the Gulf War against Iraq. Sad also was the suicide of the Lindbergh's British maid, Violet Sharp, who admitted she had inadvertently given away the time when the Lindbergh child would be at the family home in Hopewell, New Jersey. Among those horrified by the crime, and who contributed most generously to the Lindbergh fund, was Al Capone – the little fat man from Chicago who was said to have murdered 40 people, mostly other gangsters, and was for six years the USA's most notorious gangster; but then, he did also set up soup kitchens for the poor, and was at the time suffering humiliation from other inmates in Alcatraz – being called 'the wop with the mop'. From his prison cell he put up 10,000 dollars 'for information leading to the arrest of the kidnappers', but he had acquired syphilis and died at the age of 47. He managed on six occasions to avoid convictions on serious charges because – or so it was alleged – juries were afraid of him; he was eventually 'put away' in 1931 on a charge relating to the relatively minor offence of tax evasion. He was also well known for his areas of ignorance; he once said in reply to a question, 'I don't even know what street Canada is on'.

Other airmen were not so lucky as Lindbergh in their attempts to cross the Atlantic. In 1927 two planes, each carrying two people and flying in consort, vanished without trace during the flight, and, in the following year, H.C. MacDonald, flying solo, set off for Britain in his Gipsy Moth and was likewise never seen again, the only clue to his fate being a rusty can washed up on a British beach in 1929 carrying the cryptic message 'Going down in mid-Atlantic, engine trouble', followed by what looked like his scrawled signature. Another unsuccessful flight occurred in 1928, when Captain Hinchliffe and Elsie Mackay set off on March 13 to fly across the Atlantic but, likewise, were never seen or heard from again.

One extraordinary flight was that of Douglas Corrigan in 1938; he set off from New York for Los Angeles but, owing to the navigational error of forgetting to deduct 180°, he headed west instead of east, high above low cloud, landing 29 hours later near Dublin.

There was considerable competition between transatlantic fliers, not all of it aboveboard – Balbo of Italy even being suspected of trying to put castor oil in the food of his rivals – but only Boyd force-landed in Scilly. But there were other involuntary aircraft landings in Scilly, mainly seaplanes which had been catapulted off transatlantic liners such as the *Europa*, *Bremen* and *Ile de France* to carry mail to Britain and the Continent in advance of the liner's arrival, but which, owing to some mishap, were forced to land in Scilly for repair. These planes from liners usually passed safely and regularly over Scilly without incident, the islands providing them with a convenient navigation check.

* * * * *

But there were many other things to divert and amuse the public between the wars other than flying-machines. In 1929 Al Jolson – with what in the

201

Passengers about to climb aboard De Havilland Dragon G-ACPY of Channel Air Ferries
*for the return flight from St Mary's to St Just. Two of the passengers are wearing fur coats
which was not unusual in the 1930s because there was no adequate heating on the aircraft,
and cold breezes could blow over the aerodromes. Dragons – and Dragon Rapides which
succeeded them – were recognised as very safe aircraft for the times, and had the distinction
of being the first aircraft to convey a British monarch as a passenger – King George V from
Bircham Newton in Norfolk to Hendon.*

21st century would be regarded as a politically-incorrect blackened face –
made the first feature-length talking film. It was described by one 'quality'
newspaper as 'a freak, for the silent film would always be the real cinema'.
But Jolson sang *Sonny Boy* in it, a song that 'swept the world'. Then there
was the emergence of the cheap motor-car, 1931 Morris Minors were still
running in the late 1940s, and in the mid 1930s Henry Ford produced his
Model Y for £100. This led to traffic jams, not always unproductive
occasions, for Noel Coward, sitting in one in a taxi in 1928, claimed that he
had composed his waltz song *I'll See You Again*.

* * * * *

It was Claude Grahame-White in 1910 who brought the first plane to fly
over Cornwall and came as far as Mounts Bay, but not to Scilly. The initial
groundwork for starting a civil air service to Scilly was made in 1935 by the
aviator Sir Alan Cobham who, in 1927, the year of Lindbergh's famous solo
transatlantic flight, had also achieved fame by flying 23,000 miles around
Africa in the prototype of the Short Sunderland flying-boat. He was one of
the greatest pioneers of air travel, exploring and planning air routes
throughout the British Commonwealth. In 1926, he flew 26,000 miles to
Australia and back, on his return in October alighting on the River Thames
beside the Houses of Parliament, although the success of his flight on that

occasion was saddened by the news that his mechanic, A.B. Elliott, was not with him, as he had been killed by a bullet shot by a hostile Arab as they flew over the desert near the Persian Gulf. Aircraft are so universal today that it is sometimes forgotten how much many people resented them at first, if only for their intrusiveness and ghastly noise. Apropos of noise, it is sometimes forgotten how quiet the world used to be before the 1st and 2nd World Wars, and especially before the widespread use of internal combustion engines. In 1798, for instance, at the Battle of Aboukir Bay, otherwise known as the Battle of the Nile, Nelson won a great victory over the French fleet that had conveyed Napoleon and his army to Egypt. One of Nelson's ships was the was the 74-gun *Colossus* acting then as a supply ship to Nelson's fleet, and later to sink off Samson with some of the Duke of Hamilton's priceless art treasures on board – although these have now mostly been recovered, as have the ship's guns, a couple of them still serving as bollards on St Mary's quay. What happened at this battle in 1798 was that the huge French flagship, the *Orient*, blew up, in the loudest, biggest, brightest – and certainly most costly in terms of human life – of any explosion that century. There were relatively few means of making a great noise in the 18th century, so this one stood out, caused by the ignition of large quantities of gunpowder below the decks of the *Orient*. So great was the detonation that the battle ceased for a time, both sides horrified by the occurrence. English captains and Nelson sent pinnaces from their ships to help the hundreds of wounded among the enemy, such a big impression did the explosion make. After Nelson's death at Trafalgar in 1805, his coffin was made from wood salvaged from the unlucky French flagship.

* * * * *

Alan Cobham was the first to plan an air service to Scilly, and set up a company to inaugurate a service to Scilly but, before it functioned, sold out to Captain Gordon Olley, who had founded *Olley Air Service* in 1934 and had previously been a pilot with *Imperial Airways* and, before that, a pilot in the 1st World War. Olley called his new company for the air service to Scilly *Channel Air Ferries* from May 8, 1936, and selected an area near St Just for his enterprise, which soon became known as Land's End Aerodrome. Later, it was in the ownership of the Ministry of Civil Aviation but, since 1970, has been owned by the local council, with Westward Airways as their agent – its main shortcomings being the frequency of fog and water-logging of the grass, which has led to the periodic demands for tarmac. In June, 1937, a 4,000 square foot hangar from an airfield near Blackpool was re-erected on it by Olley, a man distinguished for enterprise and vision and already well known for his victory in a race against the *Flying Scotsman* – plane versus train – in 1928. In Scilly, where Olley was much respected, he persuaded St

Mary's golf-club to remove some bunkers and other obstacles from near the 5th and 7th fairways so that these areas could be used as runways by his aeroplanes. Two runways were arranged, roughly at right angles to each other to allow aircraft to land on one of them while still heading more or less into wind, and one was 1,290 feet long and the other of 1,365 feet. The service was begun on September 15, 1937, by a de Havilland Dragon (G-ADCR) – which also came from Blackpool – and it was piloted by a New Zealander, Captain D.L. Dustin. Up to four people were employed at the St Mary's airport, some to man the ticket hut and a boy to ring a handbell to warn golfers to take cover when an aircraft was approaching to land or take-off – just shouting 'fore' being judged inadequate. Golfers were sometimes co-opted to help hold down a plane's wings – when a stiff breeze was blowing – to enable passengers to alight safely.

At a time when the *Scillonian* took about 3½ hours at an average speed of 12 knots on passage to Scilly from Penzance, Olley was running scheduled flights to Scilly taking about 20 minutes. At first it was considered a safe operation, but in fog on June 26, 1938, a 'plane of Channel Air Ferries from Scilly crashed on landing at St Just, and the pilot, Captain Dustin, died. On the following December 18, another plane of Channel Air Ferries crashed on take-off, but this time nobody was seriously hurt. Both accidents were the results of pilot error in adverse conditions, and the Dragon, and its successor the Dragon-Rapide, later proved themselves very safe aircraft for the service.

Olley also improved the wartime postal service to Scilly. He arranged with the GWR and the Southern Railway Company to take post to Scilly, with a fee charged for the additional service of 4d for up to 2ozs; 7d up to 4ozs; 11d up to 16ozs.

Fares over to Scilly in the early Dragons were £1 single and a little more than that for a return, the tickets being interchangeable with the Isles of Scilly Steamship Company's tickets for the *Scillonian*. Three return flights a day were scheduled for the summer of 1938, with a free bus ride from the railway station at Penzance to St Just Aerodrome to connect with every flight. In those less serious days, it was not unusual for the pilot of the 'plane to vary his routine and amuse his passengers by 'buzzing' the *Scillonian*, flying low over the ship as she ploughed her way between the mainland and Scilly, to the delight of passengers lining her decks – and all undertaken as a contribution to the relaxed holiday atmosphere.

The wood and fabric Dragon-Rapide biplane introduced in September, 1943, with its 200 horse-power engines and a cruising speed in good conditions of up to 132 mph, was economical for the time, ideal for small grass airfields with its short take-off requirement, and was capable of carrying up to eight passengers. It was to serve as the main passenger aircraft on the Scilly route when Great Western and Southern Airways became part of British European Airways in 1947, until replaced by BEA helicopters in

1964 – and, even then, continued to be used on the route for a time by some small, independent companies. Great Western and Southern Air Lines had been formed in December, 1938, and took over the scheduled flights to Scilly – running them most of the time until 1947 – and, by the summer of 1939, operating eight return flights each day from St Just in high summer. But the conflicting claims on the use of the course from golfers led to a new landing ground being built approximately 36 metres above mean sea level at High Cross on St Mary's. It was first used on July 5, 1939, and, since the war, has developed into the present-day airport; but within two months of its original opening, Britain declared war on Germany on September 3, 1939, and so the war fought 'to end war', between 1914 and 1918, proved to have been barely two decades later, but the precursor to an even longer and greater struggle. The trouble with war – and well exemplified by the 1st World War – is that it seems, cruel, stupid and unnecessary when it is long over, but crucial, heroic and vitally important when it is all happening.

III

PART III

THE SECOND WORLD WAR, 1939-45
AND POST-WAR COMMUNICATIONS WITH SCILLY

'History is always best written generations after the event, when clouded fact and memory have fused into what can be accepted as truth, whether it be so or not!'   Theodore H. White

For the UK, the Second World War began with Britain's declaration of war upon Germany at 11 a.m. on September 3rd, 1939. Despite much discussion within the Cabinet, the wording of Britain's ultimatum gave Germany little room to manoeuvre. As Neville Chamberlain, the Prime Minister, said in his wireless broadcast to the nation at 11.15 that Sunday morning:

> This morning, the British ambassador in Berlin handed the German government a final Note stating that, unless we heard from them by 11 o'clock that they were prepared at once to withdraw their troops from Poland, a state of war would exist between us. I have to tell you now that no such undertaking has been received, and that consequently this country is at war with Germany.

Chamberlain was a product of his times, his education and his class. He came from a political family who saw the world order as right and proper, but needing smoothing at its rough edges – reform not revolution – and this he hoped could be secured by generous-minded agreements. He expected the statesmen of other great nations, such as Germany, to be kindly, well-intentioned, honourable gentlemen like himself. To him, if a nation-state had just grievances, then it was incumbent upon the leaders of the great nations to try to remove them – hence why he concluded the Munich Agreement in 1938 restoring the mainly German Sudetenland from Czechoslovakia to Germany; but he was overwhelmed by the bitterness, hatreds and fierceness of the German leaders, who were 'real' politicians, inclined to interpret generosity as weakness, and agreements, not as everlasting bonds, but as platforms from which further concessions could later be extracted. Hitler did not seek war, provided he could get what he wanted through negotiation with people like Chamberlain; but Hitler was prepared to risk war when his demands went increasingly beyond what Chamberlain could accept, seeming surprised that territorial adjustments and short struggles in remoter parts of Europe should so concern Britain that war would be declared because of them – a harping back perhaps to the Kaiser's surprise in 1914 that Britain should make war over 'a scrap of paper'. Arthur Henderson, British Ambassador to Germany, wrote a book about the situation at the time entitled

Failure of a Mission, and concluded that there was nothing more the British Government could have done to preserve peace. The result was that Chamberlain, who strove so hard for peace, ended up declaring war. There was at the time a public respect for leaders and statesmen rather lacking today; even as late as May, 1940, *The Times* was still referring to the German dictator as 'Herr Hitler'.

The political role of 'the Cliveden set' has been exaggerated, and a look at its composition reveals little homogeneity – many attended its weekends simply because they were invited by Lord and Lady Astor and enjoyed the socialising. These included such diverse people as Geoffrey Dawson, Bernard Shaw, Charlie Chaplin, Henry Ford, Mahatma Gandhi, T.E. Lawrence, and Lloyd George – hardly a set of appeasers of Hitler. Lady Astor was often critical of the Jews, but so were many people at the time, and such expressions hardly convict her of anything more than unthinking conventional prejudice. A number of British aristocracy were known in the 1930s to hold anti-communist, anti-Jewish and pro-Nazi views, with Lady Mitford, mother of the 6 Mitford sisters, expressing pro-German sentiments even after the war had started. Even Queen Victoria, in a letter to Lord Granville concerning the recommendation that Rothschild, the distinguished banker, should become a member of the House of Lords, wrote: 'To make a Jew a peer is a step the Queen could not consent to' (C. Roth's *The Magnificent Rothschilds*). However, she seemed to have overcome her prejudice by the time of Disraeli. There is the suggestion that the German Ambassador, and later German Foreign Minister, Ribbentrop, after contacts with 'top people' in Britain, advised the German government that Britain would not fight, perhaps misunderstanding that great reluctance to go to war is not in Britain sufficient reason for not doing so.

The declaration of war came when the German government was preoccupied with their blitzkrieg attack on Poland which they had begun on September 1st, and they failed even to reply by Chamberlain's deadline, and it seems a little unrealistic to have expected them to have halted and reversed their successful advance into Poland in mid-campaign. At 5.0 p.m. on September 3rd, France also declared war on Germany, but neither Britain nor France could do anything in practical terms to prevent the Germans from overrunning half of Poland in a matter of weeks. The USSR invaded Poland later in the month, but no similar ultimatum was sent to them. Indeed, for the first months of the war there was little land fighting in the west of any sort, and, even in the air, the RAF bombers sent to fly over Germany carried almost nothing more lethal than propaganda leaflets, the expressed intention being to 'rouse the Germans to a higher morality'. The Air Minister, Kingsley Wood, rejected a plan to bomb the Black Forest on the grounds that most of it was private property. But a sea blockade of Germany was immediately put into effect; and the war at sea was different, for, although the Scillies were

Newlyn Harbour showing its narrow entrance. How could Joyce have thought the Ark Royal was sunk inside it? To the right of the photograph in the foreground is the sandy bank where seaplanes were based in the 1st World War.

not directly involved, there was almost at once considerable action in the adjoining seas, the first big casualty of the war being the 13,581 ton liner *Athenia*, sunk on the day war broke out with 112 lives lost. Commander Kemp in U-30 gave no warning as he said he thought that the liner was an armed merchant cruiser because she had no lights and was pursuing a zigzag course. The sinking provoked an outcry against the Germans, so that when the *Firby* (4,869 tons) was sunk by U-48 on September 11, the submarine's commander, Herbert Schwitze, sent a personal wireless message to Churchill, who was then 1st Lord of the Admiralty, giving the exact position of the *Firby*'s lifeboats. The first U-boat to be sunk or 'destroyed' – that word being Churchill's preference – was U-39, a large, type IX submarine, on September 14, after she had made an abortive attack on the 22,600 ton aircraft carrier *Ark Royal*, Britain's only modern fleet-carrier at the start of the war. Torpedoes had been fired at the carrier but exploded only in the carrier's wake, alerting three of the escorting F-class destroyers to U-30's position, and U-30 was destroyed with depth-charges, the 44 crew being taken prisoner. Another U-boat attempted an attack on *Ark Royal* later that same day, and the carrier lost two Skua bombers trying to deal with this, and on this occasion was also otherwise unscathed. *Ark Royal* had the distinction that William Joyce (Lord Haw Haw) claimed on the German wireless many times in the war that the carrier had been sunk, even on one occasion saying that this had taken place in Newlyn harbour, a rather absurd notion given the huge size of the carrier and the small size of Newlyn. It was considered remarkable when the 600 ton Greek yacht *Panorama* came to Newlyn in 2000; how a 22,000 ton aircraft carrier could have been accommodated is farcical. The actual end of *Ark Royal* came on November 13, 1941, when she was struck amidships on the starboard side by a torpedo from U-81 – a U-boat that later sank 26 other ships. *Ark Royal* began to list quickly, and five Swordfish torpedo- bombers, which had been parked on her flight deck near her bow, slid over the starboard side one by one and into the sea. The increasing list meant that seawater covered the boiler intakes, which deprived the water-pumps of power and was the main cause of the ship sinking while being towed to port, a design fault later claimed to have been pointed out at the time of her construction, but ignored.

A dramatic early success of the U-boats came on September 17th when U-29 sank the 22,500 ton aircraft carrier *Courageous* in the Western Approaches with the loss of 518 of her crew including her captain and three young men from Penzance, the biggest number of fatal casualties in a single ship of the Royal Navy since the Battle of Jutland in 1916. The loss was felt particularly in Scilly because, from June 27 to July 3, 1933, *Courageous* had visited the Scillies, and her crew had been entertained on St Mary's in many sporting events held in competition with the crew. There were also concerts given by the ship's band, dances in the Town Hall, a variety show and tours of the ship – friendly contacts in which the crew endeared themselves to the Islanders.

The loss of *Courageous*, and the near loss of *Ark Royal* on September 14, put an end to the policy of using the Royal Navy's 7 large carriers in U-boat hunting groups, a tactic which had been advocated by Winston Churchill as 1st Lord of the Admiralty in 1939, but abandoned in favour of building small escort-carriers for convoy protection. It was one of Churchill's faults – or so some of his commanders have alleged – that he was inclined to interfere too much in operational matters; on the other hand, it has been said, by Clemenceau and others, that 'war is too serious a business to be left to the generals and admirals', and the loss of *Courageous*'s sister-ship *Glorious* on June 8, 1940, seems a case in point, for it was rather an inglorious episode in Royal Navy history, redeemed only by the heroism of the crews of the two escorting destroyers *Ardent* and *Acasta*. These sacrificed themselves by making determined torpedo attacks on *Scharnhorst*, and *Acasta* scored one damaging hit, which put the battlecruiser out of action for nearly six months; but, as for *Glorious*, it transpired that her captain, Guy D'Oyly-Hughes, was at loggerheads with some of his air officers, had omitted to have spotter aircraft airborne which could have warned him of the approach of enemy battlecruisers, and had sailed at his own insistence prematurely from Norway, with only two escorting destroyers instead of the prescribed minimum of (top) Courageous *as a battlecruiser prior to her conversion to an aircraft carrier.*

(middle) Courageous *in misty conditions in St. Mary's Road, Scilly, during her week-long visit in 1933.*

(below) Courageous *sinking on September 17, 1939, after being hit by two torpedoes from U-29.*

Courageous *was one of three battlecruisers converted to aircraft carriers between the wars. They were named* Furious. Glorious *and* Courageous, *each of about 22,500 tons and armed with 15-inch guns – although* Furious *also mounted one 18-inch gun subsequently put into a monitor. After conversion, the Navy nicknamed the three ships* Spurious, Curious *and* Outrageous. *Unlike* Furious, *the other two had full island superstructures on the starboard side of their flight decks, and could each of them accommodate about 42 aircraft in their 2 hangars below the flight deck. They retained their battlecruiser speed of up to 30 knots, which, was useful when the carriers headed into wind to assist aircraft taking-off and landing. In 1931* Courageous *was given some experimental arrester wires stretched over brake drums on her flight-deck to help check aircraft when landing, and to prevent their overshooting; these were so successful that they became the basis of the hydraulically-damped landing gear subsequently installed on all aircraft carriers.*

At the start of the 2nd World War in 1939, Furious *was based at Scapa Flow,* Glorious *was with the Mediterranean Fleet and* Courageous *was in the Western Approaches on anti-submarine patrol. Otto Schuhart in U-29 fired three torpedoes, two of which hit* Courageous *and exploded, just at a moment when the carrier captain, W.T. Makeig-Jones, was heading into wind recovering aircraft. She sank in only 15 minutes. Her loss was a case of the biter bit, because ironically she was destroyed by the very enemy she had been hunting. Schuhart escaped the heavy depth-charging of the 4 escorting destroyers, their Asdic in the early days not as helpful as had been claimed, and he even wirelessed his success back to Germany. The result was that when U-29 returned to base at Wilhelmshaven on September 28, the crew were greeted personally at the dockside by Hitler.*

Upon conversion from battlecruiser to aircraft carrier, the 15-inch guns of Courageous *and* Glorious *might well have been scrapped. In fact they were mounted in Britain's last and biggest battleship, the* Vanguard, *in 1946; but they were never fired in anger and* Vanguard *went to the breakers in 1960 – the end of an era.*

213

four, and without the company of other British warships which sailed only days later. Moreover, the Admiralty failed to pass on a warning from Harry Hinsley at Bletchley Park to the effect that increased wireless traffic indicated German naval units at sea in the vicinity, and the heavy cruiser *Devonshire*, which was not far from *Glorious* when the carrier was attacked, failed to come to her assistance – or even to pick up survivors – and later denied receiving anything but a 'garbled' signal from *Glorious*, an allegation vigorously denied by her own radio operator. The explanation for this is probably that as Admiral Cunningham (not the Admiral Browne Cunningham operating in the Mediterranean) on *Devonshire* had received orders from Churchill to bring the King of Norway and his cabinet safely to Britain, the importance of the safety of his distinguished passengers outweighed in his mind the rescue of *Glorious*'s survivors, particularly as he could have expected other naval ships to be attending the scene. These were compounded errors, all unfortunate, resulting in 1,519 men drowning from the 3 sunken British ships, and it was not until 3 days later that Norwegian fishing trawlers managed to pick up a mere 41, only one of whom was from *Acasta*.

The third of these converted battlecruisers was more lucky. When France capitulated in 1940, *Furious* was chosen to transport the gold bullion from the vaults of the Bank of England to the safety of Canada for the duration. If what had occurred to the other two carriers had befallen her, *Furious* would have been the most expensive ship loss in history; instead, *Furious* survived the war, her aircraft playing a role in April, 1944, in disabling the *Bismarck*'s sister ship *Tirpitz*; but perhaps her most famous episode was near the end of the 1st World War, when 7 Sopwith Camels took off from her flight deck on July 19, 1918, and destroyed the German airship base at Tondern and the two zeppelins, L54 and L60, the first time carrier-based aircraft had achieved such a success, although not, of course, the first time RNAS planes had been used as bombers, one of the earliest being in 1914 when they carried out a raid on the zeppelin hangars at Dusseldorf.

Two other great warships of the Royal Navy also visited Scilly in the 1930s, and similarly endeared their crews to the Islanders through social events and sporting competitions. One of these was also sunk in the war and with even greater loss of life than from the *Courageous*, only 3 men – Bob Tilburn, Ted Briggs and Bill Dundas – being rescued by the destroyer *Electra* from different Carley floats out of a total crew of 1,422, the highest loss of men ever from a Royal Navy ship. This ship was the battlecruiser *Hood*, a graceful vessel completed in 1920 and, at 42,000 tons, the world's greatest warship in the inter-war years, and regarded as the epitome of Britain's sea power. Yet, she was in action for only 8 minutes in the early morning of May 24, 1941, firing her forward 15-inch guns at a range initially of 14 miles at the German heavy cruiser *Prinz Eugen* (eight 8-inch guns), which she

(top) *In the 1930s, in misty conditions in St Mary's Sound, Isles of Scilly, the 'mighty' battlecruiser* Hood, *42,000 tons and 860 feet long, was the world's greatest warship between the World Wars. She was the largest warship ever to visit Scilly, and made a big impression, as she did everywhere she went.*

(middle)*The battleship* Rodney – *at peace. She visited Scilly from July 6-10 in 1930. The photograph is taken from her bridge looking forward. Her nine 16-inch guns are in three turrets, all forward of the bridge to keep her tonnage down to 33,000 tons. By grouping her heavy guns all together, thicker armour could be used to protect them without adding as much to her tonnage as would have been the case if the same thickness of armour had been stipulated with the guns arranged more conventionally. For example, the* Hood *and the* Bismarck *both had a traditional arrangement of 4 turrets, two guns in each turret, and two turrets placed forward of the bridge and two aft – but one ship* (Hood) *was built before the treaty restrictions and the other* (Bismarck)

completed after them. The Rodney, *and her sister-ship* Nelson, *were nicknamed 'cherry trees' because their tonnage had been cut down by the Washington Treaty which laid down a moratorium for 10 years on building battleships and later limited their size to under 35,000 tons. In the photograph the crew are lined up on her decks in neat, well-disciplined and impressive lines, where her band is playing.*

(bottom) *The battleship* Rodney – *at war. The photograph shows how Rodney would have appeared when she helped silence the guns of the* Bismarck *in May, 1941.*

mistook for the *Bismarck*, but which was actually leading that new German battleship of eight 15³/₈-inch guns. Though smaller, *Prinz Eugen* had a similar profile to the *Bismarck*, but the major reason for the mistake in identification was that when the German ships sailed from Gdynia through the Baltic to Grimstad Fiord in Norway – where *Prinz Eugen* refuelled and where they had been spotted and reported by a Swedish cruiser and by watchers on the Norwegian shore – *Bismarck* had been leading *Prinz Eugen*. Five German tankers and two supply ships were already in the Atlantic awaiting them, and then a spell of murky weather on May 22 gave the two German warships the opportunity to break out into the Atlantic without being observed, although a

Royal Navy reconnaissance aircraft from the Orkneys later that day reported that they had left the fiord. They were next spotted by the cruisers *Suffolk* and *Norfolk* in the Denmark Strait on May 23, with *Bismarck* still in the lead; but, in an effort to shake off the shadowing cruisers, *Bismarck* fired her big guns in their direction, the blast from which knocked out her own radar system, and persuaded Admiral Lütjens to place *Prinz Eugen* in the lead – so, incidentally but importantly, confusing Admiral Holland in the *Hood* as to their respective identities. This was fortuitous for the *Bismarck*; it is curious, then, that German crews felt that Lütjens was an unlucky person to have aboard.

Closely following *Hood* was Britain's newest battleship, *Prince of Wales* (ten 14-inch guns), but at 6.30 a.m., at *Bismarck*'s 3rd or 4th salvo, the *Hood* blew up in a gigantic fireball and split in two. It was said that a shell flash penetrated to the cordite in her magazine causing an immense fire, and a comparison of maximum thicknesses of deck armour suggests one explanation for the penetration: *Bismarck* 8 inches; *Prince of Wales* 6 inches; *Hood* 3¾ inches. *Prinz Eugen* was actually the first of the ships to score a hit, starting a small fire on *Hood*, but it would be too humiliating even to contemplate that hits from her 8-inch guns could have led to the explosion on *Hood*. Actually, none of the survivors heard an explosion on *Hood*, but nevertheless the ship broke in two, perhaps from her exploding torpedoes. She now lies on the seabed nearly two miles down, a depth which can be reached if the desire to know for certain the cause of her disaster ever becomes overwhelming. The *Bismarck* has also been found, and she lies on the Atlantic seabed all in one piece, sitting upright.

Many people were present at the demise of the *Hood*, but the event occurred so quickly and unexpectedly, and most were preoccupied with their various jobs or intent on trying to observe the enemy, that few saw much beyond the smoke. One person present on a destroyer was Lieutenant Commander Thomas Mervyn Dorrien Smith, who was one of the four sons of Major Arthur Dorrien Smith and the only one of the four who survived the war – the others dying on active service. He served in the Royal Navy, 1927-46, mainly in destroyers, and inherited the lease of Tresco after his father died in 1955, dying himself in 1973 at the age of 60. The Dorrien Smith family had other connections with military and naval enterprises in both world wars, including the two elder sisters of Tom Dorrien Smith: one married Vice Admiral Sir Roger Keyes, who conducted the raid by 146 small craft on Zeebrugge on April 23, 1915; the other married Viscount Trenchard, the first Air Marshal of the RAF.

Another resident of Scilly who was in action against the *Bismarck* was Norman Greening, who lived in the farmhouse on Gugh in the 1930s. He was serving on the *Prince of Wales* when she engaged the *Bismarck*, and was still on the *Prince of Wales* when she was sunk on December 10, 1941, by

Japanese torpedo bombers. He also survived another sinking later in the war.

Hood replaced the previous warship of that name, which had been deliberately sunk on November 4, 1914, to block the opening off the southern arm of Portland Breakwater against any U-boat attempting to break in – and is still there. The new *Hood*'s keel was laid on August 8, 1918, the very day that Rear-Admiral Sir Horace Hood was blown up in his flagship *Invincible*, which broke in two after an accurate salvo from the *Derflinger* in the Battle of Jutland. Two other Royal Navy battlecruisers also blew up that day – it was not a good augury – for what happened to them was not dissimilar to the fate of the *Hood* in 1941. Indeed, to some experts the loss of the *Hood* was an accident waiting to happen, because, although she had been given about 5,000 tons of extra armour, this was mainly added to her sides rather than on her deck, and made her extremely wet forward when ploughing into heavy seas without giving her the adequate extra protection she needed from plunging shells. Also, there were hidden weaknesses in her design and equipment apart from the positioning of most of the extra armour on her sides. The Admiralty had insisted that she be able to fire torpedoes, but the tubes were placed in a vulnerable position – so that exploding torpedoes may have assisted in the break up of the ship. There was also some talk after the Battle of Jutland in 1916, of British cordite being less stable than the German equivalent. There is also the possibility that her steel plates were brittle – as it is alleged that the steel on the *Titanic* had been – both coming from the same source, Colver and Company at Motherwell. Moreover, *Hood* is said to have been carrying up to 4,000 tons of wartime equipment, which added to her low position in the water; it took very little sea for her quarterdeck to become continually awash, and she shook alarmingly when heading into a swell. Yet she performed very well between the wars, as the most powerful, graceful and beautiful warship in the world – also the biggest, as the Washington Arms Control Treaty of 1922 limited the size of new warships to 35,000 tons by Britain and other signatory powers. Thus *Hood* became a superb and impressive ambassador for Britain in all the parts she visited on her world cruise – for example, half-a-million people visited her in Sydney harbour – and to serve on her became a great privilege in the Royal Navy. She was not all show; the shells in her eight 15-inch guns could be fired over 20 miles, at 1,700 m.p.h., and she was the principal unit in Force H in the Mediterranean at the start of the Second World War. In 1940, when France surrendered, she played the major part in the bombardment and destruction of most of the French fleet at Oran to prevent it falling into German hands, the French losing about 1,300 sailors in this tragic, if unavoidable, attack by Britain on a former ally.

Other reasons for *Hood*'s sinking extend back before the 1st World War, when Jacky Fisher, the First Sea Lord, championed the building of a new type of capital ship – the battlecruiser. In 1914, two of them (*Invincible* and

Inflexible) proved the worth of their greater speed and gunpower by destroying Von Spee's two crack armoured cruisers at the Battle of the Falkland Islands, something perhaps no other type of warship at that date would have been able to do. However, Fisher had the idea that speed was more important than armour, with the result that when battlecruisers were deployed in 1916 as part of Jellicoe's Grand Fleet against von Scheer's High Seas Fleet at the Battle of Jutland, their shortcomings were starkly revealed, with *Invincible, Indefatigable* and *Queen Mary* all blowing up, in a battle in which, of the 64 dreadnought battleships involved, not one was sunk. The basic weakness of the battlecruiser was that, although it may have guns as big as a battleship's and the swiftness of a cruiser, to achieve such a high speed inevitably meant sacrifice of much protective armour; in consequence, after Jutland, it was deemed unwise ever in the future to pitch a battlecruiser against a battleship – but this was exactly the situation *Hood* was in on that early morning in 1941. Yet the decision to engage at that time was probably the correct one in the circumstances, as the *Hood*, and the new but untried *Prince of Wales*, were the only Royal Navy capital ships in the immediate vicinity on May 24 with a chance of intercepting the two powerful German raiders emerging from the Denmark Strait between Iceland and Greenland. Two details from the engagement are worth mentioning; the two German ships had a higher speed – 31 knots as against *Hood*'s speed on the day of 28.5 knots; and they were on a fine bearing from the two Royal Navy ships, which meant that only the two forward turrets of the British vessels were engaged. Thus, the Germans had eight 15-inch guns and eight 8-inch guns against four 15-inch guns and five 14-inch guns – one of the guns of the *Prince of Wales* having jammed.

There is also the speculation that the concentration of Royal Navy fire upon the *Prinz Eugen* rather than at first upon the *Bismarck*, may have given the *Bismarck*'s gunners, using their radar, time and opportunity accurately to calculate their ranges without endangerment. The *Prince of Wales*, whose view was somewhat obscured by smoke from *Hood*'s funnel, was hit by four 15-inch shells and by three of 8-inch, all of which did damage – one of which killed every man on the *Prince of Wales*'s bridge – and by six other hits which did not. Two shells from *Prince of Wales* hit the *Bismarck* just below the waterline, but otherwise neither *Prinz Eugen* nor *Bismarck* were much damaged. All that is now left of the *Hood* above water are two big but old guns, removed earlier before the action, which today stand guard at the entrance to Ascension Island. Surprisingly, the first notification of the loss of the *Hood* came from a medium, Helen Duncan, who revealed the information through, as she put it, 'one of her spiritual manifestations'. At another of her seances, held in Portsmouth, she told a woman in the audience that her dead husband, who had served on the battleship *Barham*, wanted to speak to her; the woman protested that her husband was alive, but in fact a U-boat had sunk the *Barham*, with such a ghastly loss of life that the government had decided to keep the tragedy secret for a while. The government soon became alarmed by such revelations at Helen Duncan's seances lest she should also reveal other secrets at one of them, including perhaps where and when the D-Day Landings were to occur. Under the Witchcraft Act of 1735 she was put in Holloway Prison for 9 months for 'pretending to raise the spirits of the dead' – the first time the Act (now repealed) had been used for a century or so. She died in 1956, but evidence at her trial which served to convict her has since been found to have been flawed, so that, in 2001, there has been a movement to try and quash her conviction and possibly win a posthumous pardon.

After the *Hood*'s loss, Captain Leach in *Prince of Wales* was soon ordered to turn away by the Rear Admiral in a cruiser, but not before she had scored two hits on *Bismarck*'s fuel tanks – which meant that from then on *Bismarck* left a trail of oil in the water – before she and *Prinz Eugen* disappeared into the mist.

Finding a raider once it had disappeared into the vastness of the Atlantic was always the hard part. When, in 1939, *Graf Spee* was located in the Atlantic by three British cruisers, the largest, *Exeter*, had her three turrets holding six 8-inch guns knocked out by the pocket battleship's 11-inch guns, and had to retire injured to the Falkland Islands. But there were still two light cruisers, *Ajax* and *Achilles*, with only 6-inch guns but faster than the *Graf Spee*, and able, weather permitting, to follow her wherever she went until more powerful units could arrive, and this led to the *Graf Spee* scuttling herself off Montevideo.

With the *Bismarck* it was her radio call to Hitler, giving details of the *Hood*'s sinking, which roughly revealed the raider's position; but incompetent use by the Royal Navy of navigational instead of gnomic charts plotted *Bismarck* two hundred miles from her true position, which allowed *Bismarck*, heading in the direction of Brest at 28 knots, to sail undetected for almost too long. However, a lone Catalina on reconnaissance spotted *Bismarck*'s trailing oil slick on May 26 at 10.36 hours, and this was to be the key to her sinking, for it led to the attack on *Bismarck* by torpedo bombers from *Victorious* and *Ark Royal*, which, together with destroyers, scored 12 torpedo hits on *Bismarck* out of 71 launched at her. Actually the Swordfish at first mistook the Royal Navy cruiser *Sheffield* for the *Bismarck* and nearly torpedoed her; but, fortunately the waves at the time were judged too rough for them to launch a torpedo attack.

Swordfish torpedo bombers, known as 'stringbags', were old and out-of-date biplanes, their critics claiming that their maximum speed was slower than a seagull's. So, there is something remarkable that one of them should have scored a hit on the one small vulnerable area of the latest, most up-to-date battleship in the world – her rudders. However, for completeness, it

A photograph of the Bismarck *setting out on her first and last voyage, the view from her consort the heavy cruiser* Prinz Eugen, *which accompanied the battleship for the first part of the voyage.* Bismarck *was 791 feet long, with a 12.5-inch, hardened steel armour belt all around her, and a tonnage of about 45,000 tons.*

should be mentioned that *Bismarck*, for all her modernity of equipment, was actually based on a good but old design of battleship, and her rudders had been the parts of the *Bismarck* which, on her sea trials, had been shown to be a source of concern. Nevertheless, it was the torpedo hit on them which, despite the frantic efforts of her crew to free the rudders from a tangle of metal, prevented *Bismarck* from reaching the German air cover she sought. For some reason the crew did not risk blowing off the damaged rudders or using sea anchors to help control steering, with the consequence that *Bismarck* had no real hope of escape. The torpedo struck when the rudders were inclined at 12 degrees to straight ahead, and they stuck. She soon became a target for the 16-inch guns of the battleship *Rodney* and the 14-inch ones of the *King George V*, which together played the main role in bombarding the *Bismarck* and silencing all her 15-inch guns. The *Bismarck*'s gunners were entirely exhausted having spent hours firing to deter Royal Navy destroyers from getting near enough to launch torpedoes; so when they transferred their gunfire to the *Rodney*, only one shell landed on the *Rodney*, and that failed to explode. *Rodney* had been the third great warship which had visited Scilly in the inter-war years (6-10 July, 1930), with Marianne Hicks from St Agnes – daughter of Obadiah Hicks who gave his name to the 4,000-year-old barrow on Gugh – meeting and marrying Petty Officer Camp from the *Rodney*.

Having silenced *Bismarck*'s guns, *Rodney* then turned and launched a torpedo at the *Bismarck*, the only occasion in the history of naval warfare when a battleship has attempted to torpedo another battleship. In the event, it was the Germans who sank the *Bismarck*; on May 27 German engineers set demolition charges and, like *Graf Spee* before her, *Bismarck* was scuttled to remove the possibility of her failing into Allied hands, and, although she may by then have been sinking anyway, this must have speeded the process, and she went beneath the waves at about 11.00 a.m. Only 110 of the German crew were picked up by British warships – plus 3 by U-74 – out of a ship's complement of over 2,300. This was at the time the greatest-ever loss of life from a single warship, nearly twice the number lost when the *Hood* went down, although not quite equalling the 2,498 men lost from the Japanese super-battleship *Yamato* (863 feet long and over 65,000 tons with nine 18-inch guns and a 16½-inch armour belt) on April 7, 1945 off Okinawa. However, this was not quite a comparable operation, as *Yamato* had taken insufficient fuel on board for a return journey, so its voyage was more in the nature of a suicide mission, and it took something like 300 aircraft to sink her – a dramatic end to the primacy of the battleship in sea warfare. With the benefit of hindsight it should have been obvious earlier that the days of the battleship were numbered, but it took a long time for this to be universally accepted despite the fact that in neither of the World Wars - not even at the Battle of Jutland in 1916 – had a battleship sunk another battleship. The two possible 2nd World War exceptions to this are the sinking of the *Bismarck* – but here torpedoes played as large a part as shells – and the last confrontation between battleships at Leyte Gulf, but in later battles it was bombs and torpedoes from carrier aircraft which did the sinkings, not big guns.

Bismarck's one voyage has been well told by Baron von Mullenheim-Rechburg, the highest-ranking officer saved from the *Bismarck*, who had been adjutant to the captain and a gunnery officer, and whose book was published by Bodley Head in 1981 entitled *Battleship Bismarck*. In Britain ships are conventionally seen as feminine – although 'it' is sometimes used for a submarine, especially an enemy one – but Captain Lindemann of the *Bismarck* always referred to his battleship as 'he', possibly in deference to the 'Iron Chancellor', from whom the ship took her / his name.

Bismarck's companion raider, *Prinz Eugen*, had experienced some engine trouble, and escaped interception by her commander, Captain Brinckmann, taking a more southerly route towards Brest, arriving there, after refuelling from the tanker *Spichern*, without incident on June 1st. Perhaps if the two ships had not parted company, *Prinz Eugen* could have taken the *Bismarck* in tow when her steering gear was so badly damaged; but it is as likely that she too, would have been sunk by the Royal Navy. In any event, Hitler had never been keen on surface raiders, and at the loss of the *Bismarck*, cutback on raiders in the Atlantic other than U-boats.

Once at Brest, *Prinz Eugen* was the target, along with the battlecruisers *Scharnhorst* and *Gneisenau*, of massive, regular, but somewhat inaccurate RAF bombing against intensive fire from German anti-aircraft batteries. Despite this, the three ships, well escorted, sailed from Brest through the Straits of Dover to Germany with some minor damage, but this time with air cover which shot down twelve Swordfish which vainly attempted to torpedo the ships. The British authorities were taken by surprise by the audacity of the Germans in sailing the squadron up England's channel, the *Daily Express* suggesting with journalistic sarcasm that perhaps they could have stopped for drinks at Brighton Pier. *Prinz Eugen* survived the war, but her end after the war was to be blown to pieces at the Bikini Atoll in a controlled atomic bomb explosion.

Such were the major actions of the largest German surface raiders around Britain's shores and in the North Atlantic, with pocket battleships *Scheer* and *Lutzow* and battlecruisers *Scharnhorst* and *Gneisenau* all making partially successful raiding voyages in the war's early years.

Eventually all the potential German surface raiders were accounted for except one – the *Bismarck*'s sister-ship, *Tirpitz*. There was only one dock (at St Nazaire) on the German-occupied Atlantic coast big enough to service her; so a raid was planned from Falmouth for March 28, 1942, by commandos led by Lieutenant-Colonel Charles Newman of the Essex Regiment, to render the dock unusable, an enterprise called *Operation Chariot*. The dock measured 1148 feet x 164 feet and had originally been constructed to accommodate the trans-Atlantic liner *Normandie*. The object of the raid was to destroy the dock's lock-gates, and this was accomplished by modifying the old US destroyer *Campbelton* and running her into them at 20 knots. Sixteen launches, a motor gun-boat and a motor torpedo boat escorted the destroyer, but only four MLs reached port again. Saint-Nazaire was also heavily bombed by the RAF as it was a U-boat base. But the roofs of all the U-boat pens had been constructed by the Germans of sixteen feet of reinforced concrete, thick enough to withstand the biggest bombs of the time. The town was devastated; as Doenitz wrote: 'Not a dog, not a cat, is left in the U-boat town except U-boat pens.'

As it happened, the *Tirpitz* was never able to enter the Atlantic as a raider as the *Bismarck* had tried to be, for she was anchored in Alten Fiord, Norway, and attacked 8 times before three 12,000 ton gigantic bombs, designed by Barnes Wallis, finally destroyed her on November 12, 1944, a good news present for Churchill's 70th birthday on November 30; but, in the 2nd World War, it was not to be German surface warships which were the greatest threat to Britain, but the U-boats.

* * * * *

The German advance into France from May 10, 1940, brought the German army, air force and navy near to Scilly, just across the English Channel in Brittany; but the humiliating defeat of the British Expeditionary force in France also brought alarm in Scilly, although the full extent of the disaster was only apparent to the British public later. British commentators then and since have put the explanation for the success of the German advance down to the new German blitzkrieg tactics of tanks supported by Stuka dive bombers; but these tactics had been used against Poland in September, 1939, so it is strange that the British forces seemed unprepared for them. Even the Germans were amazed at the ease of their victory. However, for Britain the bad news was offset by the good news of the evacuation from Dunkirk, the extent of which so much exceeded expectations.

Although two-thirds of the ¼ million troops evacuated from Dunkirk between May 26 and June 3rd, 1940, were taken off from the mole, the rescue of those direct from the beaches has come to epitomise the event. Because of the shallow waters off these beaches, larger craft could not get near the shore, and smaller craft were needed to ferry men the mile or so out to the bigger ships. A message went out for people to volunteer their boats which, for the most part, were then operated by Royal Navy personnel once they had been towed by trawler from south and east ports to Dunkirk.

Representative of these craft was the *Sundowner*, captained by the man who had been second officer on the *Titanic* in 1912, the *New Britannic*, which later served as a holiday launch on Bryher and was called *Commodore* until restoration, and the 51 feet long *Southern Queen*, which before the war had operated as a pleasure launch out of Folkestone. *Southern Queen* had been built by Short Brothers of Leicester in 1926, had a displacement of 20 tons with a beam of 12 feet, was robustly constructed of oak with copper fastenings, and had a comparatively shallow draught of 3½ feet. She had been used before the war as the attendant boat to accompany cross-Channel swimming attempts, the first successful one being in August, 1926, by Gertrude Ederle, followed in 1927 by 25-year-old Ivy Hawke, a swimming instructor from Swindon, who landed at Dover from Cape Grisnez after 19¼ hours in the water; but her greatest notoriety concerns the traitor William Joyce. Joyce was noted by the Security Services as a Nazi sympathiser, and an MI5 report advised that Joyce should be detained in the event of war, and an order to do this was issued on September 1, 1939. But when detectives arrived at Joyce's house, they found that he and his wife had fled the country on about August 26. Joyce lived in the top flat at 83 Onslow Gardens from 1937 to 1939, having moved there from less fashionable addresses in Crystal Palace and Chelsea. No 83 was owned by a local doctor, Reginald Harvey, who let the top flat to Angus MacNab, editor of the *Fascist Quarterly*, who sublet it to Joyce. MacNab and Joyce both made some income as private tutors, even teaching Dr Harvey's sons. Joyce became known by residents of the other flats for his loud playing of Wagner records on his radiogram; what they did not know was that Joyce had constructed a small, secret room in his flat, located over a lift shaft, and to be used by him to conceal Nazi sympathisers, should the police call. This room was only discovered during a routine fire inspection of the premises soon after Joyce and his pretty, second wife, Margaret, had departed from the country. His sister, who lived elsewhere, was then contacted by the police officers and she stated that she thought her brother had received a warning by telephone from an MI5 officer some time previously. Joyce and his wife had therefore had time to arrange their affairs, and had bought tickets for the Dover to Calais ferry with the intention of making their way to Germany. But, upon arrival at Dover, they realised that they were unlikely to make it past the watchful eyes of British Security men at the docks, and so they changed their plans and journeyed along the coast to Folkestone and hired the *Southern Queen* to take them across the Channel. Eventually, they arrived in Berlin, where Joyce got a job broadcasting German propaganda to Britain for most of the war, taking over from Norman Baillie-Stewart, a lieutenant in the Seaforth Highlanders who had in the Thirties sold secrets to Germany – not very important ones – and been imprisoned for this in the years 1933 to 1937. After another 5 years imprisonment for treason after the war, Baillie-Stewart married under his new name of Patrick Stewart and settled in Dublin to write exciting novels about the American Wild West, until he died in 1966.

Joyce, in his new broadcasting role, was said to have gained the nickname 'Lord Haw-Haw' on account of his high-falutin nasal tones – although actually, Baillie-Stewart had originally been called this owing to his plummy voice, and Joyce inherited the label as the broadcaster from Germany in English. Although few in Britain ever believed what Joyce said, many were intrigued to tune in on the wireless to listen to him – even though this was forbidden – and came to recognise his usual opening remark: 'Germany calling ... Germany calling ...'.

But, as a letter in *Saga* magazine for January, 2000, revealed, Joyce had a useful side. Mrs W.A. Chadwick had a telegram from the Air Ministry in London regretfully informing her that her husband's Lancaster bomber had been shot down and that he was missing believed killed; Lord Haw-Haw, in one of his broadcasts, was able to inform her – and he did so with others in similar circumstances – that her husband was safe and in a prisoner-of-war camp. Such a service by Joyce was not one of disinterested kindness, but served essentially to increase the number of his British listeners, particularly those anxious for any news of friends and relatives missing on active service. They joined many others simply intrigued to hear the enemy propaganda but who, by so doing, left themselves exposed to its possible insidious effects. Joyce could be subtle sometimes; on one occasion he was able to announce that the clock in the centre of one English town had stopped; what puzzled many and frightened some was how he knew, given that it had only stopped on the day he made the announcement.

Why Joyce was dangerous to Britain was that the 'spin' he gave to the news he relaid was deliberately calculated to cause confusion and alarm amongst some of his British listeners. Even though all those who heard him in the UK were quite aware that he was the enemy talking, and believed that they could totally discount anything he said, there was often left in a corner of the listener's mind a nagging doubt that he might – at least in small part – be right.

Few people realise how much advertisements affect and determine their purchasing preferences, although a reflection of the costs of such advertising may make them pause; nor are they fully apprised of how much newspapers 'spin' the news so as to convey a political message, usually that of their proprietors. Newspapers do not, on the whole, convey news with any olympic detachment, but with an undeclared political agenda, and this applies as equally to the broadsheets as to tabloids, while at the same time they are bearing in mind the optimising of sales. 'Spin' is a word with a modern connotation, but it is by no means a recent phenomenon, and is equally applicable to matters past. An example of successful 'spin' which effects everyone adversely today, but came about in the 19th century owing to commercial considerations free of all politics, concerns typing. Everyone who sits down at a computer today can, in a sense, be regarded as a victim of a past 'spin'. Even the least curious person must on some occasion have wondered why the jumble of letters on the keyboard in front of them is not arranged alphabetically in the ABCDEF sequence, but are in the peculiar but now universally familiar QWERTY arrangement. The explanation is that when C.L. Sholes produced the first commercially-viable typewriter in 1873, he at first did arrange the keys in the alphabetical sequence, but found a snag in that some of the keys jammed when struck by a fast typist. He overcame this problem by arranging the letters so that those most frequently used were separated from each other, which, of course, inevitably slowed down the speed of typing, as the typist's fingers had to cover greater distances. To gain acceptance for his QWERTY arrangement, he asserted that the layout was scientifically proven to be the best and fastest, an inaccurate claim but accepted at the time for it was difficult to test. Actually, QWERTY is the slowest and least efficient distribution of the keys, and a random dispersal is likely to be better; but, like much else in human affairs, became accepted and remained so even after the initial jamming problem had been solved by other means. Thus Shole's 19th century 'spin' still determines a 21st century inefficient practice.

After the war Joyce escaped to live in Denmark but, while out walking in a wood, was stopped by two British officers who asked him for directions; when he obligingly replied, one of the officers thought he recognised Joyce's voice and asked him to identify himself. Joyce reached in his pocket for his false passport to prove he was not Joyce, but the officers thought he was trying to draw a gun on them and shot him in the leg. After hospital treatment he was brought back to England for trial, and people were surprised that the man with the big voice had a rather less imposing appearance. Joyce claimed that he was born in New York, but documents were produced showing that he had on three occasions declared his nationality to be British. He said his motives for his treachery were in no way for personal gain but out of conviction, although this hardly mitigated what he had done in the view of the British jury. After his conviction for High Treason, Joyce was executed by Albert Pierrepoint, the public executioner, who discovered that the man he was hanging had been brought up in Oldham like himself. It was unfortunate that, as the rope went taut, a facial scar on Joyce's face split open, which did nothing to improve Pierrepoint's dedication to his work.

On the subject of treachery, both E.M. Forster and Graham Greene – but neither with personal experience of making the choice – expressed the view that it is better to betray one's country than one's friends, although not easier, for the death penalty was, and still is, in force – if not in operation – for the former offence under the Treason Act of 1814, along with mutiny and violent piracy. This was strengthened by the Treachery Act of 1940, which served to remove some loopholes.

There were, however, ways of avoiding the penalty; Sir Arthur Blunt, Keeper of the Queen's Pictures, was allowed to continue his work and retain all his academic honours even after his admission of treason in 1964. He died in 1983, but explained that his treachery 'was a case of political conscience against loyalty to country: I chose conscience'.

In the case of Sir Roger Casement – one of only a handful of traitors to Britain in the 20th century who have actually suffered the death penalty – even the petition of many eminent persons failed to save him; the reasons are not really known, but it could be that the cause of Irish independence – 'England's difficulty is Ireland's opportunity' and similar talk – is felt to be especially disloyal and hurtful in Britain, where British policy of exploiting the Irish over the centuries and deliberately preventing Irish economic expansion in order that it did not conflict with British industry, is not widely appreciated by the British public; but it may also have been because of revelations in Casement's diaries of his homosexual proclivities at a time when such were publicly regarded with abhorrence. Joyce and John Amery were also executed, but both had tried to persuade Britons to form a British branch of the SS supporting Germany. Baillie-Stewart also did this, but received two terms of imprisonment, the first in the 1930s actually served in the Tower of London. In this connection, Joyce was nearly the last person in Britain executed for treason but not quite, as on the following day, Private Schurch of the RASC was hanged at Pentonville for desertion at Tobruk in 1942.

One person who should not perhaps be regarded as a traitor, although at one time in the 2nd World War and after was described as such by some people, is the comic author P.G. Wodehouse. The outcry against him was led by Duff Cooper, Minister of Information, and taken up by many journalists and by some prominent people such as A.A. Milne, who whipped up feeling against him. The circumstances of his alleged offence were as follows: when war broke out and France was defeated, he attempted to escape to England from his house near Le Touquet, but his car broke down; he was then offered one seat in an RAF plane, but had to refuse because it meant leaving his wife Ethel in France. In July, 1940, he was interned by the Germans at Loos Prison, then taken to Poland, but later transferred – after pleas by many American admirers – to the comfort of the Adlon Hotel in Berlin, where Ethel was permitted to join him. Here, he accepted an invitation to give five humorous talks on the German wireless, mainly for the benefit of his American admirers, and few people in Britain heard them, the content of the talks being unexceptional. However, some people in Britain felt strongly that it was disloyal to have made any broadcasts at all on the German wireless, and he was expelled from his London club and even had his name removed from the honours board of his old school, Dulwich College.

Wodehouse soon came to realise that he had been naive, even foolish, but there was no question of treachery. Malcolm Muggeridge, while attached to the British Secret Services, interviewed Wodehouse and confirmed this. In 1947, Wodehouse moved to New York, but it was not until 1975, when he was aged 94, that he gained his knighthood, only a matter of weeks before his death. George Orwell wrote that it was inexcusable 'to go on denouncing him three or four years after the war or ... to let an impression remain that he acted with conscious treachery'.

* * * * *

There were two BBC programmes for the UK on the wireless during the war; the Regional Programme of the 1930s became known as the Home Service and the National Programme as the Forces Programme, and later the Light Programme. The Germans did succeed, for one short period, in broadcasting on the same wavelength as the Home Service, especially during pauses in the news; so that, when the announcer claimed, for instance, that a dozen (say) of German aircraft had been shot down, a voice would chime in with the comment 'Nonsense, there was only one!'. This nuisance was dealt with from July 13, 1940, partly by the news-readers reading the news more rapidly without pauses where possible, and by their announcing their identity before every bulletin, so that listeners became familiar with their voices and were not deceived by a voice making an intrusive comment. Thus John Snagge, Alvar Liddell, Bruce Belfrage and others became household names during the war years, and represented the reassuring voice of the BBC; indeed, they played an important role, and one had only to say that one had heard it 'on the news' from one of them, for it to be accepted as absolutely true and without question. The transistor was a post-war invention, so

(top) *The* Southern Queen *when she first came to Scilly after the 2nd World War, and still with the stanchion forward, on which a gun had been mounted during the war.*

(middle) *The* Southern Queen, *going astern at St Martin's Quay after disembarking passengers in the early 1990s, before her refit and when still serving as a passenger launch.*

(bottom) *The* Southern Queen, *all spick and span alongside Albert Pier, Penzance, in early June, 2000, prior to making her way to Dover to take part in the armada of little ships voyaging to Dunkirk, to commemorate their rescue of thousands of soldiers from the beaches there in 1940, just sixty years previously.*

wireless sets were all run by valves; there was passable reception in Scilly, with the help of long, trailing, outdoor aerials. By 1955 there was one BBC TV station in black and white, and not received yet in Scilly. Broadcasts on it began at 3 o'clock in the afternoon and signed off with the playing of the National Anthem at 10.45p.m.

* * * * *

At Dunkirk, the *Southern Queen* was commanded by Sub-Lieutenant B.G.P. de Mattos, who discovered that one of her uses at the beaches was her ability, with her shallow draught, to get close to the shore and pull off other launches which had become stuck on the sand through overloading with troops. Many boatloads of men were rescued in this way by the pulling power of the *Southern Queen*'s powerful engine. One of the very last British soldiers to leave from the Dunkirk beaches was Ron Perry, who began his career with motors at a garage in Compton Road, Plymouth, but joined the army in 1939 and, after the war, as Vic Trenwith's nephew, ran coaches on St Mary's for many years.

One Scillonian who played a part in rescuing soldiers from the Dunkirk beaches, was Lloyd Hicks, who ran the pleasure-launch *Swordfish II* in post-war years. He died in 1980 aged 63, and his son, John, then ran the *Swordfish II* for many years in the Boatmen's Association, and then, later, for private day-hire for up to a dozen people with snacks provided on board. John Hicks then went to live in Bristol leaving *Swordfish II* in Scilly. His father, Lloyd Hicks, had been in the Royal Navy for twelve years and became a Chief Petty Officer gunnery instructor. At Dunkirk he was on the destroyer *Basilisk*, which was sunk while trying to pick up soldiers; Lloyd then steered back to Britain one of the smaller boats, heavily laden with exhausted troops. Captain L.D. Davies, Master of the *Scillonian* in 1968, was, in 1940, an RNR seaman, and he used a ship's lifeboat to ferry soldiers from the beaches to waiting ships, a task that he performed for seven days.

The Dunkirk evacuation had started in the last week of May but, by June 2, the German armies had pushed their way almost to the coast, and a German tank had actually fought a gun duel with an off-shore Royal Navy destroyer as early as May 25. By June 4, it had become too dangerous for the little ships even to approach the beach – something like 200 ships and 177 aircraft had already been destroyed – and six of the 38 destroyers involved had been sunk; moreover, despite the spirited resistance of nearly 40,000 Allied troops, the pocket around Dunkirk was shrinking fast. The remaining troops who had survived had little option, after burning or demolishing their equipment, but to surrender, many of them having then to endure a long and dreadful march to the German frontier, the nearest point where there were camp facilities for so many prisoners. They spent the next 4 years as prisoners-of-war. The worst single incident for Britain during the evacuation from France was the loss of the troopship *Lancastria*, an ex-Cunard liner which went down off St Nazaire with the loss of over 5,000 lives, an event judged as so appalling it was hushed up lest it should sap morale further.

The *Southern Queen* remained in naval service for the rest of the war and carried a gun on her foredeck; but, after the war, she was returned to her original owner in Folkestone and slowly resumed her peacetime role as a pleasure boat. In 1957, she was brought to Scilly to serve as a pleasure boat in the Boatmen's Association, her shallow draught again proving to be one of her assets, enabling her to navigate the shallow waters around the islands of Bryher, Tresco and St Martin's at all except low tides. In 1967, she was bought by Frank Pender who removed much of her foredeck, including the iron roof and massive stanchion, which in wartime had held the gun, and so made room to seat 81 passengers. A subsequent owner was Eric Guy, born in Scilly in 1906, who was Master at Arms on the *Queen of Bermuda* in the

Second World War and became Scilly's policeman for a while after it, and then ran the pleasure-launch *Southern Queen* with his brother Bill for several years. In retirement, until he died in 1985, he used to sit on a favourite seat on the Strand, St Mary's, on fine, summer days, and was known for dispensing to visitors uncannily-accurate weather predictions. *Southern Queen* was later sold to Alec Hicks of St Mary's, who ran her for a number of years, until his new launch *Kingfisher of St Mary's* came into service in the mid 1990s. She was then laid up in a leaky and rotting condition for a few seasons on Hugh Town beach, but was spotted by Phil Hammond from Bedford, a member of the Association of Dunkirk Little Ships founded in 1966, an exclusive yacht club of anyone who owns one of the craft which took place in Operation Dynamo in 1940. He bought her just before she was due to become the centrepiece of a Guy Fawkes night bonfire on St Mary's, and she was towed to Penzance and beautifully restored almost to her original condition at Rospeath Industrial Estate by an excellent craftsman / carpenter (Mr Carpenter), who renewed most of her oak planking. With a new engine, she then sailed for Dover and was one of the 56 little ships that journeyed together to Dunkirk on June 3-5, 2000, and took part in the televised 60th anniversary commemoration of the great deliverance of 1940 – an event which has been commemorated in this way every five years, although each time with fewer and fewer little ships. In 2000, the estimate was 150 Dunkirk Little Ships still left in existence.

Referring to the Dunkirk evacuation of 1940, the Poet Laureate, John Masefield, described it as the 'Nine Days Wonder'. About 1,300 craft altogether took part, including small launches, yachts, drifters, lighters, tugs, lifeboats, small paddle-steamers, and the captain's barge from battleship *Nelson*. They rescued about 338,000 troops, 230,000 of them British, 108,000 of them French and Belgian. Yet, it had been estimated that only 40,000 troops could be rescued from Dunkirk, so rapid had been the German advance. To take off so many seemed a miracle, but it may be partly explained by Hitler's order issued by Colonel-General von Rundstedt – but made clear by him that it came from the Fuehrer – that the panzer divisions should halt for two days, and it was this that provided the opportunity for the British. It is not clear what Hitler's motives were in halting the panzers, a decision which enabled the evacuation to proceed; but it seems likely that Hitler was hoping to conclude a peace with Britain, for he was offering terms, which were that Britain could keep her army, her navy and her colonies, providing Germany was given a free hand in Europe. He was even offering peace terms as late as October 6. In such circumstances he could hardly be destroying the entire British army with one hand and be proffering peace terms with the other and expect to be believed when he declared that he had no quarrel with Britain. Lord Halifax, the foreign secretary, was in favour of an investigation of these terms and, if he had accepted the post of Prime

The War Cabinet of the wartime Coalition Government flanking King George VI. On his left is Churchill and Anthony Eden, the Foreign Secretary, with Ernest Bevin, bulky and in a slightly crumpled suit, on the extreme right of the picture; on the King's right is the Deputy Prime Minister, Clement Attlee, leader of the Labour Party, and on the extreme left of the picture is Herbert Morrison. In the five days from May 24 to May 28 in 1940, Churchill consolidated his position and managed to prevent the Cabinet from deciding to ask Mussolini to intercede and mediate a peace with Hitler. At the same time Churchill sought an understanding with his predecessor, Neville Chamberlain, and it was Chamberlain's support for Churchill against Lord Halifax in the Cabinet which won the argument for Churchill continuing the war. The crucial point made was that only by persevering, whatever the cost, would Roosevelt and Stalin take Britain seriously.

Minister after Chamberlain's resignation, that is likely to have been British policy; but it was Churchill who became PM, and he insisted upon continuing the war ('we shall fight on the beaches ...') despite the enormity of the defeat. About 40,000 (some say up to 68,000) troops were left at Dunkirk, including many of those who had fought a valiant rearguard action and had tried to hold the German advance; but, while numbers of these had been killed, most surrendered and became prisoners-of-war for the duration. Hitler reiterated his peace offer in July, but was similarly rebuffed, the British press then and now representing the defeat as a heroic occasion – and with justification, for almost any army can advance feeling victorious, the test of true worth is how well an army retreats in defeat.

On the fall of Paris on June 14 – declared an open city to avoid war damage and casualties – some of the rescued French returned to their families in France, while others joined the Free French forces in Britain under General de Gaulle.

The hastily-organised evacuation from Dunkirk had been aided by calm seas, low cloud and even some fog, which made it harder for German aircraft to bomb the ships and, anyway, much of the evacuation was carried out at night. Winston Churchill, who had taken over on May 10 as Prime Minister from Neville Chamberlain (who had resigned mainly because of the failure

231

of Britain's Norway Campaign) had been urging the BEF to stand and break out; fortunately, Lord Gort, the commander of the BEF, was able to insist on evacuation, which saved the lives of nearly a quarter of a million British soldiers – although minus their equipment – but who, after recuperation, recovery and rearming, served as part of the backbone of the British army for the rest of the war. There was one other great military defeat of the British in the war, but this time with little glory and something like humiliation. General Perceval surrendered Singapore to the Japanese on February 15, 1942, with hardly a struggle at all; but probably he realised that his fate was to lose in the end, and he could save unnecessary casualties before too many were caused. The early surrender was a big surprise to the Japanese, who were trained not to think like that but always to put what they perceived as 'honour' first.

After Dunkirk, Britain stood alone in the war against Germany, and to some it seemed a hopeless struggle to continue. But most people in Britain were dogged in their determination to continue the war, and really thought the Home Guard could give the army the support necessary to deal with any German landing by sea or from the air. But, although tempting and, for those in the know, apparently rational, to have accepted Hitler's offer of peace would only have postponed the problem because, once Hitler had dealt with his principal enemy Russia, there was every likelihood he would have turned on Britain, for his insincerity in foreign dealings had been clearly demonstrated to the satisfaction of most Britons at the time. People knew in their hearts that there was no way of avoiding the Nazi threat other than to confront it – and history has confirmed this judgement.

It was with something akin to relief – at least to the leaders of the UK – that almost a year later, Britain found herself at last with a new ally, one who would in the end, after the bloodiest struggle in history, prevail against Germany and be the main instigator of the Nazi defeat. But it needed a statesman of the stature of Churchill to appreciate this, welcome the new ally and immediately send aid. Although privately Churchill suffered from what he called 'Black Dick', dark moods and deep depression when the war was not going well, publicly his confident voice, his talk of Britain being 'an island fortress', and his jaunty presence sustained morale in the country marvellously. He was also particularly pleasant to the dispirited Neville Chamberlain, with whom previously he had not always seen eye to eye, but whom he now allowed to remain living in 10 Downing Street until Chamberlain became ill, dying from cancer on November 9, 1940.

Like Bismarck, Churchill was a man with a commendably flexible mind, who understood the temporary nature of political alliances between states, and that the enemy of yesterday could become the ally of tomorrow sometimes without the need even of the stroke of a pen. Neither man allowed former prejudices, however stridently uttered, to stand in the way of a fresh policy if their state's best interests required it. Churchill was even willing to change political parties, even if this seemed to be abandoning political principles. He left the Conservative Party early in his career and joined the Liberals, but, in 1924, returned to the Conservatives, remarking: 'Anyone can rat, but it takes a certain amount of ingenuity to re-rat'. Bismarck abandoned policies rather than parties when he felt the need arose; having persuaded the Kaiser, Wilhelm I, in 1866 of the wickedness of Austria, and of the need to make war on that state, he was, six weeks later – once Austria had suffered defeat – urging an alliance with Austria – an attitude shift most puzzling to his King. In an even more rapid about-turn, Churchill, from being one of the harshest critics of Russia and its communist rulers, suddenly, overnight, on June 22, 1941, did a U-turn and welcomed Russia as Britain's friend and ally, and he prepared to send arms to her aid – an action explained, of course, by the launch that day of 'Operation Barbarossa', the German invasion of Russia. To the House of Commons, Churchill explained with typical impish humour: 'If Hitler invaded Hell I would at least make a favourable reference to the Devil'. Britain at last had an ally in Europe against Germany; as Churchill also pointed out: 'There is only one thing worse than fighting with allies, and that is fighting without them'.

On May 26, 1942, a 20-year alliance was concluded between Britain and the USSR after six days of negotiation between Churchill and the Soviet Foreign Minister, Molotov. Molotov stayed at Chequers under the inspired alias of 'Mr Brown', and was driven into 10 Downing Street each day for talks to thrash out the details. After the war was over, the treaty seems to have been overlooked with the onset of 'the Cold War'. One of Churchill's most perceptive speeches was made in September, 1946, when he called for 'a United States of Europe', although he could not have foreseen the strength of the later opposition in the UK to the idea or the length of time it might take to achieve.

* * * * *

The first months of the war were called the Phoney War because of relatively little war activity. That was to come in ample measure in Norway from April 1940 and in the Low Countries and France from May 10. Meanwhile, precautionary and preparatory measures were taken in Britain; in Scilly, detachments of the Duke of Cornwall's Light Infantry and the West Yorkshire Regiment were sent to the Islands – and also, later, a unit of commandos to train there. Star Castle Hotel and its annexe (later called Garrison House) were commandeered in July, 1940, to serve as the military headquarters, and the Atlantic Hotel became the officers' mess. Lieutenant Commander Perrin, who was then Lieutenant Perrin, the officer commanding RML542, recalls the impromptu inter-service 'rugby' matches played in the

Atlantic Hotel lounge, but these were stopped eventually by the Garrison Adjutant, Captain Creswell-George, after one army officer had broken his arm in the mêlée. Until the spring of 1940, hostilities consisted mainly of some intermittent sea and air activity; but the fall of France, and the German invasion of the Channel Islands in the summer of 1940, changed that. Those islands remained in enemy hands from June 30, 1940, to May 9, 1945, and most inhabitants there were obliged to become vegetarians because of the meat shortage under the occupation. They were surrendered to the Germans without a fight. Their occupation made the Scillies' inhabitants starkly conscious of the vulnerability of the Scillies, particularly when French refugees began to arrive. Some came on a lifeboat called the *Jean Charlotte*; others made the crossing from French channel ports crowded on red-sailed crabbers, vessels which had been a familiar sight fishing around Scilly in pre-war days. A plan was drawn up – fortunately never executed – which would have involved removing all remaining residents on St Mary's to Tresco, although how this would have benefited the situation is not at all clear. An atmosphere of uncertainty prevailed, and many islanders kept packed suitcases at the ready in order to undertake a hurried evacuation from the islands if this proved necessary. All local elections were suspended for the duration under the Local Elections and Register of Electors (Temporary Provisions) Act, 1939.

Although golf continued for a short time, the golf course was soon commandeered, and gun emplacements dug on its edges. Soon, the fairways were also dug, lest the enemy should try to land troops on St Mary's from the air, and an anti-aircraft gun was later placed on the course.

In 1940, much other activity in Scilly was also directed to protecting the islands from possible invasion, should Hitler decide to begin Operation Sealion – the planned invasion of Britain. Some of the pleasure launches, including *Nemo III*, *Gloria*, *Zedora* and *Sapphire I* and *II*, were commandeered for naval use and run at first by the Resident Naval Officer (RNO), but with some of the craft sent to the mainland. The launch *Springfield* was also requisitioned by the Royal Navy in the 2nd World War, while its owner, Vernon Thompson, served for five years in the Merchant Navy. Upon de-requisitioning after the war, it was brought 'home' to Scilly from Plymouth by Vernon's two brothers, Jeff and Frank, and repainted in its attractive pre-war colours of white and red – it looked like a speedboat but at the time had only a 15 h.p. engine. Already, in 1939, a store beneath Lemon Hall had been specially strengthened by the Council and made into an air-raid shelter to take up to 200 people and another one for 200 people was built on The Strand under a store. There was also an air raid shelter dug in the Parade Garden, but it was never used and was soon demolished. The Council distributed over 2,000 copies of a pamphlet telling people how to make a room at home gas-proof, and six people qualified as anti-gas instructors. Four other smaller shelters were also built, and the two sally-ports under the Garrison wall were also considered suitable as emergency shelters; but it was hoped that the granite construction of many of the buildings in Hugh Town would serve as some protection from German bombs. People could strengthen their homes with sandbags issued free of charge, and it was felt that if people stayed in their homes they would at least be dispersed and therefore there would be fewer casualties; but this did not stop some people heading for old gun emplacements during air-raids. The vicarage and Lemon Hall were offered as temporary extra hospital accommodation, if there were many casualties, and the retired Dr Addison offered to be on call in the hospital. Three air raid shelters were set up on St Martin's, one of which at the clay pit could accommodate 40 people; there was a smaller one at Middle Town and a third at Lower Town.

On St Martin's, rolls of barbed wire were assembled on Pool Green, but were never in fact unwound, but a machine-gun emplacement was made on Cruther's Hill, and a number of soldiers were billeted on the island. Coast watchers took shifts at the Daymark and there were ARP wardens, the Women's Land Army and the Home Guards with their H.Q. in the Reading Room. Nearly everybody on the island seemed to be 'somebody', but Betty Walder was the only one who became a W.A.A.F.

On St Mary's sentries were posted on the quay where checks were made on visitors' identity cards, and the ten stirrup pumps distributed in Hugh Town in May, 1939, were made available. St Mary's Hall was also earmarked as an additional emergency hospital. The Air Raid Siren on St Mary's was placed in Hugh Town at Carn Thomas and, after the war, became the fire service signal, gorse, heather and bracken fires being quite a common hazard in hot summers.

Scilly was vulnerable because there was no fighter cover for the first twenty months of the war, although some anti-aircraft guns were brought over and put in position on September 3, 1940. But German air attacks started before this: after reconnaissance over the target for some days previously, five Junkers 88 aircraft dropped bombs on August 21, 1940, on the recently-completed, direction-finding-station on Peninnis -- a station which was believed to be some sort of secret early radar station. On the following day, a Heinkel dropped incendiaries on Tresco and Bryher, and, on the 24th, seven bombs landed on The Garrison and Porthcressa, but all failed to explode. One of the enemy aircraft that day went on to drop a bomb at Telegraph, presumably aiming at the Tower, but damage was limited to one house and to two cows, which were killed. Another aircraft dropped bombs at Deep Point, but it seems more likely that it was jettisoning its load rather than aiming to sever the defunct telegraph-cable from the mainland which comes ashore at this point. However, there were two diesel generators placed at Deep Point at some time during the war, operating a radio beacon continuously as an aid to

navigation – but even this hardly seems to warrant bombing. On August 25th, the more important direction-finding-station on Peninnis was again attacked, and Matt Lethbridge recalls watching this raid from a doorway at the back of the town hall. It was by four JU88s and, for about the next ten days, they came back every afternoon just before 4.30, until eventually their incendiary bombs caused a fire from which the station burnt down. Each afternoon the four JU88s made their run-in from over The Garrison, each 'plane usually dropping two bombs before turning and dropping two more on the return run, finally machine-gunning Porthcressa as they left the islands. On the same day, Joan Kathleen Groves, a girl of 12 who suffered from cerebral palsy, had learning difficulties, and lived at No 3, H.M. Coastguard Station, was killed. Mr H.C. Taylor recalls that Joan had been sitting on her mother's lap in the base of Telegraph Tower – which, because of its substantial construction, was used by families in the nearby coastguard houses as an air raid shelter – when she was caught by a stray, ricocheting bullet from a burst of German machine-gun fire, which penetrated past the sandbagged windows and struck her in the mouth. She was the younger daughter of Charles Frederick Groves, a coastguard officer born in 1900, who served in Scilly 1939-49. Joan's grave in Old Town Churchyard was unmarked, but Alfred Trenear discovered it in 2000, situated between two other graves. It was estimated that during the week from Sunday, August 25th, 1940, about 70 high explosive bombs were dropped on St Mary's, and two launches, the *Sapphire* and the *Nornour*, were machine-gunned as they crossed from Tresco to St Mary's. Six bombs landed in the field behind the former Trinity House cottages on the Garrison, but failed to explode. The unexploded bombs were taken to an isolated spot near Pelistry and detonated safely. Another bomb landed in the middle of Porthcressa Beach and did explode, but only shattered a few nearby windows. One enemy aircraft machine-gunned a soldier on the roof of Star Castle who had been signalling to others on Tresco; he laid low below the parapet and by so doing escaped injury.

* * * * *

In 1942, a Breton trawler, *Le Dinan*, known as N51, was acquired by the British Intelligence Service (SIS) and based at New Grimsby. In June of that year, N51 rescued from the occupied French coast the head of one of the Free French Intelligence Units – a man known as Remy – together with his family, in what turned out also to be a most useful operation because a parcel Remy brought with him contained the German plans for the Atlantic Wall, which were invaluable in helping to decide the landing places of the Allied invasion of June 6, 1944. In further operations agents were retrieved or landed and supplies for them made available. It has been alleged that one or more 'mystery' ships from Tresco Channel blew up Alderney lighthouse. Then, in 1943, another boat was used; it was built with a high-speed hull capable of 28 knots, but with a French fishing-boat superstructure, and known as MFV 2023. One dark night on a secret operation from Tresco to 30 miles off Brest, a searchlight suddenly illuminated the boat, but it was not from a German destroyer but from an RAF Wellington bomber looking for German U-boats, and fortunately not prepared to waste time or ammunition dropping one of its depth-charges on an innocent looking French fishing-boat. On July 1, 2000, a plaque was unveiled at Braiden Rock, New Grimsby, Tresco, by the wife of the former French Resistance leader, Daniel Lomenach, to mark the point where, in the 2nd World War, top secret operations were launched against Hitler's occupied France, and to commemorate these clandestine missions. The location of the plaque is north of the Quay Shop, off the path heading towards Cromwell's Castle, but at steps cut into the rock by the sea at the first rock-face which the path encounters, steps which had been crudely carved out to enable crews to embark unnoticed.

When on Tresco, the crews from these trawlers were billeted either at the

(above) *From April, 1942, until October, 1943, New Grimsby Channel was the base of a secret naval flotilla keeping contact with French Underground Intelligence Organisations working in German-occupied France. In June, 1942, Colonel Renault and his family, who were in danger of discovery by the Gestapo, were rescued by N51, and brought with them to England a detailed plan of the Atlantic Wall - the German defences on the Normandy coast. This was given to Eisenhower, Montgomery and Churchill, and was crucial in ensuring the D-Day landings of June 6, 1944, were successful. The steps were cut in the granite to enable the crew and passengers on N51 to embark and disembark without anyone likely to see them.*

(below) *N51 disguised as a French fishing-boat and named* Le Dinan.

N51 Le Dinan

New Inn or at Chudleigh's cottage, and they assiduously kept up the pretence of being fishermen. The steps cut in the rocks north of New Grimsby allowed them to arrive and depart unnoticed, without the Tresco Islanders knowing what their presence was really all about.

When they journeyed to France, it was normally to the Atlantic coast rather than the English Channel coast because the latter would be too obvious to the German authorities. As well as landing and retrieving underground agents, their tasks included keeping up communications with the Free French Movement, rescuing Free French operators in danger of being apprehended by the Gestapo, and bringing information from agents in France, together with landings of items and supplies useful to their activities. The extent of these secret operations has been described in a book entitled *Secret Flotillas – The Clandestine Sea Lanes to France and French North Africa, 1940-1944*, by Sir Brooks Richards.

* * * * *

238

Eight young French refugees are shown in the photograph arriving at St Mary's in 1940 in their Breton fishing-boat Cuilvinee *in a successful escape from German-occupied France. In June, 1942, one of the principal organisers of the French Resistance, Colonel Renault, also escaped in a fishing-boat, but he transferred in the middle of the English Channel to N51, a vessel run by the British Intelligence Service. This vessel spent much time pretending to be a harmless French fishing-boat, but actually helped to service the French Underground Resistance.*

Further succour was giving to the French Resistance by the playing of the first four notes of Beethoven's 5th Symphony over the wireless on the Overseas Service. They signified 'V for Victory' in morse code, and were intended to give encouragement to people living in Europe in enemy-occupied territory. There was also a competition arranged to compose a march specifically for the underground movement. Ivor Norvello was reproached by his friends for not entering, so he hastily put together a piece that was not dissimilar to Keep the Home Fires Burning, *only written backwards. To everyone's surprise, not only did this entry win the competition, but the French Resistance Movement was happy to adopt it.* Photo : Gibson, Scilly

On the Home Front, the Government produced a flurry of national legislation and directives from September 3, 1939, one of which led to the establishment of an organisation to control air transport – actually, for a time under the management of Gordon Olley – to supervise all internal UK civilian air services. Immediately, the civil aircraft flying to Scilly – there was at first only one, G-ACPY, the others being taken for war work – was painted in camouflage and its windows whitened (blacked-out it was called), presumably lest a German spy should think of taking a trip to Scilly to look for British shipping during the crossing. To make it more difficult for German aircraft to intercept the 'plane, the flight times were varied without pattern to the certain confusion of many passengers, if not also to the enemy.

The presence of German spies in Britain was probably exaggerated, but one was certainly discovered in Scilly during the war, and before he could be apprehended was seen rowing hard in a punt towards a U-boat in which eventually he disappeared. During the war, fifteen people were executed in Britain as German spies, with one called Richter having to be held down by 4 guards before they could kill him.

At the end of 1942 there occurred an incident which for a brief while caused more trepidation than even the suspected presence of German spies. An object, which was at first taken to be a U-boat, appeared actually in St

Mary's Sound. However, upon closer investigation, it turned out to be a German Air-Sea Rescue Float, which had broken away from its moorings and drifted into Scilly. These floats were for ditched German aircrew in the English Channel, and consisted of a room below sea level, complete with bunks and supplies of food and drink, which were renewed at intervals by German E-boats.

* * * * *

The air service to Scilly continued for the greater part of the war and there were three flights a day from September 25, 1939, the plane by October, 1940, even beginning to carry the Royal Mail. But there were three interruptions; the first was in May, 1940, when the aircraft was put on standby in case it was wanted to assist in the evacuation of the British army from Dunkirk; the second was after the de Havilland Dragon (G-ACPY) piloted by a New Zealander, W.S. Anderson, a most experienced pilot, took off at about 1700 hours from St Mary's on Tuesday, June 3rd, 1941, with 5 passengers of the Leggitt family (who were on a day visit to Scilly) and then disappeared, with the loss of all on board – a tragedy which resulted in the air service being suspended until October 27, 1941, and suspended again from November 4, 1941, to January 12, 1942, after which Dragon G-ADDI took up the resumed service.

A more detailed explanation of the circumstances leading to the loss of the Dragon came in 1994. In that year a visitor to Scilly was Horst Freiheer von Luttitz, who, in 1941, was a lieutenant and the navigator in the German Luftwaffe aircrew which had shot down the Dragon. His 4-man Heinkel IIIH-4, under its captain Leutnant Walter Klenck of the German Navy, had set out from its base at Nantes in France with orders to attack the aircraft carrier *Indomitable*, then under construction at Barrow-in-Furness; but the cloud cover dissipated, removing the opportunity to hide from RAF fighter aircraft, so the mission was aborted. However, on the Heinkel's return journey down the Irish Channel, what was thought to be an RAF plane was intercepted between Scilly and Land's End and attacked from above and behind using the Heinkel's nose machine-gun, an unusual instance of a bomber attacking another aircraft. The wartime RAF camouflage of the Dragon may have played a part in this mistake in identification and certainly made the Dragon a legitimate target. Von Luttitz saw the port engine of the Dragon catch fire and the 'plane dive into the sea', after which the Germans say they twice broadcast an international distress message, but which does not seem to have been received. Rescue boats searched the sea area but only after the Dragon failed to land at St Just, and nothing was ever found, except that a body – which may have come from the Dragon – was later washed up on the shore near Newquay. The Luftwaffe crew never properly identified the plane even when they returned to base, one of their number even believing that they had shot down a triplane, a sighting which could have been an effect of the camouflage. The German crew of the Heinkel failed to see the civilian markings on the fuselage and on the upper wings of the Dragon, but they did mention during their de-briefing at Nantes, that they were surprised at the aircraft's slow speed.

Another observer of the incident was John Stanley of Surrey. Writing in *Scilly Up To Date*, No. 89, he says that he was on duty at the RAF radar station near Land's End at this time and watched the Heinkel and the Dragon plotted on his radar screen. He saw 'the two blips together and then only one left to continue its journey ...'. He adds that when regular passenger flights were later resumed 'they were only allowed to fly subject to the confirmation from our station that there were no enemy aircraft within the danger area'.

* * * * *

The Anglo-German Naval Agreement of June, 1935, had limited the size of the German navy to 35% that of the Royal Navy, although Hitler did not keep strictly to it. But, in the matter of submarines, Germany was allowed to have equal numbers with the Royal Navy, and this enabled Doenitz by September, 1939, to have 56 submarines, some of 700 tons or over of the Type VII class, which had a speed on the surface of 17 knots. About six a month was the rate of building by September, 1939. In Britain at that time, which had a population of 48 million and was dependent on imports of about 55 million tons of food and raw materials a year, there were about 5,000 merchant ships, vulnerable to any determined attack. Of Germany's 56 submarines, 30 were really for operating in coastal waters, not the North Atlantic, and Britain by adopting the convoy system from the start – the lesson from the 1st World War having been learnt – had some protection, but was so short of escort ships, particularly after Dunkirk, that many of the faster vessels opted to go it alone and not in convoy, and some fell victim to the U-boats. In the first 7 months of the war, 124 ships were sunk, followed by an interlude between March and June 1940, when German naval units, including U-boats, concentrated on the invasion of Norway. But then, after the surrender of France, there was an intensification of the U-boat war, now that the Germans had the use of the French Atlantic ports. At first the U-boats, with their low silhouette, were unlikely to be detected at night, and the Asdic devices in escort ships only detected U-boats when they were submerged. Sloops and corvettes used for escorting convoys were slower than U-boats on the surface, and when U-boats attacked in unison in so-called wolf-packs, the escorts were sometimes overwhelmed.

The evacuation of Dunkirk cost 25 Allied destroyers sunk and, subsequently, most surviving destroyers in home waters were required to be

241

The most important capture of the war – the Enigma Code from Lemp's U-110 on May 9, 1941, by the British destroyer Bulldog.

in the English Channel to try to stop the anticipated German invaders. This meant that convoy HX72 of 41 unarmed merchant ships was only lightly escorted by three 900 ton corvettes capable of only 16 knots, although they were armed with guns and depth-charges and an early form of Asdic. On reaching the Western Approaches they ran into one of Doenitz's wolf packs, losing 11 merchant ships. In October, 1940, another convoy, SC7, lost 17 of 30 ships and Convoy HX79 lost 14 ships. The British realised that something had to be done to lessen these losses, and new tactics developed by Commander F.J. Walker, helped begin to turn the situation round, so that when Convoy HG76 sailed from Gibraltar in December, 1941, 4 U-boats were sunk and two long-range Condor bombers shot down for the loss of only one escort and two merchant ships. But this was still exceptional and merchant ship losses were still too high. What was of most importance in helping the Royal Navy defeat the U-boat was the breaking of the German naval codes, which came about in fortuitous circumstances, as follows.

In May, 1941, Admiral Holland went down with the *Hood* but, earlier that month, he had planned and carried out the interception of the German weather-ship *Muenchen*. The German crew had thrown their coding-machine overboard, but the British boarding party found the coding tables for May and June still intact, and these enabled Naval Intelligence to decipher German signals until the end of June. But the really lucky break came on May 8, 1941, when the destroyer *Bulldog* brought U-110 to the surface with depth-charges. Surrounded by British warships, the 32 survivors of the 47-man German crew hurriedly abandoned the stricken U-boat, believing it to be sinking and a British warship about to ram it; in fact, *Bulldog* appeared about to ram but then went full astern and a British boarding party of 8 ratings, led by Sub-Lieutenant D.E. Balme, rushed towards it. In the water the U-boat

242

commander, Julius Lemp – he who had sunk the Glasgow liner *Athenia* on September 3, 1939 – saw what was happening and made a desperate attempt to swim back to the U-boat, but was shot dead or possibly drowned before he succeeded. The result was that inside the U-boat the boarding party found her confidential code-books and signals and her complete Enigma machine set up ready to transmit a signal. The U-boat sank later during a tow, but the Germans never knew that its Enigma machine and its cyphers had been captured – perhaps the single most important British Intelligence success in the Battle of the Atlantic, for enemy signals could now be decoded with the Germans still convinced that their communications were secret.

A film drama made in Hollywood in 1999 concerning the capture of the Enigma machine from U-571, showed Americans doing the capturing – a little rewriting of history to please transatlantic audiences. Moreover, a film entitled *The Patriot*, made in 1999, showed the struggle for freedom from Britain in the American War of Independence, 1776-83 – a great theme, but British redcoats sometimes seemed to behave little better than supposed Nazi stormtroopers in 2nd World War films, burning civilians in churches, stringing up elderly people from trees, and sometimes acting a bit like the Irish allegations against some of the Black and Tans, the British soldiers in post-1st World War Irish History. However, British film-makers had earlier made a film entitled *Breaking the Sound Barrier* starring Ralph Richardson, which showed an Englishman as the first to break the sound barrier rather than an American. Commercial considerations, it seems, outweigh the need for strict factual accuracy, for uncomplicated stereotypes are understood more easily, and films figuring them should be viewed not as historical statements but as exciting entertainment. The trouble is that the latter can often be confused in the memory with the former.

The arduous work involved in decoding was mentally exhausting, complicated and carried out in great secrecy at the Code and Cypher School at Bletchley Park by a team of dedicated mathematicians, linguists and others headed by Alan Turing – chess and bridge players were well represented – and the resulting information, known as Ultra, relayed to Churchill. Helping the decoders was Hans Thilo Schmidt, known in his private life as a philanderer, but who had once worked in the Cypher office of the German Defence Ministry in Berlin and was able to explain German cypher procedures. The most important matter was to let the Germans think that U-110 had sunk with all hands, and to so imprison the 32 survivors that they could not possibly get word to Germany that the U-boats code books and Enigma machine had been captured. Accordingly, all 32 men were sent to prison camp 23 in Canada near Hudson Bay and kept strictly confined. The immediate result was that U-boat successes declined as convoys were re-routed away from where U-boats were now known to be waiting. Doenitz was baffled, and a search for spies was made; even French night-clubs were inspected – to see if U-boat officers on leave were indulging in pillow talk – but no leak or spy was found; and yet the Germans were still convinced that their Enigma communications remained secret. Breaking the Enigma Code is credited not only with shortening the war, but in laying the foundations for the Computer Age.

May, 1943, was a crucial month when Ultra information helped in the sinking of 41 U-boats, followed in July and August by the sinking of 13 more. Eventually, the Germans changed the Enigma code to the 'Shark', and there was another interval before that was broken, but having broken one it was not so hard to break another. It was not only the war against U-boats which was helped by the cracking of the German Enigma code; at the Battle of Matapan in the Mediterranean in March, 1941, knowing the position and strength of the Italian fleet had helped Admiral Cunningham secure the victory; and Enigma also revealed the position of the 21st Panzer division at Caen after D-Day, so helping Field Marshal Montgomery. Even more important, cracking the Enigma code told General Eisenhower where the German minefields along the French coast were and where they were not, a great help in his planning of the D-Day landings in June, 1944.

The Bletchley codebreakers had a method of checking some of their deciphering. They compared an Enigma coded weather report sent from Hamburg to Berlin each day with the original weather report sent to Hamburg with the help of a German double-agent employed by MI5. Thus, despite the Germans changing their codes increasingly frequently, Bletchley could decipher them.

Bletchley Park was also able to keep track after 1941 of the movements of Admiral Canaris, head of German Military Intelligence. A section of MI6, headed by Kim Philby – who was also a Soviet agent, as it later transpired – was plotting to use this information to assassinate Canaris. However, the trouble with some secret information is that it can be partial; it turned out that MI6 had to be stopped from conducting this operation when Canaris was revealed as a member of the anti-Hitler section of the German military who were planning Hitler's assassination. In the 1st World War, Canaris was a lieutenant on the *Dresden*, and was sent to negotiate with the British when the German cruiser was cornered. He artfully won time, which enabled scuttling charges to be fitted to the *Dresden*, so that his ship was not captured. He was hanged in the last weeks of the 2nd World War for his part in conspiracies against Hitler.

* * * * *

Kaiser Wilhelm II died in Holland on June 4, 1941, with scarcely more than a note in the British newspapers, so quickly does history move on, although the Wehrmacht provided a guard of honour of 1,000 men for his funeral.

However, the end of 1941 brought a momentous new stage in the conflict which occupied newspapers for the rest of the war: Hitler declared war on the USA in support of his Japanese ally after the bombing of Pearl Harbour on December 7, 1941. The attack on Pearl Harbour was described by President Roosevelt as 'a brilliant feat of deception, perfectly timed and executed with great skill'. This seems like overblown praise because, although the Japanese sank or badly damaged eight old battleships such as the *Virginia* and *Tennessee*, no aircraft carriers – the really vital warships in the Pacific War – were affected. They had left Pearl Harbour and were at sea miles away. Moreover, five of these damaged battleships were repaired and fought again in the war, and the 4 Japanese carriers whose aircraft had attacked Pearl Harbour were destroyed at the Battle of Midway by aircraft from the very American carriers which had been absent at sea when Pearl Harbour was attacked.

The gun-club mentality of most admirals in most navies continued to build battleships, but the Pacific War against Japan proved beyond doubt that aircraft-carriers were the capital ships of the future. One success of a battleship against another battleship was in 1942, when the USA's battleship *Washington*, with excellent radar and 16-inch guns, engaged and sank the older Japanese battleship *Kirishima*, equipped with the feebler Japanese radar and smaller guns; but it was the Japanese battleship *Yamashiro* on October 25, 1944, which was the last battleship ever to be sunk by another battleship, at the Battle of Leyte Gulf by the US fleet flagship *Mississippi*. The USA's even larger battleship *Missouri* was one of the last battleships to fire her guns in war – but only against a land target – and is now kept as a museum piece.

The greater importance of the aircraft-carrier over the battleship was well illustrated at the Battle of the Coral Sea on May 8, 1942. This was the action that checked Japanese expansion in the Pacific, but the opposing ships never saw each other and never fired shots at each other; it was a conflict between carriers and their aircraft, and both sides lost one carrier in the action.

Paradoxically, the news of the sinking of the American Pacific Fleet at Pearl Harbour was a relief to Churchill, who at last felt that, with the USA in the war, victory would in the end be assured. Immediately, it meant that the United States Navy was available to help control the U-boats, in collaboration with Liberator long-range aircraft; and the building programme in the USA of 10,000 ton, massed-produced Liberty ships (about 1,500 afloat by 1943) helped to make up for merchant ship losses, if not for their cargoes. The Liberty ships were of a British design with bronze propeller – 'dreadful-looking objects' Roosevelt called them – but they served their purpose well, although over 200 were sunk during the hostilities. But the USA entering the war had some minus points: U-53 sank the United States destroyer *Jacob Jones* on December 6 within sight of the Bishop Rock lighthouse, and for a time the U-boats enjoyed what they called 'a happy time' sinking merchant vessels along the coasts of the USA. However, weapons for dealing with U-boats were improving and U-boat losses rose. Once a U-boat had been located under an area of sea by a surface warship, it would be bombarded with a plethora of depth-charges set to explode at varying depths; if an explosion took place in the vicinity of the U-boat its hull could be holed, which would either mean that it sank with all the crew, or that it came rapidly to the surface to fight its opponent with its one gun or torpedoes, but more likely to surrender – before more damage meant the pointless loss of the lives of all the crew. Some U-boat commanders fooled the surface warships by jettisoning oil to the surface as if they had suffered irredeemable damage, while making off stealthily into deeper water in another direction. The Royal Navy destroyer *Warwick* of 1,100 tons was torpedoed and sunk near Scilly on February 20, 1944, by U-413, commanded by Gustav Peol, and three drowned seamen from the *Warwick* (Peacock, Hales and Killey) are buried in Old Town Churchyard; but, on August 20, 1944, U-413 was depth-charged by the destroyers *Forester*, *Vidette* and *Wensleydale* in the English Channel and lost with all 45 hands, including its commander at that time, Dietrich Sachse, so ending its hunting career in which it had sunk 5 ships and was itself damaged twice – first from air attack by an RAF Hudson escorting Convoy MKF.IY on November 19, 1942, and second by an RAF Halifax on June 8, 1944. Such a career for a U-boat was not untypical, though many were shorter; of the 750 or so U-boats which took part in the Battle of the Atlantic, about 510 were lost and about 28,000 of their crews also. This compares with the 77 submarines of the Royal Navy lost during the war in all theatres, although, during the six years of war, 5,150 Allied merchant ships were destroyed at sea by enemy action of all types.

One of the most successful convoy escort commanders during the war was Captain F.J. Walker, who devised new tactics, including the 'creeping attack', for dealing with U-boat attacks, and died of a stroke in 1944, brought on by what was said to be overwork. Before the war he had been described as 'lacking powers of leadership' – a naval interview assessment which could not have proved further from the truth. The Scillonian, Margaret Perry, who died in 1982 and had been the wife of Ron Perry, was based at the Devonport Torpedo Depot during the war as an assistant to Captain Walker.

Sometimes unnecessary brutality occurs in war as much through misunderstandings as by an intentional wickedness. An incident of this happened on September 17, 1942, when U-156 torpedoed and sank the British liner *Laconia*, which was carrying 1,800 Italian prisoners of war. Italy was an ally of Germany at the time, and so U-156 called upon other U-boats in the area to come to help rescue as many survivors as they could; but they were spotted by an Allied bomber, which failed to comprehend what the situation was, but saw an opportunity to bomb a number of U-boats apparently caught napping on the surface. When Doenitz heard about what

It was not only goods which needed to be brought safely across the Atlantic but also service personnel and, for this purpose, some of the big passenger liners were converted into troopships, including the Queen Mary.

One of the greatest and most luxurious of the Cunard liners, and the last liner ever to be built wth four funnels, was the Aquitania, *a lucky ship which avoided the attentions of the enemy, although employed as a troopship in both World Wars. On August 7, 1914, she was commandeered by the Admiralty and armed with six-inch guns; but after she ran into another vessel, the Admiralty decided she would serve better as a troopship, disarmed her and returned her to Cunard – all this in a matter of months. For the next 35 years of unbroken service and 884 transatlantic crossings, sailing some 3 million sea miles, she became in 1949 the oldest liner still in passenger service. She became a frequent sight in Scilly as she plied her way past the Islands to Southampton.*

She did once run aground on a sandbank when attempting to enter Southampton in 1935 during a 70 mile-an-hour gale; ten tugs (five can be seen on her port side in the photograph), pulled her clear of the Knoll, a sandbank with tree trunks of an ancient, submerged forest, similar to the one in Mount's Bay.

Aquitania *probably carried more service personnel across the Atlantic over the two wars than any other ship, quite apart from the fare-paying passengers between the wars and after. She was very large and high out of the water, looking much bigger than her 47,000 tons.*

One typical, crowded transatlantic voyage started from the River Clyde opposite Greenock on Easter Sunday, 1945. She was unescorted, relying as usual on her relatively high speed of 23 knots to outpace any U-boats which might still be lurking hoping to intercept her. On this voyage, heavy gales beset her in mid-Atlantic, and she did not dare to reduce speed because although U-boat activity had much decreased by 1945, there might still be some at sea. The result of the gale was that her 4 huge propellers threshed the water and shook the ship unnervingly each time she pitched into mountainous seas. This was particularly to the discomfort of the hundreds of young RAF aircrew-under-training, who were on their way to No. 5 Air Navigation School at Portage la Prairie, 60 miles west of Winnipeg in Canada. Troops of many units were on the ship – all heading for the Canadian port of Halifax – but the RAF boys were allocated bunks in what in peacetime had been the steerage or 3rd class accommodation in the stern above the propellers, and were allotted duties such as bringing food up via greasy, stepladder-like companionways from the galley below to the mess above, where, with the heavy sea, it would not stay on the tables; but, as few were in the mood to eat it, it did not matter too much. The air cadets learnt to be glad they had joined the RAF rather than the Royal Navy, for air sickness is, for some reason, not as debilatating as sea sickness.

had happened, he ordered that there should be no more rescue attempts by U-boats.

Both the Germans and the British had trouble with faulty torpedoes. U-56, commanded by Wilhelm Zahn, had the battleship *Nelson* in his sights, on board which was the 1st Sea Lord and Winston Churchill. Two torpedoes were fired and both hit the battleship, but neither of them exploded. U-25 and U-46 reported similar failures, and U-46 aimed at *Warspite* in a Norwegian fiord and the torpedo misfired. Prien reported that he had fired four torpedoes at point-blank targets and none of them had exploded. Doenitz wrote that up to 30% of German torpedoes seemed to be duds, one explanation for which was that there had been a failure to allow sufficiently for the effects of sunspots and for the Earth's magnetism in northern latitudes, which affected the magnetic detonators. Another alleged finding was that many torpedoes had been set to run nearly ten feet deeper than designed and so went under their targets, with the detonators unlikely to work anyway; however, Oscar Wehr, the German head of torpedo testing, refused to accept this criticism.

One of the saddest parts of the convoy system was that when a merchant ship in the convoy was torpedoed by a U-boat and sunk, other ships in the convoy often found it inadvisable to stop and try to rescue survivors. Sometimes it even involved ploughing through merchant seamen struggling in the water, not daring to stop and help, for it was almost inevitable that one of the attacking U-boats would be following the convoy, just waiting for a straggler to be left behind. In December, 1942, nine new U-boats joined the U-boat fleet, making 164 able to be operational in the Atlantic, with 24 in the Mediterranean, 21 in the Arctic waters and 3 in the Black Sea. This was a formidable force to take on vulnerable merchant ships, and helps to explain why one in every 4 merchant seamen died in the war, a higher percentage than in any branch of the British armed services, and 30% of those serving in it were not of British origin. The dedication and bravery of merchant ships crews in the Battle of the Atlantic was quite amazing; they were doing their ordinary job, but they faced danger on every voyage, often without any means of replying to an attack. Even in a well-escorted convoy, they could not feel at all safe; convoy ON-127, comprising 32 merchant ships and escorts, was attacked from September 10-14, 1942, by a wolf pack of 13 U-boats, resulting in the loss of 12 merchant ships and one destroyer. On another occasion, in convoy HX.84 on November 5, 1940, the *San Demetrio* was set on fire and abandoned, the crew rowing quickly away in their lifeboats. Then, later in the day, they had what they thought was a stroke of luck; a merchant ship appeared on the horizon and they rowed towards it excitedly, only to discover that it was the *San Demetrio* again. They re-embarked, put out the fire embers, re-started the engine, and slowly reached port, and delivered the cargo intact. Altogether, 2,603 Allied merchant ships were sunk by enemy action during the 2nd World War by 1,162 U-boats of which 784 were lost. 30,249 merchant seamen have been estimated to have died as a result of the sinkings, and about 28,000 U-boat crewmen died out of an estimated 40,900 who took part. One reason for the high loss of life among merchant seamen was that iron ships tended to sink more rapidly than the old wooden ships of former wars, and to produce less driftwood on which survivors in the sea could cling to until rescued. Losses of RAF aircrews who came down in the water were also high at the beginning; the aircrew had Mae West lifejackets but, if a survivor wearing one drifted unconscious, he nearly always drowned; a firm collar was later added to the Mae West, and this much improved the survival rate.

One danger to merchant crews in convoy at the start of the 2nd World War was the shortage of escort ships for the convoys, with some large convoys, of perhaps up to 40 merchant vessels, being protected sometimes by only 3 warships. To alleviate this, some liners, which were not otherwise used as troopships, were taken over by the Royal Navy, painted grey, armed with guns and depth-charges and called armed merchant cruisers. One of these was the *Jervis Bay*, which was unlucky enough to be the escort of the homeward-bound convoy HX.84, of which the *San Demetrio* was a member. In the Atlantic Approaches on November 5th, 1940, the German pocket battleship *Admiral Scheer* attacked it. *Jervis Bay*, with guns able to fire shells only about 10,000 yards, sacrificed herself – as good guards should – by engaging the enemy, whose shells from six 11-inch guns were able to hit the *Jervis Bay* at about twice that range. But 34 ships of the convoy escaped by scattering, including the *San Demetrio*, and only 5 were sunk by the *Admiral Scheer* – after the *Jervis Bay* had been sunk.

One of the worst convoy disasters was what happened to convoy PQ-17 on July 10, 1942. It arrived in Archangel, but only contained 4 ships, the remnants of a convoy of 33 ships. Contrary to normal practice, which left decisions to the convoy commander, there was a belief of the First Sea Lord in London that the convoy was about to be attacked by surface enemy warships. He issued the catastrophic order for all ships to disperse, which provided the perfect opportunity for the Germans to pick off the merchant ships unprotected by the Royal Navy. Sometimes intelligence information can be quite wrong and lead to complete disaster as happened here.

It is sometimes assumed that the danger to Allied merchant ships came only from U-boats, surface raiders and German aircraft. But, in fact, E-boats were also a menace, even quite late in the war. In 1944, seven E-boats, directed by a German reconnaissance aircraft, met Allied convoy WP457. Under the command of Lieutenant Commander Karl Muller, the E-boats attacked from the shelter of the Cornish coast near Porthcurno, which confused those aboard the convoy's escorting destroyer HMS *Mackay*, her captain at first assuming from the direction of their approach that the E-boats were British air-sea rescue craft or similar. A number of the ships in the convoy were sunk, the E-boats then hurrying away, taking advantage of their high speed after a short successful action, without casualties or damage to themselves. A few days later, E-boats again successfully attacked another convoy, but the Allied invasion of France from June 6, 1944, ended the E-boat attacks on convoys, except for one last one on March 15, 1945. A memorial on St Agnes makes clear that one of the men from that island lost his life in a battle with E-boats. It reads: 'A/B Leslie Legg, HMMTB 671. Posted missing, presumed killed in action with German E-Boats in the English Channel near the coast of France on 24th April, 1944, aged 19 years'.

Germany began the war with a fleet of raiders of British merchant ships in the Atlantic, including the two battlecruisers *Scharnhorst* and *Gneisenau*, the three pocket battleships *Graf Spee*, *Admiral Scheer* and *Lutzow* (formerly *Deutschland*) and the heavy cruisers *Admiral Hipper* and *Prinz Eugen*; but they also had over half-a-dozen armed merchant ships operating as raiders, usually disguised as merchant ships but armed with guns up to 5.9 inches calibre and torpedo tubes and carrying one or two aircraft. The best known are probably the *Orion*, *Widder*, *Kormoran*, *Atlantis*, *Pinguin*, and the *Thor* (which sank the British armed merchant cruiser *Voltaire*) and all these were assisted by tankers and supply ships such as the *Nordmark*.

In this war against these surface raiders one problem was providing enough convoy escorts of sufficient power to take on powerful raiders. It was not solved by building corvettes – useful though these were against U-boats – for they were slow and not well armed, nor by converting liners not required as troop carriers. One of the first of these latter was the *Rawalpindi* which, on November 23, 1939, sacrificed herself to save most of the ships in the convoy she was escorting to Britain by taking on, in the Western Approaches, the battlecruiser *Scharnhorst*. Despite having only 6-inch guns against the German raider's 11-inch, she scored at least one hit before being sunk in 14 minutes. Altogether, 55 former passenger-liners were converted into armed merchant cruisers during the war and, by the end of 1941, 15 of these had been sunk, and in one of them sunk on May 13, 1941, Lieutenant Commander Arnold Nance of Scilly was drowned. The eventual solution to the problem was for the Admiralty to allocate a battleship to convoys in vulnerable areas. That this lesson had been learnt is shown by the response of the *Scharnhorst* and *Gneisenau* who, sailing together under command of Admiral Lütjens, encountered a large convoy on February 22, 1941. As the two battlecruisers closed to attack, they spotted the tripod masts of the old battleship *Ramillies*, and immediately steered away from the convoy. Then, they met a convoy without a battleship escorting it, and sank five of its ships but, shortly afterwards off the west coast of Africa, they came upon another convoy, this time escorted by the old battleship *Malaya*, and again they withdrew. Finally, when approaching the Canadian coast, they found another convoy without a battleship escort and sank 16 ships, returning afterwards to Brest on March

22. This raiding voyage had obliged Admiral Tovey to commit too many of the Royal Navy's battleships of the Home Fleet to convoy duty, and thus provided the opportunity for two other powerful German raiders, the heavy cruiser Admiral Hipper and the pocket battleship Admiral Scheer, to return to Germany unimpeded from their raiding voyages. However, even a reinforced Home Fleet would probably not have caught one German raider, the *Komet*, which was operating in the Pacific and which returned safely to Germany by navigating through the North East Passage and the Bering Sea.

There was also the point that the warships of the Home Fleet at Scapa Flow composed a fleet-in-being, inactive, but *by their presence* helping to maintain the sea blockade on Germany which, by 1945, was having a considerable effect on Germany's capacity to make war. It is sometimes assumed that a warship must be doing something to justify its cost, despite the fact that everyone is aware that, with nuclear weapons, their mere possession is important in world politics. The case is not dissimilar to those who oppose putting more uniformed police on the streets, using the statistic that a police officer on the beat only walks past a crime being committed on average once every 8 years, thus overlooking that a uniformed policeman *by his very presence* may be deterring many criminal activities, quite apart from inspiring confidence in the law-abiding.

Another menace to Allied shipping at the start of the war was the German development of the magnetic mine, which did not wait to be run over by its victim, but was actually attracted to it, and the battleship *Nelson* was badly damaged by one of these mines. However, one of these mines which had not exploded was recovered intact off Shoeburyness in the autumn of 1939, and it was found that by degaussing ships – i.e. running an electric current around the hull – the magnetic mine became no more hazardous than an ordinary mine. Even the *Scillonian* received this protective treatment. Ordinary mines were quite as hazardous in the 2nd World War as in the 1st. One laid by U-31 was run into by the cruiser *Belfast* (built 1937, 9000 tons, 32 knots, nine 6-inch guns) on October 31, 1939, and broke the cruiser's back; after a long repair, *Belfast* did eventually see action against the *Scharnhorst* and is now moored in the Thames as a visitor attraction. Along her companionways today are some paintings of her action with the German battlecruiser, the artist being John Hamilton who lived in Scilly and did all his paintings in the Islands. Barely a month after the *Belfast* was damaged, a mine laid by U-33 also put the battleship *Nelson* out of action for many months – the second time a mine had disabled her.

Mines were also hazardous to submarines, but sometimes it was not mines, aircraft, or any other anti-submarine activity which claimed a U-boat and the lives of its crew, but an older enemy – the rocks around the Scillies. On March 3, 1945, U-681, commanded by Werner Gebauer, struck a ledge in the Western Rocks and was holed above the waterline. The U-boat was then able to make progress only on the surface and set off towards Ireland, but was spotted by a Liberator bomber of 103 Squadron of the 7th Fleet Air Wing of the US Navy from Dunkeswell in Devon, which proceeded to attack it. At that the crew scuttled their vessel and surrendered. Eleven crew had been killed but 38 survived and were brought into St Mary's. The U-boat's location was positively identified on the seabed in 1999 and some items recovered.

* * * * *

The Government made some war preparations after the Munich Agreement in 1938, but failed to draw up a comprehensive rationing scheme like the Swiss Government had done, or to give sufficient boost to the expansion of aircraft production. Even the Spitfire was at first developed by private enterprise without government support. But there was a strong belief in the late 1930s, when Baldwin declared that 'the bomber will always get through', that poison gas would be used in any future conflict and that some protection for civilians must be organised; so, in 1938/39, thirty million gas masks were issued in the UK – in three sizes – to ensure that the nation was prepared, and Scilly's inhabitants joined the rest of the UK population in being issued with gas masks as a precautionary measure, with a gas contamination centre set up in Church Street. Respirators arrived in Scilly on August 26, 1939, and at the same time came sirens for erection on each of the inhabited islands to give warning of when enemy bombers were in the vicinity. In the event there was neither a gas attack nor armed invasion, and it may be that one of the reasons poison gas was not used by either side had little to do with the precautions taken to combat it, but because of its remembered tendency in the First World War to blow about indiscriminately, threatening friend and foe alike. It may also be relevant that, in 1918, a 29-year-old, so-called corporal in the trenches on the Western Front – Adolph Hitler – was a victim of a gas attack and spent some time in hospital recovering. Actually, Hitler was never corporal; he was a Private 1st Class, a gefreiter, equivalent to the British Lance Corporal in the army or Leading Aircraftman (LAC) in the RAF; he won the Iron Cross, first class, but was later gassed, which brought his 4-year, military career to an end. The legend of his being a corporal may have arisen out of an attempt to draw a parallel with Mussolini, who had been a corporal, and with Napoleon who was nicknamed 'the little corporal'. As someone on the Brains Trust on the wireless once remarked, 'many of the highest world leaders were corporals in their army service'.

On one occasion Churchill was said to have contemplated the use of poison gas in retaliation against the German use of V1s and V2s, but British military chiefs advised that conventional weapons were more effective, so the idea was dropped. One other reason why the Germans did not use it, despite having large stocks of it and having developed a more deadly nerve gas, was because movement on the battlefield was much faster in the Second World War than in the First, and therefore the risk to one's own forces of using it was potentially greater.

Others have suggested that the reason for poison gas not being used in the Second World War was partly that civilians and military personnel on all sides were protected, but mainly the fear of retaliation by the other side. In a war where no risk of retaliation existed – as for example when Iraq used it against Kurds – there seems to have been little hesitation in employing it. Hermann Goering talked in 1940 of employing a 'sleeping gas' to put all the inhabitants of the South of England to sleep – but without causing lasting harm to them – long enough for the German army to invade without casualties on either side; but nothing came of the idea, which is reminiscent more of a Bond film than the German Wehrmacht.

* * * * *

As the war progressed, Britain's major war advantage and her major war weakness both became increasingly apparent. Her advantage was the English Channel, a natural moat and just sufficient an obstacle to save Britain from invasion and probable defeat in 1940 – with, of course, the crucial help of Fighter Command denying the Luftwaffe air superiority. Air supremacy was something which Hitler had laid down to Goering as a pre-condition of invading across the Channel, especially as Goering is said to have assured the Fuehrer that he could achieve it. The major disadvantage of Britain was its heavy reliance upon imports, mainly of weapons, fuel, raw materials and food. In 1940, Britain produced only 30% of the food the British people consumed, the rest had to be imported in merchant ships mainly from non-European countries, while the Germans were able to produce 80% of their food and obtain much of the rest not by ship but by land. Therefore, it was almost inevitable that the Battle of the Atlantic would become one of the major war theatres, and that the Scillies, because of their geographical position, would play a part.

The main weapon the Germans used in the blockade was the U-boat, together with long-range aircraft such as the Condor, a few surface war-ships (which were not of much use after the first two years), mines and E-boats; in defence, Britain had flying-boats, such as the Sunderland, and, later, the Catalina, aircraft of RAF Coastal Command, particularly Wellington bombers, and about 1,300 various warships (the majority destroyers and corvettes) to escort the convoys that suffered assault in the Battle, usually from wolf packs.

Commenting upon the lack of preparedness for submarine warfare of the British navy – and indeed all navies – before the 2nd World War, Admiral Doenitz in his *Memoirs* (p. 23) wrote: 'It shows how difficult it is for a naval officer who has been educated and trained for surface warfare clearly to appreciate and assimilate the importance of any other method of fighting such as submarine warfare ... Notwithstanding the fact that German U-boats in the First World War had confronted Britain with the greatest crisis in her history,' and Doenitz quoted Captain Roskill (Vol. 1, p. 355) in saying 'defence was also considered chiefly from the point of view of attack by enemy surface units'. But it is fair to say that both sides had learnt by the time of the sinking of the *Bismarck* in May, 1941, that the U-boat was Germany's main weapon of war at sea; and the sinking of the battleship *Barham* by U-331 on November 25, seemed to confirm this.

Altogether, 76 Allied warships were sunk during the war in every theatre, and about 10,000 men of the Royal and Commonwealth navies died, this was not as many as in merchant ships where nearly 2 out of every 3 merchant seamen died. The pay of these men – all volunteers – was £9 a month for an ordinary seaman plus, after the war began, 2 shillings and sixpence a day danger money.

At the start of the war the rules of war still obliged submarines to sink merchant ships only after warning and after allowing their crews time to get safely into their lifeboats. For example, on September 7, 1939, Wilhelm von Dresky, commanding U-33, met the 4,060 ton *Olivegrove* west of Land's End; he let her crew and passengers get into their lifeboats before sinking the ship, and then he had Captain Barnetson from the *Olivegrove* aboard the U-boat, shook hands with him, apologised for the sinking, radioed a passing American ship to come to assist the lifeboats, and in such ways made sure all would be safe. The minesweeper *Gleaner* depth-charged U-33 to the surface on February 12, 1940, but, after scuttling, only 17 of the crew were taken prisoner as 23 had been killed in the explosions, including Dresky. However, 3 Enigma machine-rotors and some documents were recovered from the U-boat wreck and were of help in the initial stages of deciphering the Enigma code.

That a single U-boat could be dangerous to a convoy is illustrated by the experience of Otto Kretschmer, who was later to be Chief of Staff of Nato Naval Forces in the Baltic, but who, at the start of the Second World War, was a young officer in charge of U-99. On November 3, 1940, his U-boat sank 4 merchant ships in Convoy OB237 and, in addition, the armed merchant cruiser *Laurentio*, which had been escorting it; when the other escort, the armed merchant cruiser *Patroclus*, stopped a little later to pick up survivors from the *Laurentio*, U-99 sank her too. On the other hand a battleship might sink a submarine, not necessarily by gunfire but, in the case of the *Warspite* in April, 1940, rather unusually by launching its one amphibious Walrus 'plane which sank U-64.

The most dangerous time for Britain was when Admiral Karl Doenitz adopted the wolf-pack tactic as a counter to the Allied convoy system, his U-boats nearly winning the Battle of the Atlantic – and thus the war as far as Britain was concerned – but losing the battle partly because his craft had too often to fight on the surface, the German Schnorkel device being developed too late in the war to make the crucial difference.

The Germans had rarely more that 60 U-boats at sea at any one time, with only about half of these active in the North Atlantic and Atlantic Approaches; but in 1942 these were particularly successful. However, on August 27, 1941, one aircraft of Coastal Command actually captured a U-boat (U-570) after it had been damaged by depth-charges, could not submerge in the rough seas, and had lost power. The crew emerged out of the conning tower holding a white flag, but the aircraft had to circle around the submarine for several hours until the armed trawler, *Northern Chief*, arrived to take the formal surrender, and have the submarine towed to a British port, repaired and recommissioned as HMS *Graph*. The Royal Navy found no Enigma cyphers on the U-boat – the German crew had destroyed them – but they were surprised to find that the U-boat had a hull made of 1 inch high-tensile steel, with every joint riveted and capable of withstanding water pressure of 14 tons per square foot at a depth of 500 feet. The Royal Navy then decided to have all their detonators on depth-charges altered so that they could be triggered below 500 feet – so the capture was particularly fortuitous for them in the war against the U-boat.

The danger that the U-boats posed is acknowledged by Churchill in his book *The Second World War*. He wrote (Vol. II, p. 529): 'The only thing that ever really frightened me during the war was the U-boat peril.' The trouble with convoys was that they were difficult to handle, and seven to nine knots was the average speed of most of them, because the convoy's pace was limited to that of the slowest vessel; moreover, keeping station, particularly in stormy weather, taxed the skills of even the most experienced merchant officers. U-boats could easily catch convoys because they could do over 17 knots on the surface. Often a pack of them would lie in wait positioned ahead of the convoys, submerged but spread out over 10 miles to maximise the likelihood of interception. To keep contact with one another they usually had to radio Admiral Doenitz, who from 1940 had the use of the French Atlantic ports for his craft, and who would relay commands; so, while the Royal Navy codes were fairly easily cracked until 1943, the Germans believed their Enigma 'Dolphin' code was safe, and for a long time had no idea that it had been broken – so they tended to give away some of their U-boat movements.

Some idea of the state of the battle can be indicated in the following figures: in 1942 about 600 merchant ships were sunk by U-boats, but in 1943 the figure had declined to nearer half that number. The USA coming into the war after Pearl Harbour, although it resulted in a short-term field day for the U-boats sinking American ships along the American Atlantic coast, in the long term gave a boost to the British; the acquirement of long range Liberator bombers by RAF Coastal Command, meant that at last the gap in the mid Atlantic, where the U-boats had felt fairly safe and where merchant ships felt particularly vulnerable, was closed. The use by Coastal Command of other new planes, especially the Mosquito and the Beaufighter, was also important and helped to reduce German coastal merchant ships, over 200 of which they sank in 1944/45, many in Norwegian fiords.

* * * * *

Around Scilly in the early years of the war, the main attacks were not by U-boats but by aircraft, and there was at first little defence capability, although, fortunately, these attacks were intermittent and somewhat casual. The exception was the German determination to destroy the wireless communication post on the Peninnis peninsula, which eventually they achieved, after a number of what seemed like random attacks. On August 29, German aircraft dropped high explosive bombs first on The Garrison, then on Tresco (where the lounge windows in the Abbey were broken) and on Round Island, causing 5 minor casualties. On September 6th, an aircraft dropped bombs near the power station on St Mary's and, on October 29th, November 3rd and November 10th, Dornier 17s machine-gunned Porthcressa and other parts of Hugh Town. The civilian population in Scilly felt most vulnerable, and it is estimated that by the middle of 1941 up to half the pre-war inhabitants of Scilly had evacuated to the mainland. But the attacking aircraft also paid a price; two Heinkel 111s were shot down on July 18th, 1941, and another on August 16th. Then, on August 26th, 1941, a bomb hit Bona Vista in the Strand, Hugh Town, a house whose site is now occupied by the Scillonian Dairy. The bomb was said to be of the armour-piercing sort, and was big enough to send a rock through the church roof, landing in the chancel. Sylvia Banfield Jenkins, aged 29, was killed, the daughter of Richard and Jane Jenkins of Ennor House in Old Town, with whom Roy Wright was billeted; and the bomb resulted also in the death on the following day of a nurse, Dorothy Agnes Paice, aged 22, daughter of Gerald and Agnes Paice, Gerald being one of the local bank managers. Sylvia Jenkins was particularly remembered for her generosity in using her food coupons to make cakes for RAF personnel. Mrs Paice and a boy were rescued from the ruins of the house, and 6 other bombs dropped at the same time damaged Dora Moul's house and Mincarlo, and stopped the church clock at 9.05. There were one or two minor injuries, and one bomb exploded in Cothayes Garden.

Apart from the little girl who died at Telegraph, there were no other civilian deaths in Scilly as a direct result of enemy machine-gunning but the Germans did once machine-gun St Agnes – where some of the islanders sought shelter under the pews of the church, one of whom was Lilian Trenary – and they also bombed some boats at Bryher, set fire to some of the vegetation on Round Island, machine-gunned Star Castle (where the soldiers there returned fire with their Bren guns and other weapons), and attacked the Coastguard post at the Daymark on St Martin's, but here succeeded only in damaging a nearby rock. German aircraft also set light to the bracken on St Helen's, but it is not clear why they bothered, although it may simply have been the result of jettisoning bombs to lighten their aircraft for a faster homeward flight, particularly if they were short of fuel or were apprehensive that they might be chased by RAF fighter aircraft. The burning had the incidental beneficial effect of exposing the remains of the 10th century oratory on the island. Bombs on Round Island set fire to the island's vegetation, and obliged rabbits and other wildlife to huddle near the sea on the rocks until the fire had burnt itself out and they could return to their burrows and other 'homes'.

To guard against enemy invasion, the main beaches of St Mary's, where landings of enemy forces could be anticipated, were, early in the war, lined by the military with barbed wire, and poles were stuck in the fairways of the golf course to prevent any attempt by enemy 'planes to land there. Barbed wire was also placed on The Garrison (particularly at The Woolpack), above the beaches of Portheressa, Old Town, Pelistry, Watermill and Bar Point, and at several other places inland on St Mary's including Newford Island. 27 concrete pill-boxes were constructed at points where machine-gunners inside could rake possible landing beaches with fire, and a few of these pill-boxes still exist around St Mary's today – there is, for instance, a well-positioned one at Porth Hellick and another above the centre of the beach at Old Town. During the war the foreshores of Scilly were placed out-of-bounds after dusk to all inhabitants unless they had permission from the military authorities. Members of the West Yorkshire Regiment stationed on Scilly had instructions that, in the event of an enemy landing, the Garrison should be the final resort of the defending forces, which was to be held until help from the navy and from reserve troops at Falmouth could arrive. Later in the war, the garrison in Scilly consisted mainly of old soldiers aged 50 and over.

On January 13th, 1941, a German reconnaissance aircraft machine-gunned some boats fishing around the Scillies and, on March 10th, one German aircraft dropped 7 high explosive bombs aimed at Telegraph Tower, killing one pony owned by Bill Phillips. The tail fin of one of these bombs which failed to explode was subsequently made into a decorative flowerpot-stand. On April 4th, when a passing Allied convoy was under attack, one of the attacking aircraft tried to drop two bombs on Peninnis lighthouse, but missed the target, as did two more bombs dropped on April 12 – probably jettisoned. On Sunday, June 8, 1941, many islanders were in church on St Mary's at Evensong, when a German aircraft was heard machine-gunning. The Chaplain reported that he had just finished his sermon, but the congregation seemed more than usually quick to get on their knees, he assumed in order to

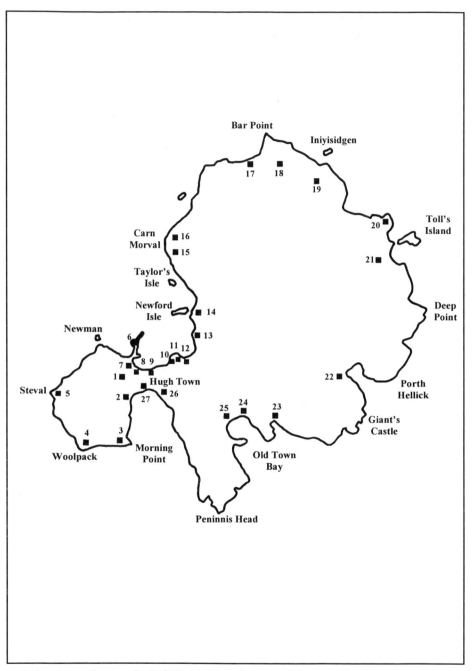

A sketchmap showing the 2nd World War defences on St Mary's. The above diagram indicates the position around the coastline of St Mary's where 27 concrete blockhouses were constructed in anticipation of a German invasion. They are carefully positioned for the most part above beaches where German landing craft might reasonably seek to land troops, and where machine-gunners or riflemen could direct their fire at them through the slits in the blockhouse walls. At one stage in the war, when a German invasion was still a possibility, the pill-boxes on St Mary's were manned every night.

find some safety between the pews rather than through any excess of devotion. Then, on August 26th, a high-explosive bomb fell near St Mary's church, and – as Matt Lethbridge confirms above – incendiary bombs were aimed at and landed on the direction-finding-station on Peninnis, so completing that station's destruction. On August 27th, a Heinkel III dropped 4 high-explosive bombs on the aerodrome, but with little damage and no casualties. The Seven Stones lightship was machine-gunned, as was the Trinity House Vessel *Satellite*, when sailing off the Wolf lighthouse; as a consequence *Satellite* was given a 12-pounder gun on subsequent voyages, for buoys and lighthouses had still to be tended, even if there was a war on.

The Heinkel III was a handsome and versatile aircraft which entered service in the Luftwaffe in 1936. It was classed as a medium bomber, with a top speed of 258 m.p.h., and carried a crew of 4. Its most distinctive feature was not visual but aural, for it had two unsynchronised engines which created a throbbing noise. It became known not only to Scillonians but to millions of British people, particularly to those who lived in the Greater London area; at one period of the war one Heinkel would fly over London back and fore every evening, arriving about 9 p.m. and departing before midnight, droning away overhead and dropping just the occasional bomb. It was certainly a nuisance, but not particularly undermining of morale as the enemy intended, rather the opposite as people became familiar with its presence, even if this stopped short of contempt. It was believed that it was a Heinkel which dropped eight high explosive bombs on Porthloo early in the morning of May 12, 1941; but they caused no casualties, although damaging several of the houses nearby. During this early period in the war, Star Castle came in for frequent machine-gunning. After all, it looked impressive and was indeed the headquarters of the army (mainly territorials) in the islands. The troops returned the fire from the ramparts using Enfield rifles, Bren Guns and two 2-inch mortars, plus up to four Boyes Anti-Tank rifles and plenty of ammunition. One of the Boyes Rifles was mounted in the castle's north-west ramparts, and its operators claimed to have brought down an enemy aircraft.

* * * * *

The war on the Home Front in Britain was conducted by the Government with the object of the civilian population managing on limited imports and resources, with equality the keynote in the distribution of these resources. To achieve this ration books were issued to every citizen and, rather than the wealthy at their desks having the ability to buy greater rations, it was people who were registered as involved in vital heavy manual work who were entitled to have increased rations – a reversal of normal peacetime priorities and a practical demonstration of the socialist dream of creating a society where each 'gives to it according to his ability and receives from it according

One surprising visitation to Scilly was of half-a-dozen Landing Craft Tank in 1943. One of them, LCT 354, ran on the rocks off Newford Island,and the lifeboat Cunard *rescued the 17 crew on board. The landing craft was one of 24 LCTs (Landing Craft Tanks) which were being escorted by an armed trawler from the Mediterranean back to Britain after taking part in the successful landings of Allied forces from North Africa in Sicily and southern Italy. The squadron left Gibraltar in good weather and headed out into the Atlantic in order to avoid passing through the Bay of Biscay on the journey home, as they had been notified that U-boats had been active there. Unfortunately, the 25 boats ran into rough seas, for which the LCTs were not built; although 112 feet long, empty of vehicles and each with twin 500 h.p. engines, they were slow and their flat bottoms and 15 feet wide bow, which enabled them to land tanks onto beaches, meant great hardship in rough seas for their 12-man crews.*

Two sank but, after 10 days, the rest succeeded in reaching the calmer waters within the islands of Scilly, five of them hauling up on Porthmellon on November 14. They eventually reached Falmouth, Liverpool or Swansea and later took part in the greatest seaborne invasion in history, when 850,000 men and over 1,000 vehicles landed on a 50-mile stretch of the coast of Normandy on June 6, 1944, and during the subsequent week. The invasion was a success, although there were inevitably many casualties, and the cemetery at Bayeux is consequently the largest in Europe. George Hicks of Scilly, known as 'G', a pleasure-boat operator in the Boatmens' Association until his death in 1980 aged 69, was skipper of a landing craft in the RASC during the war. The landing drill was that before the LCT reached the beach to unload its 6 to 10 Churchill tanks or equivalent, it would drop its kedge anchor, so that it could pull itself off the beach again and out to sea under power of its capstan engine. What happened to LCT 354, and caused her to have a hole which had to be given a temporary repair before she sailed to the mainland, was that on the way into the Scillies, despite having no keel, she had scraped the Bartholomew Ledge. The reason for this was a navigational error; many of the crew happened to be Belgians, who, like the French at that time, had the opposite buoy system to the British. Photo: Gibson, Scilly

to his needs', which is, of course, still the philosophical basis of the National Health Service. However, the wealthy could supplement their rations by buying occasional meals in hotels and restaurants, which were permitted special supplies in order to keep in business; but this was hardly an option for the Scillonians as most such establishments in Scilly were closed for the duration.

Rationing came in as shortages appeared. On September 23, 1939, petrol rationing began by coupons for it being issued, and on October 4, the Dig for Victory Campaign was inaugurated. But it was not until January 8, 1940, that sugar, butter, bacon and ham were rationed – and milk from the summer of 1941. Everyone had to register for rations at a local shop – a simple matter in Scilly, where Chirgwins (a shop which returned to this name in 2000) was the main provision store on St Mary's. There was no tinned milk, and oranges were only sold for children. One way in which the wealthy – and some of the not-so-wealthy – evaded the severer effects of petrol rationing was by licensing two vehicles but only using one. One vehicle could be a big-engined car, such as a Vauxhall 25 (cost £298 to purchase new in 1937 and advertised – by Welch's Garage Redcliffe Street, Bristol, with the words 'every ride a glide') and the other a small one, such as a Fiat 500; the greater number of coupons issued for the larger car could then be used to fuel the smaller one. The coupons were not supposed to be interchanged in this way, but most forecourt assistants had neither inclination nor incentive to check that the coupons presented along with payment matched the number-plate of the car into which they had pumped petrol – there being no self-service at pumps at that time. But this hardly applied in Scilly where few people had or needed cars anyway.

The first bomb on Britain was dropped in November, 1939, on the Shetland Islands and killed a rabbit; but all this was, of course, the relative calm before the storm. This is why sea activity was given much press coverage, and why the defeat of the German pocket battleship *Graf Spee* in the South Atlantic in December, 1939, by the three Royal Navy cruisers *Exeter*, *Ajax* and *Achilles* was an occasion for great celebration; while the loss of the battleship *Royal Oak* on October 14 to a daring U-boat commander, Kapitanleutnant Gunther Prien in U-47, who somehow penetrated the protected anchorage at Scapa Flow, was an event of great national sadness – 823 men drowning and only 396 saved when the ship went down in 13 minutes and while still at anchor.

Prien had one patrol in the summer of 1940, when his U-47 sank ten merchant ships, representing a total of 66,588 tons; but he and his U-boat were destroyed in March, 1941, by the destroyers *Verity* and *Wolverine* working together, one locating the U-boat's underwater position and movements with Asdic, the other dropping depth-charges.

Churchill had written in 1936 that Asdic 'removes from the submarine that cloak of invisibility which was its principal weapon'. But he was a bit premature in his judgement for, in the first two years of the 2nd World War, Asdic's range was less than a mile, its beam narrow and at a more or less a fixed angle, and it did not work properly on a vessel doing over 8 knots or when the sea was rough. It also picked up echoes from submerged objects other than U-boats so confusing its operators, who were regarded anyway as rather inferior on board warships as compared with gun or torpedo operators. But, by 1941, many of these drawbacks to the Asdic had been remedied – hence the successful destruction not only of U-47, but of the U-boats of other German ace submarine commanders.

* * * * *

Very soon after war began, the Government prepared the population for the worst. Stirrup pumps became available and every household was urged to have a bucket of water handy in case of fire. Ten stirrup pumps had already been distributed in Hugh Town in May, 1939, while, in September, sirens were fitted to Carn Thomas School and shutters added to Town Hall windows by S.M. Treneary (who was paid £57 19s 5d for the work). Public Information leaflet No. 1 even urged everyone to carry a luggage label with their name and address on it, in case they became a casualty away from home. Black curtain material was made available and each evening there was the ritual of seeing that no light was exposed outside the home, and each morning this blackout was taken down. The public were urged to buy war bonds to help pay for the war and as a guaranteed investment, and car headlamps had to be covered so that slits only two inches wide projected light forward. 2¼ million Anderson shelters were built for people's back gardens in cities, and huge concrete sections of round drainage-pipes were placed in large open fields to prevent their use by German gliders landing troops.

Mrs Beeton's book *Household Management* of 1861 had much influence even into the 20th century, but it was her publisher husband, Samuel Beeton, who should perhaps take the blame for any overcooking of vegetables the book is alleged to recommend. He also published the first fashion magazine in 1852, *The Englishwoman's Domestic Magazine*, giving away a paper dress-pattern with each issue. With the coming of the 2nd World War, the world changed, and most of Isabella's book's purposes no longer applied, with 'household management' now consisting mainly of 'make do and mend' and 'how to eke out rations'. Such pre-war disputes as to whether the milk or the tea should enter the cup first seemed to become unimportant, particularly as all tea was blended and with no longer a choice between China and Indian. Moreover, tea was limited on ration to 2 oz. a week from July, 1940. Technically, i.e. chemically, it is said that the milk should be put in first; but, before the war, it was a class matter, with the upper middle-classes tending to add the milk first and the lower middle-classes the tea – but even this has been disputed, perhaps by those not quite in the class to which they aspire. Aristocracy may have the tea poured for them, of course, and the pre-war working-classes were mostly unaware and unimpressed by such distinctions within the middle classes. Anyway, many of the pre-war working-classes were inclined to stir their tea so vigorously they instantly alienated themselves from the middle classes, as when they said 'Pleased to meet you' instead of the acceptable 'How do you do?' or murdered English tenses by saying 'When I was sat in the chair...' instead of 'When I was sitting in the chair...'. Younger generations of the 21st century seemed noticeably relaxed about such matters, and are no longer plagued to say 'thank-you', 'please' and 'sorry' all the time – if, indeed, at any time.

The feeling grew in the Second World War that Mrs Beeton's ideas no longer applied, being entirely outdated. Certainly this could be said about most of the recipes in her publications, given the extent of wartime food rationing; and her homilies concerning live-in domestic servants hardly seemed to apply any more as that class largely disappeared during the war, to be replaced eventually by daily helps and, in the 1950s and subsequently, by electrical appliances and convenience foods. The standard wartime joke that in her recipes Mrs Beeton had said 'take 6 eggs ...' was not strictly accurate, although it produced some hollow laughter among those enduring the limitations of rationing. Mrs Beeton's idea of the world was, of course, a typical Victorian one, reflecting the views of the more prosperous quarter of that society, remnants of which still lingered on into the Second World War; however, most people during the war came to aspire to something better and fairer being created after the war (particularly returning ex-servicemen) and expressed in the Beveridge Report, which was largely a blueprint showing how to create social security 'from the cradle to the grave'. The Beveridge Report is more accurately, if unexcitingly entitled *The Report on Social Insurance and Allied Services*. It was published on December 2, 1942, and aimed to create in British society 'freedom from want'. Almost the entire population welcomed it as something decent to look forward to, but there were a few who termed it 'the way to moral ruin', as in a letter to *The Times* from O.J. Falk of December 5, 1942. The Report was partly in order to make the wartime suffering at least seem to contribute to something worthwhile. Many people had experienced 'a good war', and rose to positions of power, prestige, responsibilities and pay they could never have achieved in peacetime; they had seen for themselves how life could improve under a government obliged to pursue egalitarian policies. This helps to explain the landslide to the Labour Party at the 1945 general election, which was so hurtful to Churchill because he did not understand it. He felt people had turned against him – which was not the case – but they had rejected his party's policies which were felt to be backward-looking. To understand the attitudes of many of the more comfortably-off during the 2nd World War, who accepted a measure of egalitarianism only as part of wartime exigencies and sought to abandon it when peace came, a film such as *Mrs Miniver* (portrayed by Greer Garson), is illuminating. So also is *Mrs Beeton's Household Management*, despite being written in mid-Victorian times. It promoted an image of Mrs Beeton as a sort of Mrs Bridges (of the TV programme *Upstairs, Downstairs*), which is quite remote from the truth; her achievement was really in her writing rather than her recipes, for she was not distinguished as a cook, but the recipes included under her name were for the time remarkably clear in their instructions, although there was little that was original in the recipes themselves.

Isabella Beeton (her maiden name was Mayson) was born on about March 13, 1836. Her father died when she was 5, and her home, in her later childhood years, was the accommodation under the grandstand of Epsom Racecourse, where her stepfather, Henry Dorling, was Clerk of the Course. Eventually, the family moved to a residence in Epsom's main street big enough to house Dorling's 21 children and stepchildren. Isabella attended a school in Heidelberg for a time, where she became proficient in languages, as a pianist and in pastry cooking. She went on to become a journalist, and in 1855, at the age of 20, married Samuel Beeton, a publisher, and lived at 2 Chandos Villas, a semi-detached house in Pinner. They had 4 servants (one was her cook), and here they conceived the idea of a book about how to manage servants and containing recipes – a book for middle-class brides; and this is the origin of the most famous of all cookery books, *Mrs Beeton's Book of Household Management*, published by her husband in 1861. The book had a phenomenal popularity, selling 2 million copies by 1868, and it introduced Victorians to foreign recipes (translated by Isabella) and to new manufactured food products, but concentrated mainly on plain, homely meals. Three chapters were not written by Mrs Beeton – the two on medical matters and the one on legal – and this last one clearly looked to the future. It is remarkable that the book accompanied Captain Scott's ill-fated expedition to the South Pole in 1910, and was even found as the reading material in the prisoner-of-war camps of the Japanese in the 2nd World War, although what use it was to either readership is speculative. A copy was also found among a number of other rather tatty volumes on a shelf in a St Mary's café, close by a copy of *Hall and Knight's Algebra*, a well known school textbook in its time, now similarly unread, and, to many, unreadable.

The success of Mrs Beeton's book seems largely to have been based on the nearly 2000 recipes it contained, many contributed from readers of Beeton's *Englishwoman's Domestic Journal*. Much of the book is based on earlier works, particularly Eliza Acton's *Modern Cookery* of 1845 and *Modern Housewife* by Alexis Soyer, 1809-58, the chef of the Reform Club, who invented soup kitchens for the destitute, although he is most famous for having gone out to the Crimean War, 1854-56, and improved the diet for the troops in a manner similar to the way Florence Nightingale improved their nursing. Mrs Beeton was able to include in her book some of the points from Miss Nightingale's *Good Sense on Nursing*.

Mrs Beeton had four children, the first two dying young, but the last two both surviving until 1947. She died in 1865 at the early age of 29, soon after giving birth to her fourth child. Although exceptionally and commendably fastidious about hygiene, she died on February 6, 1865, of puerperal fever, most likely owing to less than adequate medical attention, the doctor present at the birth is alleged to have come straight from medically examining a corpse.

Two maxims Mrs Beeton coined and for which she is still well known are 'a place for everything and everything in its place', and 'in cooking, clear as you go'.

A flavour of her book may perhaps be gleaned from the following sentences – extracted from Chapter I, entitled *The Mistress*: 'Good temper should be cultivated by every mistress, as upon it the welfare of the household may be said to turn. ... every head of a household should strive to be cheerful, and should never fail to show a deep interest in all that appertains to the well-being of those who claim the protection of her roof' (from the Oxford World Classics series, an excellent abridged version of *Mrs Beeton's Book of Household Management* by Nicola Humble, 2000).

From the above extracts it could reasonably be concluded that Mrs Beeton was out-of-date long before the 2nd World War; but an indication of how opinion in Britain has changed since the 2nd World War is the recollection that there were then in Britain a few people so anti-communist in their political and social attitudes, that they wondered, when Germany fought Russia, whether Britain might have been on the wrong side. Curiously, there actually was a short period during the 2nd World War when Germany and the UK seemed to be on the same side; the occasion was when Russia invaded Finland on November 30, 1939, and both Germany and Britain sided with and sent aid to the Finns.

* * * * *

The crime rate tripled in the UK during the war despite the absence on active service of most young men. The blackout assisted nefarious acts, and there were so many regulations to break. Looting from a bombed house, although carrying a heavy punishment, could be mitigated in one's mind by the thought that all might have been lost in the bomb blast anyway.

UK letter postage rose from 1½d to 2½d, and unemployment fell below one million for the first time since the First World War. The blackout was applied in Scilly as rigorously as on the mainland, and *The Island News*, issue No. 13 (costing one penny), urged householders to paint white any obstructions on paths and pavements around their homes which might represent a hazard to pedestrians after dark. It was claimed in the same edition that the blackout seemed more complete in Old Town than in Hugh Town – thus, incidentally, stoking up an old rivalry between these two settlements – and it was suggested that the reasons for this might be that the people of Old Town went to bed earlier or because the windows of Old Town houses were smaller on average than those in Hugh Town. Neither explanation seems very plausible today, when the greater number of business premises in Hugh Town at that time would seem adequate to explain any perceived difference.

The Union Flag flew from Buzza Tower from the start of the war to assert the Islands allegiance. It is incorrect to refer to it as the Union Jack – although frequently and acceptably this is done – because, strictly speaking, the jack is the flagpole from which the flag flies; but few observe this nicety, while, at the same time, sometimes being incensed if the flag is flown upside down which, again, strictly speaking, is a distress signal.

* * * * *

An essential task in modern war seems to be the promotion of one's own side's morale. This is not achieved just by flying flags and issuing propaganda, but also by creating statistics which seem to show that one's own side is not only better than the enemy but also winning.

However, even when figures produced in wartime are accurate, they can sometimes be a little misleading in their interpretation. Consider, for example, the daily national newspapers, all cut down in the number of pages they were allowed but, in terms of circulation, the *Daily Express* had relatively high figures, certainly pleasing its proprietor, Lord Beaverbrook. It is easy to conclude that it was the newspaper's content which attracted so many people to buy it, and no doubt this was usually the case; but there is another factor, rarely mentioned, which may well have affected that newspaper's circulation figures; the paper on which the *Daily Express* was printed made effective firelighters – better, it was alleged, than some other newspapers – burning easily when folded in the traditional way – and this at a time when persuading the coal, coke, wood or other fire in the grate to light was one of the necessary and painstaking winter morning chores in most British households, central heating being then rare in modest homes. Whether it was easier to fold the *Daily Express* into the firelighter shape, or whether the paper used was more combustible than others, is not altogether clear; but, in either eventuality, the newspaper's circulation figures could have been affected and an erroneous conclusion reached.

One national newspaper, the *Daily Worker*, was banned from publishing from January 8, 1941, on the grounds that it was too defeatist, particularly when it attempted to tell people some of the stark truth as to the extent of the war damage. Also threatened with suppression under Defence Regulations for criticising the war effort, was the *Daily Mirror*, which had called some of the army chiefs 'boneheads'.

As well as the national daily newspapers, children's weekly magazines continued in the war, *Beano* and *Hotspur* being favourites. *Beano* humour was of the type: Question: 'Why does Mussolini never change his socks?' Answer: 'Because he smells defeat'. For older boys the *Magnet* by Frank Richards – about Harry Wharton, Bob Cherry, Frank Nugent and others at Greyfriars School, an independent boys boarding school – where Billy Bunter was actually not the principal character – and the *Gem* by Martin Clifford – about Tom Merry and Arthur Augustus D'Arcy and other boys at a similar school called St Jims – were popular in the 1930s, the *Gem* running from 1907 to 1939 and the *Magnet* from 1908 to 1940. Few people at the time realised that both magazines came from the pen of the same author, Charles Harold St John Hamilton, 1875-1961, who must surely have been one of the world's most prolific writers, writing under many pseudonyms.

In December, 1941, women between the ages of 21 and 45, who were not in reserved occupations such as nursing, became liable to be directed into war work – the armed forces, factories or the land army – a government capacity to direct the labour of women which the German government did not possess. In Hitler's Germany, all girls from the age of ten, were expected to join the Youth Movement, but those who later joined the civil service were obliged to resign their jobs if they later wished to marry, which has an echo in the UK, where women teachers before the 2nd World War were expected to resign before marrying. However, in 1938, married women in Germany, who had 4 or more children, were rewarded with a state loan. Training leading to a diploma, was available in Germany to all married Aryan women, and included instruction on how best to manage the roles of wife, mother, housekeeper and child carer. Thus motherhood was much valued, but only for Aryans, not for gypsies, Jews or Slavs; and a sterilisation programme was instituted for the severely mentally challenged and schizophrenics. Some proof of racial purity was sought before a marriage license was issued, and instruction given in 'racial awareness'. Abortion and the sale of contraceptives were strictly forbidden.

In Britain, strikes were forbidden and, in 1943, 10% of new servicemen were redirected by ballot to serve as miners – the so-called 'Bevin Boys' after the able Minister of Labour, Ernest Bevin, to whom Churchill left much of the Government's home front matters. This resulted in some boys from public schools being sent to work down the mines.

Food rationing was welcomed in the war because it was seen to be fair when foodstuffs were short; but, more important still, the economically bottom third of the population were for the first time able to afford an adequate diet. The reason for this – and why the health of the nation generally, despite rationing, was improving, was because the government kept the prices of essential food commodities on ration deliberately low. Despite the post-war junk-food phenomenon, this improvement has continued, partly because of the inauguration of the National Health Service in 1948, which meant that medical costs were no longer obstacles to medical advice and treatment. A measure of this improvement is provided by the number of people in the UK living to the age of 100 and receiving a congratulationary message from the Queen. At the end of Victoria's reign in 1901, telegrams were sent to 105 people; in 1953, when Elizabeth II ascended the throne, this figure had risen to 251, but the total population had also risen by over ten million. In the year 2000, by which time letters or cards had replaced the telegram, that figure had leapt to over 9,000.

Great advances were made in medical treatments also during the war, and one event on February 12, 1941, not widely understood at the time but having wonderful implications for the future, concerned a policeman with septicaemia; he was treated with penicillin, the first person to receive it, and made a full recovery.

Food shortages during the war also obliged or tempted people to vary their diets and to eat things they had never tried before. Three fresh pigeon's eggs would make an attractive-looking substitute for a hen's egg, fried or poached; and, in Lyons Corner House in Leicester Square, it was possible to order the large egg of a herring gull served on toast, and it tasted well, if one did not reflect too much on the wide-ranging diet of that unfussy bird. Some items had originally owed their popularity to legendary aphrodisiac qualities, even the humble potato being one of those when first introduced into Spain from the New World in 1534; and the tomato, although out of fashion for nearly two centuries because of a suspicion that it might be a trifle poisonous, was back in favour from the 1830s and much grown in Britain during the 2nd World War. Sea foods such as oyster, octopus and mullet, together with rhino horn, soup made from sea swallows' nests, various spices and even honey, were at one time – and still are by some folk – considered aids to the mating game, although with varying efficacy; but, in Britain, it was fresh vegetables, with little to recommend them other than their availability, cheapness, ease of growing in the garden however small, and reputation as 'good' food, that won for them the widest acclaim during the war. Once accepted in the diet, habit helped to perpetuate their consumption with generally beneficial effects upon the health of the population; however, after the war, the consumption of many vegetables came to be seen as representative of wartime shortages and restrictions, and, sadly, their range and quantity of consumption declined, particularly with the rise of relative affluence from the 1960s.

By 1940 weekly rationed foods per person were as follows:

sugar	12 oz
butter	4 oz
tea	2 oz
margarine	2 oz
cooking fat	2 oz
meat (including bacon)	16 oz approx.

Luxuries, such as cake-icing, were prohibited, by 1941,
   cheese was only   1 oz, and
   eggs had been reduced to one a fortnight.

Restriction, rationing, prohibitions and shortages played a part in reducing imports to Britain to 30 million tons by March, 1941, all of which were designated as essential foodstuffs and materials.

However, the prices of non-essential and unrationed items increased, and many formerly imported goods, such as bananas, disappeared for the duration. But vegetables were never rationed, so that agricultural counties such as Cornwall benefited commercially and, in Scilly, vegetables were grown plentifully. In towns people were urged to transform formerly trim suburban front-lawns into plots for growing carrots, turnips, swedes and the like, and the campaign to 'Dig for Victory' produced the heyday of the kitchen garden. 4½ million extra acres of land in the UK were brought under the plough by farmers, in addition to the many allotments which appeared on much of the waste ground around towns. Many of the allotments on the slopes of the Peninnis peninsula beside the coastal path overlooking Porthcressa were intensively cultivated in the Second World War and much of the land here continues to be farmed in this way today. By contrast, potatoes were rationed in Germany from April 6, 1942. A black market – particularly in foodstuffs – flourished in Britain during the war, and provided some welcome, perhaps inevitable, alleviation to the stringency of rationing, with many a city briefcase returning home in the evening with the addition of an illegitimate pot of jam secreted amongst its important papers, and articles of clothing were still being sold, without coupons given, in Petticoat Lane in June, 1941. The most important downsides to this activity were the profits of black marketeers, the deterioration of morals and the resulting unfairness; but, in Scilly, the inhabitants could at least fish for their supper, an advantage denied those in inland areas. The extent of food rationing in Britain was determined by the findings of research into food values conducted by Lord Boyd-Orr and, after the initial restrictions outlined above, a points rationing system was introduced in 1941 for items such as tinned fruit, and sweets or chocolates. Food such as bread, flour, potatoes, fish and fresh vegetables were not rationed during the war, but restaurants had to limit the number of their courses to three, and a maximum charge of five shillings for a meal was established. Local Authorities started British Restaurants in areas which had been heavily bombed, but then extended them to towns throughout much of the country to provide 3-course hot meals for upwards of a shilling. The soup was somewhat watery, the meat course had but a slither of meat, the whole bulked out with as many as four or five fresh vegetables – turnips, swedes, cabbage, parsnips and the like – and the pudding was often something that resembled jam tart and custard. But the meal was cheap, had sustenance and was much more than many people had been able to afford for lunch in the

In postwar Britain, Queen Elizabeth, the Queen Mother, came several times to Scilly. In this photograph she is being shown the goldfish pond in Tresco Abbey Gardens by Lieutenant-Commander Tom Dorrien Smith. It is not the most attracive feature of the gardens and she must have seen far bigger and better ones elsewhere; but it demonstrates her charming capacity to be genuinely interseted in everything she was shown, a quality which endeared her during her long life, and helped gain the Royal Family great popularity during the Second World War.

Thirties, and it was better for them. Moreover, British Restaurants were patronised by all classes – they were more like canteens than soup kitchens. On February 9, 1944, the King and queen partook of a one-shilling lunch with a group of mineworkers at a pit canteen; rather unbelievably they were reported as saying: 'It is a long time since we had a better meal' – a demonstration of *noblesse oblige*, the primacy of good manners over strict accuracy. Another example was in May, 1967, when the Queen visited Penzance; she described her welcome as 'one of the warmest she had ever received' (*The Cornishman*, 3 August 2000). She could hardly have said fairer than that.

Churchill realised the importance of a name and had a gift for choosing the right one. He had the uninspired 'Local Defence Volunteers' changed to 'Home Guard' in 1940, and the awful sounding, if accurate, 'Communal Feeding Centres' replaced by 'British Restaurants', with the comment: 'Everyone associates the word "restaurants" with a good meal, and they may as well have the name if they cannot have anything else.' Churchill also had a gift for impish humour; in the summer of 1940, the British army had been defeated and withdrawn from the beaches of Dunkirk, France had surrendered and Britain stood alone facing likely invasion. Churchill delivered a rousing speech on the wireless: 'We shall fight on the beaches, we shall fight on the landing grounds, we shall fight in the fields and in the streets, we shall fight in the hills; we shall never surrender'. He then covered the microphone with his hand and in an aside added 'And if we can't do that, we'll hit them on the head with bottles'.

The weekly rations on February 23, 1942, were as follows:

Bacon and ham	4 oz
Sugar	8 oz
Butter	6 oz
Cooking fats	2 oz
Meat	1lb.
Tea	2 oz
Cheese	3 oz
Preserves	1lb.
Points ration in a month together with:	20
for adults	3 pints of milk
	3 eggs a month
plus, for children	2 oranges
	cod liver oil for children up to the age of 6.

There was also a packet of dried egg mixture every 2 months. Apples remained unrationed during the war, but the import of fruit from overseas was forbidden, and queues for anything off-ration were common. White bread disappeared, and there was an unrationed national loaf – a mixture of nearly all the flour, off-white in colour but tasty and nutritious and better for people to eat than pure white – but even this was rationed in the days of post-war austerity from July 2, 1946 to July 24, 1948. Beer was never rationed, but it was 'watered down'. Because Britain relied so heavily on imports, rationing seemed more stringent than in some other war-involved countries; Japan, for instance, had been at war with China since 1937, yet her first rationing was of sugar (and matches) on June 2, 1941. Milk was unrationed in Germany and the meat ration was about a pound a week, very similar to the amount in Britain, where dried milk and dried egg powder helped to eke out the other rations. Some of the Dutch are said to have been reduced to eating their tulips, which are claimed to be palatable but rather indigestible.

As the war progressed there were restrictions on coal, and clothing was rationed, beginning on June 2, 1941, and not taken out of rationing entirely until 1949, when the then President of the Board of Trade, Harold Wilson, abolished it; and furniture and fabrics were manufactured during the war to an economical standard laid down by the Government, although of good

The Utility Kite Mark dates from 1941, when clothing, furniture and soft furnishings were manufactured in Britain to a utility standard. This meant that they were well made for their purpose, but without decoration or unnecessary embellishments, and this kept down the price. The distinctive mark can still be found underneath some items such as chairs, which may have survived from the era.

serviceable quality. In 1942, an exhortation limited the amount of water people were supposed to put in their baths to a depth of 5 inches, and it was suggested that people paint a line around the inside of their baths to indicate this amount. Such proved a patriotic hope rather than an enforceable law, but so strong was the wartime siege-spirit and the sense of duty to the community, that most people responded willingly and kept more or less to the limitation even in the privacy of their home bathrooms, although rather fewer bothered to paint the bath line. The King and Queen set a good example by having the line painted on the baths in all the royal palaces. In Germany their water shortage was solved in a different way: they banned the taking of baths except at the weekend. Six bombs which fell on the night of September 10, 1940, on Buckingham Palace, destroying the chapel and damaging other parts, although not actually the royal quarters, gave rise to the remark – credited to the Queen – that she felt she 'could now look the East End in the face'. The royal couple's early visits to the bomb sites of the East End of London had not always been well-received, but after this well-publicised event, the King and Queen were lauded with praise for it seemed they showed sympathy with the London poor and their popularity rose. However, when mention was made on one visit that their home had also been hit, one impertinent bystander spoilt the feeling of solidarity somewhat by asking pertinently: Which one?

Even Goebels, master of spin and PR, never arranged for Hitler to visit bombed areas in Germany. It was claimed or assumed that the royal couple were in residence when the bombs fell on Buckingham Palace, although most nights during the Blitz they wisely spent at Windsor; nonetheless, the general perception among the public was that the King and Queen were sharing in some of the dangers and hardships of their subjects; but they did not, as may have been popularly imagined, stick to the ration book food allowance or clothing rationing, for this would have been setting an example too far. The cellar beneath the private apartments at Windsor Castle was the Royal air raid shelter; also stowed safely in it were some of the Crown Jewels wrapped in old newspaper for the duration. The Queen, with her beatific countenance, was particularly adept at talking to ordinary people in a warm way, and did much to help her diffident husband who dealt stoically with a difficult

272

stammer. Thrown unexpectedly into the job of Queen on the sudden abdication of Edward VIII in 1936 'to marry the woman I love', Elizabeth was a tower of strength to the high principled, if somewhat irascible, George VI, and both put 'duty' high in their scheme of things, a priority clearly passed to their elder daughter.

Price controls to stop profiteering were imposed on coffee, cocoa, rice, spaghetti, biscuits and custard jelly, but many working-class families still found prices high, as many were still surviving on under £5 a week. Sweet rationing began on July 27, 1942, and, on October 10, the milk ration was reduced to 2½ pints a week. On March 3, 1942, the maximum price of a suit was £4 18s 8d, with sleeve buttons, double breasting and turn-ups made illegal on new suits; however, it was still possible for the wealthy to obtain from Saville Row tailors almost anything they liked to pay for, although possibly not embroidery on women's underwear and nightwear, this being banned on April 15, 1942. Those who complained about restrictions or regulations or shortages or inconveniences were quickly silenced with the oft-heard rhetorical question: Don't you know there's a war on!'

In 1914, at the outset of the 1st World War, some owners of dachshunds gave away their dogs, fearful lest they be suspected of being enemy spies. German shepherds were known as alsations, so the same did not apply to them. However, a slightly different aspect of the old problem occurred in the 2nd World War, as a letter to *The Times* by D.L. Murray on August 29, 1939, explained. Murray pleaded with caricaturists to cease using the dachshund as a symbol for Germany in their drawings, which he alleged was likely to lead to instances of thoughtless cruelty to what are only harmless and affectionate little pets.

* * * * *

Rationing did not end with the coming of peace in 1945; indeed, in some ways, it became worse. The austerity that Britain had in the immediate post-war years was largely a consequence of the intensive war efforts and sacrifices made by the population over the period 1939-45, and some have argued that perhaps the price paid for demanding 'unconditional surrender' by Germany was unnecessarily high, and that the war could have been shortened with less damage to Britain's and other countries' economies if an honourable peace had been negotiated. However, this view is disputed, for such a peace would have had to include the overthrow of Hitler and the Nazis, and it is not at all clear how this could have been achieved by negotiation; and, anyway, few would have seen such a peace as honourable.

The ration quantities for one week in 1946 were as follows:
8oz sugar
9oz fats
2oz cheese
4oz bacon
2 pints milk
1 egg
2oz tea
4oz preserves

Plus six points of any of the following foods:

Points per pound weight	
meat and meat products	16
tinned soups	4
tinned fish	16
tinned or bottled fruit	4
tinned or bottled vegetables	4
condensed milk (per pint)	2
dried fruits	16
nuts	12
biscuits	4
cereals	8
oatmeal	4
dried peas or beans	4
rice, sago, tapioca or semolina	2
macaroni or spaghetti	4
salad oil, salad cream or olive oil, per fluid ounce	1
table jellies, cornflower	C
custard or blancmange	C
cake, pastry, pudding mixture, dried egg	8
tinned peas or beans	3
tinned stewed steak	20

Hotel guests were obliged to hand over their ration books to the hotel for the duration of their stay.

* * * * *

After the war, demobilisation was undertaken slowly and methodically so as not to create a rush of unemployed, but soon National Service was introduced, joining restrictions on foreign travel and continuing rationing as acceptable peacetime limitations on personal freedom. This late 1940s conscription was pressed strongly by the Service chiefs because Britain still hung on to a world-wide Empire and had responsibilities to defend, so few young men were excused from this civic duty other than those disabled or in poor health. But this 'imperial policy', as it was called, was costly and undertaken at the expense of the country's economic recovery; indeed, it was decades before the people of Britain finally accepted that the 'Great' in 'Great Britain' was actually a geographical description, signifying the inclusion of the cluster of islands off the north European coast, rather than a political term of proud power. As Professor D.W. Brogan pointed out in a letter to *The Times* of January 3, 1949: '"Britain" has been the name of our island since the beginning of recorded history. "Great Britain" is a new term'. James I invented it, ostensibly to distinguish it clearly from Brittany, but the French often talk of 'l'Angleterre'.

There were often pious wishes expressed by the good-hearted in the 1930s that something should be done to improve the living of the poor, but little was actually done after Neville Chamberlain's earlier reforms, for which today he is given little credit because they were overshadowed later by what are viewed as his failures of foreign policy. The alleged main obstacle to helping the poor was that there was not enough money to do so, yet when the 2nd World War took place it was soon costing £14 million a day – which suggests that what had been lacking in the 1930s was not the money but the will. 'The poor you always have with you' – John, chap.12, v.18 – was never meant to signify that poverty need not be addressed. By March 10, 1942, the 2nd World War was estimated to have cost Britain over £9,000 million, and that figure was already above what the entire 1st World War cost Britain in comparable terms.

Raising money for the war effort by holding 'weeks' was one way of footing the bill and these were organised as elsewhere in collaboration with the National Savings Committee. *War Weapons Week* in 1941 in Scilly raised £32,000 which was not bad from a population of only about 1,500 or fewer. *Wings for Victory Week* in 1943, opened in Scilly by Jean Batten, one of the first women to become a pilot, raised just over £20,000, enough to build two Hurricane fighter aircraft. *Warship Week* raised enough to purchase motor gunboat No 77, which had 5 encounters with German E-boats, and *Salute the Soldier Week* in 1944, had a target of £10,000, which was easily attained – enough to buy 8 Bren-gun carriers and 8 army ambulances.

The problem of paying for the war was also partly met by raising the standard rate of income tax. In September, 1939, it was up to seven shillings and sixpence in the pound, but on April 17, 1941, rose to ten shillings in every pound. The distinctive feature of income tax is that it is paid by those who have enough income to pay it, whereas many other taxes, of the sort which are levied on everyone alike irrespective of income, inevitably bear hard on the poor. Thus the majority of people saw increases of income tax as a fair tax, and its rise nowhere seemed to be a disincentive to working hard as has sometimes been alleged that it does; indeed, the opposite seems often to have been experienced, since many were induced to work harder to take home the same amount as before, something many did willingly to assist the war effort. Nonetheless, the end of the war inevitably found Britain with very large debts, and one of the most important challenges with the coming of peace was to improve the economic situation, and this meant a continuation of wartime stringencies, especially as the ending of the war saw the immediate termination of wartime aid from the USA. In response to Churchill's grandiloquent plea to the Americans 'to give us the tools that we may finish the job', the importance of America's Lend-Lease Act of March 11, 1941, can hardly be overstated; it enabled Britain to order materials from the USA without having to pay for them – at least until after the war.

The first food ship from the USA arrived on May 31, 1941, and it was a milestone and, without such American generosity and economic and military support, it is difficult to see how Britain could have survived, a conclusion reached in a contemporary report by Arthur Greenwood. Some British commentators were annoyed by Britain's indebtedness to the USA in the war, but rarely has a country given so much to help another, and such deserves acknowledgement and appreciation.

Moreover, some of the convoys from America were to suffer devastation, and US merchant seamen were also to suffer proportionately more losses than their Service personnel. On September 21, 1940, convoy HX72 of 41 merchant men was attacked by a wolf pack which included U-boat aces Schepke (U-106) and Kretschmer (U-99), who overwhelmed the five escorts and sank eleven of the merchant ships bringing supplies to Britain, followed by a similar attack on convoy HX79 on October 19, which destroyed a further 13 ships. Altogether, the year 1940 saw about 4 million tons of such shipping destroyed by U-boats, and 5,621 seamen drowned. When the *City of Benares*, sailing to America, was torpedoed on September 27, 1940, by U-48, 77 children died and only 13 were rescued, half of these after drifting in a lifeboat for almost a week under the supervision of Miss Cornish. They were mainly children of wealthy parents, on their way to supposed safety in the USA and Canada, and their fate tended to halt this form of evacuation. All this was achieved by Germany despite the fact that in November, 1939, only 15 U-boats were operational, and this figure was down to 11 in January, 1940; subsequently, this figure was much increased, but never by enough to win the Battle of the Atlantic. Had Germany concentrated on building U-boats instead of wasting effort on Hitler's pre-war project of a fleet of surface warships, the war might have been still harder to win, for Britain only produced enough food to sustain the population for 3 days a week; for the other 4 days reliance was on imported foodstuffs.

In the 21st century it is estimated that there are still nearly 1 in 7 of the world's population who go hungry every day. This is only partly a lack of food production – there is said to be enough for everyone with the help of soya beans and genetically-modified food. But one meal a day – which is what the poorer quarter of the world tend to rely upon – is not enough nor does it have the quality and variety necessary to maintain good health. The real problem is distribution, with the poorer countries able to afford too little and the richer consuming too much, and incorporating in their diet too high a proportion of fat and sugar, known to be deleterious to good health. Food is a little like money; unless it is distributed more evenly, there is likely to be suffering, leading to trouble of all sorts.

During the war the people of Britain learnt to be even-handed in the distribution of many goods and services, and after the war to retain this spirit until the last vestiges of rationing were removed in 1954. People came to appreciate fairness above a free-for-all in society, and this is one reason why the Labour Party came to power in 1945 with the Conservative Party out of office until 1951.

Sir Stafford Cripps, the Labour Chancellor of the Exchequer, has been held to have been the architect of the post-war programme of austerity, which the ending of American Aid necessitated, and which, hard though it was, secured the return of Britain to something like economic solvency. Bread had not been rationed during the war and the National Loaf was the only one available; but, in 1947, Cripps introduced rationing even of this loaf. Then, the meat ration was reduced – it was smaller after V.E. Day than it had been in 1944 – and the bacon ration was reduced from 4 oz. to 3 oz., and cheese cut to 1 oz. a week, even until March 1952. Cripps was a dedicated, hardworking man who loved Scilly and visited the islands for short holiday breaks quite often in the post-war years. Sadly, he died – it is said through overwork – before he could see all aspects of his rationing removed and the economic recovery under way. War changed the nature of society in the UK considerably, and it became acceptable in the national interest for the government to dictate in what had formerly been areas of personal freedom, including the direction of labour of all except those in reserved occupations or outside the age-ranges or incapacitated. In December, 1941, single women aged between 20 and 30 and not in reserved occupations, were 'called up', and women between the ages of 16 and 45 were later obliged to help by being put into organisations such as the Land Army. Orders, directions and restrictions continued of necessity to increase during the six years, and early on in the war signposts were removed and the names of villages over shops were painted over everywhere in Britain, so that invading German parachutists would not know where they were. This restriction never affected Scilly, where there were no signposts at that time; even by the 21st century there were no signs in Hugh Town showing the street names. The signpost restriction was repealed on June 30, 1943, when the danger of invasion was past.

Compared with the two million homes destroyed or badly damaged in Britain during the war, and the 80,000 British civilians killed, Scilly escaped relatively lightly with only 3 civilians killed. Apart from London, the worst-hit city was Plymouth. Coventry had its big raid which destroyed the cathedral and killed about 1,000 citizens on November 14, 1940; this was followed by raids on Portsmouth, Southampton and Sheffield. But Plymouth suffered seven big air raids in March and April, 1941, in which about 600 people were killed, 30,000 people lost their homes and a quarter of the inhabitants left the city each evening to camp in the open on Dartmoor, where at least they felt safe. Plymouth's centre was systematically destroyed by the bombing, and many of the inhabitants were obliged to do their shopping on Mutley Plain, a mile north of the city, which escaped most of the devastation. So great was the damage in the city centre, that even the old street plan was not followed at the post-war rebuilding, which set itself against the old and picturesque and succeeded in creating shopping areas open, spacious and with vistas, but rather windy and predictable – with not a curve in sight. Home Office advice issued to citizens on July 17, 1944, reads oddly now. It read: 'Do not be afraid to be the first to take precautions when you hear a bomb coming'.

One tragic aspect of the raids is that Plymouth had been designated a safe or neutral zone by the authorities, and some evacuee children from the London area were killed in the raids. Evacuation of some children from Plymouth began in May, 1941, but there was some reluctance in Cornwall to taking them in, and the police had to threaten some people with prosecution before they would house them. Only 3 evacuees are known to have come to Scilly, but they came under private arrangements, not public ones. The Ministry of Health had asked for accommodation for evacuees in the Islands in January, 1939, but, once the war had begun, concluded that Scilly was not a safe or suitable area for their reception.

* * * * *

Scilly's principal contribution to the war was to serve as a base for Royal Navy and Royal Air Force craft to rescue airmen from ditched planes and sometimes seamen from sunken ships. The development of these rescue services took place because of the needs of war. In 1939 and 1940, fewer than 20% of ditched RAF aircrew were being rescued, and in October, 1940, the RAF lost 260 airmen, mostly in the sea. Such high losses of highly-trained personnel was the reason behind the expansion of the RAF Air-Sea Rescue Service, whose own personnel were drawn from a mixture of wartime volunteers, regular servicemen, and from civilians with merchant navy qualifications.

The Royal Navy's rescue craft were well-armed, usually carrying 3-

pounder guns; but the RAF launches at first carried little armament as they were rarely attacked. The Germans were the first to use the colour yellow on their launches to indicate craft on rescue missions and facilitate aerial recognition, but such practice was at the time simply one of convenience and not recognised in international law. Then, in 1941, two of the RAF's high-speed launches were attacked and sunk by German aircraft, and High Speed Launch 108 was attacked on July 1, 1941, by a German floatplane, and its engines were stopped. The German plane then landed and took the injured British crew to hospital, while a German trawler was summoned by the German plane to take possession of the launch. So, subsequent to this event, the launches were equipped with defensive armament, often two .303 Browning machine-guns, which were an improvement over the Lewis guns of the First World War. The Luftwaffe were the first to equip their aircraft with one-man dinghies inflated by CO_2 cylinders, while RAF crews had only Mae West lifejackets to float around in. However, after a German dinghy was captured in 1940, Britain began to produce them complete with a flag for the ditched crew to wave. The Germans were also the first to moor rescue floats in the English Channel and North Sea, and this idea was taken up by the Air Ministry in 1941, and 16 were anchored in British estuaries, together with 5 German ones which had been captured when they broke loose from their moorings in gales and drifted to the British coast. In 1942, the larger RAF aircraft had multi-seat dinghies, whose equipment included spray covers, waterproof distress flares, a Verey pistol, water instead of fruit drinks, a whistle, chocolate, first-aid kit, yellow caps for identification and some protection, paddles, drinking cups, a baler, dinghy leak stoppers, a telescopic mast and flag, a knife with a curved blade and a cork handle so that it would float. The largest dinghies were six feet in diameter and, from 1942, were equipped with a transmitter in a waterproof bag – a copy of a German one which had been captured and found to be efficient. The dinghies also had an aerial raised by a gas-filled balloon or kite.

RMLs of the 10th flotilla of the Royal Navy's Coastal Forces served in rotation in the islands, together later with RMLs of the 63rd flotilla. The naval craft also operated at times from Falmouth, Newlyn, Appledore and, at first, also from Padstow, until the RAF launches took over at that base. When stationed in Scilly, one of the Royal Navy launches always lay alongside St Mary's Quay in readiness to respond to an emergency call. They were of the B-type Fairmile class, 112 feet long, of 80 tons displacement, with a crew of 18, and could do 20 knots. At times these naval launches were joined by two RAF air / sea rescue launches, although the RAF HSLs were hard-chinned and not as sturdy in rough seas as the round-hulled naval craft; they were 63 feet long and had been designed by Scott-Payne. There was more than a hint of rivalry between the crews of the two services, especially as on calm water the RAF craft proved considerably faster, although they had to make do with

The first steamroller ever to appear in Scilly was the one in the photograph, which was brought over to St Mary's to improve the runway on the aerodrome to help Hurricanes land and take-off safely. In the photograph it is shown on St Mary's Quay, driven with typical wartime high spirits by Lt. Cdr. Perrin, who commanded RML 542, but is here seen riding under the White Ensign hoisted aloft on the roller.

In June, 1942, No50 Works Flight arrived in St Mary's to extend the runway. They brought the steamroller to Scilly shipped over by Trinity House. The first area of tarmac was laid down and a small extension to the airfield was made by the Works Flight, who took over the cottage known as Nowhere in Old Town near the church as their living quarters. A Tiger Moth, piloted by Pascall, came over on June 4 to bring Mr Reece, the Air Ministry's section engineer, to plan the airfield changes, but, on taking off for the return flight, the engine failed and Messrs Pascall and Reece found themselves in 17 fathoms of water in the bay at Porth Hellick. Reece was picked up by a naval launch and Pascall swam ashore – both none the worse for the dip – but the aircraft was wrecked. Fortunately, when Air-Vice Marshal Orelebar – pilot of the British winning aircraft of the pre-war Schneider Trophy – came for a day's inspection on June 6, he praised the station personnel and nothing went amiss.

Photo: Lieut. Commander C.R. Perrin

civilian rations while the RMLs' crews had full navy rations. In particular, the RAF crews had margarine while the RN crews had butter. Friendly banter between the crews was sometimes heard at the two popular bars on St Mary's, the Atlantic Bar and Jack's Bar at Holgates; one story was that when one of the RAF boats first came into service in 1942, a navy crewman remarked that it looked like a Hants and Dorset bus, and the nickname stuck. But bus or no bus, the basic design of the RAF boats proved so successful that some of the boats served worldwide and were still in use in 1955, although with a wider range of duties, including target towing. In shortened form, a development of their classic design can be seen in the Arun class lifeboats of the RNLI.

The RAF craft often used their speed to be first on the scene at accidents,

(Above): RML 542 *at anchor in Hugh Town Harbour, showing the power-operated Pom-pom mounted forward. The gunner was K.L. Morley who, after the war, opened his shop in Hugh Town selling men's and women's wear, and which his family continued to run after his death in 1992.* RML 542 *was 112 feet long, had a top speed of nearly 20 knots, carried depth charges, and had a crew of 18. She was paid off at the close of the war in 1945. Both photos are by courtesy of Lt. Cdr. C.R. Perrin who skippered* RML 542 *for 2½ years.* RML 542 *held the record for the number of aircrew rescued by Scilly's rescue launches.*

(below): *an aerial photograph from an RAF Tiger Moth showing two of the Royal Navy's air-sea rescue launches alongside St Mary's quay during*

the Second World War. The two RAF high-speed launches stationed in Scilly in 1942 were 68 feet long and had been designed by Scott-Payne from prototypes tested by T.E. Lawrence.

but, as Ken Morley (who was naval pompom gunner on RML542) has pointed out, for most of the time in the years 1942-45, the naval launches of 63rd RML Flotilla were often the only air-sea rescue boats in Scilly, as the RAF boats were more usually operating out of Padstow and Newlyn. The launches in these two ports may have been faster but were not as near many happenings as the RN craft in Scilly, which were as far into the Western Approaches as it was practicable for them to be based.

Two new 25-ton, high-speed, Scott-Payne-designed launches of the RAF were brought to Scilly from the builders, Vospers at Southampton, by William Pilling early in 1943, and two more delivered to Newlyn, their identification numbers being 2552 (F/O West), 2553 (F/O O'Brien), 2554 (F/O V.I. Creasey), and 2555 (F/O Senator). Every Saturday morning in the summer months, one at Newlyn was exchanged for one in Scilly, so that all four had served on both stations within a few weeks. They had a range of about 500 miles, were 68 feet long, were said to be able to do between 25 and 40 knots, and took a crew of between 10 and 12. They replaced the smaller, relatively slow pinnaces, which were really supply craft to seaplanes pressed into air / sea rescue work at the start of the war. The new boats were painted

The photograph shows Leading Aircraftman T.E. Lawrence piloting a prototype launch across Plymouth Sound, accompanied by his Wing Commander's wife, Mrs S.W. Smith, who was being taken for a 'spin'. S.P.B. Mais told the story of an elderly Scillonian, whom he met in 1934, who had been most disappointed upon meeting Lawrence a few years earlier; he had asked the great man for his autograph, but Lawrence would only sign it as 'Aircraftman Shaw', as he then was, rather than 'Colonel Lawrence', as he had once been. Thomas Edward Lawrence, 1888-1935, was the illegitimate son of an Anglo-Irish landowner, who became the archaeologist to the British Museum expedition to Egypt before the 1st World War. This, and his detailed knowledge of the Arab world, led to his appointment as Intelligence and Liaison Officer to Arab chiefs in the 1st World War when they rebelled against their rulers, the Turks, who had become Germany's allies. Lawrence wore Arab dress to help his good relationship with the Arab leader, Sherif Husan and his son Feisal.

Disappointment for Lawrence came when he accompanied Churchill to the Cairo Conference in 1921, and found that his promises to the Arabs were set aside, especially by the giving of Syria to France. He started a new life by enlisting as Private Ross in the Tank Corps and then as Aircraftman Shaw in the RAF, where his love of speed led to his developing fast launches in Plymouth Sound, at first as seaplane tenders. In 1930 the RAF was offered a 37 feet, twin-engined, hard-chine launch by Scott-Paine for testing. Although only 200 horsepower, it had a speed of 23 knots, and it was Shaw, whilst serving at Mount Batten, who put this craft through its tests and improved it, resulting later in Scott-Paine's firm gaining an order for the first High Speed Rescue Launch (called a crash-boat). Scott-Paine went to the USA, but many of his later craft were supplied to the Royal Navy under Lend Lease in the 2nd World War, his designs being incorporated in most of the RAF and RN high speed launches of the war, some of which served importantly in Scilly.

In 1940, the MTB3 *was equipped with a Rolls Royce Merlin engine like a Spitfire. Lawrence wrote* The Seven Pillars of Wisdom, *which described his adventures and experiences in liasing with the Arabs in the 1st World War, and the book became almost compulsory reading for 6th formers in the 1930s, although now not as favoured, being thought, not perhaps unsurprisingly, to have somewhat exaggerated Lawrence's role.*

When Lawrence attended the early Schneider Cup Race, he was given a speedboat by Colin Cooper which he called Biscuit, *and gained much of his experience overhauling her until she could obtain a speed of something like 45 knots He was also given the task of writing the original manual for the operation and servicing of the early RAF marine craft, but it seems unlikely that the crews of the air / sea rescue craft in the Second World War were aware that the original edition of their manual had such a distinguished author.*
Photo reproduced by kind permission of the Bodleian Library (MS, Res, C54, fol89r).

bright yellow and unarmed, but later were repainted grey and given two Browning machine-guns and an Oerlikon, after some similar boats from another station had been attacked despite their yellow colour. On St Mary's quay was a telephone-box which was the link with RAF Newlyn and with Coastal Command; the telephone would ring and at least one boat would be ordered out to an area of sea where a square search would be made to locate a dinghy from a ditched RAF aircraft. Sometimes an RAF Walrus aircraft (a small flying-boat biplane) would have reached the ditched airmen first, and would either have rescued them itself, or have dropped a smoke-float to make the task of finding them easier for the HSL. Sometimes there was a bit of a race with the Navy's RMLs to be first to the scene, but cooperation was usually excellent.

Some of the testing and development between the wars of the first launches – called seaplane tenders in the early days, which was the original air / sea rescue concept – was carried out by Thomas Edward Lawrence. Because of the later 2nd World War, it turned out to be some of his most important work, yet his fame today is more as a scholar, soldier and author. Born in 1888, he carried out archaeological excavations at Carchemish in the Middle East until, as Colonel Lawrence during the 1st World War, he was appointed to liase with the Arabs and persuaded them to defeat the Turks in that region. Films made about him have given the impression that he rode everywhere by camel in Arabia; but actually his preferred mode of transport – except in the desert – was an armoured Rolls Royce. He wrote an account of his exploits in his book *The Seven Pillars of Wisdom*. Siegfried Sassoon and E.M. Forster both read the book in manuscript and had input to it; in return, Lawrence had influence on *A Passage to India*. To secure Arab help against the Turks, Lawrence came to understandings with the Arab leaders on behalf of Britain concerning what they could expect after the war; but, in 1921, at the Cairo Conference, which he attended with Winston Churchill, who invited Lawrence because of his knowledge of the Middle East and charm in dealing with Arab leaders, Lawrence found to his dismay and disillusionment that these understandings were not to be honoured. In 1922, he became an advisor on Middle East affairs to the Colonial Office and a Fellow of All Souls College; but, after a spell in the army as Private Ross, he enlisted in the trade of a mechanic in the Marine Branch of the RAF with the name of Shaw, a name he took by deed poll in 1927. His passion for speed (he once had a race on his motorcycle with a Bristol Fighter) led him to be posted to Mount Batten, Plymouth, and it was here that his duties, in the rank of LAC (leading aircraftman), involved testing and improving fast motor-launches, such work helping in the development of the later air / sea rescue craft of the 2nd World war. In the 1930s Scott-Paine constructed the launches, and then, after he had gone to live in the USA in 1939, built more which were used by Britain during the Second World War under lend-lease arrangements. 'Teddy'

Burling was also interested in the design of air / sea rescue craft, and rose to be a Group Captain in the RAF in command of the seaplane base at Mount Batten at Plymouth when Lawrence was serving under him as LAC Shaw. Both men were slim and about 5foot 6½ inches tall, and, despite a large difference in their ranks, the two remained on friendly terms. Burling had gone up to Cambridge University and then into the RNAS, where he learnt to fly floatplanes; he had known Lawrence during the 1st World War, when he was a pilot in the RNAS at Jedda assisting 2nd Lieutenant Lawrence by bombing Turkish-held bridges in the Middle East. The rank differential at Mount Batten did sometimes cause problems: on one occasion Burling refused Shaw's application for a fourth successive weekend's pass, because he felt that Shaw was obtaining unfair privileges over other aircraftmen; but Shaw then produced a letter he had received from Winston Churchill inviting him for the weekend – and at that, his request for leave was instantly granted.

Group Captain E.J.F. Burling, D.S.O., D.F.C., A.F.C. had an interesting career. As a young man, he designed a floating-dock for the use of seaplanes at Tresco in the 1st World War. He was later to be the RNAS pilot of the first aircraft ever to be catapulted from a battleship – actually off HMS *Vindictive* in order to locate a pirateship, *Vindictive*, closing to capture all eleven of the pirate crew off Byas Bay, Hong Kong. Burling was at one time made Admiral of the select RAF Sailing Club at Singapore, and was Station Commander at Felixstowe from 1936, where experimental work was carried out culminating in Britain winning the Schneider Trophy with Mitchell's Supermarine S5. Almost as important was Burling's association with Uffa Fox, the yacht designer, which led to Burling helping to develop the airborne lifeboat, which was dropped to ditched airmen by parachute from 1942. This was based on the lifeboat of George Selman, chief designer to Scott-Paine, who made the first one for the Swedish Air Force and then a different version for the RAF. During the war it was mainly carried by Wellington bombers and is said to have saved the lives of a great number of aircrew.

Burling was also present at the first practical demonstration of detecting aircraft on a radar screen. Watson-Webb, who invented radar, asked Burling to send some of the Mount Batten flying-boats into the air space covered by his new machine, and they both watched the screen on which the flight of these aircraft made blips. During the 2nd World War, Burling was involved in the security of General de Gaulle, and was President of the RAF Selection Board at the Air Ministry at Adastral House in London. Burling's mother was a nurse called Chrissie, who came down from London with her son to live at Sandy Nook in 1895, and to whom, after she died in 1925 he dedicated a fine window to be seen today in St Mary's Church in Hugh Town. It is said that she had played a part in nursing Edward VII when, as Prince of Wales, he had been a patient in the late 1880s or early 1890s – at about the same period when a popular song of the day contained the words 'Burlington Bertie'; and she met Edward VII again when he visited Scilly in 1901. Like other nurses, Burling's mother benefited from the work of Florence Nightingale, who, in 1907, was the first woman to have the Order of Merit conferred on her. When Florence died in 1910, many people were amazed to find that she had been alive so long, for the Crimean War, 1854-56, with which she was popularly associated as 'the lady of the lamp', seemed so long ago. In later life, Florence was confined much of the time to her couch by ill-health, yet she became an authority on India – which she never visited – although, arguably, much her most important work was in improving the status and training of nurses, a profession for long associated with prostitution, which was one of the main reasons Florence's parents had opposed her original involvement in it.

Little of this concerned the Royal circle of Prince Edward – called 'Bertie' by his family – whose sources of amusement seem today wasteful and their humour somewhat infantile. For instance, Lillie Langtry (a clergyman's daughter and a tomboy when young, but later one of Edward's numerous lovers, which included Alex Keppel) once told one of her hosts that the soup was cold, causing him to burn his lips as he tasted it; the mother of the Duchess of Marlborough placed bits of soup amongst the cheese portions and even tied a full inkpot over a door used by her husband. Soapsuds were sometimes added to sweets instead of whipped cream, and great hilarity accompanied battles with soda syphons or tobogganing downstairs on trays. Apple-pie beds and leaking hotwater bottles also provided endless sources of merriment, but nobody was allowed ever to play jokes upon Prince Edward – as heir to the throne he was strictly off-limits. Instead he became – in the words of Marot Tennant – 'a professional love-maker', with Alexandra, the beautiful Danish princess he married in 1863, putting up with his unending succession of infidelities wherever he went on his extensive excursions about the country, almost as if his seducing of pretty women was a hobby like stamp-collecting. The slim Alexandra, one day looking through the palace window, observed her husband approaching in his open carriage with, seated beside him, one of his lovers, Lillie Langtry, who had by then grown decidedly plump; Bertie had acquired the nickname of 'Tum-Tum' (Rudyard Kipling, when in the USA, had accurately described him as the 'corpulent voluptuary'), and the sight of these two made Alexandra burst into laughter and call over her lady-in-waiting to witness it. It was a time when it was accepted among the upper-classes that male Royals would have relationships with women outside of their marriages, and it was not until the latter part of the 20th century that middle-class morality had reached up to the upper-classes and promoted criticism of the latter-day Prince of Wales for admtting such a relationship – Edward's great, great, grandson, Charles, with Camilla Parker-Bowles, Alex Keppel's great, great, granddaughter.

Nurse Burling, as some called Burling's mother, later married E.J.

Mumford and helped run Holgate's Hotel with him – her brother, Albert Poynter, being employed as a member of the hotel staff before himself becoming a hotelier – of the Atlantic Hotel in Hugh Street, formerly known as Bickfords. Burling went to command at Calshot in 1944 to prepare for the D-Day landings and, after the peace, it is alleged that he took some German yachts and gave them to the Solent Yacht Club.

Between the wars, Holgate's Hotel on St Mary's was the most impressive building on Hugh Town's harbour front. It had been built in three stages, 1899, 1920, and 1938. It was owned by Bertie Mumford but requisitioned at the start of the 2nd World War for billeting service personnel. After the war the building was refurbished after de-requisitioning, and re-opened on March 15, 1949, as a 50 bedroom hotel, which Burling inherited from his stepfather and went to live in upon retirement from the RAF. He was a familiar sight in Scilly, cruising around the islands nearly every fair-weather summer day in his graceful, white sailing yacht *Spero* – or sometimes in his racing yacht *Wizard* – and always accompanied by his one crew member, Charles Forester MacDonald. Burling suffered a stroke in 1964 and eventually closed the hotel, so that – apart from servants and companions – he was the sole occupant during his remaining years; however, to his immense irritation, the Council of the Isles of Scilly continued to charge him high rates, as if the building was still an hotel rather than his private residence.

Charlie MacDonald had served in the Royal Navy, and, when his ship was sunk, lived in an open lifeboat for 4 days before being rescued. He also served in the merchant navy, and two of the ships in which he was serving were sunk by the German battlecruiser *Scharnhorst* within days of each other. He finished the war in the RAF Air / Sea Rescue Service. After demobilisation, Charlie became, not only boatman to Burling but servant-companion, tending his master after his stroke, and was at his deathbed on November 27, 1974, when Burling was 85 years old. Burling was buried in his mother's grave in the churchyard at Old Town, MacDonald living on in retirement in Scilly until 1997.

In his will Burling left Holgate's Hotel to the Cheshire Homes but, although the great white building had looked imposing, its structure was not considered sound and was deemed to be too costly to repair. One of its defects was that when E.N. Mumford had the extension made in 1920, some of the concrete blocks used in the construction came from the old seaplane base on Tresco, from whence they were available and cheap; but they were said to have been of Tresco sand mixed with cement and rather too brittle. So the building was totally demolished and the area grassed over and now known as Holgate's Green, with the hotel's sprung maple-floor saved and found of use when building the squash court at Porthmellon, not being replaced until 1999.

* * * * *

This ditched aircrew from a Whitley bomber were rescued by an air-sea rescue launch from St Mary's on August 16th, 1942.

Hypothermia is one of the greatest dangers to crews of ditched aircraft and sunken ships, for survivors can quickly be overcome from their experience in the cold sea, even after they have been rescued by lifeboat, rescue launch or climbed aboard an inflatable. In the Second World War experiments were carried out by the Germans using

the inmates of concentration camps such as Dachau – not necessarily Jews, but people from many other groups such as gypsies, homosexuals, asylum residents, persons of mixed race and others. It was with these that German doctors determined that hot water was the quickest, least costly and most effective treatment for the hypothermia condition, a remedy also believed in by the allies; this was not an unexpected conclusion but neither was it very helpful because, while hot water could be supplied in abundance once survivors reached hospital, it was not something always easy to supply beforehand, and therefore the speed with which the rescue boats reached survivors came increasingly to be seen as crucial. This is one of the reasons why the fast Royal Navy and Royal Air Force rescue launches based in Scilly became so important.

The first rescue by the 63rd Flotilla occurred on Christmas Day and Boxing Day in 1942, when the crew of six from a ditched Whitley bomber were picked up safely by RML 542, 65 miles south-west of Scilly. There was another danger to be faced in the English Channel from 1940 onwards, when German E-boats began operating from French ports such as Cherbourg. At times these E-boats were as great a menace to Allied shipping as U-boats and, on one occasion, four Norwegian merchant ships were sunk by them within sight of Land's End. Leslie Legg, of Annet Farm on St Agnes, was one of those killed when his motor torpedo boat 671 was in action with German E-boats in 1944.

One successful E-boat operation – kept secret in the war, but by the 21st century widely known – was the surprise E-boat attack on American landing craft taking part in Operation Tiger on April 28, 1944. This was the code name of an American army rehearsal a few weeks before the projected D-Day landings in Normandy, when eight landing craft, full of troops and equipment, set out from Plymouth and made a circuit of the bay almost as far as Portland – a sea trip designed to replicate in length the planned cross-channel voyage on D-Day. In fact, the troops on board the landing craft were not informed whether the operation was a practice or the real thing. After the voyage it was planned to land the troops on Slapton Sands, a beach selected because it resembled in length and in other ways, the beaches of Normandy on the other side of the Channel.

But the Germans at Cherbourg were listening-in to the increased wireless activity Operation Tiger generated, and decided to send 9 E-boats under Gunther Rabe across the Channel to investigate.

E-boats had a beam of 17 feet and a draught of 4½ feet, and were built of teak on aluminium hulls. They had Daimler-Benz diesel engines capable of over 40 knots; neither Britain nor the USA had craft as fast as that. They were also well armed with guns and torpedoes. They met the convoy of landing craft about 12 miles west of Portland and torpedoed NO.507 and caused an ammunition explosion on No.531, the tail end of both ships going down with all their equipment and together with most of the troops on them, hemmed in as they were below deck. A third landing craft, NO.289, was also severely damaged. LST 496 actually fired upon LST 511 thinking it was the enemy.

Much of the blame for the tragedy can be laid at the door of slipshod administration, and a failure by those in charge to realise the danger from E-boats. The Royal Navy which actually had the destroyers *Onslow* and *Saladin* not far away, had supplied the convoy with pathetically poor escorts from Plymouth, consisting of one destroyer, the *Scimitar* – which, upon receiving slight damage in a minor collision, turned back to Plymouth without even informing the convoy – and one corvette, the *Azalea*, which was slow and had no means of wireless communication with the American troop commander, as no frequency had been agreed. *Azalea* also was not informed of the departure of the destroyer and fired no shot or played any part in the short action which followed, so the E-boats returned to Cherbourg without any loss. Indeed, if they had continued their attacks, they might have secured even more damage; but, as it was, they had created a shortage of LSTs and this postponed D-Day a while, and it revealed, not for the first time, some poor staff work, particularly among Admiral Moon's naval officers at Plymouth, who gave him poor support. Moon went on to help the Normandy landings, but later committed suicide. Some lessons were learnt however, and, although the Americans suffered huge casualties at the Omaha beach landings in Normandy, at Utah only 197 men died.

A worry to the Allies immediately after the tragedy was that the Germans would note the similarity between Slapton and Normandy beaches and would realise where the real invasion was to take place, and the Allies had in mind their ill-fated attack on Dieppe on August 19, 1942, which was a failure and with heavy casualties. Fortunately for the Allies, the enemy remained convinced that the main attack would be in the Pas de Calais, so they did not reinforce Normandy defences unduly. Relatives of the dead from Operation Tiger were simply informed that they were 'missing in action', and nobody was allowed to say anything at all about the disaster in which 749 American servicemen died, with some of the survivors struggling in the water for up to six hours before a rescue operation was mounted. Many died because they had not been shown how to operate the lifeboats in the LSTs.

But such a disaster was not the fault or the business of RMLs of the Royal Navy, although the naval launches possessed offensive capabilities beyond their purely air-sea rescue role. RML542, for instance, was 34 metres long and carried depth-charges, machine-guns, a 2-pounder pompom gun on the foredeck and an Oerlikon gun aft, and could thus be said to have been nearly as powerful, if nowhere near as fast, as the E-boats.

Communications between the launches and St Mary's was through the Custom House in Hugh Town, which had been taken over by the Royal Navy at the start of the war and used to receive coded messages by phone from the mainland. These, after decoding, were relayed to the telephone box on the quay and thence to the rescue-launch on standby, This craft was kept in condition ready to sail immediately when required – sometimes even to as far away as the Bay of Biscay – to pick up ditched aircrew from their dinghies, for speedy rescue was often crucial to survival. These rescue missions were always secret, which helps to explain why the bravery of the launch-crews and their persistence in finding lost airmen may not always have received as much recognition as deserved. The launches maintained radio contact with St Mary's Custom House, which was itself in contact with the radar station the RAF had built at Newford, thus enabling the launches to be warned of the approach of enemy aircraft. They could also talk with escorting or searching aircraft via VHF, but the launches were still vulnerable to air attack and had no means of concealment as had submarines. The natural dangers of the sea and the many rocks of Scilly's waters were also hazards to these craft, particularly as all navigation lights around Scilly had been extinguished for the duration. However, in certain circumstances, lights could be put on by request in order to help the launches find their way back into Scilly, rather than having to rely on dead-reckoning. Lieutenant Commander C.R. Perrin, the commanding officer of RML542, recalls one night asking for the Bishop Rock light to be turned on for a couple of minutes to help him find his way back to Scilly. He had been out in the Atlantic for two days on a search-and-rescue mission and, although he believed his dead-reckoning navigation was reasonable (considering the unreliability of dead-reckoning), that night was particularly dark and nothing whatever could be seen. At the stroke of 0100 hours the Bishop light was switched on for him as he had requested and, to his amazement, instead of an expected distant beam on the horizon, the lighthouse was right in the path of his launch less than a mile away. Other exceptions to the blackout were that Peninnis and Round Island lighthouses were sometimes also lit at night to help guide a passing Allied convoy. There was also a beacon on Woolpack Fort from 1943 called centimetre wave equipment – a sort of radar – and operated by Colin Gordon of a Canadian

RAF unit – Woolpack being massively defended by barbed-wire entangle-
ments, as with other parts of the Garrison, to guard against an enemy landing.

The Islands were also used during the war by Short Sunderland flying-
boats of RAF Coastal Command as an emergency base, convenient if they
were damaged when flying in the Western Approaches or found themselves,
with insufficient fuel to reach their home base at Pembroke Docks or at
Plymouth. Algy Guy, Jim Lethbridge and Matt Lethbridge (junior), who
served in the RNA, tended the Sunderlands; and later, after he had joined the
RAF, Matt Lethbridge was posted to St Mary's as an RAF launch-coxswain,
and again, for a while, tended the Sunderlands. These Sunderland flying-
boats were wonderful aircraft in their time; they had a top speed of not much
more than 205 m.p.h., yet in the Second World War, speed was not
everything. From his launch alongside St Mary's quay, Lt. Cdr. Perrin one
afternoon watched a Sunderland being pursued but not caught by a much
faster Messerschmitt. The Sunderland dodged in and out of some big, woolly,
cumulus clouds, such hide and seek proving so frustrating to the pilot of the
Messerschmitt that he eventually gave up the chase and flew away. In fact,
the Sunderland did not have to rely purely on evasive tactics for it was well
capable of looking after itself in a fight. It had two gun-turrets as well as
several dorsal-guns behind normally closed hatches, which could be flung
open by its ten-man crew, if they were challenged to battle by enemy aircraft.

Sunderland flying-boats were in service in the RAF for 21 years, a length
of time unmatched by any other operational aircraft. To its crew the
Sunderland served as a home as well as a fighting-machine, for it often gave
them board and lodging for days on end and, at least on one occasion
remembered by Wing-Commander G.R. Leatherbarrow, for over a month; in
consequence, close comradeship was a notable feature of the crews,
especially because their patrol flights were sometimes long and not
necessarily eventful, consisting only of long vigils over trackless oceans
meeting neither friend nor foe. Yet German records verify that Sunderlands
may have accounted for up to 39 U-boat worldwide during the war, with
many other U-boats being damaged by their attacks.

They also had a role in air-sea rescue; on September 18, 1939, two
Sunderlands, one from Pembroke Dock, the other from Mount Batten,
Plymouth, rescued all the survivors from the torpedoed merchantman
Kensington Palace, which it might have taken surface craft a great deal
longer to reach.

Sunderlands were developed from the Short Brothers' Empire class
passenger-carrying flying-boat, which had a great range, and they came into
service with the RAF in 1938, the base at Mount Batten receiving them in
1939. Their principal battle weakness was a blind spot under the belly, and
this explains why Sunderlands, when under attack from enemy aircraft,
tended to dive to near-zero height, if there were no clouds nearby into which

The clean, impressive lines of the RAF Sunderland flying boat, a graceful machine which, in its pre-war 'Empire' form, epitomised luxury air travel.

The first Sunderlands flew in 1937, a development of the 'G' class Empire Flying Boats. They saw much service with the RAF's Coastal Command and, as early in the war as 21st September, 1939, two of them rescued 34 seamen from the torpedoed merchant ship Kensington Court. *In 1940, in the hasty evacuations of retreating British forces from Norway – and later from Crete – up to 60 service personnel were carried in a Sunderland at a time. But their main work was reconnaissance – to locate U-boats and to give convoy protection. They could hold their own against enemy aircraft for they had a nose turret with a single gun, guns on either beam (later models had a dorsal turret instead), and a four-gun tail turret. They flew low when under attack to safeguard their vulnerable hull, and there were occasions when enemy aircraft attempted to deal with them by dropping bombs on them as they flew along relatively slowly. They carried a bomb and depth-charge load of only about 2,000lb, but their great value was a huge range of about 1,800 miles at their slow cruising speed of 130 m.p.h. Spacious quarters provided for a crew of nine, sometimes more; they had a wing span of nearly 113 feet and mounted 4 Pegasus engines.*

The Sunderland was also the first British aircraft to mount a power- operated gun-turret, and was, in 1940, the only British aircraft able to fly 500 miles from its base.

they could disappear. They also had a problem when attacking U-boats, especially as the war progressed and U-boats became better able to deal with air attack, for Sunderlands had of necessity to expose their undersides to U-boat gunfire in order to reach a position where they could drop depth-charges near or on the submarine. However, this did not deter Sunderlands from attacking, as was demonstrated by the sinking of U-243 on July 8, 1944, by a Sunderland captained by Flying Officer W.B. Tilley, and by the sinking of U-325 on April 30, 1945, by a Sunderland of 201 squadron. The optimum operational flying height for spotting U-boats was found to be about 1,000 feet, and some squadrons, of which No 230 was one, added two gun-positions in the galley of their Sunderlands, firing under the wing downwards. This gave the aircraft some protection underneath, but it was not unknown for one of the gunners in this position accidentally to shoot off one of the wing floats. U-boats under attack from Sunderlands often took to staying on the surface and fighting it out; one aircraft – from 230 squadron was shot down in this way, and the two survivors from the plane's crash had to complete the rest of the U-boat's operational cruise as its on-board prisoners. In 1940, another Sunderland from this squadron, captained by Flight Lieutenant Campell, claimed a U-boat sunk, but at the de-briefing was awarded only a 'possible kill'; the following week he sank another U-boat, only this time he managed to land on the water beside the stricken submarine, and bring back to base some of the U-boat survivors including the captain as prisoners on his Sunderland in order to prove his 'kill'.

One of the strengths of the Sunderland was that it could take a fair amount of punishment and still be capable of flying and retaliating. In the first air action involving a Sunderland in the Second World War, N9046 was intercepted by several Junkers 88s on April 3, 1940, and several of the German attacking aircraft were 'downed'. The Sunderland then flew home with leaking fuel tanks, a bullet-ridden hull, the instrument panel shattered, and two aircrew badly cut by flying-glass. The Junkers 88 was a formidable German twin-engined, reconnaissance bomber with a crew of 4 and a top speed of just over 300 m.p.h., which was considerably faster than the Sunderland; but the numerous gun-positions on the Sunderland proved effective, and after this engagement the Luftwaffe pilots were said to have dubbed the Sunderland 'the flying porcupine'.

In another engagement over the Bay of Biscay on July 2, 1943, Sunderland N-NAN was attacked by eight Junkers 88s, four on each beam; the Sunderland jettisoned all her depth-charges and then suffered from about 20 systematic assaults from the enemy, an engagement lasting almost non-stop for an hour. At this action's close, three Junkers 88s had been shot down, but the Sunderland's interior was a mess and several crewmen had been injured. The navigator was mortally wounded, yet gallantly managed to give the pilot a heading for home before he died; the aircraft then limped 300 miles to Cornwall and, after making a landing on the sea off Praa Sands near Penzance, her engines were able to drag her peppered hull out of the water and up the beach to terra firma.

Three men from Scilly flew in Sunderlands of 204 Squadron based at Mountbatten. Jack Hayward of St Martins had come to St Martins in 1928 as an orphaned boy seeking work; he joined the RAF in 1938 and trained as an air-gunner, but died when his Sunderland hit Plymouth Breakwater during a night landing only a fortnight after the war began. Don Hicks from St Agnes also served in Sunderlands with 204 Squadron, but was later posted to a Catalina Squadron where he won the George Medal. Raymond Lloyd, a Flight Sergeant air-gunner from St Martin's, flew over Scilly frequently

Matt Lethbridge recalls a Sunderland in sinking condition at a mooring placed for it off Shark's Pit (Porth Harry), which had to be beached on Town Beach where temporary repairs could be carried out. After these, the Sunderland was placed out at one of the harbour buoys and partly refuelled in readiness for a test flight. But the following night a gale sprang up and the flying-boat sank – a total loss.

On June 24, 1942, Sunderland RB-B with an Australian crew came into Scilly having lost both propellers of its engines on one wing. Lt Cdr. Perrin recalls 'talking the pilot down' by radio, so that he landed without further hazard. It was a dark night, so a flarepath of dinghies with lights on them had to be hurriedly organised to guide the pilot in, and this worked well, the plane landing 'like a bird', although the pilot reported that he could hardly keep the plane balanced. The Sunderland was then brought in to St Mary's and onto Town Beach – as in the photograph above – and, after temporary repair, the Sunderland was towed by RML 542 all the way to Mount Batten for major repair. When operating once more in August, 1943, this Sunderland sank U-454 with depth charges, but not before the U-boat had shot down the Sunderland by gunfire – both craft thus being destroyed.

during the war on Atlantic patrols in Sunderlands. Owing to strong head winds on one trip early in the war, the flying-boat ran out of fuel 40 miles off the Bishop Rock and had to land on the sea, but broke a float in doing so. Lloyd and the rest of the crew climbed out on the wing to keep the boat in trim, until rescue came in the shape of a Dutch freighter, the S.S. *Biderdyke* en route to the USA on October 13, 1939, which picked them up and then transferred them to the destroyer *Icarus* which landed them all safely back at their base at Mountbatten at Plymouth.

Not all Sunderlands made safe landings in Scilly even when undamaged, for landing 25 tons on water was never easy especially in rough weather. On February 24, 1945, a RAF Sunderland landed before daybreak and tore her bottom out on the Pots; the crew were rescued, but the flying-boat drifted on to the Mare Ledges and became a total loss. Another, almost new Sunderland with a New Zealand crew, overshot its run-in to St Mary's Road and wrecked itself on Tobaccoman's Ledge off Tresco; one of its four engines, complete with propeller, could still be seen wedged high on the rocks there until well into the 1970s.

Another Sunderland ripped her hull open on Newman Rock when taking off, but landed successfully alongside a grass runway at her mainland base. Another flying-boat, which was not a Sunderland but a Catalina, used Scilly on Christmas Eve, 1943, as an emergency halt while on a flight from Gibraltar to Scotland. By chance, the Catalina's pilot was Flight Lieutenant A.P. Hamilton, brother of the late Scillonian marine artist, John Hamilton, whose paintings of Second World War naval and air battles of the Pacific War are hung along the corridors of the Pentagon in the USA. This Catalina was badly damaged and had only one of its two engines working, yet it was landed safely despite a choppy sea. Sunderlands had a range of over 500 miles but Catalinas had an even greater one. However, although reliable, Catalinas were poorly-armed, with two machine-guns in blisters on their sides, and a speed of only about 130 m.p.h. By contrast, Sunderlands had power-operated gun-turrets, fore and aft, and beam guns also; but the depth-charges carried were only of 250lb, which meant that even a direct hit on a U-boat did not guarantee its destruction, and, as these were set to explode at 22 fathoms, this was usually too deep to harm a U-boat still on the surface.

To moor the flying-boats in Scilly safely, red-coloured rubber buoys were anchored securely in St Mary's Harbour and in Porthcressa Bay, moorings which had to be serviced regularly, a job carried out at the time by Roland Morris, a diver who was later to become better known for his search for the wreck of the *Association* in 1707. But the position of these flying-boats at these moorings was unsafe in heavy seas or gales, in Porthcressa being too exposed to a blow from the south and in St Mary's Harbour to a north-westerly one, and two flying-boats were wrecked at their moorings in Scilly during the war as a result of high winds. On July 1st, 1940, U-26, commanded by Heinz Scheringer, was crippled in an attack by Sunderland P9603/H commanded by Flight Lieutenant William Gibson just south-west of the Bishop Rock, and, when the Royal Navy corvette *Gladiolus*, escorting convoy OA.175, rushed to the scene, the U-boat crew had little option but to scuttle their submarine and become prisoners-of-war. Of the submarine's crew, 7 died in the Sunderland's attack, but 40, including Scheringer, were made prisoners. Even after the war was over, Sunderlands performed an important role in an unlikely major event – the Berlin Airlift of 1948. Their salt-resistant fuselages meant that they were ideal for lifting salt into Berlin, 4 tons at a time, which they accomplished by landing on a large lake close to Berlin, making about 1,000 such trips altogether during the East / West crisis. Production of Sunderlands ceased in 1946, but those still in service participated in the Korean War. The last RAF Sunderland flew in 1959, marking the end of all flying-boats in the RAF; by 1993, only one Sunderland in the world was still in flying condition. This was named *Fantasy of Flight*, formerly of Coastal Command, GBJHS/ML814. Edward Hulton purchased and restored the aircraft at a cost of over £1 million, and then sold out to aircraft collector Kermit Weeks who placed it in his aviation museum in the USA.

The Boeing 314 was the American equivalent of the Short Empire Flying Boat of Imperial Airways that developed into the Sunderland. In 1942, one of the American Boeings had a hazardous journey: it was flying Winston Churchill back to Britain from across the Atlantic, where he had had a meeting with President Roosevelt in Virginia, when the aircraft missed sighting Scilly and Land's End and discovered – on re-calculating its track – that it was heading straight for Brest, where massed German anti-aircraft guns would almost certainly have shot it down. The Captain immediately turned and headed northwards, but then the plane appeared on British radar coming from the direction of occupied France and was interpreted as hostile. Six Hurricanes took off to intercept it and try to shoot it down but, because of some fortunate rapid changes of direction by the Boeing on sighting the English coast, the Hurricanes failed to find the Boeing, which was thus able to land safely without incident at Plymouth, its important passenger unaware of the perils he had survived.

* * * * *

By August, 1940, upwards of four hundred of Scilly's residents had of their own accord left the islands for the mainland for the duration of hostilities. They had decided not to wait for any order for compulsory evacuation, in the belief that living in Scilly had become too great a risk, especially without air cover. Indeed, it was not until the Luftwaffe bases had been established in the Cherbourg peninsula and in the Channel Islands that action was taken to improve Scilly's air defences by basing in the islands a flight of Hawker Hurricane fighter aircraft from 87 Squadron. These were sent from Exeter to St Mary's on May 19, 1941, and stayed there until September 17, 1944, and consisted initially of six aircraft with their pilots and 34 ground crew – many of the pilots already well experienced through participation in the air battles of 1940.

Fighter pilots of the RAF were particularly honoured for the part they played in the Battle of Britain when, though few in numbers, they saved Britain from invasion. Their heroism became recognised, not only by the public view of their dog fights over southeast England, but when it was revealed that by the end of September, 1940, 537 pilots, that is nearly half the pilots of Fighter Command, had experienced being shot down or wounded, although, because they usually took to their parachutes and were fighting above home ground, very many lived to fly and fight again another day, but an increasing number also lost their lives.

At the start of the war, pilots still wore collars and ties, but the need to turn one's head around quickly, to keep an eye on any hostile aircraft on one's tail, led to the abandonment of the tie, and sometimes its substitution by a silk scarf of a design not covered by regulations. In a broadcast on the wireless at that time, Winston Churchill said: 'Never in the field of human history has so much been owed by so many to so few'. He was paying tribute to the pilots of RAF Fighter Command who had prevented Goering's Luftwaffe from obtaining easy air supremacy over the south of England, thus deterring the German army from invading as Hitler had demanded air supremacy as a prerequisite for invasion. Churchill was the master of the grandiloquent phrase and he is said always to have taken a great deal of trouble over his speeches because they were so important in fostering the spirit of the nation; but the wording of this famous speech was not entirely original. It has been suggested that he may have seen a letter from Sir Francis Godolphin to Lord Burghley of August 6th, 1593, in which he commends the work of Robert Adams in building Star Castle with the words: 'the work considered, so much has seldom been performed at such small charge, and with so few hands in so short a time'. But, original or not, Churchill's words were timely and perfectly expressed the debt and gratitude of the nation to a few hundred pilots with their ground crews – among them some of those later posted to the Scillies.

The Battle of Britain in the summer of 1940, which took place after the evacuation from Dunkirk, was a struggle for the supremacy of the skies over the southern part of England. The Luftwaffe won over the English Channel, but RAF Fighter Command denied them supremacy anywhere beyond the British coastline. The Luftwaffe had a numbers advantage but the ME109 had a limited range, as did the Stuka; both had less than 30 minutes over England before they were obliged to return to base to refuel. Moreover, the German bombers carried too small a bombload for what was expected of them, and the Germans were slow to appreciate the advantage which radar gave to the Hurricanes and Spitfires, enabling them to be in the air and above the Luftwaffe bombers and fighters almost by the time they had reached the British coast; and the British had the home ground, whereas if a German bailed out he became a prisoner-of-war. The Luftwaffe concentrated on bombing airfields in an attempt to destroy Fighter Command, and on August 31 they actually succeeded in destroying 39 aircraft more than they lost, although usually the balance was the other way round. Hitler had excluded London from being bombed – he may still have had hopes of a peace with Britain on his terms – but two German bombers dropped bombs on London on August 24, presumably in error – perhaps to achieve a faster flight home by jettisoning weight to escape British fighters. This occasioned the raid by British bombers the following day on Berlin, with leaflets as well as bombs, and on the following three nights but without doing great damage. However, it is claimed that these raids diverted the Luftwaffe's attention from British fighter airfields (Croydon, Biggin Hill, Kenley, North Weald, etc.) and to the bombing of London in retribution for the RAF's bombing of Berlin, and thus led to the postponement and later cancellation of the invasion of Britain which had been planned to start on September 21. For a whole week from September 7 the Luftwaffe raided London at night, causing about 2,000 casualties in the city. The Germans had planned a raid on the East End of London on the night of December 29, 1940, intending to drop large numbers of incendiary bombs to coincide with a low spring tide, when there would be maximum difficulty for fire brigades to obtain water from the Thames to quench the fires. The raid took place, but with less effectiveness than planned, because poor weather had grounded many bombers on German airfields.

Raids continued throughout the winter and one of the very worst on London was on April 16, 1941, when 440 tons of bombs were dropped. This can be compared with one of the biggest of Air Marshal Harris' Bomber Command raids on May 31, 1942, when about 1,000 planes targeted the city of Cologne, dropping about 2,000 tons of bombs. However, a moonlight raid on London by the Luftwaffe on May 11, 1941, left the House of Commons, together with many other buildings, a pile of rubble, and also left 1,400 people dead. The Commons thereafter sat in the Lords, and the Lords sat in Church House, Westminster. The present Commons chamber, designed by Gilbert Scott, was first used on October 26, 1950, but was deliberately made too small to seat even threequarters of the present 655 members, allegedly in order to preserve an intimate, if confrontational, atmosphere across the despatch box. In the television age it may merely emphasise 'yah-boo' politics.

Although London suffered hugely, the diversion from the airfields in September, 1940, was a relief for Fighter Command, which was desperately short of pilots and aircraft towards the end, with training on Hurricanes and Spitfires becoming far too short, so that losses of the newly-trained pilots were unacceptably high. Indeed, 3 hours was sometimes all that could be managed to show newly-trained pilots how to fly the Hurricanes and Spitfires, and they were given little instruction on how to fight with them. Although not initially welcomed, pilots of other nations joined Fighter Command, with over 1 in 10 being Polish or Czech by September, and there were also 56 Fleet Air Arm pilots, 23 of whom died in action. The 145 Polish pilots were noticeably better trained and battle-experienced, so that may explain why only 35 of them died in the battle. Among the RAF officer pilots there were sometimes alleged signs of a reluctance to share their hard-won battle techniques with junior pilots, when five 'kills' meant a pilot was regarded as an ace. At first many new pilot officers came from public schools, and they were sometimes not too happy if they were ordered to be led in formation into battle by a grammar-school type with the rank only of sergeant, however experienced he might have been. It took time for these matters to be sorted out. Attitudes like this were certainly not experienced among the Battle of Britain pilots who came to Scilly.

One of 'the few', who had fought in the Battle of Britain in his Hurricane, was Squadron Leader George Woodwark, who died in Scilly in 1975, aged 62. Another was Ian Widge Gleed who had won the Distinguished Flying Cross and the Distinguished Service Order, and shot down 4 ME109s and 6 other aircraft in the Battle of Britain, two of them at night.

Gleed was born in 1916 in Finchley, the son of Dr and Mrs Seymour Gleed. He was educated at Epsom College, commissioned in the RAF in 1936 and became one of that select band of highly-respected ace fighter-pilots in the war. He took part in attacks on the *Scharnhorst* and *Gneisenau* and wrote an account of his life in the air entitled *Arise to Conquer*, his air log book being now retained in the RAF Museum at Hendon. He came to Scilly in May, 1941, and was the first to land his Hurricane on the alarmingly short 450 yard runway, which 'encouraged' the others to follow him. A little surprisingly, sailing was still unrestricted in Scilly in 1941 despite the war, and Gleed was able to borrow a 4-ton local boat and enjoy some of his leisure time in this yacht; but he always ensured that during daylight hours, two of his pilots would be at cockpit readiness, seated in their Hurricanes, ready to take-off the moment a red flare from the Bishop Rock lighthouse or elsewhere signalled that an enemy aircraft was approaching the islands. A piece of the propeller from Gleed's Hurricane (his favourite called *Figaro*, with initial letters LK signifying 87 Squadron), which shot down the Dornier 18 in 1941, is preserved in St Mary's excellent museum.

As Squadron Leader, Gleed was appointed to command the Hurricanes sent to Scilly in 1941, and it is sad that, after his later promotion to Wing Commander and subsequent posting to the Mediterranean in 1943, he was shot down and killed over Tunisia at the age of 26. On September 29, 1998, an hour-long, BBC documentary in the Timewatch series, showed that Gleed had been a friend of Beverly Nicholls and had been homosexual – according to his friend and fellow pilot Chris Gotch – but few, if any, of those who served with him were aware of his orientation, and all had enormous respect for him. The revelation today is scarcely of any consequence or even of much interest; but at that period (the 1940s), had it been known, it would have been regarded as shocking.

Accompanying Gleed to Scilly on May 19, 1941, were Flight Lieutenant Rayner, Flying Officer Beaumont, Flying Officer Watson, Pilot Officer I.J. Badger and Sergeant Thorogood. Soon after they had landed on the new airport at High Lanes, a signal from Devon informed them that an enemy aircraft had been seen in the vicinity. Badger immediately took off in his Hurricane (P2798) and intercepted a German flying-boat (a Dornier 22 or an

Arado 196), which was approaching Scilly at about 50 feet above the waves. Badger descended upon it and shot it down. Then, on May 24, Gleed and Thorogood in their Hurricanes were coming in together to land after a patrol, when a Dornier 18 flying-boat suddenly appeared from a low cloud base and its front gunner cheekily opened fire on them from one of its 13mm blister guns; both Hurricanes opened their throttles, clearing the runway and evading the bullets, and then chased the Dornier and shot it down into the sea. On May 28, Gleed and Watson, while patrolling in their Hurricanes spotted a Junkers 88 and gave chase, but they had to abandon this when 60 miles out from Scilly because they were near the limit of their Hurricanes' range. However, they believed that hits had been scored because they had seen some smoke emanating from the enemy. As an important result of this incident, the Hurricanes were temporarily withdrawn on May 31 and long-range fuel tanks fitted, returning on June 16 to Scilly with their range restriction solved; but otherwise the pilots felt that in their first month they had well justified their posting and saved the Scillies from some enemy attacks.

The De Havilland Hawker Hurricane, although still made of wood and fabric, was Britain's first monoplane fighter aircraft; previous fighters, such as the Gloster Gladiator, had been bi-planes. Compared with the Messerschmitt 109E, known to Luftwaffe pilots as 'Emil', the Hurricane was not quite as fast or as manoeuvrable, but had other estimable qualities, including a high rate of climb. It was equipped with eight, fixed .303 Browning machine-guns in its wings, and could fire 2,400 rounds in 14 seconds, usually in 2-second bursts when an enemy aircraft was within its sights.

When France surrendered to Germany in 1940, Britain was virtually fighting the war alone, and it really is to 'the few' fighting in their Hurricanes and Spitfires that saved the war for Britain in 1940; for what is believed to have changed Hitler's plan to invade Britain in 1940 (Operation Sealion) was the Luftwaffe's inability to secure air superiority over England's south coast. Goering claimed he could gain it in 3 weeks, and then the German invasion barges, massed on the French coast, would be able to land German troops without attack from the RAF. It was the resistance of Fighter Command which apparently persuaded Hitler that Britain could be dealt with later and with fewer German casualties, and that Russia was the main enemy and must be tackled first. Britain could meanwhile be subjected to aerial bombing, which was thought likely to persuade the UK government to seek peace without the need for any costly invasion.

It was the conflict of aircraft over Southern England between about July 10 and October 10, which Churchill called the Battle of Britain, and which was fought by pilots of France, Australia, Canada, South Africa, Rhodesia and Jamaica as well as Britain, Poland, and Czechoslovakia, mainly in Hurricane fighter aircraft, with a smaller number of Spitfires. About 650 RAF fighter planes in 55 squadrons at the start were ranged against 1,480 fighters and 1,350 bombers of the Luftwaffe. In this battle of Britain, the pilots (the few) and their supporting ground crews, must take most of the glory for their tenacity and bravery; but the Rolls Royce Company deserves some credit also.

Charles Rolls and Henry Royce formed a partnership in 1904, beginning a Manchester workshop as pioneers in the motor-car industry, and a year before Austin started at Longbridge. Eton-educated Rolls was salesman, and ex-railway apprentice Royce was the engineer, with an able administrator, Claude Johnson, in charge of office work until his death in 1926. Their Company's achievements consisted not only of the world's top car – Lord Northcliffe declared 'best people buy only Rolls-Royces' – but engines for aeroplanes. The motor side of the business was sold to Volkswagen in the 1970s, but aero-engines, beginning with the Eagle in the 1st World War, to the Merlin in Hurricanes, Spitfires and Wellingtons in the 2nd World War, and through to jet engines since, have been and are the most profitable venture. Much of the company's later success was due to Ernest Hives, Rolls' chauffeur in 1903, who became General Manager from 1936, and to whom the Air Ministry gave praise with the words 'God knows where the RAF would have been without him'. He deserves recognition because the Merlin engine helped win the Battle of Britain; and, in Scilly, the success of the Hurricanes from 1941 depended upon it.

The Hurricane's main rival, the Messerschmitt 109, had a top speed of 317 m.p.h. (the Hurricane Mark I's was 308 m.p.h.), and was armed with cannon; but the Hurricane could out-turn the Messerschmitt and could take more punishment than either the ME109 or the Supermarine Spitfire. Moreover, to build a Hurricane took an estimated 10,000 man-hours, as compared with 15,000 man-hours for the Spitfire, so more Hurricanes could be built in a given time. In the Battle of Britain, Hurricanes are credited with shooting down 807 German aircraft and the Spitfires 485 – a reflection of the greater numbers of the Hurricanes in service in RAF Fighter Command in the summer of 1940. The most crucial day of the battle was September 15, when 32 Hurricane squadrons plus 18 Spitfire squadrons faced 315 German bombers and fighters. German losses on this day and subsequently were great enough for Hitler on September 17 to postpone plans for the invasion of Britain, eventually to abandon them altogether. Between July 10 and October 31, 1940, the Germans lost 1,733 aircraft while attacking Britain, compared with 915 British aircraft lost defending Britain. Hurricanes later served in the Arctic, the African deserts, Burma, the Mediterranean and were even catapulted off merchant ships; but of 14,300 Hurricanes built, only 3 survived in flying condition into the 21st century.

Air activity by the Germans continued over Scilly through the summer of 1940 independently of the Battle of Britain raging over Southern England. On July 18, a Heinkel III was shot down into the sea, its crew surviving in a

1) Pilots of the Hurricane fighter aircraft at St Mary's.

2) The sturdy Hurricane that won the Battle of Britain and later protected the Scillies.

3) The faster Messerschmitt 109 - its German equivalent; but speed is not everything.

4) The Messerschmitt 110 was a twin-engined fighter with a long range (unlike the 109) and was intended to provide escort for the bombers. It was well-armed, with two 20mm cannons, four 7.9mm machine-guns and one free-mounted 7.9 gun. Its maximum speed was 349 m.p.h. But it lacked the manoeuvrability of the Hurricane which performed surprisingly well against it.

5) The Heinkel III was the Luftwaffe's standard bomber. Its maximum speed was 258 m.p.h.

6) The Dornier 17 (called the Flying-Pencil in both Germany and Britain) first saw action in the Spanish Civil War. It had a maximum speed of 249 m.p.h., in some models but proved a little vulnerable to Hurricanes attacking from the rear or from below.

7) The Junkers 88. The JU88 was the Luftwaffe's most versatile aircraft, but those which flew over Scilly were mostly reconnaissance planes or medium bombers. The aircraft was well-armed with machine-guns, and had a top speed of about 292 m.p.h. By the middle of the war, German factories were producing up to 2,000 JU88s each year. They were designed to carry a crew of between 2 and 5, depending upon the version and task of the aircraft, and all the crew were seated close together in the forward

Messerschmitt Bf 109

compartment, a situation, which Goering believed, would promote high morale and a comradely spirit. Some German aircraft seen over Scilly were sometimes misidentified as Junkers 88s, but it was not until 1943 that the Luftwaffe made many offensive patrols with them, when their range capability had been increased to over 2,000 miles. An example of misidentification was the shooting down of the Dragon on June 3rd, 1941, which was ascribed at the time to a JU88, but the attack was actually carried out by a Heinkel III.

A not unusual picture of fighter pilots – somewhere in Britain – rushing to their aircraft when the word came through that they had to 'scramble'. But, in Scilly, Gleed went one better and, on days when the weather suggested enemy aircraft might be expected, had a couple of pilots sitting in their Hurricanes awaiting a signal that enemy aircraft were approaching, in order to make a fast take-off to intercept them.

dinghy to be picked up by a launch from St Mary's, two of the German survivors still proudly wearing their iron crosses, 1st class. It was not until Scilly possessed Hurricanes based on its own aerodrome on St Mary's from May, 1941, that enemy air sorties over Scilly could be properly opposed, but it took the Luftwaffe sometime before they learnt to avoid Scilly's air space. On August 1st, 1941, enemy aircraft dropped bombs in the sea off Wingletang at night, the purpose being obscure. Locals thought a shoal of mackerel moving in the moonlight must have attracted them, but there were no reports of large numbers of dead fish washed up on the Islands. That month a Junkers 88 was shot down by Flying Officer Forsyth in his Hurricane, and another one, on August 16, by Pilot Officer Musgrove. October saw a Heinkel III set on fire, and one of the new and fast Messerschmitt 110 fighters was also shot down. In January, 1942, the flight commander, Ian Gleed, was promoted to Wing Commander and became, for a time, commanding officer at Middle Wallop. He was replaced in Scilly by Squadron Leader Smallworth from 87 Squadron at Exeter, who in turn was later succeeded by Flight Lieutenant Jewell. In January, 1942, came the first RAF casualty, when Flight Lieutenant Roscoe was killed in an accident during a mainland training flight shortly after his marriage to a WAAF cypher officer. He had been demonstrating to soldiers holding exercises on St

Mary's, showing them what it was like facing a low-flying aircraft, when his plane collided with some overhead wires. Hurricanes which were successful in 'downing' an enemy aircraft often returned and gave 'a victory roll' before landing – which never was the cause of a mishap, but gave pleasure to those on St Mary's who saw it.

Another accident occurred in the middle years of the war, when the danger of attack from German forces in France was at its height. It was the routine that a Hurricane from St Mary's or from a base on the mainland was always detailed to provide some air cover for the *Scillonian* when she sailed to or from Scilly; on August 12th, 1943, in order to liven up proceedings, one of these Hurricanes made a mock attack on the Scillonian as she was en route from Scilly to Penzance. The pilot was a Canadian, Flight-Sergeant T.B. Hunter, known as 'Johny' and described as a 'likeable, dare-devil sort', who tried to fly between the masts of the *Scillonian* – it is alleged for a bet or a boast, although another story has it that he was showing off to a young lady travelling on the *Scillonian* – after he had practised the feat between some masts on the aerodrome; however, these latter masts were steady, whereas those on the *Scillonian* heaved up and down as the ship negotiated the Atlantic swell, with the tragic result that the port wing of his 'plane just clipped the top of the *Scillonian*'s foremast, causing the aircraft to crash into the sea killing the pilot. Neither the plane nor the pilot's body were ever recovered.

On March 14, 1942, the force on St Mary's was re-organised and called 1449 Flight; it's call sign was 'Garbo', and it still had six Hurricanes, with up to 43 air and ground personnel altogether (ten of them pilots). One of the pilots, who had flown Hurricanes in Scilly from 1941, was John Strachey (1901-63), who had been educated at Eton and Oxford. He was the son of the editor and part-owner of *The Spectator* magazine and, before the 2nd World War, was MP for Birmingham. He joined the RAF in 1940, became Adjutant to 87 Squadron and later rose to the rank of Wing Commander. In 1945, he entered Parliament as MP for Dundee, joining Clement Attlee's Government in the Ministry of Food, 1946-50, and then as Secretary of State for Air, 1950-51. His colleague, Roy Jenkins, upon reviewing Strachey's biography by Professor Hugh Thomas, called him 'one of the most privately attractive figures in the House of Commons'.

The tasks of Flight 1449 remained unaltered. They were to provide convoy patrols, to escort damaged Allied aircraft to their bases, as well as to deter German aircraft from approaching the Scillies; but facilities and equipment at their base at the aerodrome at High Cross also remained rather basic, consisting in the main of two Nissen huts on the aerodrome's south-east corner, a tent, a telephone, a fire-tender and a windsock. This was soon increased by a Blister hangar, a wooden watch tower, another Nissen hut and an H.Q. block. A GCI radar station was established, which now gave some timely warning of enemy aircraft approaching. This station on Newford Island of Porth Looe, St Mary's, was set up as a RAF radar unit called a Ground Controlled Interception Station. It had an all-round sweep and could pick up anything up to 45 miles away, even 90 on occasion. It was useful in guiding fighter aircraft to intercept enemy aircraft and for locating ditched aircraft so that their crews could be picked up by MLs. There was a direct line to the RAF and Navy MLs and to RAF Portreath which, later in the war, had Mosquitos and Beaufighters.

In the event of the station being bombed, a mobile unit was placed on the golf course; there were also homing beacons at Deep Point and at Woolpack which gave out a Morse signal to help returning aircraft, supplemented by a searchlight to give further helpful direction after dark.

Pilots in Scilly continued to use Grant's Castle to practise their shooting skills, targets having been specially erected for them among the ancient rings of what are now earthen walls, but nothing of these targets now remains.

The actions of the Hurricanes against enemy aircraft between May 19, 1941, and July 16, 1942, are summarised below:

		(Pilot)	(Enemy Aircraft)		(Hurricane)	
1941	19th May	P/O I.J. Badger	Heinkel, Dornier or Arado	Destroyed	P2798	LK:A
	24th May	S/Ldr I.R. Gleed D.F.C.	Dornier 18	Destroyed	W9196	LK:B
		Sgt. L.A. Thorogood				LK:S
	28th May	S/Ldr I.R. Gleed D.F.C.	Junkers 88	Probable	P2798	LK:A
		F/O R.L. Watson				
	18th July	Sgt. A. Thom	Heinkel III	Destroyed	V7136	
		F/O G.L. Roscoe			W9139	LK:N
	16th Aug.	F/O C.M.A. Forsythe	Junkers 88	Destroyed		
	26th Aug.	F/O G.L.Roscoe	Junkers 88	Destroyed	W9139	LK:N
	20th Oct.	Sgt. A. Thom	Heinkel III	Probable	W9139	LK:N
	Oct.	Sgt. A. Thom	Messerschmitt 110	Destroyed	W9196	LK:B
		F/O E.G. Musgrove			W9139	LK:N
1942	8th July	P/O B.S. Thompson	Junkers 88	Damaged		
		Sgt. D. Rogers				
	16th July	P/O B.S. Thompson	Junkers 88	Damaged		
		Sgt. D. Rogers				

The table above was compiled with the help of the excellent wartime diary kept by Mr Osborne, headmaster of the school on St Mary's, and which is a model of its kind, and its help is most gratefully acknowledged.

* * * * *

Hurricane fighters, although single-seaters, were relatively large aircraft for the time, as big as the twin-engined de Havilland Dragon bi-plane – whose military version was known as the Dominie – and much heavier. They were preferable to Spitfires for service in Scilly because of their wider

304

undercarriages, which made them better able to cope with the rough surface of St Mary's airfield. They had a wooden fuselage, covered with starched Irish linen fabric, which could take a great deal of punishment without preventing the aircraft from flying. Bullet holes were easily and quickly patched by ground crews between operations. The Spitfire was all metal, which had some advantages, but the Hurricane was a steadier platform when firing its guns. Its wings were unusually thick, thus providing room to house the undercarriage, which retracted inwards and had big, low-pressure tyres, ideal for use on uneven, grass runways – a considerable contrast with, for instance, Germany's Messerschmitt 109 fighter, which had a narrow track and was subject to relatively more frequent collapses of its undercarriage upon landing. Another difference was that the Hurricane had a hump- backed fuselage, which gave a better view when taxiing and landing, whereas the ME109 had a cramped cockpit with a relatively poor field of vision. Hurricanes were also remarkably robust and could continue flying not only after receiving battle damage, but could also withstand pilot mishandling; it was not all that unusual for a Hurricane to be seen on the airfield at St Mary's with its nose in a hedge and its tail in the air after a badly-judged landing – usually having suffered only quickly-repairable damage. The airfield on St Mary's was not the easiest to land upon, particularly in rough weather; it was short and bumpy, and suffered also from a dome effect – a hillock in its middle with a 1 in 20 incline at its steepest part – the opposite problem from the well-known one at the 330 acre Battle of Britain airfield at the former Croydon Aerodrome, where aircraft taking off disappeared for a few moments into a shallow dip half way along the runway. There is a story connected with the frequency of the landing mishaps of the Hurricanes on St Mary's airfield: apparently the RAF's commanding officer at Portreath became so concerned by the frequency of these accidents that he decided to fly to Scilly himself to instruct the pilots there on safe landing techniques. Unfortunately, on making his run-in at St Mary's, he finished up in a daffodil field, unhurt but a little wiser. He was immediately ferried back to Portreath in a Walrus piloted by Flight Lieutenant R. Dimbleby – and seems to have abandoned any further thought of giving his talk.

From 1942, long-range Focke-Wulf Condor 200 aircraft made sorties in the area of the Scillies and, when spotted on radar, Hurricanes took off on patrol to deter them from coming near the islands. Hurricanes also escorted back to base crippled bombers of the RAF and USA which had been sent to destroy German installations in occupied France, and sometimes gave cover to Air / Sea Rescue Walruses of 276 Squadron based at Portreath, amphibian aircraft which could reach ditched air crews quickly, but were vulnerable if attacked by German aircraft unless chaperoned home by Hurricanes.

On June 13, Flight Sergeant Reid, flying the Canadian-built Hurricane AG239, developed an oil leak while escorting a convoy and had to bale out.

The aircraft was lost, but the convoy escort ship, HMS *Pearl*, picked up the pilot. Three weeks later, on July 8, Pilot Officer Thompson and Flight Sergeant Rogers, in their Hurricanes, gave chase to a JU88 for 80 miles and, although they believed they had damaged it, they had to return to base because they were low on fuel; the situation was repeated on July 16 in an exactly similar chase. More positive results occurred when Flying Officer Roscoe in Hurricane N9139, and Flight Sergeant Thom in Hurricane E7136, chased a Heinkel III south-west of Scilly and shot it down into the sea; while, on August 5, Beaufighters from the mainland shot down a German floatplane – an AR196 – near the Bishop Rock lighthouse. Meanwhile, for the aircraft on St Mary's there were always the near-daily patrols to be made over the steamship *Scillonian* to ensure that she was not attacked en route – although, once alongside the quay at St Mary's, the *Scillonian* was protected from attack by flying a balloon up to 200 feet above her foremast – and to escort the Avro Anson V, which arrived almost daily with RAF stores, equipment and relief personnel. On August 16, Flying Officer Forsyth in Hurricane V7011 chased a JU88 south of Scilly, attacked it and saw its port wing break off and the aircraft cartwheel into the sea. On August 26, when two JU88s dropped eight bombs killing the two young women on St Mary's, Sylvia Jenkins, the 29-year-old, and Dorothy Agnes Paice, the 22-year-old nurse, at Bona Vista on The Strand, Pilot Officer Musgrave in Hurricane N9130 was able to give chase and he shot down one of the raiders. On October 20, Flight Sergeant Thom was in Hurricane N9139 and met and attacked a Heinkel III, when he had to turn away and so lost it; he did subsequently report that some smoke had been seen, but he could only claim it as a 'possible' downing. The following day, Thom in B9196, and Pilot Officer Musgrave in N9139, spotted a fast Messerschmitt 110 fighter bomber and brought it down into the sea. On November 1, Pilot Officer Rogers was forced to ditch his Hurricane in Smith Sound because of engine trouble, but was quickly rescued by Mr Hicks of the Turks Head, St Agnes, who, fortunately, was nearby in his motor boat.

Another task which fell to the St Mary's Hurricanes was escorting damaged Allied heavy bombers such as Flying Fortresses and Stirlings when they were returning from bombing raids on targets on the French coast, and had been hit by anti-aircraft fire. In fact it has been estimated that the Hurricanes of St Mary's played some part in nearly 300 such rescues or escorts during the war.

October, 1942, had seen the erection of the 3 Nissen huts on the airfield at St Mary's, and the expectation of receiving some Hurricanes Mark 2B, which were equipped with cannons, some of them having been built in Canada and shipped to the UK in sections. February 23, 1944, saw a 4-engined, big Liberator BZ777 of RAF 547 Squadron of Coastal Command forced by fuel shortage to crash land on the airfield and overshoot. The crew of 7, and the one passenger, survived because the runway had previously been lengthened;

but Flying Officer T.G. Dixon at the controls was killed by one of the plane's 4 propellers breaking off and flying into the cockpit. The Liberator was shipped from the islands to the mainland in separate sections, and its crash certainly justified the runway being extended.

The success that Flight 1499 had in protecting the Scillies is evidenced from maps taken from a shot-down German aircraft in March, 1942. These showed that the Luftwaffe had by then imposed on its aircraft a 90-mile daylight exclusion zone around the Scilly Islands – sure testimony indeed, of the effectiveness of the Hurricanes in guarding Scilly. By 1943, 1449 Flight had received Hurricanes Mark IIB with cannons (Z3426, Z3682, AM275, BW993 and JS264) and also an Avro Tutor K611 for communications; moreover, there was an air of expectancy that a Second Front was soon to be opened up against the Germans in Western Europe to relieve the strain on the Russians fighting the Germans alone in Europe in the East; so that, even before D-Day, German air activity around the Scillies had much diminished. One piece of evidence of the air activity over Scilly and mainland Cornwall in the years 1940-44, was discovered by a holidaying couple strolling on the beach at Perranporth in 1988; they spotted an aircraft tyre poking out of the sand at low tide. They summoned help and, after digging, they found a wartime Spitfire of a Czech pilot which crashed on April 12, 1942, after it had been in accidental collision with another Spitfire, both pilots being killed as their aircraft plummeted into the sea. The Spitfire the visitor couple found had been buried in the sand, and then, after 46 years, it had been washed ashore; its remains were collected and they now lie preserved in Perranporth Museum.

One Liberty ship, the *Mando*, ended her days in Scilly on the Golden Ball Bar north of Tresco in dense fog – but this event was on January 21, 1955. Another Liberty ship, the American *Jonas Lee*, was seen to be sinking off Scilly on January 12, 1945, after being torpedoed in a U-boat attack on a convoy in which she was sailing from Swansea. St Mary's lifeboat rescued survivors and brought them into St Mary's where the islanders looked after them. 43 years later, in June, 1988, one of them, Frank Pulaski of Chicago, wrote to Scilly to try to contact the police constable at that time who took him into his house when Pulaski was suffering from a head injury and had problems eating. Apparently, Pulaski needed confirmation of his condition for an insurance claim he was making. Another action came on March 11th, 1945, when a submarine, U-681, was sighted on the surface off Bryher, and was bombed and sunk by a Liberator off Mincarlo, 42 of her crew of about 50 also being landed in Scilly. During these years it was not uncommon for wreckage from sunken ships to come ashore, and the launches would sometimes go out to collect the bodies of drowned seamen when these were spotted drifting in the sea around the islands.

* * * * *

Some idea of the later air activity around the Scillies from 1943-45 is revealed in the following, based upon a compilation undertaken by Dr Martin Parsons of Reading University, and which he has kindly permitted to be included here:

January 27, 1943:	A Whitley bomber with engine trouble overshot the runway on St Mary's airfield while attempting a landing, and ended up in Longstone Quarry. There were no casualties.
January 27, 1943:	An Australian pilot, when flying low, allowed his aircraft's wing-tip to hit a wave; his 'plane crashed and he was injured, but he recovered fully.
June 4, 1943:	21-year-old Flight Sergeant D.A.F.K. Hyde's Hurricane developed engine trouble some 40 miles south of Scilly, and he ditched it in the sea. He was rescued from the water, but died later.
June 23, 1943:	Flight Sergeant Capel was killed when his two-seater Defiant, engaged in target-towing, crashed on Eastern Villa at Pelistry. The aircraft's air gunner was rescued by Sergeant Green of the St Mary's Home Guard, who was subsequently awarded the British Empire Medal.
October 3, 1943:	A Wellington bomber crashed in the sea off Scilly, but there were no survivors from the 6-man crew.
October 8, 1943:	A twin-engined Messerschmitt 110 was shot down into the sea 53 miles from the Bishop Rock by a Spitfire which had been searching for some missing RAF aircrew. The two German aircrew were rescued and became prisoners-of-war.
February 24, 1944:	A Dakota crash-landed on the airfield but with no casualties. The American crew happened to have ham and cider on board their plane, also a jeep; these they used to make a sightseeing tour of St Mary's and have a picnic.
April 17, 1944:	A search was made for a Wellington bomber which had gone down in the sea near Scilly. The crew were found but all had drowned – they had no dinghies.
April 26, 1944:	A United States Air Force Lightning made a belly-landing on the airfield. The pilot had lost his way and surrendered to those who came to help him, as he thought at first that he was in enemy hands.
May 10, 1944:	Two lots of survivors from a sunken ship were found and rescued from the sea.
June 19, 1944:	Flying Officer Turner 'pranged' his Hurricane on landing on St Mary's airfield.
July 6, 1944:	Another Hurricane on landing damaged its port undercarriage.
August 6, 1944:	A Hurricane stalled upon landing and was badly damaged.
August 7, 1944:	Another Hurricane damaged a wheel-fairing and a wing-tip on landing. These accidents were partly owing to the shortness of the runway, which obliged those pilots who

	were a little late in making contact with the ground to turn their aircraft at a right angle at the end of the runway, a manoeuvre which sometimes resulted in damage to their 'plane's undercarriage.
August 15, 1944:	A Sunderland landed safely on the seas at St Mary's, but with damaged engines; its top-turret had been shot away and its rear gunner was dead.
Later in August, 1944:	Another Sunderland became short of fuel and landed south of St Agnes in poor visibility; it damaged its float and sank while it was being towed in to St Mary's. Another Sunderland, upon landing, overshot the flare path and ran on to the Mare Ledges; the crew were rescued safely, but had difficulty making the aircraft's depth-charges safe. A Wellington, piloted by Flying Officer Bayley, crashed off St Martin's, the crew being rescued by an air-sea rescue launch from St Mary's. A rumour circulated in Scilly that the aircraft was carrying bullion; if so, it must have been quickly removed by the authorities for none was ever found by the Scillonians.
September 13, 1944:	A Hurricane came in to land on the airfield at too high a speed and 'pranged'.
September 17, 1944:	Unit disbanded in Scilly.
March, 1945:	A damaged Dakota crash-landed on the aerodrome, but without casualties.

* * * * *

The Normandy landings began on June 6, 1944, and, with the opening of this second front, war effort of all sorts shifted from Scilly elsewhere, as the Luftwaffe had problems nearer home and no incentive to fly sorties over Scilly. So, on September 17, 1944, the RAF unit in Scilly was disbanded and relocated at Portreath, where the pilots were retrained to fly the new Typhoons and Tempests. By this stage of the war, aircraft were improving considerably: a design by Frank Whittle for a turbo-jet engine was beginning to revolutionise flying, and, in 1944, a Vampire in level flight exceeded 500 m.p.h. for the first time. This made Hurricanes and Spitfires seem slow, but the only RAF jet aircraft which actually served during the Second World War were the Gloster Meteors of 616 Squadron. They proved valuable in catching and shooting down the 400 m.p.h. German V-1 pilotless jet-engined bombs (doodle bugs), of which, by the end of the war, fighters claimed to have shot down 1,842 and anti-aircraft guns 1,866. Between June 13 and September 1st, 1944, the Germans launched 2,419 V-1s which flew towards the Greater London area at nearly 400 m.p.h., killing 5,126 British civilians, a greater number of fatal casualties than in the entire London Blitz of 1940 / 41, the last raid of the London Blitz being on May 10, 1941.

Balloon cables, stretching in lines south of London and near the coast, 'downed' some more, saving London but often hitting places to its south such as Croydon, the borough that suffered most with 142 V-1s falling on it, killing 211 people. Their successors, the V-2s, of which 517 were sent between September 8, 1944, and March 27, 1945, with Ilford receiving 35, were unstoppable until advancing Allied armies in France and the Low Countries overran their launch sites; but only 3 fell in Croydon – they were so fast that the noise of their coming was heard actually after the sound of their explosions. Sites on the Cherbourg peninsula for V-2 weapons to be able to target Scilly and the West Country were overrun by Allied forces before they were scheduled to start operations on June 12. Altogether, from all sorts of enemy action, 28,890 people in London lost their lives during the Second World War.

Considering the war activities in the Scillies as a whole, the RAF losses are known exactly. Altogether eight Hurricanes were lost in Scilly between 1941 and 1944, and there are eight graves of RAF personnel with identical, white headstones in Old Town churchyard, four of which are of pilots. It is said that if islanders – who became used to the faces of the RAF Hurricane pilots in Hugh Town – should ever ask the whereabouts of one of the lost airmen whom they had not seen recently, the euphemistic reply given was that 'he had gone fishing', originating perhaps because the code name of the detachment in the Scilly was 'Fishing'. One of the Hurricane pilots who survived, David Rogers, who married a Scillonian girl, Nancy Stedeford of Lunnon Farm, was commissioned in 1942 while with 1449 Flight, and settled in Scilly after the war to become a flower farmer. From the launches, the late Ken Morley, a gunner on RML542, settled in Scilly to run an outfitter's shop in Hugh Town; Matt Lethbridge, a Scillonian on one of the RAF launches, became coxswain of St Mary's lifeboat in the later years following his father of the same name and his grandfather; and Roy Wright, from the RAF base, also settled in Scilly after the war. In his youth he had been a schoolboy international footballer; in the war he was an RAF engine and air frame fitter and came to Scilly in May, 1941, with 87 Squadron, rising to the rank of warrant officer. He married a Scillonian girl in 1942 and, after a spell at RAF Portreath, returned to Scilly in September, 1944, just before 1449 Flight in Scilly was disbanded. After his billeting at Ennor House, he lived in one of the Nissen huts – eventually increased to 4 – built on the corner of the airfield. After the war he settled in Scilly and worked for 36 years in the Island Supply Stores.

A surprising number of Scillonians, or of people who later came to live in Scilly, served in North Africa in the 2nd World War. The earlier stages of the conflict there saw up to 200,000 Italians surrender, until the German Afrika Corps landed in Tripoli and were, for a time, worryingly successful. But then Churchill sent out much war equipment, so that, after a war in which British forces had everywhere done the retreating, the tide turned. On October 23, 1942, at the start of what came to be called the Battle of El Alamein, Montgomery and the 8th Army, with 1,229 tanks to Rommel's 496, began advancing – eventually to victory. Curiously, *Lilli Marlene* became the hit song with both the 8th Army and the Afrika Corps.

Among those who took part in the North African war was John R. Smith in the 1st army, and possibly William Fleet, who started the Strand Guest House and died there in 1979; he had been for a short time General Montgomery's batman, although this could have been in 1944. Bob Davison, who farmed Garrison Farm and ran the campsite on the Garrison until his death in 1969, aged 69, had been an RASC captain in the army in North Africa, and Raymond MacLaren, who retired in 1980 after being the Duchy of Cornwall land steward in Scilly for 24 years, had served in the Indian Army from 1937-48, and had served as a major in the 8th army in North Africa. William Rowett, who was Chaplain of the Isles of Scilly, 1966-70, served in Africa as a brigadier on General Montgomery's staff. Danny Sexton also served in the Desert War.

Another veteran of the Desert War was Walter Groves ('Fuzz' to many on Scilly on account of his beard), who had, at various times, a multiplicity of occupations in the Islands, including Secretary to the Boatmen's Association, local auctioneer, debt collector, agent in Scilly for a building firm, one-time golf club steward and press correspondent. In this last role, a national newspaper editor telephoned him during the Cold War period and asked him what was happening on board a Russian cruiser, which was on a goodwill visit to the Islands and was anchored off Old Town bay. Fuzz looked out of the window of his bungalow (Nowhere) and replied: 'They are training their guns straight at us'. Unfamiliar with Scillonian humour in replies to somewhat absurd questions, the London editor 'held the front page' in his excitement. Sadly, Fuzz died in 1976 aged 62 – he was a heavy unrepentant smoker, a habit acquired during army service.

Nowhere was requisitioned during the war from 31 October, 1941 to 5 April, 1944. In the past its site had been the Dumpling Inn, where Israel Pender lived. His son, also called Israel Pender, had a donkey and cart and cleaned the streets of Hugh Town; his grandson, Jack Pender, fought in the Desert Campaign in the 8th Army, but was taken prisoner by the Italians; when freed on the Italian surrender, he tried to get home via Switzerland, but was caught by the Germans and imprisoned in Stalag Luft 7 in Poland, where the advancing Russians eventually released him.

When Jack returned to Scilly he was very thin, having lived mainly on black bread and cabbage in the prisoner-of-war camp. He brought a couple of London taxi cabs to Scilly, but in later life lived quietly on the Garrison, remembered mainly for entertaining by playing the melodeon until his death at the age of 73 in 1988. He had spent nearly 4 years all told as a prisoner-of-war, and Bernard Smith nearly as long. Jack Pender, when describing his capture, used to say 'they came at us with Tiger tanks and we replied with rifles'; it raises the question of why the Italians captured him when only the Germans were believed to have had Tigers?

R.D. Patmore was one of the ground-crew of 1449 Flight and billeted with Mr and Mrs Jenkins of Old Town, at what was later named Bay Tree Cottage, and at Middle Carn at Tolman, which later became the retirement home of Kenneth Sisam, former Secretary of the Oxford University Press and, in his time, the best authority on the history of Scilly. Patmore's mess hall was at Airport Lane Corner.

Another who served in the Desert War was Lord William Arthur Bampfylde, 6th Earl of Onslow, who was there between October, 1941, and June, 1943, and wrote a book about his life in the Territorial Armoured Regiment entitled *Men and Sand*. In his book he wrote: 'If one has to take part in a war, desert is by far the best place in which to wage it; there the opposing armies are the only population, and there are no women or children or property or buildings of beauty to destroy, no ghastly havoc to make'. Writing today, he might well have been tempted to add 'no wildlife to decimate, no crops to ravage, no countryside to despoil'. Onslow also landed in Normandy in 1944 on D-Day plus one, but became a prisoner-of-war.

The Onslow's had leased St Agnes lighthouse since 1920, to enable them to be able to take 4 or 5 month summer holidays there; the 6th Earl also leased the parsonage next door in 1964. In the summer terms, the Onslow children were taught to read and write in St Agnes School. During the war, the army manned the tower of the lighthouse and had wireless apparatus there, but it was felt that St Agnes school-house was rather near the lighthouse should German aircraft machine-gun it; so, for the early years of the war, the school was held in Rose Cottage.

Many Scillonians served on ships or in planes. From St Martin's, Foster Raine was lost at sea, and Jacky Russell went down in a minesweeper. William Ellis, who was born on St Mary's and died there 95 years later, was one of many who were torpedoed on merchant ships in the Atlantic. He was one of the lucky ones who survived, but had to endure 10 days in an open boat before he was picked up. Cyril Hicks flew Spitfires and Bernard Smith of St Agnes was an RAF air gunner, but was shot down in 1943. Donald G.M. Hicks, of the same island, was a mechanic in Sunderlands and was in one of the Sunderlands that searched for the *Bismarck* after the loss of the *Hood*; while Dr John Wells, who was the Isles of Scilly doctor in 1936 – only one in Scilly in pre-war days – and was largely responsible for designing the present hospital, became, during the 2nd World War, a medical officer in the navy, but, after the war, left medicine to work as a distinguished artist in Newlyn, and died in 2000. Not many realised that he had limited sight in one eye, or that he was the son of the bacteriologist who had worked with

312

The photograph is of rows of similar gravestones of service personnel who died in or around Scilly in the Second World War and are buried near each other in Old Town Churchyard. 23 servicemen lost their lives on or around Scilly during the 2nd World War, but those buried in Old Town Churchyard are Bush, Capel, Hales, Hyde, Jones, Killey, Menary, Norcliffe, Page, Peacock, Prowse, and Sergeant T.S. Rowan, an RAF aircrew observer whose body was recovered from the sea and buried October 13, 1941, RAF Sergeant S.I. Sanders, whose body was recovered from the sea and buried on May 27, 1940, Pilot Officer Ian Campbell Miles Sanderson, whose body was also recovered from the sea and buried on July 18, 1941, and two unknown sailors 16 in all. Altogether it is estimated that 262 Scillonians – or those who were living on Scilly just prior to the outbreak of war – served in the armed forces during the war (according to figures compiled by W. Hopwood, Clerk to the Council of the Isles of Scilly at the time), of whom 26 died, according to the War Memorial in Old Town Churchyard.

Alexander Fleming to discover penicillin. A later prominent member of the Scillonian community was Derek Pickup who was a flying instructor during the war, commanding officer of an Initial Flying Training School with a rank equivalent to Wing Commander, but then became Lloyd's Bank Manager in Scilly, 1954-70. Jimmy Soar, who died in Scilly aged 73, became a noted surveyor, and in the war had helped to build the Pluto pipeline (Pipeline Under the Ocean) and the Mulberry Harbours for the Second Front of 1944. One large section of the Mulberry Harbour, on tow up the English Channel in May, 1944, broke its tow and eventually came ashore intact at Perconger. A tug took it away and it was used off Normandy after D-Day, June 6, 1944, – there are still pieces of the Mulberry Harbour to be seen off Arromanches. Pluto was completed on August 12, 1944, and ran from the Isle of Wight to Cherbourg, supplying fuel for the army in France. Flying Officer Huckin and Flight Sergeant Graham, flying in a Mosquito, were shot down over the Bay of Biscay on January 12, 1944; they managed to get aboard their airborne

313

lifeboat and were rescued by an RML coming all the way from St Mary's. John Williams, who had worked as a clerk in the Council Offices on St Mary's, became a Sunderland flying-boat observer with 201 Squadron, and Dr John Kelly, who had been the medical officer to His Majesty's Forces in Scilly during the 2nd World War, loved Scilly so much that he became the Islands' family doctor after it. There were, of course, many others, and also many who, like Sergeant Vic Trenwith, served in the Home Guard in the Islands. Roland Phillips, who was Chief Executive Officer of the Council of the Isles of Scilly from 1954 to 1976, had been a navigator in the RAF, flying in Mosquitos, a night fighter used to escort RAF bombers over Germany, and Lt. Cdr. A.J. Stanton was on the destroyer *Kelly*, serving under Lord Mountbatten, while Francis Watts took part in the D-Day Landings of June 6, 1944.

William Duncan came from Aberdeen and served in armed trawlers based in Scilly in the 1st World War, receiving a medal for the rescue of crews from Dutch ships on February 22, 1917. He was called up in 1939, together with many other Scillonians including Kitchener Sherris, Fred Sherris, Jack Toomey, Bert Ball, Leonard Jenkins and Bert Williams. He served in the destroyer *Witch*, which was employed on escort tasks, and on sinking a big cargo-ship to make a breakwater at a right-angle to an invasion beach-head on D-Day on June 6, 1944. He was invalided out of the RNR that September owing to eyesight deterioration, and, as his family had been among those who had evacuated from Scilly to Penzance in 1940 when German aircraft were attacking Scilly, he joined them. Later, he bought Mincarlo, when it came up for sale upon derequisitioning by the RAF, and re-opened it as a guest house.

* * * * *

Important as they were, the activities of the air-sea rescue launches and the Hurricanes were only part of the war around the Scillies. Between 1939 and 1945, a total of 2,775 Allied merchant ships were sunk by enemy submarines world-wide and 781 German U-boats were destroyed, a substantial proportion of these U-boat sinkings taking place in the Western Approaches. One unusual event was the sinking of a U-boat near the Wolf Rock; it happened on December 18, 1944; U-1209 is thought to have been endeavouring under cover of darkness to place itself in a good position to attack a convoy from the landward side, but sailed just too close to the Wolf Rock lighthouse. Accidently the submarine grounded itself on an ebb tide right below the lighthouse, to the consternation of one of the lighthouse keepers who, despite the Wolf being the first pillar lighthouse to have built-in lavatories, went out on the balcony at dawn for 'relief', and found himself gazing down at a conning tower. The commanding officer of RML542, Lieutenant Perrin, recalls that he was at Newlyn at the time, when a message came through from Trinity House at Penzance reporting a U-boat stuck on the Wolf. Admiral Pilcher, at the Royal Navy Office in Newlyn, agreed that RML542 should be sent to investigate; but, when Perrin arrived, he found the submarine had floated off the rocks on the flood tide near dawn and had been depth-charged by the Canadian destroyer *Montreal*, while attempting to crash-dive. The U-boat's hatch had been left open and 44 out of 51 crew made their escape through it.

Of the German crew rescued, some were taken to Newlyn for interrogation, but this did not include the unfortunate U-boat commander, Ewald Hiilsenbeck, who suffered a heart attack and died soon afterwards. Four of the U-boat survivors were picked up by RML542 and the other forty by the Canadian destroyer. Among them was Georg Polil, who was in a POW camp for 2½ years, and also the U-boat wireless-operator, Paul Gerhart Jeszkoviak, who, after a time as a farm worker after the war, came to live in London as Paul Gerhart and became a London bus-driver. They were lucky, for the horrific fact is that, unlike U-1209, most of the crews of destroyed U-boats died trapped within them.

What happened to U-boats in the later years of the war, 1944 and 1945, can be illustrated by the fortunes of the following 8 U-boats, all the events taking place within striking distance of the Scillies:

(1) U-1199, under its commander Rolf Nollmann, was one of the more advanced German U-boats; it was equipped with the Snort System, which enabled it on its first patrol in September, 1944, to remain submerged for 50 days. It sank one ship and damaged another, but on January 21, 1945, was discovered 16 miles off Land's End by the Royal Navy's destroyer *Icarus* and the corvette *Mignonette* and was sunk with all its crew not far from the Wolf Rock.

(2) U-480, under its commander Hans Joachim Förster, sank 4 ships and damaged another; on June 13, 1944, it shot down an aircraft which tried to attack it. But, on February 24, 1945, it was detected by the frigates *Duckworth* and *Rowle* as they were escorting convoy BTC.78. As it approached the Scillies, the U-boat was depth-charged and sunk with all 48 crew, only 11 miles south-west of Land's End, about midway between St Mary's and the Wolf.

(3) U-1018, under its commander Walter Burmeister, sank the 1,317 ton Norwegian ship *Corvus* on February 27, 1945, but was immediately depth-charged by the Royal Navy frigate *Loch Fada* escorting convoy BTC.81 of which the *Corvus* had been a member. U-1018 sank south of the Lizard with all 51 crew.

(4) On February 27, 1945, U-327, under its commander Hans Lemcke, was spotted by a Liberator of the United States Navy, which was escorting convoy ONA.287. The aircraft directed the Royal Navy frigates *Loch Fada* and

Labaun to the scene, and they depth-charged the submarine which sank with all 46 crew south of the Wolf.

(5) On March 3, 1945, U-683, under its commander Günther Kebler, was on patrol somewhere in the area of sea between Land's End and the Scillies, when it went missing with all 49 crew. This may have been as a result of an accident rather than Allied action.

(6) On March 11, 1945, on its first cruise-mission, U-681, under its commander Helmet Bach, struck the Crim Rocks in the Scillies and was holed. It immediately surfaced and tried to head in the direction of Ireland, but was spotted helpless on the surface by a Liberator of 103 Squadron piloted by Lieutenant Field, and immediately surrendered to prevent being bombed. Of the crew, 11 were lost, but about 40 were taken prisoner by the Royal Navy's *Loch Fada* and MLs from St Mary's, which had hurried to the scene.

(7) U-399, under its commander Heinz Buhse, and equipped with Snort, sank the 7,184 ton United States ship *John R. Park* on March 21, 1945, and the 362 ton Netherlands motor vessel *Pacific* 5 days later; but, on that same day, when attacking another ship, it was detected and depth-charged by the Royal Navy frigate *Duckworth*, and sank with all 46 crew some 6 miles WSW of the Lizard.

(8) U-247, under its commander Gerhard Matschulat, sank the 207 ton British vessel *Noreen Mary* on July 5, 1944; but, on September 1st, 1944, it was located 10 miles SSW of Land's End by the Royal Canadian Navy frigates *St John* and *Swansea*, as it headed out for a raiding patrol from its base at Brest to the Bristol Channel. It was sunk with the loss of all 52 crew. Rather unusually, U-247 was claimed as depth-charged a second time on March 12, 1945, by Royal Navy escort ships which confused U-247 with U-683.

(9) U-246, under its commander Ernst Raabe, damaged the 1,370 ton British ship *Teme* on March 29, 1945, but was depth-charged and believed sunk between Land's End and the Lizard. Actually, U-246 was only damaged but, after repair, was bombed on April 30, 1945, by Sunderland ML783/H captained by Flight Lieutenant Foster of 201 Squadron RAF, and was sunk with all 48 crew.

These nine examples illustrate how by 1944 / 45 the war against the U-boats had virtually been won because, although they still managed to sink some ships, their own losses were far too great to continue doing so.

Of about 40,000 conscripted U-boat crewmen, 28,000 were lost, possibly the highest proportion of any arm of any service of any nation in any war.

For each two U-boats lost only about 5 merchant ships were sunk, the highest period of German losses being between April and July 1943. This was the time of the turning of the tide against the submarine menace, when

WAR DEAD in the 2nd World War

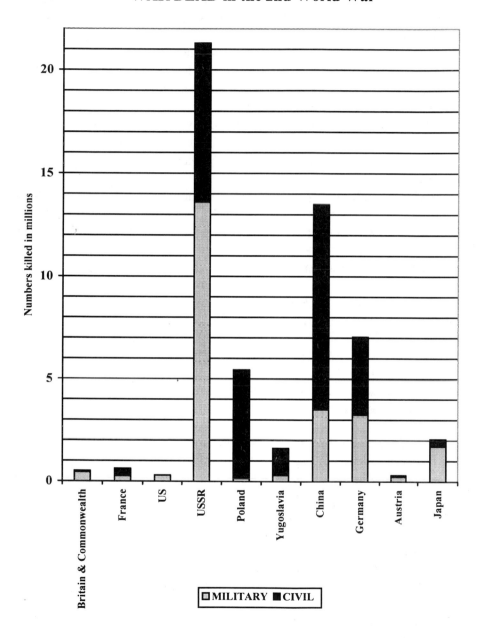

Enigma intercepts helped the Royal Navy and the US Navy, and as many as 108 U-boats were sunk and 4,700 U-boat crewmen died. Incredibly, the German U-boat crews continued to set out, even though they must have been aware that 200 U-boats had been sunk on their first voyage; their courage was sustained by their belief that Allied merchant ship losses were far greater than was actually the case, and by German propaganda that if they just kept going, victory was just around the corner. German inventions to help U-boats, such as the torpedo that could direct itself towards the sound of a target ship's engines, and snorkels which allowed U-boats to re-charge their batteries while submerged, were developed successfully but too late in the war. The actual losses show that 866 German and Italian submarines were sunk during the war – that is 70% of the total sent to sea. 156 U-boats surrendered in 1945, but about 221 had been scuttled by their German crews before their surrender. As for lives lost in battle, these may be a little misleading, if used to judge the effectiveness or otherwise of a military or air attack: for instance, conventional air raids on Japan during the Second World War killed more people than in all the RAF and American bombing raids made on Germany, plus the two atomic bomb air attacks on Japan, all combined, and this includes the 350,000 German civilians killed by Allied bombing of German towns in the last 15 months of the war.

In Britain, between 60,000 and 80,000 civilians died in air raids between 1939 and 1945, a large figure in British terms and one wisely not widely reported until after the war in case it should tend to sap morale. 55 million lives have been calculated as having been lost on all sides as a result of the Second World War. The Jews are believed to have lost up to six million people in concentration camps and one figure which indicates their suffering is that, although there were estimated to be 131,838 Jews still living in Germany on January 1, 1942, by April 1, 1942, the figure was down to 51,257; but this was not all, as half a million gypsies, 15,000 homosexuals, 200,000 disabled people (especially the mentally retarded) together with catholic priests, Jehovah's Witnesses and many others were also killed in an horrific attempt to 'purify' the Aryan race; but even these figures pale when compared with the 15 million Russian civilians killed by the Germans, which is in addition to the 5 million military personnel of the USSR who died.

One of the beneficial effects of the Allied Victory in the 2nd World War was the recognition – and this is enshrined in international institutions and agreements – of equality between people of differing races, nations, colours and creeds, without discrimination – at least in theory, even if not always achieved everywhere in practice.

When the first atomic bomb was dropped on Hiroshima on August 6, 1945, 100,000 people are estimated to have died that day with perhaps 50,000 or so subsequently; but nearly as many, 83,000, died in the 'conventional' raid on Tokyo by heavy US bombers on March 10, 1945. As a matter of comparison, the Battle of the Somme on the Western Front in 1916, lasting 142 days from July 1st, resulted in nearly 1¼ million deaths, counting those on both sides. Yet, in the 2nd World War, over a million were killed just in the Battle of Stalingrad. In the 1st World War it is estimated that 10% of fatal casualties were civilians; in the 2nd World War, the figure is 60%. The difference is ascribed to technological developments. The trouble with figures is that when they become really big – as with these casualties – they also become harder to grasp, and the MEGO effect (My Eyes Glaze Over) sets in.

* * * * *

Telegraphy had been invented by Watson in 1842, but its weakness, from the point of view of use in war, was that it was liable to be monitored by the enemy. Pigeon post was believed to be more secure, even though the birds were liable to 'interception' from predators and other natural hazards. And this was despite the fact that there was a secure cable across the English Channel by 1850, and another one across the seabed of the Atlantic Ocean from Porthcurno to America in 1866, by means of which Queen Victoria sent a first message to the American President. Most army units stationed in Scilly during the 2nd World War were concerned with manning searchlights, machine-gun posts, and anti-aircraft guns; but a few were a part of one of the more bizarre units – an RAF peregrine falcon detachment stationed in the Islands.

From the outset in 1939, there was a belief, held firmly by the British authorities, that German spies in the UK were being sent homing pigeons – under a scheme they believed to have been suggested by Himmler, a pigeon fancier, and were releasing them back to Germany with secret messages. As a result, all people keeping homing pigeons in this country were inspected by the police, and an RAF unit with peregrine falcons was stationed near Star Castle on St Mary's to intercept the enemy birds; but the only pigeons brought down by these falcons proved to be two lost French birds, which had probably been blown across the English Channel by high winds. Pigeons had been used successfully to convey messages from the provinces to the besieged defenders of Paris in 1870, and pigeon messages had been used occasionally on the Western Front in the 1st World War, when despatch riders and runners could not get through or were unavailable. In the 2nd World War, they were sometimes provided in reconnaissance aircraft as a back-up means of communication when all else had failed, but were not much use for summoning assistance when an aircraft came down in the sea, and until 1942, when a floating pigeon-basket replaced the previous ordinary wicker-one, pigeons were unlikely to survive a ditching. Moreover, they were a somewhat uncertain and relatively slow means of communication and useless in darkness. However, one pigeon called Winkie was different; it escaped from a ditched Beaufort on February 23, 1942, and returned to its pigeon loft at its air base, although without a message on its leg. But, by using the time that the bird arrived and an assessment of the bird's condition, those at the base concluded that the missing aircraft must be within 50 miles of the base. A square search of this sea area was started and, as a result, the dinghy from the Beaufort was located, an RAF high-speed launch directed to the spot from Scilly, and all the Beaufort's aircrew rescued safely. This was, however, an isolated instance, and no other RAF rescues were recorded in the war afterwards as having been made with the help of the pigeon service. Nevertheless, the first news of the ill-fated raid on Dieppe in August, 1942, reached Britain across the English Channel, not by radio which was thought likely to have been intercepted by the Germans, but by carrier-pigeon. There were about 20,000 birds in the Pigeon Service altogether, covering all three armed Services, and 32 of these were awarded the equivalent of the birds' Victoria Cross during 2nd World War for delivering messages which saved lives.

One of the principal army units which came to Scilly in 1940 was of Independent Companies, forerunners of the Commandos. Their training had taught them to 'live off the land', so, in the Islands, they tended to practise a little of what they had been taught – to the loss and frustration of some of Scilly's civilian inhabitants, who were somewhat relieved when they were later replaced by a battalion of garrison troops. There is a legend that on June 6, 1944, this Scilly garrison received the signal: 'Spearhead landed Normandy'; it is said that the St Mary's Hospital was ordered to prepare for casualties, while a successful assault was made by the garrison troops on the imposing St Mary's farmhouse called 'Normandy', its residents being taken completely by surprise. Only later that morning did news come through of the Allied D-Day landings on the north French coast.

As the end of the war approached and the military presence in Scilly was reduced, requisitioned property was restored to pre-war owners. Star Castle, and it's annexe for instance, requisitioned in July 1940, was handed back to its pre-war owner in December, 1944, together – eventually – with a sum of money to cover the costs of damage or wear caused by the army occupation. The travel ban to Scilly was lifted at the end of 1944, and this enabled some of the hotels to prepare to re-open. Gradually some prosperity began to return to the islands as the two complementary industries of flower-growing and tourism revived and expanded, enabling the Government to extend income tax to Scilly in 1953 and to introduce motor taxation in 1969.

The Ministry of Transport's ban on the export of flowers from Scilly from 1943 had led to one or two enterprising attempts to circumvent it. One mainlander tried to pack his numerous suitcases with them, and an American pilot took off with many boxes of them concealed on his Dakota, but was unfortunate in pranging his aircraft upon take-off, which led to the discovery

320

of his smuggling activities.

In February, 1944, Scilly flower farmers gave boxes of flowers to the Red Cross, but some are said to have been smuggled to market for sale, making use of a coupon system which allowed growers to sell a limited quota of their flowers – a loophole which enterprising Scillonian farmers with flowers on their hands would almost inevitably wish to exploit. Pre-war, the flowers had been exported to the mainland in wooden boxes from Scandinavia; one artful strategem was to 'adapt' these boxes so that they were slightly bigger, and so would hold more flowers. However, as A.J.P. Taylor commented in his *English History, 1914-55*, p. 551: 'The Ministry of Transport stopped the special trains bringing cut-flowers from Cornwall and the Scilly Isles. The ban was defied. Enterprising traders travelled on passenger trains, their suitcases loaded with flowers. In March, 1943, Churchill intervened and had the special trains restored.' A.J.P. Taylor was actually criticised by some fellow historians after the war for writing history in an interesting way in popular newspapers, for its study was believed too hard and complex for average readers and best confined to academia. This was a touch of arrogance and was also found in some other disciplines in the 2nd World War and for decades afterwards, one example being education, a subject which has been criticised rather severely as puffed up with pretensions, at least in its philosophical if not in practical aspects, and with little of worth to offer much beyond common sense.

* * * * *

By 1945 the war was seen to be moving to its conclusion even by its losers, and in Germany there were desperate attempts to organise the country for what was called 'total war'. All men aged 16 to 65, not already in uniform or reserved occupations, had already been mobilised for compulsory labour in January, 1943, but Nazi belief that women should be homemakers meant that they were still largely excluded. However, over seven million workers from other countries were employed within Germany, including skilled Russians, Jews and Poles, and some half a million girls from the Ukraine and elsewhere were employed as domestic servants. The inmates of some concentration camps provided labour for many farms and factories, but many of the above were treated roughly by the German authorities, if not by individual German families. By the end of the war much of the defence of the homeland was organised by the Volkssturm, the German Home Guard, which was composed mainly of grandfathers and boys – a last-ditch recruitment to save the Fatherland.

Some leading Nazis could be exceptionally brutal, particularly if their own safety was at stake. The details of the aftermath of the assassination of 38-year-old Reinhard Heydrich, an efficient but hard-line Nazi official, formerly a Luftwaffe fighter pilot and then Chief of Security Police, is indicative of the worst of the German regime in Europe. Heydrich became the German Protector of Bohemia, and was alleged to be one of the advocates for 'The Final Solution of the Jewish Problem', as they termed it. He used to drive himself to his office near Prague each morning without an escort. Two volunteers from the Free Czech Organisation in Britain saw this as an opportunity and were parachuted into Bohemia by an RAF plane, and one morning, as Heydrich was passing in his 3.5 litre Mercedes, they threw some bombs, which killed him. The two assassins were later cornered by the police and died in a gun battle; but Himmler was not satisfied with this, and had the German Security Police surround the village of Lidice near Prague – where they thought the two assassins had been hiding prior to their deaths – and they destroyed all its houses and killed all its 173 men inhabitants. The remainder of the village population, comprising 198 women and 98 children, were sent to concentration camps. What strikes as particularly unpleasant about this episode is the vengeful treatment of so many innocent people in the village, merely to set a fearful example – without reference to law or natural justice – lest anyone else should contemplate putting at risk the lives of other leading Nazis.

* * * * *

In the USA, the development of the Mustang fighter did as much to help the US bombing campaign against German cities as the development of the Hellcat and the Corsair did in mastering the Japanese Zero in the Pacific. In particular, what the Mustang had, apart from a Rolls Royce Merlin engine, was long-range capability, supplied by papier-mâché extra fuel tanks, which enabled it to escort the bombers to Berlin and to other distant German cities, and then jettison these extra tanks when needing to engage in combat with German fighters. With armies advancing into Germany from west and east, and supremacy of the air over Germany thus becoming attained by the Allies, it is not surprising that surrender soon became the only viable option open to the Germans and culminated in VE Day on May 8, 1945. On that day, with Hitler having committed suicide, Admiral Doenitz, as the new Fuehrer since April 30, brought final resistance to an end (Doenitz received a ten-year sentence at his trial at Nuremburg, was released in 1954 and died in 1980). But what really broke the Germans was the Russian army's success on the Eastern Front – the exact moment when the tide of war turned being the surrender of von Paulus and his 6th Army to a young Russian lieutenant in the basement of Stalingrad's former largest department store on January 31, 1943. This was followed, in 1944, by the war on two fronts that the Germans had always feared; and it was the advance of the Allied armies that brought the German collapse rather than the bombing, extensive though it was with something like half-a-million German civilians dying in the war as a result of Allied air attacks.

Various events and changes took place on the Home Front in 1944. The ban on women teachers getting married and staying in their profession was lifted on March 26, and the House of Commons voted on the 'desirability' of giving women teachers equal pay with men. Yet, on March 31, four people were found guilty under the 1735 Witchcraft Act, for 'pretending to be mediums'. On April 6, 1944, Pay-as-you-earn (PAYE) was introduced and proved to be a less painful and more assured way of paying tax; and then on August 3, 1944, it was agreed that secondary education for all was to be established.

On April 1st, up to ten miles inland on the South coast was placed out-of-bounds, not to residents but to visitors – because the Second Front armies were being prepared there; and, on Hitler's birthday on April 20, 4,500 tons of bombs were dropped by the Allies on Germany.

The D-Day invasion came none too soon, because it was only by overrunning the V-1 and V-2 launching sites that their attacks could finally be stopped. One successful stratagem employed to minimise the damage caused by V-1s was to make public in the British press – and therefore to the German authorities – the whereabouts of V-1s that happened to fall in the countryside north of London. This persuaded the Germans that their range on the V-1s was set too long and they shortened the setting on many of them – with the result that these fell – at any rate for a time – harmlessly on the Kent countryside instead of on urban London.

There was disappointment among the Allies when it was learnt that Stauffenburg's briefcase bomb, which, on July 20, he had placed carefully under a table near Hitler at the Fuehrer's East Prussian headquarters, had gone off but had failed to kill Hitler; and horror when, after being found guilty at a trial, a gruesome story was circulated that eight generals and other plotters had been executed by strangulation from piano wires, their bodies suspended from meat hooks. Rommel had known about the plot but, to save embarrassment, he was allowed to avoid trial by committing suicide on October 14 through taking poison.

On September 9, the first V-2 rocket bomb landed in Britain, killing three people. The British authorities let it be known that it was a gasworks explosion, so as not to cause alarm. On September 17, the blackout was lifted except near the coast, where it was still a dimout. On September 25, the airborne attack on Arnhem proved 'a bridge too far' and, on December 3, 1945, the Home Guard were 'stood down' – at its peak it had included 1,701,208 men and 31,824 women, with officers given honorary ranks.

A tragedy not learnt about until after the war was the sinking in the Baltic of the German liner *Wilhelm Gustloff* by the Russian submarine S13 on January 31, 1945; German civilians and technicians were trying desperately to escape the advancing Russian army in Prussia, and over 4,000 (possibly nearly 7,000) of them were crowded on this ship which set sail for neutral Sweden. Nearly all of them drowned, the greatest loss of life from a single ship in history.

The other great action of early 1945 – and in retrospect a tragedy, but possibly almost an inevitable one in the war circumstances when Stalin had continually been reproaching Churchill for doing so little to aid the Russians in the war effort – was the air raid on Dresden on February 14, 1945. Dresden seemed remote from Britain and was thought safe by the Germans from air attack, so that the normal population of about 600,000 had been swelled by up to 400,000 German refugees fleeing from the advancing Russians. Around 800 RAF Lancaster bombers and 400 American B-17s took part and met little resistance, the city being devastated, with about 100,000 civilians thought to have died.

The other dramatic news of early 1945 was of the suicide on April 30 of Hitler, who is said to have shot himself through the mouth as he sat on a sofa, his girlfriend, Eva Braun, having previously taken poison. He was 56, but is said to have shown signs of physical and mental deterioration for some months previously, unable to understand what had gone wrong. The tragedy – and perhaps the product of his hatreds and early influences – is that he seemed unaware of or unconcerned by the evil his policies created, his intentions apparently being to employ any means to make Germany the greatest power on earth – but not for himself, his personal life seeming to be somewhat dull as dictators go. Mussolini and his girlfriend Clara Petacci were shot with machine-guns by Italian partisans, after being discovered hiding on April 28 under a pile of coats on the back of a lorry; their bodies were then strung up by their feet. Hitler avoided similar public posthumous humiliation by arranging that his body, and that of Eva's, should be burnt outside the underground bunker in Berlin, which had been his headquarters.

President Roosevelt died a little before the war ended. He suffered from polio and could not stand unaided, yet, out of respect and politeness, American newspapers avoided showing his infirmity or said much about how grievously he was disabled. He died, aged 63, while he was having his portrait painted in the bedroom of his small bungalow in Warm Springs at Pine Mountain, where he attended for treatment of his polio. He had two doctors with him, complained of a headache, then suddenly fainted and never regained consciousness. His vice-president, Truman, took over and, to many people's surprise, proved most able in the job.

At his meeting with Churchill aboard the battleship *Prince of Wales* in August, 1941, Roosevelt had said he would in effect 'wage war on Hitler without declaring it' and he did this by massive aid to Britain. Earlier, at the end of 1940, Roosevelt was told by Kennedy, the American ambassador in London, that Britain was likely soon to have to surrender, and so, Roosevelt said that in that event the Royal Navy could come to Canada – to fight on from overseas – but that the Royal Family should come no closer than Bermuda, as 'the American republic may be restless if they came to Canada' – a sign that memories of the American War of Independence against George III had not yet been finally forgotten.

Blackout and dimout in the UK ended entirely on July 15, 1945, and on August 6, an atomic bomb, strangely called *Enola Gay* after the pilot Tibbet's mother, was dropped on Hiroshima, followed by another on Nagasaki on August 9. Japan surrendered to General MacArthur on August 14, with huge weeping crowds in Tokyo begging the Emperor for his forgiveness for letting him down by losing the war. The result of the General Election in the UK on July 26, in terms of seats in the House of Commons, was as follows:

Labour	393
Tories	213
Liberals	12
Independents	22

Many people could not understand what they saw as the ingratitude of the nation to Churchill; but, in fact, Churchill was a war horse and never outstanding as a Prime Minister in peacetime, even if superb as the war leader. Moreover, it had been a Coalition government which had won the war, not merely one of Conservatives. Attlee had been deputy Prime Minister, and Bevin, Morrison and others had played prominent roles. Attlee took over as Prime Minister on July 26, 1945, and proved very effective. Labour offered a new and better world; the Conservatives seemed happy to restore the old world of the 1930s – not a pleasant prospect for the working classes of that era. However, the 1944 Education Act had pledged secondary education for all, and the Beveridge Report of December 1, 1942, offered hope of a better society through its plan for a welfare state. But recovery from the efforts of the war, although dogged, was slow: the average weekly wage in the UK in 1950 was £6.8s.0d (£6.40); petrol was still rationed, and food still on points; there was still a spending limit for each person taking meals in restaurants, and the meat ration was only 8 ounces. Moreover, bread was rationed, which it had not been in wartime – all this was part of the price paid economically for six years of war, the longest any country on either side had been in the war.

* * * * *

With the ending of the war, there was, as elsewhere in UK seaside resorts, a rapid increase in tourism, if limited accommodation to provide it, for holidays were something that had been much curtailed in the war years.

In Scilly, there were, of course, no such thing as *en suite*, and some of the re-opened hotels could only offer rooms out in houses in Hugh Town for

sleeping, with meals taken in the hotel – a situation that lasted at least until the early 1950s. Moreover, for single girls, they were often offered only a double-bed in the only room available – not always with an interior-sprung mattress. The meals in the hotels were usually at strict times and set ones – Brown Windsor soup still appearing – with few choices in the main course, although, in Scilly, lobster salad – and generous amounts of it – was on the menu every Sunday evening at Star Castle Hotel, a reflection partly of the more abundant stocks of that delicacy in the waters around Scilly at that time, but mainly because chef had 'that evening off'. Rather surprisingly, hotel staff of good quality were hard to find in post-war Britain; but to have a holiday at all was wonderful, and visitors were prepared to put up with any small inconveniences, knowing nothing else and with nothing else on offer; they could not have foreseen the superb provisioning and pampering of holidaymakers in Scilly which came in the second half of the 20th century and is such a delight today.

Such increase in tourism led to changes in the provision of transport services to Scilly. On February 1st, 1947, the air service, which had, on a small scale, operated almost continuously throughout the war, was absorbed into British European Airways, which had been formed by the post-war Labour Government to take over independent internal air lines. From 1961, a number of independent airlines also started up an air service to Scilly, but few lasted long because the difficulties and costs of providing it were never quite matched by the level of fares that were charged. Scillonian Air Services began in 1962, but ceased in 1964. One entrepreneur who tried very hard was Squadron Leader Philip Cleife; he founded Mayflower Air Services in 1961 with one de Havilland Dragon Rapide piloted by himself, and for the first time Scilly was connected with Exeter and Plymouth airports, Cleife making his first flight on July 8th, 1961, with seven passengers. By 1963, the airline seemed to have become established and was looking forward to returning reasonable profits, so a second Dragon Rapide was bought and a second pilot, Peter Loat, recruited, which made it possible for one 'plane to fly from Scilly to Plymouth and the other from Scilly to Exeter, so cutting out the wasteful leg between Plymouth and Exeter. But disaster struck the viability of the airline on July 20th, 1963; on taking off from St Mary's, a rapidly deflating tyre caused Cleife's Rapide to swing to port and robbed the aircraft of sufficient speed at a crucial moment in its take-off. In the subsequent crash, the passengers emerged with only minor injuries, but the top of the control column had broken off at the moment of impact and pierced Cleife's thigh, pinning him to his 'plane. The aircraft burst into flames, but firefighters used a hacksaw and sawed through the column so that they could remove it and Cleife from the fire. Cleife also had bad burns from which, with the help of plastic surgery, he recovered; but he could never qualify for a professional pilot's licence again. His wife, Virginia, stepped in to run the airline's administration for the rest of the season, and the remaining aircraft, with Peter Loat as pilot, covered the bookings; but the situation could not last and Mayflower Air Services, with its one remaining aircraft, was sold to Scillonian Air services in December, 1963, who, thwarted in their attempts to buy better aircraft from Kuwait, in turn resold Mayflower in May, 1964, to British Westpoint Airlines. This company also acquired the three redundant BEA Rapides which had run the St Just to Scilly service before the introduction of the helicopters, and operated the 'planes until 1966, when this company also went into liquidation. Scillonian Airways then purchased and operated two of the Dragon Rapides for a while, but it too, soon ended its services, and closed down in 1969.

The failures of these companies was related to the replacement by BEA in May, 1964, of its 8-passenger Rapides with two (at first) American-built Sikorsky S-61N helicopters, each seating 25 passengers (later increased to 32) – aircraft whose naval version was known as the Sea King. Each of the Sikorsky's rotor blades is 31 feet long, and its load-carrying capacity is 20,500lbs; it carries two pilots and a cabin attendant. The inauguration of the helicopter service on 1st May, 1964, roughly coincided with the Isles of Scilly Steamship Company's purchase of a second ship, *Queen of the Isles*, for the Penzance to Scilly route; but the success of the helicopter in attracting passengers away from the sea route, and the new building restrictions which reduced the cargo this ship was permitted to carry, affected its economic viability and led in 1968 to the sale of the *Queen of the Isles*. At first the helicopters operated from St Just Aerodrome (return fare to Scilly £5.30) until September, 1964, when the new heliport at Eastern Green, Penzance, became ready for service as the first self-contained heliport in Europe with maintenance facilities serving a scheduled helicopter service. The heliport proved an immediate improvement on St Just because, although further than

St Just from Scilly – 37 statute miles as against 30.5 – it suffers less from fog and is much nearer the Penzance railway terminus. The extra distance the helicopter has to fly is also partially offset in terms of time – if not in cost of fuel – by the fact that the helicopter flies at least 10 m.p.h. faster than the bi-plane did (about 140 m.p.h. as compared with about 130 m.p.h.). Although an average trip by the Sikorsky helicopter between Scilly and Penzance takes about twenty minutes – once, against a gale-force headwind, it took 49 minutes to Tresco – a following wind can much reduce flying time, and gales can produce flights lasting as little as twelve minutes, the record flight in 1998. The helicopter service to Scilly is now the longest-established regular helicopter service in the world.

Faster than either of the above aircraft was the 9 passenger, Britten-Norman Islander (cruising speed 160 m.p.h.) of Brymon Airways, which began scheduled services to Scilly in June, 1972, from Newquay and Plymouth, and from Exeter in 1973. Brymon Aviation had been founded in 1969 by freelance journalist Bill Bry and racing-driver Chris Amon, a junction of parts of their surnames giving the new airline its name. In 1981, they had a Dash 7, a 4-engined aircraft which connected London with Newquay, but Brymon were taken over by British Airways in 1993, and they continued to operate the same aircraft on the route although in different livery. Flights to Scilly by Brymon from 1972 had been scheduled to connect with the flights of aircraft of other airlines to and from airports in London and the Midlands until, in 1974, Brymon Airways started its own 19-seat de Havilland twin Otter Service to Newquay, but British Airways did not continue with this integration of services with other airlines.

Westward Airways operated to Scilly a de Havilland 89A Dragon Rapide G-AIYR from 1977, but not for long; the aircraft was the last Dragon-Rapide to fly commercially in the UK and is now in the Imperial War Museum at Duxford.

In 1972, BEAH (British European Airways Helicopters) became BAH (British Airways Helicopters), and, in April, 1975, as a result of the increase in traffic, a new terminal building was opened on St Mary's on the west side of the airport overlooking Old Town to replace the old terminal to the east, which was subsequently demolished in 1976 with only traces of its foundations remaining today. The Council of the Isles of Scilly took over the running of the airport in September, 1982, paying a peppercorn rent for the lease from the Duchy: but they ran into a public outcry in 1991, when they proposed (and in 1992 built) the extension of the main airport runway, thus complying with an ultimatum from the Civil Aviation Authority to make the airport safer for take-off and landing or else be obliged to close it down. In August, 1983, Isles of Scilly Skybus, a subsidiary of the Isles of Scilly Steamship Company, began operations, and from 1984 carried flower-boxes in winter to the mainland as well as operating a charter service for

Increased air traffic put a strain on the old terminal building on the east side of the airport, so the present one was built to replace it and opened by Harold Wilson on April 1st, 1975, the old terminal buildings being demolished in 1976. The red telephone box in the centre of the departure lounge was retained for a time, but passengers came to regard it as decorative rather than functional, so it was removed. The control tower of the new building now has good all-round vision, as can be seen in the photograph above; three motorised luggage trolleys wait at the ready to take luggage off the helicopter and replace it with luggage of passengers returning to the mainland. The turnaround is now so practised and slick that it can be done, including the changeover of luggage, in the time taken for one group of passengers to disembark and another to embark.

passengers. Skybus was to prove a success despite the relatively poor weather at St Just compared with that at Eastern Green, and despite another major hindrance to the service – the short and sometimes somewhat soggy grass of the aerodrome at St Just, which precluded the use of heavier aircraft. However, once Skybus had been granted its licence by the CAA, a scheduled passenger service from Land's End was started on April 6, 1987, and was most successful.

The flower trade has always used the winter air service from Scilly to speed some boxes of early flowers to market, but the helicopter proved particularly helpful, not only because of the extra loads it could carry, but because it could land on off-islands such as St Martin's and load flower-boxes direct. On one day in the winter of 1988, nearly 2,000 boxes of flowers were flown to the mainland.

Helicopters have proved useful to Scilly in other ways, from servicing the Bishop Rock lighthouse by landing on the helicopter-pad built specially on top of it, to lowering old cannon and their carriages onto gun positions on Cromwell's Castle, Tresco, and on The Garrison, St Mary's, and even

The main work horse of the Isles of Scilly helicopter operation for 20 years has been G-BCEB. The photograph is of this aircraft, called 'Isles of Scilly' – but also called Echo Bravo *after her 1994 refit – on the tarmac at St Mary's having taken on board her passengers and ready to take off for the return journey to the heliport at Penzance.*

airlifting salvage equipment in 1967 to the *Torrey Canyon*. BEAH helicopter *Echo Bravo* in November, 1986, behaved as an aerial crane – it is designed to be able to lift 2½ tons of equipment – and obligingly lifted from Penzance three huge new Axminster carpets slung underneath its passenger cabin, and lowered them onto a lorry on St Mary's quay for delivery to Tregarthen's Hotel. With such an unwieldy underslung load, speed was limited to 40 knots, and the flight took over an hour.

Another use – until environmental concerns ended it – was in assisting in getting rid of old cars. Until the Second World War, any old vehicle for disposal, together with other island rubbish, was deposited by the lorry load at Porth Minick off Old Town, a beach considered of little merit by the visitor and relatively hidden, yet close enough to Hugh Town to be but a short journey for the dustcart. Even today the rusting remains of old back axles and gearboxes still impart a reddish tinge to the surrounding grey granite boulders. Later, old vehicles on Scilly were disposed of by tipping them off the cliff at Deep Point, where it was believed the sea bottom was far enough below to hide them for ever. Inevitably, some cars pushed off the cliff top became stuck in gullies on the way down and never reached the sea – a bizarre sight, and one which did not commend itself to visitors. So, to eliminate the danger of falling cars wedging themselves in this way, and to ensure that the cars were disposed of where the sea was deepest, an operation involving dumping about 80 old St Mary's vehicles off Deep Point was carried out in 1980 by a Royal Marines' helicopter as part of a training exercise. Subsequently, environmental concerns have forbidden this type of dumping at sea, and so old vehicles have now to be shipped to the mainland at the owner's expense or broken up in Scilly.

Accidents since the 2nd World War involving the air services to Scilly have been relatively few, but there was one helicopter which made a forced landing an October 31st, 1968, next to the heliport at Penzance, but without injury or damage – so it hardly counts. In 1969, Westward Airways began a service to Scilly, but on February 23rd, 1970, their Islander aircraft overran the runway on St Mary's and hit a wall – since removed – after which they suspended operations. The most serious accident – the first in twenty years of operation – was to a S-61N helicopter G-BEON on Saturday, July 16th, 1983, which, in foggy weather, flew into a calm sea after descending from 2,000 feet to about 250 feet as it made ready for landing just two miles from St Mary's. The Sikorsky helicopters have sealed hulls and normally will float; but on this occasion the helicopter hit the sea and somersaulted, sinking quickly in 200 feet of water. Out of 23 passengers and three crew, there were only six survivors, who after an hour in the water spent clinging to debris and floating luggage, were rescued by the St Mary's lifeboat, whose coxswain was Matt Lethbridge. His skill in finding them in the foggy conditions was remarkable. The subsequent inquiry revealed that pilot error had been responsible for the crash, and criticised both the lack of audio equipment in the aircraft to warn the pilots when they were flying too low, and the inadequacy of some of the operating procedures. Against this tragedy it is recorded that by 1968 three-quarters of a million passengers had been carried safely on this route – the first scheduled helicopter service in the British Isles, and by May, 1994, this figure was over 2¼ million. The transport of boxes of flowers in the winter – extra space being made by removing some passenger seats from the helicopter – proved a valuable winter supplement to income, and ensured an even speedier delivery of flowers to markets. An extension of the service came in 1983, when direct helicopter flights to Tresco were begun, a heliport being established on Abbey Green with the old tea-hut serving as operations control.

By 1992, the Sikjorsky S-61NM helicopter *Echo Bravo* (G-BCEB), which was the mainstay of the operation, had achieved one of the highest records for technical reliability of any scheduled European airline. It had luggage lockers in the lower hull which enabled a quick turnaround of only about five minutes for unloading passengers and their luggage, and then loading other passengers and their luggage for the return flight. The engines were kept running during the turnaround to cut out the time wasted stopping and starting them, and to reduce the wear on the brake-pads and the cost of replacing them. The original annoyance to passengers of exposure to exhaust fumes when they boarded the aircraft was reduced by their being able to enter and leave the aircraft by a forward passenger door. In 1986 BAH was sold and became BIH (British International Helicopters) owned principally by the now-disgraced business tycoon Robert Maxwell, who used its helicopters to Service North Sea oil rigs from Scotland, as well as operating the scheduled line to Scilly from Penzance. But, already in 1982, Sikorsky had ended the manufacture of S-61s, and by 1992 *Echo Bravo* was beginning to show its age. It was joined in 1990 by a smaller 18-seat Westland W630 helicopter, which in 1991 inaugurated a helicopter link between Newquay and Scilly, but which was terminated in 1992 when the Westland helicopter was sold. Brymon Airways ceased their services to Scilly on September 29, 1990, but still flew from Heathrow to Exeter and Plymouth and on to Newquay, so it was still possible to fly from London to Scilly by changing airlines at Newquay. When British Airways took over Brymon's Heathrow to Newquay route in 1993 (operating the same 4-engined Dash 7 aircraft but repainted in their own livery) the link was maintained by a 50-minute long taxi-bus service from Newquay Airport to the heliport at Penzance. The start of a service in 1991 by Skybus from Exeter to Scilly created an alternative air route from London. In 1992 BIH located a second S61N at Penzance, but it took only 28 passengers (against *Echo Bravo*'s 32) and lacked the forward door. With the collapse of the Maxwell business empire in 1992, BIH was taken over by administrators, who found the company viable and profitable. They were able to sell it to a management buy-out team in 1993 which, from that year, operated one helicopter only to Scilly, the reliable *Echo Bravo* (G-BCEB), which had been operating the service since 1975. This aircraft was named *Isles of Scilly* by Lady Wilson at a ceremony in 1989 to mark the 25th anniversary of the helicopter service to Scilly and, at the beginning of 1994, was not only given new engines and a new gearbox – these are required about every eleven months – but a complete refit to enable it to remain in service for many years ahead until its eventual replacement, possibly by a faster, quieter, EH101 Heliner, carrying 30 passengers at a top speed of 193 m.p.h.

Routine maintenance at the Penzance heliport has inevitably to be carried out at unsociable hours in the evenings or on Sundays when the helicopter is not flying; but this is not a problem, for great pride in the helicopter service is shown by all who work in it, as was demonstrated at its celebration of thirty years of 'the longest-running scheduled helicopter service in the world' in May, 1994. BIH later became part of Brintel Helicopters Limited, formed on January 27th, 1993, which had about 16 helicopters, running flights to North Sea oil and gas rigs and platforms, and in 1998 operated two S61 helicopters from Penzance Heliport to Scilly under the operating title of British International. British International was soon part of the Canadian Helicopter Corporation which had about 200 helicopters world-wide, the two helicopters at Penzance being given a red-coloured cockpit and the logo of a humming-bird. In 2000, ownership changed again, with the two S61 helicopters owned by Veritair Ltd but still operating as British International.

There was a great fuss made in Scilly in opposition to the extension of the runway on St Mary's as shown in the photograph above. Many Scillonians were concerned that a longer runway would enable larger planes to bring even more visitors to Scilly, so threatening still further the peace and quiet of the islands, which is what attracts many people in the first place. The campaign failed to stop the building of the runway – in fact it had to be constructed for safety reasons – but it succeeded in alerting everyone not only to the dangers of over-commercialisation but to the need for vigilance in preserving Scilly's uniqueness. Fears about possible damage to the headland and inevitable closure of footpaths have fortunately proved groundless.

On April 1st, 1992, the fire service, baggage handling and air traffic operations at St Mary's airport were taken over by the Council of the Isles of Scilly, who carried out a refurbishment and extension of the airport terminal on St Mary's. With the new runway completed in 1992, a new booking-hall and airport lounge opened in 1993, the way seemed open for an expansion of the air services to Scilly, and from May, 1994, Skybus began operating a 19-seat, DH-6 Twin Otter aircraft from Exeter and Plymouth to Scilly, which meant that for the first time it was possible on some days of the week in the season (and with a 'plane change at Exeter) to reach Scilly from London in not much more than two hours; and, from December 19, 1994, Skybus began operating a scheduled passenger service from Bristol, and later on from Southampton. St Just airport buildings were refurbished in 1994, as were the Penzance heliport buildings in 1997 and 1999, so that the comfort of passengers on the air routes was much improved. A corresponding improvement by the inauguration of a new type of passenger vessel on the sea route is anticipated in years to come, but meanwhile *Scillonian III* was refitted, although the plan to lengthen her was not pursued. With the *Gry Maritha*, or similar vessel carrying goods to the Scillies three times a week, there is no longer the same need for a passenger ferry with a large goods-carrying capacity other than for passenger luggage, mail, urgent items and perishables. Looking to the longer term, a vessel which did not have to include in its design such considerable load capacity as *Scillonian III* would be less expensive to run and could be still more attractive to passengers. A 37 metre length catamaran has been suggested as *Scillonian III*'s eventual replacement, which would be capable of making the trip from Penzance with up to 450 passengers at 30 knots taking 1½ hours; but it would have to be of substantial construction to weather the stormy seas often met on the crossing, and without the discomfort to passengers which in past times on previous ferries to the Scillies they have often had to endure, putting up with turbulent seas in order to reap the reward of landing in such magical and beautiful islands.

* * * * *

Polonius: What do you read, my Lord?
Hamlet: Words, words, words.   *Hamlet*, Act II

APPENDIX I
THE ARCH-ENEMIES: NAZI v. COMMUNIST

Hitler and Stalin were the two outstanding protagonists in the 2nd World War. In Britain, Hitler, as the enemy, was regarded as the devil incarnate (Churchill called him 'a guttersnipe'), while Stalin, as the ally, was 'Uncle Joe'. History now judges them equally as ruthless dictators, who had more than their fair share of hatred in their natures, although in some ways they were markedly different.

Stalin was hardworking whereas Hitler was indolent even as a schoolboy. Hitler grew to hate his father, who was given to hitting his children – not an unusual practice in Germany (and elsewhere) in the first half of the 20th century – but he adored his mother. He dropped out of school, wanting to be a painter – and, in 1908, went to Vienna, but was rejected for a place at the Viennese Academy of Arts. However, he listened to the debates in the Austrian Parliament, and absorbed the prevailing criticisms he heard of Jews and of parliamentary democracy. In Vienna, he lived a poor, rather lonely life in a hostel, where he read quite a lot, mainly war books. He tried to make a living by illustrating picture-postcards, and worked with Jews in this endeavour. In 1914, at Munich, he enlisted in the army and proved a good soldier, winning the Iron Cross, 1st class. He was twice wounded and once gassed, and learnt, from nearly 4 years of service, how life was a struggle to survive. Hitler was furious when he heard the news of Germany's surrender in November, 1918, while he was recovering in hospital from gassing, and he sought scapegoats for the defeat and grew to hate them and what he saw as the humiliating treaty imposed on Germany by the Allies at Versailles. Although an Austrian with an Austrian accent, he discovered he had a talent for oratory, and he joined a group of similar-minded malcontents, who, in 1923, made an abortive attempt to seize power. They failed and Hitler fled, but was caught and imprisoned, which gave him the opportunity to write about his beliefs in his book *Mein Kampf* (My Struggle). It seems amazing that the historian, A.J.P. Taylor, who wrote *The Origins of the Second World War*, is alleged not to have read *Mein Kampf* before he wrote it.

In January, 1933, Hitler became Chancellor of Germany by means of the democratic process. He became popular with the German people and his speeches were carefully crafted to please them. He was teetotal, a vegetarian and a non-smoker, who objected to raucous and ill-mannered behaviour, and seemed blameless in his personal life. He had a particular rapport with children and kept an alsation dog, but had no close family; when his niece shot herself, he was for a time devastated. He met Eva Braun when he was 40 and she was 17, and they had a genuine friendship; but, as chancellor, Hitler tended to lounge about all day doing nothing in particular. What he did like doing was designing German cities, an activity which always took precedence over boring matters of state. What galvanised and sustained him was his obvious early popularity, for he loved being the showman and, in the early years mingled with crowds without apparent fear of attack. But, when the war started to go badly for Germany, Hitler aged rapidly and was an old man at the age of 56 when he last appeared in public in March, 1945. In the end he blamed the German people for his failure. On April 30, 1945, he committed suicide and had his body burnt to avoid capture and its humiliation by the advancing Russians.

Stalin, like Hitler, also adored his mother, who was quite strict with him and sent him to an Orthodox Seminary for his education. There, he hated the Jesuit discipline, but was able to read Karl Marx before he left in 1899. He believed in the class war, and, for trying to incite violence, he was exiled several times to Siberia as punishment. In 1905, he met Lenin, who employed him because Stalin showed a talent as an organiser. When war started, Stalin was unfit for military service because of a withered arm, the result of smallpox in earlier life. But, in 1917, he took over the editorship of *Pravda* at St. Petersburg, read Byron's works, composed poetry, fell in love and married – but not to Lenin's sister as Lenin had wanted.

Stalin had come from Georgia and was only 5 foot 4 inches tall and not impressive-looking. However, 1922 saw him appointed General Secretary of the Communist Party. Lenin suffered strokes – his first in 1922, his last in 1924 – but he never seems to have envisaged Stalin as his successor; it was Trotsky who was the great orator, a talent Stalin never possessed. Behind the scenes, Stalin 'organised' Trotsky out of his way, showing a hard determination beneath his surface geniality. Once in power, Stalin was much more of a purger than Hitler, eliminating potential opposition and confining in gulags (labour camps), nearly two million people, who came to represent a convenient source of labour for road, rail and canal building. In November, 1932, Stalin's wife left him and then shot herself, and he did not attend her funeral; it was said that Stalin became even more cruel after this. Unlike Hitler – at least in his pre-war days – Stalin was from the outset distrustful of everyone around him, and constantly feared assassination, although, during the war, Hitler became a bit paranoid like this, because there were many failed attempts on his life. Stalin worked hard nearly every day in his study in the Kremlin, one of his few relaxations being watching films. Stalin agreed to the partition of Poland – Poland's fate, twice previously in history at the hands of Russia and Prussia – but was taken by surprise by Hitler's attack on Russia on June 22, 1941, a rather inadvisable date for Hitler to choose – as it turned out – for it was the same day of the year that Napoleon had invaded Russia and was to end with similar catastrophic results. Stalin had no stomach for the horrors of war and only visited the Front once; but his organising ability was used to the full and eventually he emerged the victor in the awful titanic struggle between them.

APPENDIX II
EDUCATION

Another opinion change since the 2nd World War concerns what constitutes intelligence. There were some, even in Britain, who believed that the level of intelligence in the nation was threatened by the alleged greater proclivity of the working classes to have children as compared with the middle and upper classes. The assumptions underlying this were that people who were working-class had less intelligence – and that was one reason why they were working-class – and that intelligence was inherited and unchangeable. Even after the 2nd World War, intelligence was still regarded as a distinctive quality of the brain, measurable by intelligence tests, and it was only later that intelligence came to be recognised more as the creation of intelligence tests and not necessarily any innate and separate aspect of the brain. After years of being told that intelligence could not be improved, parents and schools began giving children practice in tests – such as old intelligence tests used for the 11+ exam – and even the educationalists had eventually to admit that the scores of such children rapidly improved – as, indeed, common-sense had always held that they would.

Sir Cyril Burt, the charming professor of psychology from 1932-50 at University College, London, claimed to have found from his researches that working-class people overall were less intelligent than people in the classes above them, and that this was a reason they were poorer. This was a finding acceptable to much right-wing prejudice, and can be seen reflected in the otherwise reforming Butler Education Act of 1944, which divided secondary education – established in 1944 for all – into 3 types of secondary school, grammar, technical and modern, pupils being selected for each by an 11-plus exam in which an intelligence test had a place.

Burt died in 1971 aged 88, and the following year, Leon Kamin, a psychologist at Princeton, discovered flaws in Burt's research, and in 1976 *The Sunday Times* revealed that the published reviews praising Burt's work, supposedly by his research assistants, Margaret Howard and J. Conway, had actually been written by Burt himself. Moreover, the two researchers were fictitious. However, so slowly does the revelation of truth undermine treasured, longstanding beliefs, that it took some time before the British Psychological Society seemed fully to acknowledge the implications of the fraudulent research. Even an article published on June 17, 1982, in the *New Scientist* stated that 'Burt's crime ... was manufactured to feed his and our prejudices' – the 'our' being significant.

The extent of the damage, if any, resulting from Burt's work is hard to assess, and there were other fashionable but dubious educational theories since the 2nd World War which, while having some beneficial influences, may also have been damaging to British schools. Some of the ideas of John Dewey and some of the extreme interpretations of the Plowden Report, for instance, while contributing to a happier atmosphere in schools, may have had adverse educational implications – seeing education as 'child-centred', of 'development from within' and discounting the importance of the assimulation of facts, information and skills acquired from a teacher as their central dispenser. There has been a tendency to favour group activity rather than view learning as an individual experience in an attentive classroom, perhaps arising originally through making a virtue out of necessity when the class wouldn't keep quiet. Boring lessons, unsuitable material, poor delivery – all have much to answer for.

The introduction of a formal education before the age of five is widely believed to be damaging – even six may be too soon – the early years being best served by play; and reading schemes that are not based on phonics seem to have been detrimental. Some damage may have also arisen through the replacement of traditional classroom furniture by tables and chairs which are in some ways more convenient. There used to be an individual desk for each student facing toward the lesson-provider and in an area of space of the student's own. This focused attention on the class teacher but, with the coming of the new furniture, the arrangement altered, with some pupils even with their backs to the teacher, and the length of their attention span has certainly decreased – although other reasons, such as television viewing habits, can also be advanced for this. Swiss schools in the 21st century, along with those of most other countries, use traditional furniture arrangements and rely on whole-class teaching, with what is claimed to be a 4-year lead on average in their students over UK students by the time they leave school. It may be that UK teachers, through lack of practice or lack of coaching in communication skills in training, have become less proficient than formerly in giving 'talk and chalk' type lessons or in how to inspire those they teach in a simultaneous one-to-one relationship with each class pupil before them. Television lessons may be some substitute for this role, but something is lost.

If a decline in educational standards since the 2nd World War is disputed, a comparison between examination papers for GCSE with ones in similar subjects for School Certificate before and during the 2nd World War, may help to dispel them. On the other hand, such a comparison may not be a fair one, for those who sat the Schools Certificate were all from schools which had pursued an academic education, at a time when the vast majority left school at 14 without having had more than elementary education, and with no examination. At least with GCSE most pupils leaving school are examined. Moreover, the range of subjects available to study has widened greatly, and it may be that some 'progressive' education changes are a price worth paying, if they achieve the goal of enthusiastic involvement of half the population to graduate status.

338

APPENDIX III

OLD TOWN WAR GRAVES

Sixteen War Graves of Service Personnel of the 2nd World War
in Old Town Churchyard

1. 404680 Flight Sergeant L.J.S. BUSH Wireless Operator/Air Gunman
   R.N.Z.A.F., 12th September, 1942, Age 23.
2. 953919 Flight Sergeant C.F. CAPEL, Wireless Operator/Air Gunman,
   Royal Air Force, 23rd June, 1943, Age 23.
3. L.J. HALES, Able Seaman, R.N D/JX 368912, H.M.S. 'Warwick',
   20th February, 1944, Age 20.
4. 427237 Sergeant D.A.K.F. HYDE, Pilot, Royal Air Force,
   14th June, 1943, Age 21.
5. E.H. JONES, Engineman, R.N.P.S., LT/KX 125189, H.M.S. 'Mutin',
   23rd May, 1942, Age 28.
6. W.E. KILLEY, Able Seaman, R.N. D/JX 306361, H.M.S. 'Warwick',
   20th February, 1944, Age 20.
7. 748613 Flight Sergeant H. MENARY, Pilot, Royal Air Force,
   27th August, 1941.
8. D 27753 J.T. NORCLIFFE, The West Yorkshire Regiment,
   9th November, 1941.
9. Flight Lieutenant H.C.S. PAGE D.F.C., Pilot, Royal Air Force,
   31st January, 1942, Age 27.
10. R. PEACOCK, Stoker 2nd Class, R.N., D/KX 161772,
    H.M.S. 'Warwick', 20th February, 1944, Age 20.
11. A60002 Sergeant T.S. ROYAN, Air Observer, Royal Canadian Air Force,
    27th August, 1941, Age 21.
12 741012 Flight Sergeant S.I. SANDERS, Pilot, Royal Air Force,
    24th April, 1941, Age 24.
13. Flying Officer I.C.A. SANDERSON, Pilot, Royal Air Force,
    11th July, 1941, Age 27.
14. 588188 Corporal H. PROWSE, R.A.F., 11th April, 1942, Age 26.
15. A Sailor of the 1939-1945 War, Royal Navy. Buried 9th March, 1944.
16. A Sailor of the 1939-1945 War, Royal Navy. Buried 6th December, 1939.

APPENDIX IV

SCILLY'S WAR MEMORIALS
List of War Memorials in the Isles of Scilly,
collected for the Imperial War Museum, 2000

Island	Building	Memorial Title
ST AGNES	PARISH CHURCH	L. LEGG PLAQUE
ST AGNES	PARISH CHURCH	W. MORTIMER AND L HOUNSELL
ST MARTINS	PARISH CHURCH	A. CHICHESTER
ST MARTINS	PARISH CHURCH	J.J. HOYER
ST MARTINS	PARISH CHURCH	WW1 OBELISK
ST MARTINS	PARISH CHURCH	WW2 PLAQUE
ST MARYS	METHODIST CHURCH	ST MARYS METHODIST CHURCH WW1
ST MARYS	OLD TOWN CHURCHYARD	ST MARYS MEMORIAL CROSS - WW1 AND WW2
ST MARYS	PORTH HELLICK BEACH	ADMIRAL SIR CLOUDESLEY SHOVELL
ST MARYS	ST MARY THE VIRGIN CHURCH	BANFIELD WINDOW
ST MARYS	ST MARY THE VIRGIN CHURCH	PTE G. ADDISON
ST MARYS	ST MARY THE VIRGIN CHURCH	PTE H.T. TRENWITH
ST MARYS	ST MARY THE VIRGIN CHURCH	WW1 AND WW2 BOARD
TRESCO	PARISH CHURCH	DORRIEN SMITH PANELS
TRESCO	PARISH CHURCH	MEMORIAL TO RNAS MECHANICS
TRESCO	PARISH CHURCH	PLAQUE -WWI
TRESCO	PARISH CHURCH	ROLL OF HONOUR - WW1
TRESCO	PARISH CHURCH	ROLL OF HONOUR - WW2
TRESCO	PARISH CHURCH	WW1 CROSS

APPENDIX V

On the other inhabited islands, there are other memorials to those who served and died in the wars. In St Martin's churchyard are the graves of 4 seamen whose ship was sunk near the island by a U-boat, and a War Memorial cross commemorates 3 men of that island – all surnamed Ashford – who died on active service in the 1st World War. For the 2nd World War, Foster Raine, John Kessell, Jack Hayward, Arthur Taylor, Roy Brance – all men who had resided on St Martin's before the war and died on active service – are also commemorated.

APPENDIX VI
ROLL OF HONOUR
The War Memorial in Old Town Churchyard
Roll of Honour

Henry G. BACKWAY
Edward G. BARRETT
J.T. Sullivan BENNETT
Roy BRACE
A. Robert A. DORRIEN SMITH
Francis A. DORRIEN SMITH
Lionel R. DORRIEN SMITH
John ELLIS
Jack HAYWARD
William HAYWARD
Francis HICKS
Sylvia B. JENKINS
John KESSELL
Leslie LEGG
Charles NANCE
Dorothy PAICE
Stanley O. PHILLIPS
Henry PROWSE
Foster RAINE
Richard ROSCHOLAR
Francis RYAN
J. Roger STIDEFORD
Arthur TAYLOR
Herbert TAYLOR
Marcus TRENEARY
Barbara WATTS

To the honour of the sons of these Islands who served in the Forces
and lost their lives in the World Wars, 1914-1918, and 1939-1945

INDEX